D1572652

Documents of Political Foundation
Written by Colonial Americans

From Covenant to Constitution

Edited by
Donald S. Lutz

A Publication of the
Institute for the Study of Human Issues
Philadelphia

MTB

To Stephen A. Lutz and Eva B. Lutz

Manufactured in the United States of America

Library of Congress Cataloging in Publication Data

Main entry under title:

Documents of political foundation written by
Colonial Americans.

    1. Law--United States--Sources. 2. United States--
Constitutional history--Sources. I. Lutz, Donald S.
II. Institute for the Study of Human Issues.
KF350.D64 1986   349.73   85-25604
ISBN 0-89727-066-5   347.3

For information, write:

Director of Publications
ISHI
210 South 13th Street
Philadelphia, PA 19107

4/1/88

CONTENTS

ACKNOWLEDGMENTS

It goes without saying that the author must bear
the responsibility for the choices, editing, and
analysis that are represented by this volume. At the
same time, the seven year research effort was aided
and abetted by many who must be recognized for their
skills and generosity. While the identification and
collection of the documents begain in 1976, the full
significance of my project and the final form it took
resulted from my participation in a series of workshops on convenants organized by the Center for the
Study of Federalism at Temple University. Daniel
Elazar is director of the Center, and for his support,
insight, and skill at organizing and conducting such
workshops I am extremely grateful. There were liter-
ally dozens of people whose criticism and insight
during the meetings assisted my thinking, but special
note should be taken of John Kincaid of North Texas
State University, Ellis Katz of Temple University, and
Charles S. McCoy of the Pacific School of Religion.
The University of Houston has provided me a con-
genial atmosphere in which to carry forward my research, as well as much more direct support than can
be expected by a member of the academy. The University Faculty Development Leave Committee provided me
with a semester free of teaching duties during which
the manuscript was essentially completed. The University Publications Committee provided typing funds
for preparation of the manuscript, as well as a
generous subvention grant which made publication
possible. At a critical point the Department of
Political Science, under the leadership of Richard
Hofstetter, provided funds that permitted me to
continue work despite having two broken arms. Ms.
Martha Knutson for a time became my arms and hands,
and her attention to detail and skill at textual

analysis improved the manuscript. Last but not least at the University, Ms. Lawrence Verdell White Barnes (L.V.) typed the original manuscript in an accurate, intelligent, and timely fashion. Denice Reddick ably prepared the final manuscript for publication.

Linda Westervelt, my wife, shared the little triumphs and disasters that daily make up long term research such as this, and despite her own ambitious research schedule provided continuous encouragement and intellectual stimulation.

This volume is about communities, especially their beginnings. We each learn most of what we know about community from our respective families. Being the oldest of seven children, I must credit my brothers and sisters for an especially rich education in this regard. Mary, Larry, Jim, Brian, Yvonne, and Stephen are the unwitting source of my interest in communities, as are my parents. Since the focus of this volume is the origin and development of communities, it seems more than appropriate to dedicate it to those who are responsible for my primary and enduring experience of community, my parents.

PREFACE

This volume has a foundation story that needs to be told since it comprises an essential part of the book's significance. Rather than being just another collection of documents assembled in the hope of illuminating general historical trends or eras, the items contained within this volume result from a set of decision rules based upon a theory of politics. The theory of politics is drawn from the work of Eric Voegelin, although Willmoore Kendall and George Carey first introduced this author to Voegelin, and then interpreted Voegelin's work in a manner that pointed to the possibility of and need for this volume.

Eric Voegelin stresses that political analysis should begin with a people's attempt at self-interpretation, a self-interpretation that is most likely to be found in their political documents and writing. While one can analyze the brute fact of a political system's existence, at some point, if a political system is to endure, a people constitute themselves as a people. The crucial point is that at some point, either before or after creating a political society, a people reach a shared psychological state wherein they recognize themselves as engaged in a common enterprise, a people bound together by values, interests and goals. It is this sharing, this basis for their being a people rather than an aggregate of individuals, that constitutes the beginning point for political analysis.

Essentially what is shared is a common set of symbols and myths that provide meaning to their existence as a people, and links them to some transcendent order. This shared meaning, and shared link to some transcendent order, allows them to act as a people, to answer the basic political questions such as: How do we decide what to do? By what standards do we judge

our actions? Through what procedures do we reach collective decisions? What qualities or characteristics
do we strive to encourage among ourselves? What
qualities or characteristics do we seek or require of
those who lead us? Far from being the repository of
irrationality, these shared myths and symbols constitute the basis upon which collective, rational action
is possible.

These myths and symbols become at the same time
the basis for action as a people, and the means of
their self-illumination as a people. Furthermore,
since these myths and symbols are frequently expressed
in political documents, they tend to structure the
documents, determine the content, and define the
meaning of the words in these documents. Voegelin
also says that these shared myths and symbols can be
found in embryonic form in the earliest political
expressions made by a people, and in "differentiated"
form in later writings. Put another way, by studying
the political documents of a people, we can watch the
gradual unfolding, elaboration, and alteration of the
embryonic myths and symbols that define a given
people. He calls this process "differentiation," but
also refers to it as "self-illumination" and "self-
interpretation."

Finally, in a brief synopsis that cannot begin to
do credit to such a profound theory, Voegelin argues
that in Western Civilization basic symbolizations tend
to be variants of the original symbolization of the
Judaeo-Christian religious tradition. Without getting
into a discussion of where this leaves the Greeks and
Romans, suffice it to say that Voegelin's analysis led
Kendall and Carey to reexamine early American political documents, and what they found was a variant on
the symbolization of the Judaeo-Christian tradition.

Using only a few of these early documents of
foundation, they identify a number of basic symbols
which are present in all of them, and can be found in
documents of the 1770's and 1780's as well: higher
law, supreme representative assembly, deliberation,
and a virtuous people. This is not the place to
explicate what each means; the important point is that
Kendall and Carey argue that there are basic symbols
which can be found in the earliest documents of
foundation in embryonic form, and a hundred and fifty

years later in differentiated form. While provocative
and convincing, the position taken by Kendall and
Carey cannot be considered firmly established unless
and until the early American documents of foundation
can be comprehensively analyzed and the symbols traced
through succeeding documents.

This author, engaged in a project to analyze the
theory underlying the state constitutions written
between 1776 and 1789, was pushed by the evidence of
historical documents to seek that theory in earlier
American practices and thought rather than in European
institutions and theory.[1] Later research did indeed
show the continuity in symbols running from the
Mayflower Compact to the constitutions of the late
eighteenth century, and the embryonic basis for this
political tradition clearly evolved from basic symbols
in the Judaeo-Christian tradition.[2] Thus finding
support for the Kendall and Carey application of
Voegelin's theory, the author was led to identify and
collect the documents of political foundation written
by colonial Americans in order to conduct a detailed
analysis of them and the symbols they contain. This
long-term project is still underway, and it is clear
that the documents collected for purposes of the
analysis contain far more than any one researcher can
identify or digest. Therefore, having for the first
time identified a comprehensive collection of foundation documents, and having established at least in a
preliminary way the common threads running among them,
these documents are presented here so that others may
become familiar with them and advance our understanding of their contents.

There is much for us to learn. For example, the
Pilgrim Code of Law (1636) is probably the first true
written constitution in the English language. Covenants, compacts, and oaths of allegiance are prominent
among our earliest documents. Those writing on political obligation have been quite taken with John Locke,
but here we have people solving the problem of political obligation in a modern context before Locke was
born. The concepts of equality, popular sovereignty,
majority rule, representation, and constitutionalism
are just a few of those whose meaning and origins
could be illuminated by reference to these documents.

Until now most of these documents have been lost
to public view, and the few studied in depth have been
studied in isolation from the others. It is hoped
that the publication of this volume will lead to at
least two things: first, that this important aspect
of our political tradition will become well known to
students of American politics; and second, that we
will learn to read these documents together rather
than as separate statements. This is not a book of
readings. It is the foundation story of a people told
by themselves.

[1]Voegelin's basic works are *The New Science of Politics* (Chicago: University of Chicago Press, 1952; and
Order and History, 4. vols. (Baton Rouge: Louisiana State
University Press, 1956, 1957, 1957, and 1974). The book
by Willmoore Kendall and George Carey is *The Basic Sym-
bols of the American Political Tradition* (Baton Rouge:
Louisiana State University Press, 1970).
[2]Donald S. Lutz, *Popular Consent and Popular Control:
Whig Political Theory in the Early State Constitutions*
(Baton Rouge: Louisiana State University Press, 1980).
[3]Donald S. Lutz, "From Covenant to Constitution in
American Political Thought," *Publius: The Journal of
Federalism*, Vol. 10, No. 4 (Spring, 1981), 101-133.

INTRODUCTORY ESSAY

PART I

FROM COVENANT TO CONSTITUTION

Local government in colonial America was the
seedbed of American constitutionalism. This simple
fact has never been appreciated by those writing in
American political theory or constitutional theory.
Evidence for this neglect can be found simply by
examining any book dealing with American constitutional history and noting the absence of any significant reference to colonial documents written by
Americans. Rather, at best there will be brief
references to the Magna Carta, perhaps the English
Constitution, and probably the Declaration of Independence. If the authors of these books go so far as
even to discuss the source of American constitutional
theory beyond these few documents, they will almost
inevitably mention European thinkers, John Locke being
prominent among them.[1] This attitude toward the
colonial portion of American political thought is so
prevalent, that one writer recently remarked that,
"For theoretical as well as practical purposes the
origin of the American track can, therefore, be
assumed to begin in 1776. The thinkers, issues, and
events prior to 1776 have never really had a central
impact on the conduct of American politics."[2] It is
the purpose of this volume to end such neglect and
reverse such attitudes.
Recent work by historians has pointed us in the
direction of reexamining the colonial roots of our
political system, but the implications of this work
have not been absorbed by political scientists.[3]
Furthermore, historians themselves are not inclined to
put their questions in such a way as to lead to the

comprehensive examination of colonial documents of
political foundation. Intellectual historians almost
immediately look to Europe and the broader Western
Tradition when seeking the roots of constitutionalism
for the simple reason that there is a profound constitutional tradition there to examine. There has also
been a tendency to view the American Revolution as the
fundamental watershed in American history, closely
followed by the Civil War, which introduced an
unavoidable discontinuity in American thinking and
affairs. Rather than suggest that the perception of
such discontinuities should be rejected, it is argued
here that we should look for continuities as well.
One fundamental continuity to be found runs from the
earliest colonial documents of foundation to the
written constitutions of the 1770's and 1780's. We
should look to our own shores when seeking a constitutional tradition for America.

     One important caveat must be mentioned. This
author has argued elsewhere that there are two constitutional traditions running through colonial documents.[4] The first can be found in the charters,
letters-patent, and instructions for the colonists
written in England. In certain respects, the United
States Constitution favors this tradition. The second
tradition is found in the covenants, compacts, agreement, ordinances, codes, and oaths written by the
colonists themselves. While the U.S. Constitution
embodies aspects of this tradition as well, it is in
the early state constitutions that we find the full
flowering of this second tradition.

     These traditions, while in certain respects
distinct, also interpenetrate each other. Most of the
early colonial charters provide for the colonists to
design their own political institutions and practice
self-government, and most of those that did not so
provide at least permitted the colonists to fill in
the blank spots themselves. Charter revisions and
colonial document writing took each other into
account, and often one was the result of the other.
Nevertheless, it needs to be emphasized that the
former set of documents was handed down to or imposed
upon the colonists, while the second derived from the
colonists themselves. The asymmetry in power implied
by a charter is significantly different from the

symmetry of power implied by a compact mutually agreed upon.

There is a fundamental sense in which the two traditions worked together to produce a constitutional perspective uniquely American. The fact that American colonists were invariably here as the result of a written charter that could be amended, led to their becoming used to having a written document defining the context of their politics, and having a document that could be altered through some legal process. The English had a written constitution, but it was composed of the vast corpus of common law and legislative ordinance. English colonists in America became familiar with the idea of a single document being the focus of their link with that vast corpus.

At the same time, English colonists in America became used to being involved in the writing of their own documents to flesh out the particulars of their governments. This was partly the result of necessity -- time and distance between England and America did not permit close control from England. It was also the result of choice. The religious dissenters who were prominent in the first waves of migration came here to establish their own communities where they could practice their religion free from outside interference. This desire plus the structure of their churches led them to use self-written covenants as part of their political definition. It is a very short step to move to a blending of these two traditions wherein Americans would find themselves writing single, amendable documents as the focus of their political systems and calling them constitutions.

We will in this volume be concentrating upon what has been here termed the second tradition. We will be looking at those documents of political foundation written by the colonists themselves. The charters are already well known and easily accessible.[5] The documents written by the colonists are not well known and are generally not easily accessible, even where they are identified. Nevertheless, the reader should keep in mind that the documents presented in this volume are only part of the picture, although they are the most neglected portion of the picture.

Nor should the reader conclude that every document of political foundation is here included. There

are doubtless others that remain buried in obscure
collections, and perhaps future researchers will argue
that some that are known and not included in this
category should be. All that is claimed for the
present collection is that it probably represents most
of such documents, and that those reproduced here are
typical for and representative of American colonial
documents of political foundation.

   We have spoken of a "constitutional tradition."
Others have suggested that the Pilgrim Code of Law
(1636) was the first constitution in the English
language. We speak of the Massachusetts Constitution
of 1780 and the Pennsylvania Constitution of 1776 as
if such titles were not problematic. All three kinds
of statements assume that we know what is meant by the
term "constitution." From the very first, it is best
to consider this term something to be determined
rather than something assumed. It is because we start
off thinking that we know what a constitution is that
we have not given these documents the close textual
analysis they deserve.
   To illustrate what is meant, consider the 1776
Virginia Constitution. It is always reproduced with
the title at the beginning as "The Constitution of
Virginia." This is immediately followed by the title
to the first part, "Bill of Rights." Sixteen sections
later we come to the second part which is labelled
"The Constitution or Form of Government, Agreed to and
Resolved Upon by the Delegates and Representatives of
the Several Counties and Corporations of Virginia."
Here we have a puzzle. If the part after section
sixteen of the Bill of Rights is the Constitution,
then is the Bill of Rights properly part of the
constitution, and if not, why is the entire document
called a constitution? If the Bill of Rights is part
of the constitution, then why is the second part
labelled the way it is? The 1776 Maryland Constitution uses the same format, as does that of New Hampshire (1784), and North Carolina (1776). Pennsylvania
(1776) and Vermont (1776) label the second part "The
Plan of Government" or "The Frame of Government," as
does Massachusetts (1780). Furthermore, this last
document, considered the most influential state
constitution ever written, describes itself internally

as a "compact" and not a constitution. Are these early state documents that we habitually label "constitutions" in fact constitutions or something else?

It is neither feasible nor appropriate to answer this question here in detail, but this author is not alone in concluding that many of the early state constitutions were in fact compacts.[6] This raises the question of what a compact is, and in turn leads us to the early colonial documents, for many of them were compacts. At the same time, many of these colonial documents were not compacts. In order to assist the reader in reading the documents contained herein, and also to lay out categories of thought useful in tracing the developments that were part of our early constitutional tradition, it is necessary to do two things. First, we must define the terms commonly used internally to describe these colonial documents. Second, we must provide categories which allow us to describe what kind of foundation document each is. This will be followed by a list which describes each of the documents in this volume so that the reader may trace the developmental history, as well as compare documents that are similar in kind or contrast those that are dissimilar.

Let us perform the second task first since it is more fundamental. Even though we are examining a constitutional tradition, since the nature of a constitution is problematic and something to be settled in the future by those who study these documents, we will use the term "foundation documents" to describe the contents of this book. Once this term is adopted, it is reasonble to ask what it is that each document founds. It is possible to identify four distinct foundation elements, and any document can contain one, all, or any combination of these elements. The elements are: 1) the founding or creation of a people; 2) the founding of a government; 3) the self-definition of a people; and 4) the specification of a form of government. Let us consider each in turn.

Sometimes a document of foundation will create a people but not a government. It is as if those signing or agreeing to it were saying, "Here we are, a new people, one distinct from all other peoples,

declaring that we are ready to take our place on the
stage of life." The individuals composing the people
were, of course, already alive as individuals, but the
document creates a new life -- that held in common.
One could also speak of their creating a society, but
this term is not quite strong enough since it implies
a pattern of social interaction whereas to create a
people is to imply the creation or affirmation of a
culture as well. A society may have rules for inter-
acting, but a people has common values, goals, and
meaning to its life. While some social scientists
will point out that all known societies have had
shared values and meaning or they would not function,
the crucial fact of a foundation document containing
this element is that it is a celebration and conscious
affirmation of that which is shared. There is the
implication of a link with something transcendent that
ties them together as a people. It is the difference
between working together to build a wall to keep out
enemies and creating a church in which to worship the
god of the land enclosed by the wall.

Other documents will create or establish a
government. The Providence Agreement (1637), Document
23, is a classic instance. An existing people agree
simply to form a government to make collective decisions. It is easy to see the dead hand of John Locke
in the distinction between the creation of a people
and the agreement to create a government, but it
should be pointed out that colonists in America were
both making and blurring the distinction before Locke
was born. The Plymouth Combination (1620) and Cambridge Agreement (1629), Documents 3 and 7 respectively, contained both elements, whereas Documents 20
and 23 contained only the latter.

Those documents which contain the element of
self-definition are in some respects the most
interesting of all. It is unusual for a document to
create a people without also outlining the kind of
people they are or wish to beome, although some
documents contain further illumination of a people
that already exist. This self-description of a people
is the foundation element usually overlooked, yet it
is from this element that what we later call bills of
rights will evolve. Documents 1 and 2 contain only
this element and are typical in that the values of the

people are implicit in the prohibitions enumerated.
Commitment to godliness, order, and cleanliness are
obvious. Despite its name, the Massachusetts Body of
Liberties (1641), Document 41, will also imply
commonly held values, largely through a set of
explicit prohibitions. That it is called a "Body of
Liberties" points toward what this element will
become. In other documents, such as Salem's Enlarged
Covenant (1636), Document 19, the values and
self-image of a people will be spelled out explicitly
with no need for inferences on the part of the reader.
Whether explicit or implicit, this foundation element
represents a people's self-definition or self-illumination, and later in our history we will be unable to
exclude this element from what we will come to call a
constitution.

The fourth foundation element, the specification
of a form of government, present only embryonically in
documents like the Plymouth Combination (1620),
gradually comes to occupy a larger and larger proportion of our foundation documents. The word used
internally to identify this element is often "constitute." That is, within colonial documents the writers
usually "agree" to form a people or a government, but
"constitute" a form of government. That this part of
state constitutions, the part describing specific
forms and institutions, is usually termed "The Constitution or Form of Government" thus becomes quite
understandable. It is the fourth foundation element
grown to prominence in a foundation document, and it
is still being introduced by the term used in early
colonial documents of foundation. Some colonial
documents contain only this element, others combine it
with other foundation elements. In either case, we
can watch the development of American political
institutions later found in our constitutions --
institutions like elections, majority rule,
bicameralism, and checks and balances.

Because one or more element may be present in a
given document, if only in embryonic form, it is often
arguable just how the document should be categorized
with respect to these foundation elements. As a
further aid to comparative analysis, it is both useful
and interesting to consider the various legal forms
used, a task to which we now turn.

PART II

DEFINITION OF TERMS

It has been said that humans have a tendency to develop a multiplicity of terms for things that are prominent in their lives so as to distinguish subtle yet important variations. Thus, for example, Eskimos have many words to identify types of snow, and in classical Athens there were many gradations of community identified, each with its own descriptive term. If we turn the logic around, then it is apparent that the English speaking people of the seventeenth and eighteen centuries considered political agreements to be of great importance as they regularly used over a dozen different terms, sometimes interchangeably, but often to distinguish subtleties which they considered noteworthy. We will need to examine some of these linguistic alternatives, partly in order to comprehend what the issues were, and partly because the more general words we have inherited were not used to describe the documents as written. For example, when we examine the documents in this volume, we discover that the word "covenant" is rarely used to describe a document by those writing it, even though a number of the documents were understood to be covenants by their respective authors and had the covenant form internally. "Covenant" was too broad a term, and the authors often preferred a more restrictive, precise title.

The same is true for "Compact." The term is not used in any of the titles of these colonial documents, at least not by those who wrote them. The Mayflower Compact was not so named until 1793 and was referred to by the inhabitants of the colony as the Plymouth Combination, or sometimes simply as The Combination.

To make sense out of these documents, then, we will first need to define the broad categorial terms of covenant, compact, contract, and organic act, and then recover the understanding in use at the time for charter, constitution, patent, agreement, frame, combination, ordinance, and fundamentals. Since the colonists were not always consistent in their use of these terms, it will not be enough to conclude that, for example, since an agreement definitionally was a form of compact that all agreements were therefore compacts.

A contract usually implied an agreement with mutual responsibilities on a specific matter. A contract carried with it a restricted commitment such as in a business matter or a marriage, and involved relatively small groups of people. The contract could be enforced by law, but did not have the status of law.

A compact, on the other hand, was a mutual agreement or understanding that was more in the nature of a standing rule that, if it did not always have the status of a law, often had a similar effect. A compact implied an agreement that affected the entire community in some way, or relations between communities. The word had the root meaning of "knitting together" or "bringing the component parts closely and firmly into a whole." A compact, therefore, was an agreement creating something that we would today recognize as a community. Because a compact was not as precise as a contract, and more like a settled rule than an agreement with specific, reciprocal responsibilities, we do not find talk of a marriage compact or a Mayflower Contract.

A covenant could be viewed as having two distinct though related meanings. As a legal term in England, it referred to a formal agreement with legal validity made under the seal of the crown. This denoted an agreement of a serious nature witnessed by the highest authority. The religious counterpart to this secular or civil covenant was any agreement established or secured by God. The formal agreement made and subscribed to by members of a congregational church in order to constitute themselves a distinct relligous community had God as the witness and securer of the agreement. A religious covenant thus was essentially

an oath, and if it established a political community,
political obligation was secured by the oath rather
than merely resting upon the fact of consent having
been given. Note that both the civil and religious
meanings of covenant were related in that each was
characterized by being witnessed and therefore secured
by the highest relevant authority. Presumably any
compact with both God and the crown as securer would
be simultaneously a civil and religious covenant. A
civil covenant would require the presence of the royal
seal, while a religious covenant could be invoked
merely through the use of an oath.

Even with this restricted discussion two things
become apparent. First of all, calling John Locke a
"contract theorist" would have been considered a
misnomer by colonial Americans. He was more properly
a "compact theorist." Secondly, the relationship
between a covenant and a compact was a complex one.
Both were based upon the consent of those taking part.
Both created a new community. Both implied a
relationship that was stronger, deeper, and more
comprehensive than that established by a contract.
However, a compact required simply the consent of
those taking part, while a covenant required sanction
by the highest relevant authority as well. In this
regard, compact is the more modern of the two
concepts, while covenant was the more natural term to
use in a religious context or in a medieval context
where the authority hierarchy was well defined and had
a clear apex. A compact could be turned into a
covenant merely by calling upon God to witness the
agreement, which also turned consenting to the
agreement into an oath. If a people found themselves
in a situation where a mutual agreement had to be
drawn up, and where it was impossible to obtain the
royal seal in order to give the document legal,
binding status, the easiest solution for a religious
people was to call upon God as a witness to bind those
signing until the king's legal sanction could be
obtained. If, for some reason, a people reached a
mutual agreement that was covenant-like, but chose to
call upon neither God nor the king, they must have,
for some reason, considered themselves completely
competent to establish the document's legality. This
last instance would be one where legality was viewed

as resting upon the authority of the people, indicating an understanding of popular sovereignty. A compact was just such an agreement, one resting only upon the consent of those participating. For this reason, Blackstone could say, "A compact is a promise[8] proceeding from us, law is a command directed to us." The fact that most of the early colonists were a religious people, a religious people primarily from Protestant religions practiced in forming their own communities and familiar with the covenant form for doing so, becomes an important part of the background to American constitutionalism. That these people were often thrown by circumstances into situations where they had to practice this skill of community building through covenant writing, and that the charters under which they sailed often required that they provide for self-government in detail, or at the very least permitted such activities, must be viewed as another historical circumstance of considerable importance for American constitutionalism.

An agreement between God and his chosen people, then, was a covenant. The judicious Hooker refers to[9] "christ's own compact solemnly made with his church." While this was not the Jewish covenant, the Protestants writing the colonial documents in question viewed their work as equivalent to the Jewish biblical covenants.[10] It was certainly equivalent in the sense that calling upon God to witness a civil union not only turned a compact into a covenant, it also indicated an accord with the broader covenant in the Bible between God and his chosen people. Giving one's consent to join a civil community with this kind of covenant was in part an act of religious commitment, and elections to choose "the elect" were also acts of consent with religious overtones.

Consent becomes the instrument for establishing authority in the community and for expressing the sovereignty of God. God transmits his sovereignty to the people through the broader covenant, and they in turn convey his sovereignty to the rulers on the basis of the specific covenant creating the civil community. The people's consent is the instrument for linking God with the rulers, whose authority then is viewed as sanctioned by God, but because this authority comes through the people the rulers are beholding to God

through *them*. This, the original basis of popular
sovereignty, had been independently developed by both
Protestant and Catholic thinkers by the seventeenth
century.[11]

Given these characteriziations, it can be seen
that a covenant is simultaneously a compact as it
contains everything essential to a compact. A compact, however, is not simultaneously a covenant,
because it lacks the explicit link with the higher
authority, even though the idea and form for a compact
are derived from covenants, and the kind of community
established is similar enough so that one could call a
compact a near-covenant. Furthermore, there are
circumstances in which an apparent compact is really a
covenant in the complete sense. For example, suppose
a people form a society under a covenant in either or
both God's and the king's name. They then later form
a government for this society in a document that does
not mention any authority other than themselves as a
people. Since the first document that formed them as
a people also automatically establishes them as
expressing the higher authority whenever they act
through their own popular sovereignty, all subsequent
documents by that people could be considered covenants
as well since the link with the higher authority is
understood. Nor is this implied covenant status always
left for the reader of the document to infer. The
Pilgrim Code of Law (1636), Document 21, is a good
example. After, in the first paragraph, establishing
the legal basis for holding the assembly that will
write the Code, the first sentence in the second
paragraph says: "Now being assembled according to the
said order, and having read the combination made at
Cape Cod the 11th of November 1620 . . . as also our
letters patents confirmed by the honorable council,
his said Majesty established and granted the 13th of
January 1629 . . . .' The combination of November 11,
1620 referred to here is, of course, what we now call
the Mayflower Compact. The letters-patent refers to
the charter from the king that was then in effect. The
former document is a religious covenant, and the
latter is a civil covenant. This sentence in the
Pilgrim Code of Law serves the double function of
first establishing the legal basis for their having
the power to write such a Code, and secondly it brings

the Code under the umbrella of the earlier covenants thereby making it an implied mixed covenant. There is on pages 29 - 30 of this section a table containing a selective description of the documents contained in this book. The reader will note that the Pilgrim Code of Law is not described as a mixed covenant but as a civil covenant. This is because the first paragraph of the document establishes it explicitly as such, even though it is implicitly a mixed covenant. The rule followed in the table is to categorize each document on the basis of a reading of what is explicit in a given text so as to avoid confusion. At the same time, it is being pointed out here that a careful textual analysis in conjunction with earlier, related documents can lead to an implied status somewhat different from what is listed. This is one more reason why such documents of foundation should not be read in isolation. In any event, it is worth emphasizing here that the writers of the Pilgrim Code of Law saw reason to place the document in the context of both their legal charter and their self-written document of foundation. This is one document where the two constitutional traditions come together.

It is perfectly possible for a contract to be elevated to compact or covenant status. For example, the king could place his seal upon a contract, perhaps charters come most easily to mind, or a marriage contract could be witnessed by God in an oath. However, such a document would imply quite a different kind of community than a simple covenant. Since all of the details of the relationship would be spelled out, the result would be less a community where the partners are required to go beyond the legally defined relationship to develop fully the relationship, and more one where the partners are minimally required to fulfill the obligations specifically mentioned. Such a contractually-based compact or covenant would first of all not be a true covenant as understood in the Jewish tradition, and secondly, it would be inclined toward legalistic wrangling over the meaning and intent of specific words and phrases. The emphasis upon the letter rather than upon the spirit of the agreement would destroy community as implied by covenant or compact, and result in something less -- an association for specific, limited ends. True covenants and compacts, without any contractual elements, are thus communitarian oriented, while contractual variants are inclined to be legalistic. One manifestation of the latter would be the tendency of a people to produce longer and longer specifications for the agreement which are more and more precise and limited. However, this should not be pushed too far as an identifying characteristic of a contractual society since there is another, non-contractual form of agreement that may resemble it superficially.

An "organic act" is one that codifies and celebrates an agreement or set of agreements made through the years by a community. In this way, a "common law" comprised of legislative and judicial decisions made over a number of years can be codified, simplified, and celebrated in dramatic form, thereby also renewing the consent-based oath upon which obligation to the community rests. The early state constitutions adopted in 1776 could be viewed as organic acts as well as compacts as they usually summarized and codified what the colonists of each state had evolved over the previous one hundred and fifty years. In the case of Connecticut and Rhode Island the colonial charters were formally re-adopted as constitutions -- charters which had been essentially written by the colonists. Massachusetts did not adopt or readopt anything in 1776 but continued to live under the 1725 charter as a continuous community. Examples of an organic act include The Laws and Liberties of Massachusetts (1647), the Connecticut Code of Laws (1650), and the Puritan Laws and Liberties (1658), Documents 53, 58, and 60, respectively.

These organic acts are long and contain precise terms for limited categories of behavior. Various provisions, for example, might regulate behavior in church, after dark, or in dealing with Indians under specific circumstances. While highly legalistic, they are laws after all, they are not contracts in the strict sense since there generally are not provisions for reciprocal obligations. These are more properly "ordinances" but not organic acts, because rather than being a summary and codification of what came before they each are sets of rules made *de novo* . The Capital

Laws of Connecticut (1642), Document 44, is similar in
this regard to Documents 1 and 2.

We now have the basic characterizations for the
analytic categories of religious covenant, civil
covenant, mixed religious-civil covenant, compact,
contract, and organic act. As was noted earlier,
these terms were generally not used to describe
colonial foundation documents, at least not by those
writing them. It is necessary, therefore, to provide
a brief characterization for each of the terms that
were prominently used -- agreement, combination,
frame, fundamentals, ordinance, patent, charter, and
constitution.

An "agreement" in the formal, political sense
referred to an arrangement between two or more persons
as to a course of action, a mutual understanding, or a
common goal. The term was usually used to describe a
document that we would recognize as a covenant or
compact. Indeed, documents frequently use the phrases
"to agree," to compact," and "to covenant" interchangeably in their internal wording. Treaties were
sometimes termed agreements. However, while an
agreement was legally binding on the parties making
it, the term more properly implied a sense of harmony
or concord that transcended a purely legal relationship. To refer to a treaty as an agreement meant at
the very least that there was no dissention, but it
usually implied more -- a level of mutual pleasure
that approached atonement, whether in the sense of
reconciliation or of propitiation. An agreement,
then, at least during the period in question, was far
more than a contract. It clearly suggested a
relationship that moved beyond the letter of the
agreement toward mutual support and pleasure,
something close to the "knitting together" implied by
a compact or the spirit of community carried by a
covenant.

A "combination" was viewed as a bringing together
of two or more entities into a whole. The banding
together or union of persons was usually for the
prosecution of some common, broad objective. The term
was often used interchangeably with agreement and
compact, and sometimes with alliance and treaty. As a
legal term it had neither consistent nor widespread
use, but American colonists were quite consistent in

using it as the equivalent for agreement as just outlined. The document later to be known as the Mayflower Compact, which was clearly a covenant in form, was known to those who wrote it as the Plymouth Combination.

During the era in question, a "frame" referred to an established order, plan, scheme, or system, especially of government. It strongly implied a definite form, regular procedure, order, and regularity. It also implied an adapted or adjusted condition in the sense of changing to take into account new factors or conditions affecting the older form, plan or system while not rejecting that older one. Thus, a frame tended not to be a document of initial founding as much as it was one of refounding, and hence was similar to an organic act. Document 69 uses "frame" in its title.

The use of "fundamentals," as in New Haven Fundamentals (1639), Document 37, implied the base upon which something is built. It was used primarily to refer to immaterial rather than physical things, and thus was used to describe leading principles, rules, laws, or articles which served as the groundwork for a political system. Such a statement of principles might be an addition to a covenant or compact, a preface to a frame or ordinance, or it might constitute the agreement itself. Document 37 is the classic example. Documents 32, 41, 46, 52, 53, and 66 are further examples.

An "ordinance" usually referred to an authoritative command, although in a more restricted sense, narrower scope, and less permanent nature than a law or statute. The term was sometimes used to refer to the founding or instituting of something, but in the sense of making conformable to order, rule, or custom -- as in placing or arranging in proper sequence or proper relative position. It would not be improper to view an ordinance as sometimes attempting to establish "orders" of people according to class, merit, ranking, status, importance, duties, rights, etc. As with fundamentals, political ordinances could be covenantal in form, compacts, contracts, or something else depending upon the content. The words "ordain" and "order" were used as operative words in a documents that legally produced an ordinance. Document 1 is an

ordinance that is especially inclined to produce
"orders" of people. Many of the ordinances reproduced
in this volume are simple legislative acts, such as
Documents 15, 24, 31, and 44.

A "patent," as in letters-patent, had the root
meaning of a public letter or document, as opposed to
a private one, usually from a sovereign or person in
authority. It had a variety of uses -- e.g. to put on
public record some contract, to command or authorize
something to be done, to confer some right, privilege,
title, property, or office. Whatever its use, it
usually implied a monopoly of some sort, as in
exclusiveness of use. Obviously a patent was related
to a contract, but it was also related to a law in
that it was handed down by some authority. It was
unlike a contract in that it did not necessarily imply
reciprocal duties but often simply recorded a grant
with no duties assigned the grantee.

The word "charter" is derived from the Latin word
meaning a leaf of paper, a writing, a document. Often
it was a legal document or deed written upon a single
piece of paper by which grants, cessions, contracts,
and other transactions were confirmed or ratified. It
was also used to refer to a written document delivered
by the sovereign or legislature to grant privileges
to, or recognize the rights of, an entire people, a
certain class, or specific individuals. The Magna
Carta comes to mind here as an example since it
recognized the rights of the nobility   the
king. In the Leviathan, Hobbes says that charters are
not laws but exemptions from the laws, which also fits
in with the purpose of the Magna Carta or other bills
of rights. Charters were also used to grant pardon,
and create or incorporate boroughs, universities,
companies, or other corporations. They were a written
instrument or contract applied especially to documents
or deeds relating to the conveyance of property. The
word "charter" was used as a linguistic alternative
for privilege, immunity, or publicly conceded right.
To say that something was chartered was to say that it
was founded, privileged, or protected. Charters and
letters-patent were similar, although the latter term
was broader in that it could refer to any authoritative document. A charter was invariably a patent,
while a patent was not necessarily a charter. Charter

was also closely related to contract as a legal term
in that it effectively constituted a contract between
the authority granting it and the person(s) to whom it
was granted. However, unlike a simple contract, a
charter often included so many statements of a general
nature that it transcended the notion of a contract.
A contract, for example, would not be an appropriate
description for a document which contains statements
as broad and vague as, " . . . and the proprietors
shall establish a government whereby differences among
the planters may be settled." The peculiarity of a
charter was that it often contained strong contractual
elements linked to many or most of what we would
recognize as foundation elements of a broader nature.

Although rarely used to describe early colonial
documents, the word "constitution" is worth examining
in order to compare its usage with some of the other
terms we are examining. Related to the term "consti-
tuent," which refers to that which makes a thing what
it is in the sense of being formative, essential,
characteristic, or distinctive, it is more immediately
drawn from "constitute," which means to establish,
ordain, or appoint in the sense of providing legal
form and status. Constitution, proper, referred to
the action of making, establishing, decreeing, or
ordaining something, usually in the sense of having
been made by a superior civil or ecclesiastical
authority.

Additionally, it had been used historically to
denote limitations. For example, the Constitutions of
Clarendon in England, a set of propositions drawn up
at the Council of Clarendon in 1164, defined the
limits of civil and ecclesastical jurisdiction. Used
in this way it was similar to a charter as exemplified
in the Magna Carta. The term constitution had also
been used to describe the mode in which a state was
organized, especially as to the location of sovereign
power; as well as to describe the fundamental principles according to which a nation, state, or body
politic was organized and governed. For example,
there was the Declaration of the Estates of Scotland
(1689): "Whereas King James the Seventh did by the
advice of wicked and evil counsellors invade the
fundamental constitution of the kingdom, and altered
it from a limited monarchy to an arbitrary despotic

power . . . ;" or Lord Viscount Bolingbroke's definition, "By Constitution we mean, whenever we speak
with propriety and exactness, that assemblage of laws,
institutions, and customs, derived from certain fixed
principles of reason . . . that compose the general
system, according to which the community hath agreed
to be governed.[12]

In summary, we find the word constitution associated with making or establishing something, giving
it legal status, describing the mode of organization,
locating sovereignty, establishing limits, and describing fundamental principles. Not unsurprisingly, it
was often used in association with charter, law,
statutes, ordinance, frame and fundamentals. In our
usage today, it encompasses part of all that these
words imply, plus some of what we associate with
compact. Although the usage of the word during the
seventeenth century sounds familiar to our ears, the
various components had not yet been brought together
in any complete fashion. Also the term "constitution"
was not used to refer to a specific document as we are
inclined to do today. The English had developed the
concept of a written constitution, but the writing was
scattered over thousands of documents, and no one was
quite sure which documents should be included. When
Americans finally brought all the elements together in
single documents in 1776, the term constitution was to
include far more than was outlined by Bolingbroke.
Indeed, the early state constitutions would derive
their elements from agreements, compacts, and covenants, as well as from frames, charters, fundamentals,
and ordinances. The word constitution is not used in
any of the documents duplicated in this volume, but
the word "constitute" is used in five. They are Documents 3, 20, 26, 55, and 66.

This completes our characterization of the
various terms that can be used to describe the colonial foundation documents. As an aid to comparative
analysis, as well as for seeking out those documents
of special interest to any given reader, we have
provided a table which categorizes each document
according to the types of form it contains or is
consistent with, as well as the foundation elements it
contains. While the author has been careful in
assigning each category, readers should not consider

the table as definitive. Because of overlapping
meaning and the uncertainty of word use, the
characterization of a document as containing or
embodying a given legal form is often open to
challenge. The assigning of categories is designed to
be suggestive and helpful. Each document is also
categorized in terms of who was acting in writing it.
This information is important, and will be utilized in
the discussion to follow in Section IV.

SELECTIVE DESCRIPTION OF DOCUMENTS

Code for Types of Documents (with respect to form):

A - religious	H - combination
B - civil covenant	I - fundamentals
C - oath	J - ordinance
D - compact	K - patent
E - contract	L - charter
F - organic act	M - constitution
M - agreement	

Code for Foundation Elements:

1 - creation of a people
2 - creation of a government
3 - provision of a self-definition
4 - creation or description of
   a specific form of government
   or set of political institutions

Document Number and Short Name	Type of Document	Foundation Elements	Who is Acting
1 Articles, Laws	I & J	3	executive
2 Laws Enacted	I & J	3	legislature
3 Agreement	A,D,G&H	1,2,3,&4	people
4 Laws and Orders	J	3&4	legislature
5 Plymouth Oath	C	1&3	people
6 Salem Covenant	A	1&3	people
7 Agreement	A,D&G	1&2	people
8 Watertown Covenant	A & G	1&3	people
9 Mass. Election	G & J	4	people
10 Oath of a Freeman	C	1&3	people
11 Mass. Agreement	G	4	people
12 Cambridge Agreement	D & G	4	people
13 Dorchester Agreement	D & G	4	people

Document Number and Short Name	Type of Document	Foundation Elements	Who is Acting
14 Cambridge Agreement	G & J	4	people
15 Mass. Agreement	G & J	4	legislature
16 Oath of a Freeman	C	1&3	people
17 Salem Oath	C	1&3	people
18 Watertown Agreement	G	4	people
19 Enlarged Salem Covenant	A & F	1&3	people
20 Plymouth Agreement of 1636	D,G&H	2	special body
21 Pilgrim Code of Law	B,D&J	3&4	special body
22 Dedham Covenant	D & G	1,3&4	people
23 Providence Agreement	G	2	people
24 Orders	J	3&4	legislature
25 Act for Establishing the House	B & D	4	leg.& people
26 Government of Pocasset	A & D	1,2&3	people
27 Plantation Covenant at Quinnipiack	A & D	3	people
28 An Act for Church Liberties	J & G	3	prop.& people
29 Act for Swearing Allegenace	A,C&J	3	legislature
30 An Act What Persons	B & J	4	legislature
31 Act for the Liberties	J	3	legislature
32 Fundamental Orders of Conn.	A,D&I	2&4	people
33 Newport Agreement	D & G	1,2&4	people
34 Government of Portsmouth	B & D	2&4	people
35 Guilford Covenant	A & D	1&3	people
36 Structure of Town Governments	H	4	legislature
37 Fundamental Articles of New Haven	A,D&I	2,3&4	people
38 Agreement of Settlers	A,D,G&H	1,2&3	people
39 Plantation Covenant	G & H	3&4	people

Document Number and Short Name	Type of Document	Foundation Elements	Who is Acting
40 Connecticut Oath of Fidelity	C	1&3	people
41 Mass. Body of Liberties	D,I&J	3&4	legislature
42 Piscataqua Combination	D & H	1,3&4	people
43 Government of R.I.	D & G	2&4	legislature
44 Capital Laws of Conn.	J	3	legislature
45 Government of Guilford	D & G	1,2,3&4	people
46 New Haven Fundamentals	D,G&I	1,2,3&4	people
47 New England Confederation	D,G,&H	2,3&4	legislature
48 Mass. Bicameral Ordinance	J	4	legislature
49 Mass. Ordinance on the Legislature	J	4	legislature
50 Majority Vote of Deputies	J	4	legislature
51 Warwick Agreement	D & G	2&3	people
52 Acts and Orders	D,I&J	2,3&4	people
53 Laws and Liberties	F,I&J	3&4	legislature
54 Mass. Ordinance	J	4	legislature
55 Charter of Providence	J & L	2&4	legislature
56 Maryland Toleration Act	J	3	legislature
57 Towns of Wells	D & H	2&4	legislature
58 Connecticut Code of Laws	F & J	3	legislature
59 Cambridge Agreement	G	3&4	people
60 Puritan Laws and Liberties	F & J	2,3&4	legislature
61 An Act of General Court	J	3&4	legislature
** Charter of Conn.	B & L	1,2,3&4	king &leg.
** Charter of R.I.	B & L	1,2,3&4	king &leg.

Document Number and Short Name	Type of Document	Foundation Elements	Who is Acting
** Concessions and Agreement of N.J.	D & G	1,2,3&4	leg. &props.
** Concessions and Agreement	B,D&L	1,2&4	leg. &props.
62 Letter from Governor	J	3&4	governor
63 General Assembly of R.I.	J	4	legislature
64 Preface to General Laws	F & J	3	legislature
** Concessions of W N.J.	D,G&I	3&4	people &props.
65 Laws and Liberties of N.H.	F,I&J	3&4	legislature
66 Fundamentals of W N.J.	D,G&I	3&4	people &props.
67 Concessions to PA.	D,E&J	3	people &props.
68 Laws & Liberties of N.H.	F,I&J	3&4	legislature
69 Frame of Gov. of PA.	B,I,J&L	4	proprietor
70 Act for Freedom	G & J	3	prop. &leg.
** Frame of Gov. of PA.	B & J	4	prop. &leg.
** Laws on Personal Freedom	J	3	legislature
** Fundamental Constitutions	B,D,I&L	2,3&4	proprietors
71 Charter of Liberties			
72 Articles of Agreement	I & J	3&4	gov. &leg.
** Admonition for Reformation	F,G&J	3	gov. &leg.
** Frame of Gov. of PA.	F,I&J	4	governor
73 Division of Conn.	J	4	legislature
** Charter of Privileges	F,G&L	3&4	prop. &leg.
74 Act to Ascertain	J	4	gov. &leg.

** These are part of the documentary history under analysis here, but are not reproduced in this volume because of space limitations. The Appendix to this volume indicates where each of these documents can be found reproduced.

PART III

ANALYTIC OVERVIEW

Although one major purpose for publishing these
foundation documents is to lead others to analyze them
individually and together, it is not inappropriate to
initiate that analysis by presenting here some of the
apparent developments that they embody. Let us
briefly outline some of the things that a reading of
these documents together leads us to conclude.

1.   The use of the covenant form for political
foundation is derived from the use of covenants for
the foundation of religious communities.
2.   The political covenant evolved rather
quickly into the compact form.
3.   The use of the compact form for documents of
political foundation was a fundamental step in the
development of popular sovereignty.
4.   The secular "agreement" was a variant of the
compact form.
5.   The covenant and compact forms were used in
such a way that they could contain any or all of the
foundation elements.
6.   With few exceptions, when the covenant or
compact forms are used it is the people who are
acting.
7.   When the legislature acts it usually uses
the ordinance form, of which the "fundamentals" form
is a variant.
8.   With few exceptions, the ordinance form is
used primarily so as to include only the last two
foundation elements.
9.   The formal oath, when used by itself,

contained the first and third foundation elements, and when embedded in a longer document such as a constitution, it contained only the third element.

10. Although present mainly in embryonic form at the beginning, the fourth foundation element becomes prominent in later documents.

11. While this fourth foundation element was prominent in the early state constitutions, the other three elements were often present also so that these documents in effect were using the compact form.

12. The third foundation element evolved into a form we now call a bill of rights.

13. In 53 instances the third and fourth elements are separated, ie. one is found in a document without the other. In 28 instances they are found together in the same document. Thus, colonists were twice as likely to separate these two elements as combine them.

14. Number 13 led to some confusion as to whether state constitutions should include bills of rights. Some combined the third and fourth elements in the body of the document, many separated the two elements into two sections, calling only that section containing the fourth element the "constitution," and some did not contain a bill of rights at all.

15. The colonists were willing to let the legislatures speak for them in matters of foundation, except when forming themselves into a people and founding a government. The exception to the latter is found in those documents founding a federation of existing towns.

16. Number 15 leads to the natural expectation that legislatures could write state constitutions, although when these documents were in the compact form, and thus contained all four foundation elements, the expectation was that the people should also approve them. When the first two elements were not present, such popular ratification was not excpected.

Undoubtedly, other general developments could be abstracted, but these possibilities should be suggestive enough to encourage further analysis. It is not appropriate in a volume of this sort to engage in an extended analysis to support the sixteen trends abstracted above,[13] but there is some additional

discussion which might prove useful for any reader
seeking to understand the documents. In particular,
while most of the above can be tested by direct
examination of the documents reproduced herein, the
first point requires a bit more information.

Protestants, Catholics, and Jews should all be
familiar with the notion of the Bible as containing a
covenant between God and his chosen people. This is,
of course, the archetype for the concept of covenant.
The political aspects of the covenant idea, however,
may not be as well appreciated. Ignoring for now the
Bible itself, it is instructive to look at what the
Jewish themselves derived from the covenant model in
the Bible. Drawing upon their tradition, the Jewish
people have tended to recur to covenants as the basis
for the formation of their communities. For example,
consider the following preamble from a model document
written during the Middle Ages for creating a congre-
gation-community.

> We, the elders and leaders of the community of
> -x-, due to our many sins we have declined and
> become fewer and weaker, and until only few have
> been left of many, like a single tree at the
> mountaintop, and the people of our community have
> been left with no head or   , or head justice
> or leader, so that they are like sheep without a
> shepherd and some of our community go about
> improperly clothed and some speak obscenely and
> some mix with the Gentiles and eat their bread
> and become like them, so that only in the Jewish
> name, are they at all different. We have seen
> and discussed the matter and we agreed in assem-
> bly of the entire community, and we all, great
> and small alike, have gone on to establish this
> charter in this community.[14]

The document then goes on to outline the institutions
through which they will govern themselves. Several
aspects of this document warrant further comment.
First of all, the operative word, the word that
creates the force of the document or gives it effect
is "agreed," at least as it is translated. Secondly,
the agreement is made by everyone in the community.
While a system of representation was used for
deliberation and framing, the words imply that
everyone in the community explicitly agreed to the

covenant. Thirdly, we can identify all four foundation
elements as being present. Following an extended
explanation of why the document is needed, it creates
a people set off from other people. It creates a
government for making the collective decisions
required by the community, and then specifies the form
of government, its institutions and principles, in the
part not reproduced here. The self-definition of
themselves as a people is implicit in the preamble as
well as later. They are a religious people who need
leaders to keep them close to God. Their relationship
to God is reflected in their clothing, their food,
their speech, and their behavior. While these are not
spelled out here, this document links them to a
broader covenant where such things are spelled out in
detail. In addition to being a religious people
determined to live by a common moral code, we see a
free people bound only by their own consent, a people
dedicated to calm, deliberative processes for
collective decision-making. The self-definition runs
through all parts of the document, from the colorful
complaint of why a new community is needed, to the
form of taxation to be used.

     With the coming of the Protestant Reformation and
its attendant emphasis upon direct biblical
interpretation, we find the covenant form becoming
prominent among them as well. The more radical the
Protestant sect, it seems, the closer they approached
the Jewish covenant tradition. For example, the
Scottish Presbyterians signed the "national Covenant"
at Edinburgh on February 28, 1638 for the defense of
Presbyterianism against the Episcopal system that had
been introduced by James I and Charles I. The "Solemn
League and Covenant" was accepted by the General
Assembly of the Church of Scotland on August 13, 1643,
and the Westminster Assembly of Divines, and English
Parliament on September 25 as a league between England
and Scotland on the basis of the establishment of
Presbyterianism in both countries. The bonds
subscribed to at Edinburgh by the Lords of the
Congregation and their followers on December 3, 1557,
and at Perth on May 31, 1559, in order to carry out
the Protestant Reformation was also termed a covenant.
It is to be noted that the covenant form they used was
in a mixed religious-political context, and that it

was used to define a people and its values as well as
its form of government. These grand covenants made
the history books, but there were many others made to
form specific congregations or local communities.

    This brings us to the initial colonization of
English America. As is well known, small religious
communities were prominent among the first settlements. Often an entire church community would migrate
to American shores together, and they would either
bring their church covenant with them or write a new
one upon arrival. Just as the Scottish and English
covenants would begin with something like, "We the
undersigned, in the name of the most just Lord, do
hereby agree . . . ," a typical church government
would read like that of the Charleston-Boston Church
(July 30, 1630):

> In the name of our Lord Jesus Christ, & in
> Obedience to His holy will & Divine Ordinance.
>
>   We whose names are hereunder written, being
> by His most wise, & good Providence brought
> together into this part of America in the Bay of
> Massachusetts, & desirous to unite ourselves into
> one Congregation, or Church, under the Lord Jesus
> Christ our Head, in such sort as becometh all
> those whom He had Redeemed, & Sanctifyed to
> Himself, do hereby solemnly, and religiously (as
> in His most holy Presence) Promise, & bind
> ourselves, to walke in all our ways according to
> the Rule of the Gospell, & in all sincere confor-
> mity to His holy Ordinances, & in mutual love, &
> respect each other, so near as God shall give us
> grace.[15]

Here we have an explanation of why the document is
needed, the creation of a people (all those undersigned), the creation of a church instead of a
government, and the definition of themselves as a
people who intend to walk in the ways of the Gospel,
God's ordinances, and in mutual love. The comparison
of this church covenant with the Jewish model earlier
reproduced, and with the early political covenants
reproduced in this volume, illustrates the easy
appropriation from Jewish covenant to colonial
compact.

    Furthermore, the growth of these early covenants
into more complex documents can be traced. The Salem

Covenant of 1629 (Document 6), perhaps the briefest
and most attenuated covenant on record, was expanded
into The Enlarged Salem Covenant (1636), Document 19.
This expanded covenant not only has the four foundation elements noted in the Charleston-Boston Church
Government, but the element of self-definition has
been considerably expanded so that it now takes up
most of the document in a list of nine articles. This
can then be compared to later documents such as the
1641 Massachusetts Body of Liberties, Document 41.

Finally, the operative words found in these colonial church covenants, as exemplified by the one
reproduced above, are typically "covenant," bind,"
"agree," and "promise." In almost every significant
detail the church covenants written in early colonial
America resemble Jewish covenants, with one important
exception -- they do not establish a specific form of
government. When colonists found themselves in the
position of having to create a government, or having
to flesh out a government granted in a charter, they
tended simply to add this element to the church
covenant form and thereby completely recover the
foundation elements found in Jewish covenants. They
did not do so consciously, perhaps, but the radical
Protestant return to biblical sources for ordering
their lives led to their becoming, to a far greater
extent than they realized, precisely what they saw
themselves as metaphorically -- a modern version of
the Jewish people.

The evolution of political covenants into compacts is also worth a brief discussion. The first
political covenant written by American colonists has
come to be known by us as the Mayflower Compact.
Although not termed a compact until 1793, it may be
properly so termed as it does contain everything that
the compact form requires. The first foundation
element, the creation of a people, is accomplished in
traditional English fashion with the words "We whose
names are underwitten . . . ." The second element,
the creation of a government, is accomplished with the
passage combining themselves into a "civil Body
politick." The third foundation element, a
self-definition of themselves as a people, can be
found scattered throughout the document. The people
defined by those signing the document see themselves

as "Loyal Subjects of . . . King James," as a
Christian people seeking the Glory of God and the
advancement of the Christian religion, as having the
freedom and capacity to make their own laws, and as
those possessed of a unique mission -- to plant the
first colony in northern Virginia.

    The fourth foundation element, the specification
of a form of government with its institutions and
operating principles, is found only in embryonic form.
The document tells us that the laws of the colony
shall be made with the participation of all those
undersigned, implying a kind of democratic system,
that the laws shall affect all equally, and that the
laws shall be made for the general good of the colony.

    This much would make the document a political
compact, but the opening words, "In the name of God,
amen" transform it into what is more properly termed a
covenant. This calling upon God to witness their
agreement is echoed later in the words where they
"covenant and combine" themselves. The Mayflower
Compact thus has all of the elements that are required
for a compact form, plus the calling upon God needed
to make it a covenant. That the Mayflower Compact can
be viewed simultaneously as a covenant and a compact
is further supported by the use of both "covenant" and
"combine" as operative words. The former is generally
associated with the covenant form, the latter with the
compact form. Since not all of those signing the
document were Puritans, it makes sense that the
covenant form is present to bind those who were
religious, and the compact form is present for those
who were not religious. Later in the text the authors
similarly use a number of words to cover the linguistic territory: " . . . and by Virtue hereof do enact,
constitute, and frame, such just and equal Laws,
Ordinances, Acts, Constitutions, and Officers . . . ."
These were not lawyers writing the text, and they were
in an ambiguous setting with no clear precedent. The
Mayflower Compact reads like an agreement written by
cautious minds bent upon taking no chances.

    In 1633 the settlers at Dorchester, Massachusetts
wrote an agreement that did not call upon God at all
but used the simple compact form (Document 13). This
was not a complete foundation document, however, as it
lacked the first and third foundation elements. In

1636 the people of Plymouth wrote what has come to be
known as the Pilgrim Code of Law (Document 21). This
is considered by many to be the first true constitution written by Americans, and consisted of a detailed
description of governmental institutions and their
operating principles, in other words, the fourth
foundation element. The Plymouth Agreement (Document
20), passed the same day and inserted as a preface to
the Code of Law, contains the other three foundation
elements, so that together the two documents constitute the first complete foundation document in developed form. As noted earlier, this was explicitly a
compact, but also implicitly a covenant as the religious and civil covenants legally founding the settlement were read at the beginning of the proceedings to
justify their being able to write such a document.
The compact and covenant forms are still intertwined.
     The covenant form predominated for a while and
can be found represented in such documents as the
Fundamental Orders of Connecticut (Document 32), and
Quinnipiack Plantation Covenant (Document 27), the
Fundamental Articles of New Haven (Document 37), the
Agreement of the Settlers at Exeter (Document 38), and
the Government of Pocasset (Document 26). The Newport
Agreement (Document 33) was a compact pure and simple,
but lacked the first and third foundation elements.
The Government of Portsmouth (Document 34) was a
compact but also lacked the first and third elements.
The Piscataqua Combination (Document 42) is apparently
the oldest pure compact in American political history
that is also complete as a foundation document.
Whether complete or incomplete, the similarity between
these early compacts and covenants is striking. The
only real difference is the presence or absence of God
as a witness to the agreement. This is no small
difference for the history of political thought, as a
pure compact form implies complete comfort with the
concept of popular sovereignty.
     In like manner the other propositions listed at
the beginning of this section can be established
through a careful reading of the documents. That, and
any further discoveries, are left to the reader.
Tracing the development of bills of rights should
prove especially interesting. Any such examination
would give more than pause to those who assume that

documents like the Declaration of Independence and the
Virginia Bill of Rights, both written in 1776, suddenly sprang from the heads of their respective authors
in a fit of theoretical creativity.

PART IV

EDITORIAL DECISIONS

Whenever one is faced with transcribing historical documents there are a number of decisions that
need to be made. One is whether or not to use the
original spelling and grammar. In the case of these
documents it was decided to introduce as few emanda-
tions as possible, and to identify the emendations
that might have been introduced earlier by others.
The only emendations introduced by this transcriber
involve the occasional deletion of lists of names at
the end of a document. These instances are noted by
comments in brackets. Anything else in brackets
constitutes an alteration introduced by an earlier
transcriber that this one cannot eliminate by reference to the actual text. In many instances this is
because the original text no longer exists and we are
limited to some transcription in its place. The use
of a caret indicates a blank or an undecipherable word
or words in the original text. In some instances the
text that was transcribed had been systematically
altered by an earlier transcriber. For example, the
oldest surviving text may have been printed during the
eighteenth century using the printer's convention of
substituting the German "u" for "v" or an "i" for "j."
For a while it was common practice when transcribing
to emend these printer's conventions, and where an
earlier transcriber has done so, and that is the text
being here transcribed, such transpositions are noted
in the remarks introductory to the document.
    In every instance the effort has been made to
locate a facsimile or accurate transcription for each
document. Since there are often competing versions,
the text that is being used for transcription here has

been identified in the introductory remarks and then
faithfully transcribed. The original text often does
not have a formal title at the beginning. In these
instances the title used is either the one by which
the document has traditionally come to be known, or
else a simple descriptive title is attached. Where
the traditional title is different from the formal one
actually on the original, this is reflected by using
the traditional title after the document number, and
then placing the original title at the top of the
transcribed text immediately after the introductory
remarks. Document 1 provides an example of this. The
single spaced title after the introductory remarks
represents the beginning of the transcription.

If one is going to engage in close textual
analysis it is crucial that the complete text be made
available. This is the practice followed in all but a
few instance in this volume. A few documents, such as
the Connecticut Code of Law, are so lengthy that to
reproduce them completely would extend this volume by
several hundred pages. In those few instances where
the complete text is not transcribed, that fact is
noted, what is missing has been identified, and the
place where the complete text can be found is listed.
The editing of these few documents has been based upon
the presence of repetitive material or material in a
given text that is judged at best marginal to the
political content. In the instances where editing has
been used it was judged better to present a partial
text of an important but little known document rather
than exclude it entirely because its length precludes
reprinting all of it.

The documents are here reprinted in the historical order in which they were written. While the
result furnishes a good sense of how political thinking stood in a particular year, it should be noted
that the early colonies were largely cut off from each
other. Therefore, there is good reason to read the
documents of a particular colony together when seeking
the development and differentiation of political
thought and symbols rather than reading them dispersed
through a more general reading of colonial documents.
To assist the reader in this colony by colony reading,
the following listing reorders the documents in terms
of the state that resulted from a particular series of

colonial foundation documents. In a few instances, towns that produced more than one document in a given state are also separated out for a listing.

State or Town	Documents
Connecticut	27, 32, 35, 36, 37, 40, 44, 45, 46, 50, 58, 64, 74
Guilford	35, 45
New Haven	27, 37, 46
Maine	42, 57
Maryland	24, 25, 28, 29, 30, 31, 56
Massachusetts	3, 5, 6, 7, 8, 9, 10, 11, 12, 13, 14, 15, 16, 17, 18, 19, 20, 21, 22, 41, 48, 49, 53, 54, 59, 60, 61
Cambridge	12, 14, 59
Plymouth	3, 5, 20, 21, 60
Salem	6, 17, 19
New Hampshire	38, 65, 68
New Jersey	66
New York	62, 72
Pennsylvania	67, 69, 70, 71, 73
Rhode Island	23, 26, 33, 34, 39, 43, 51, 52, 55, 63
Providence	23, 39, 43, 55
South Carolina	75
Virginia	1, 2, 4

Finally, a note is in order concerning dates. The calendar in use through most of the seventeenth century began the new year on March 24. This resulted in every day between January 1 and March 23 being a

year earlier than on our current calendar. Historians
frequently list a double date such as February 19,
1634/1635 to indicate that it is 1635 according to our
system of reckoning but 1634 according to theirs. In
every instance in this volume the date given in the
title of a document reflects our current calendar
system. The date internal to the document may reflect
one year earlier. Also, it was common to list a date
as "the second day of the first month," or "the second
day of the seventh month." Since new year fell in
March, the second day of the first month translates as
March 2, whereas the second day of the seventh month
translates as September 2.

FOOTNOTES

1
     Most books on constitutional law in America
begin with the United States Constitution and devote a
few paragraphs, or at most a few pages, to constitutional history before 1787. Also, they invariably
analyze only national developments, ignoring the state
constitutions. There are four notable exceptions to
this charge. They are: Alfred H. Kelly and Winfred A.
Harbison, *The American Constitution: Its Origin and
Development* (New York: W. W. Norton and Co., Inc.,
1976), fifth edition; Breckinridge Long, *Genesis of the
Constitution of the United States of America* New
York: The Macmillan Company, 1926), Andrew C.
McLaughlin, *The Foundations of American Constitutionalism* (New York: The New York University Press,
1932); and Hannis Taylor, *The Origin and Growth of the
American Constitution*(New York: Houghton Mifflin
Company, 1911). However, these four books together do
not begin to provide a complete and sophisticated
discussion of American constitutional origins, at
least in part because a list of colonial constitution-
like documents is not developed. Also, there is no
analysis of the terms used in these colonial documents, the foundation elements found in them, or the
legal status of such colonial documents.

2

Gordon Lloyd, "Textbooks in American Political Theory," *Political Science Reviewer* V (Fall, 1975), 314.

3

See, for example, Bernard Bailyn, *The Ideological Origins of the American Revolution* (Cambridge: Belknap Press, 1967); H. Trevor Colbourn, *The Lamp of Experience*(Chapel Hill: University of North Carolina Press, 1965); Paul K. Conkin, *Self-Evident Truths* (Bloomington: Indiana University Press, 1974); George Dargo, *Roots of the Republic: A New Perspective on Early American Constitutionalism* (New York: Praeger, 1974); Jack P. Greene, *The English Colonies in the Eighteenth Century: 1689-1763* (New York: Oxford University Press, 1969); Michael Kammen, *Deputyes and Libertyes: The Origins of Representative Government in Colonial America*(New York: Knopf, 1969); Lawrence H. Leder, *Liberty and Authority: Early American Political Ideology, 1689 - 1763* (Chicago: Quadrangle Books, 1968); Wilson Carey McWilliams, *The Idea of Fraternity in America*(Berkeley: University of California Press, 1973); J. R. Pole, *The Seventeenth Century Sources of Legislative Power*(Charlottesville: University Press of Virginia, 1967); M. J. C. Vile, *Constitutionalism and the Separation of Powers*(Oxford: Clarendon Press, 1967); E. Neville Williams, *The 18th Centry Constitution, 1688 - 1815* (Cambridge: Cambridge University Press, 1971); and Gordon S. Wood, *The Creation of the American Republic, 1776-1787* (Chapel Hill: University of North Carolina Press, 1969).

4

"From Covenant to Constitution in American Political Thought," *Publius: The Journal of Federalism,* forthcoming in 1981.

5

They are most easily accessible in Francis n. Thorpe, ed., *The Federal and State Constitutions, Colonial Charters, and Other Organic Laws of the United States* (Washington, D. C.: Government Printing Office, 1907; 7 vols.).

6

Ronald M. Peters, Jr., *The Massachusetts Constitution of 1780: A Social Compact*   (Amherst: University
of Massachusetts Press, 1978).

7

The characterizations of the terms which will be
developed are derived from an examination of the
writing of the period, the usage of each word during
the era as described in the *Oxford English Dictionary,*
and an examination of various legal documents.

8

Sir William Blackstone, *Commentaries I*, 1765,
45.

9

Richard Hooker, *Of the Laws of Ecclesiastical
Polity*(Everyman's Library, 1954), book V, section 15,
lxii.

10

For an excellent introduction to the role of
covenants in the Jewish political tradition, see
Daniel J. Elazar, "Covenant as the Basis of the Jewish
Political Tradition, " *The Jewish Journal of Soci-
ology* Vol, 20 (June, 1978), 5 - 37; and Delbert R.
Hillers, *Covenant: The History of a Biblical Idea*
(Baltimore: The Johns Hopkins University Press,
1969).   For the appropriation and development of the
covenant idea by Protestants one might consult Cham-
plin Burrage, *The Church Covenant Idea: Its Origin and
Development*   (Philadelphia, 1904); E. Brooks
Holifield, *The Covenant Sealed: The Development of
Puritan Sacramental Theology in Old and New England,
1570-1720* (New Haven: Yale University Press, 1974);
and Dagobert D. Runes, ed., *The Hebrew Impact on
Western Civilization*(New York: Citadel Press, 1965).
For the nature and development of covenants in
America, one might consult any of a great number of
volumes.   Among the better are: Peter Ymen DeJong,
The Covenant Idea in New England Theology, 1620-1847
(Grand Rapids: E. B. Erdmans, 1964); Richard P.
Gildrie, *Salem, Massechusetts, 1626-1683: A Cove-
nant Community*   (Charlottesville: University Press
of Virginia, 1972); Perry Miller, *The New England Mind:
The Seventeenth Century*   (Boston: Beacon Press,
1961) 398 - 431, 464 - 78; Perry Miller, *The New
England Mind: From Colony to Province*   (Boston:

Beacon Press, 1966), 21 - 28, 68 - 78; Herbert W.
Schneider, *The Puritan Mind*   (Ann Arbor: reprint,
1966), chapter 1; Cushing Strout, *The New Heavens and
New Earth: Political Religion in America* (New York:
Harper and Row, 1974), and Harry M. Ward, *Statism in
Plymouth Colony*(Port Washington: Kennikat Press,
1973) 3 - 14, 52 - 63.

    11
        See Otto Gierke, *Political Theories of the Middle
Ages*   (Cambridge: Cambridge University Press,
1900; and Gierke, *Natural Law and the Theory of Society: 1500 to 1800*   (Cambridge: Cambridge University Press, 1934) for the Catholic tradition.   See
Sanford A. Lakoff,   *Equality in Political Philosophy*
(Boston: Beacon Press, 1964) for the Protestant
tradition, especially chapter 3.

    12
        Lord Viscount Bolingbroke, *On Parties*(1735),
108.

    13
        See the article by Lutz cited in footnote 4
above for a more extended discussion.   Portions of
this discussion are taken from that essay.   For more
extended discussion of the contents of the early state
constitutions see Donald S. Lutz, *Popular Consent and
Popular Control: Whig Political Theory in the Early
State Constitutions*(Baton Rouge: Louisiana State
University Press, 1980).

    14
        Elazar, "Covenant as the Basis of the Jewish
Political Tradition," 6.

    15
        Arthur B. Ellis, *History of the First Church in
Boston, 1630-1880* (1881), 3.

DOCUMENT 1:   Articles, Laws, and Orders, Divine,
                Politic, and Martial for the Colony in
                Virginia, 1610 - 1611

Text taken from D. H. Flaherty, ed., *Laws Divine,
Moral, and Martial Compiled by William Strachey* who
retained the original spelling and puncuation except
to transpose "i" and "j" and "u" and "v" to correspond
to modern usage. The usual practice is to reproduce
only pp. 9 - 25 of the Strachey version, as is done
here, but the complete document is 101 pages long.
The balance of the document contains a detailed
discussion of the colony's martial laws and specific
instructions from the marshall to every rank concerning duties and bearing. The Flaherty volume contains a
discussion of the historical context surrounding this
document, as well as the complete text.

Articles, Lawes, and Orders, Divine, Politique,
and Martiall for the Colony in Virginea: first
established by Sir Thomas Gates Knight, Lieutenant Generall, the 24th of May 1610. exemplified
and approved by the Right Honourable Sir Thomas
West Knight, Lord Lawair, Lord Governor and
Captaine Generall the 12th day of June 1610.
Againe exemplified and enlarged by Sir Thomas
Dale Knight, Marshall, and Deputie Governour, the
22nd of June, 1611.

Whereas his Majestie like himselfe a most zealous
Prince hath in his owne Realmes a principall care of
true Religion, and reverence to God, and hath alwaies
strictly commaunded his Generals and Governours, with
all his forces wheresoever, to let their waies be like
his ends for the glorie of God.

And forasmuch as no good service can be performed, or warre well managed, where militarie discipline is not observed, and militarie discipline cannot
be kept, where the rules or chiefe parts thereof, be
not certainely set downe, and generally knowne, I have
(with the advise and counsell of Sir Thomas Gates
Knight, Lieutenant Generall) adhered unto the lawes
divine, and orders politique, and martiall of his
Lordship (the same exemplified) an addition of such
others, as I have found either the necessitie of the
present State of the Colonie to require, or the
infancie, and weaknesses of the body thereof, as yet
able to digest, and doe now publish them to all
persons in the Colonie, that they may as well take
knowledge of the Lawes themselves, as of the penaltie
and punishment, which without partialitie shall be
inflicted upon the breakers of the same.
1   First since we owe our highest and supreme duty,
our greatest, and all our allegeance to him, from whom
all power and authoritie is derived, and flowes as
from the first, and onely fountaine, and being especiall souldiers emprest in this sacred cause, we must
alone expect our successe from him, who is only the
blesser of all good attempts, the King of kings, the
commaunder of commaunders, and Lord of Hostes, I do
strictly commaund and charge all Captaines and Officers, of what qualitie or nature soever, whether
commanders in the field, or in towne, or townes, forts
or fortresses, to have a care that the Almightie God
bee duly and daily served, and that they call upon
their people to heare Sermons, as that also they
diligently frequent Morning and Evening praier themselves by their owne exemplar and daily life, and
duties herein, encouraging others thereunto, and that
such, who shall often and wilfully absent themselves,
be duly punished according to the martiall law in that
case provided.
2   That no man speake impiously or maliciously,
against the holy and blessed Trinitie, or any of the
three persons, that is to say, against God the Father,
God the Son, and God the holy Ghost, or against the
knowne Articles of the Christian faith, upon paine of
death.
3   That no man blaspheme Gods holy name upon paine
of death, or use unlawful oathes, taking the name of

God in vaine, curse, or banne[1], upon paine of severe
punishment for the first offence so committed, and for
the second, to have a bodkin[2] thrust through his
tongue, and if he continues the blaspheming of Gods
holy name, for the third time so offending, he shall
be brought to a martiall court, and there receive
censure of death for his offence.
4.   No man shall use any traiterous words against his
Majesties Person, or royall authority upon paine of
death.
5   No man shall speake any word, or do any act,
which may tend to the derision, or despight[3] of Gods
holy word upon paine of death: Nor shall any man
unworthily demeane himself unto any Preacher, or
Minister of the same, but generally hold them in all
reverent regard, and dutiful intreatie[4], otherwise he
the offender shall openly be whipt three times, and
ask publike forgivenesse in the assembly of the
congregation three several Saboth Daies.
6   Everie man and woman duly twice a day upon the
first towling of the Bell shall upon the working daies
repaire unto the Church, to hear divine Service upon
pain of losing his or her dayes allowance for the
first omission, for the second to be whipt, and for
the third to be condemned to the Gallies for six
Moneths. Likewise no man or woman shall dare to
violate or breake the Sabboth by any gaming, publique
or private abroad, or at home, but duly sanctifie and
observe the same, both himselfe and his familie, by
preparing themselves at home with private prayer, that
they may be the better fitted for the publique,
according to the commandements of God, and the orders
of our Church, as also every man and woman shall
repaire in the morning to the divine service, and
Sermons preached upon the Saboth day, and in the
afternoon to divine service, and Catechising, upon
paine for the first fault to lose their provision, and
allowance for the whole weeke following, for the
second to lose the said allowance, and also to be
whipt, and for the third to suffer death.
7   All Preachers or Ministers within this our
Colonie, or Colonies, shall in the Forts, where they
are resident, after divine Service, duly preach every
Sabbath day in the forenoone, and Catechise in the
afternoone, and weekly say the divine service, twice

every day, and preach every Wednesday, likewise every
Minister where he is resident, within the same Fort,
or Fortresse, Townes or Towne, shall chuse unto him,
foure of the most religious and better disposed as
well to informe of the abuses and neglects of the
people in their duties, and service to God, as also to
the due reparation, and keeping of the Church hand-
some, and fitted with all reverent observances thereunto belonging: likewise every Minister shall keepe a
faithful and true Record, or Church Booke of all
Christnings, Marriages, and deaths of such our people,
as shall happen within their Fort, or Fortresses,
Townes or Towne at any time, upon the burthen of a
neglectfull conscience, and upon paine of losing their
Entertainment.⁵
8   He that upon pretended malice, shall murther or
take away the life of any man, shall bee punished with
death.
9   No man shal commit the horrible, and detestable
sins of Sodomie upon pain of death; and he or she that
can be lawfully convict of Adultery shall be punished
with death. No man shall ravish or force any woman,
maid or Indian, or other, upon pain of death, and know
that he or shee, that shall commit fornication, and
evident proofe made thereof, for their first fault
shall be whipt, for the second they shall be whipt,
and for their third they shall be whipt three times a
weeke for one month, and aske publique forgivenesse in
the Assembly of the Congregation.
10   No man shall bee found guilty of Sacriledge,
which is a Trespasse as well committed in violating
the abusing any sacred ministry, duty or office of the
Church, irreverently, or prophanely, as by beeing a
Church robber, to filch, steale or carry away anything
out of the Church appertaining thereunto, or unto any
holy, and consecrated place, to the divine Service of
God, which no man should doe upon paine of death:
likewise he that shall rob the store of any commodities therein, of what quality soever, whether provisions of victuals, or of arms, Trucking stuffe,⁶
Apparrell, Linnen, or Wollen, Hose or Shooes, Hats or
Caps, Instruments or Tooles of Steele, Iron, etc. or
shall rob from his fellow souldier, or neighbor, any
thing that is his, victuals, apparell, household
stuffe, toole, or what necessary else soever, by water

or land, out of boate, house, or knapsack, shall bee
punished with death.

11   Hee that shall take an oath untruly, or beare
false witnesse in any cause, or against any man
whatsoever, shall be punished with death.

12   No manner of person whatsoever, shall dare to
detract, slaunder, columniate, or utter unseemly, and
unfitting speeches, either against his Majesties
Honourable Councell for this Colony, resident in
England, or against the Committees, Assistants unto
the said Councell, or against the zealous indeavors,
and intentions of the whole body of Adventurers for
this pious and Christian Plantation, or against any
publique book, or bookes, which by their mature
advise, and grave wisdomes, shall be thought fit, to
be set foorth and publisht, for the advancement of the
good of this Colony, and the felicity thereof, upon
paine for the first time so offending, to be whipt
three severall times, and upon his knees to acknowledge his offence and to aske forgivenesse upon the
Saboth day in the assembly of the congregation, and
for the second time so offending to be condemned to
the Galley for three yeares, and for the third time so
offending to be punished with death.

13   No manner of Person whatsoever, contrarie to the
word of God (which tyes every particular and private
man, for conscience sake to obedience, and duty of the
Magistrate, and such as shall be placed in authoritie
over them [1], shall detract, slaunder, calumniate,
murmur, mutenie, resist, disobey, or neglect the
commaundments, either of the Lord Governour, and
Captaine Generalle, the Lieutenant Generall, the
Martiall, the Councell, or any authorised Captaine,
Commaunder or publike Officer, upon paine for the
first time so offending to be whipt three severall
times, and upon his knees to acknowledge his offence,
with asking forgivenesse upon the Saboth day in the
assembly of the congregation, and for the second time
so offending to be condemned to the Gally for three
yeares: and for the third time so offending to be
punished with death.

14   No man shall give any disgraceful words, or
commit any act to the disgrace of any person in this
Colonie, or any part thereof, upon paine of being tied
head and feete together, upon the guard everie night

for the space of one moneth, besides to bee publikely
disgraced himselfe, and be made incapable ever after
to possesse any place, or execute any office in this
imployment.

15   No man of what condition soever shall barter,
trucke, or trade with the Indians, except he be thereunto appointed by lawful authority upon paine of
death.

16   No man shall rifle or dispoile, by force or violence, take away any thing from any Indian coming to
trade, or otherwise, upon paine of death. 8

17   No Cape Marchant, or Provant Master, or Muni-
tion Master, or Truck Master, or keeper of any store,
shall at any time imbezell, sell, or give away any
thing under his Charge to any Favorite, of his, more
than unto any other, whome necessity shall require in
that case to have extraordinary allowance of Provisions, nor shall they give a false accompt unto the
Lord Governour, and Captaine Generall, unto the
Lieutenant Generall, unto the Marshall, or any deputed
Governor, at any time having the commaund of the
Colony, with intent to defraud the said Colony, upon
paine of death.

18   No man shall imbezel or take away the goods of
any man that dyeth, or is imployed from the town or
Fort where he dwelleth in any other occasioned remote
service, for the time, upon pain of whipping three
severall times, and restitution of the said goods
againe, and in danger of incurring the penalty of the
tenth Article, if so it may come under the construc-
tion of theft. And if any man die and make a will,
his goods shall be accordingly disposed; if hee die
intestate, his goods shall bee put into the store, and
being valued by two sufficient praisers, his next of
kinne (according to the common Lawes of England [1],
shall from the Company, Committees, or adventurers,
receive due satisfaction in moneys, according as they
were praised, by which means the Colonie shall be
better furnished; and the goods more carefully preserved, for the right heire, and the right heire
receive content for the same in England.

19   There shall be no Capttain, Master, Marriner,
saylor, or any else of what quality or condition
soever, belonging to any Ship or Ships, at this time
remaining, or which shall hereafter arrive within this

our River, bargaine, buy, truck, or trade with any one
member in this Colony, man, woman, or child, for any
toole or instrument of iron, steel, or what else,
whether appertaining to Smith Carpenter, Joyner,
Shipwright, or any manuall occupation, or handicraft
man whatsoever, resident within our Colonie, nor shall
they buy or bargaine, for any apparell, linnen, or
wollen, householdstuffe, bedde, bedding, sheete
towels, napkins, brasse, pewter, or such like, eyther
for ready money, or provisions, nor shall they exchange their provisions, of what quality soever,
whether Butter, Cheese, Bisket, meal, Oatmele, Aqua-
vite, oyle, Bacon, any kind of Spice, or such like,
for any such aforesaid instruments, or tooles, apparell, or householdstuffe, at any time, or so long as
they shall here remain, from the date of these presents upon paine of losse of their wages in England,
confiscation and forfeiture of such their monies and
provisions, and upon peril beside of such corporall
punishment as shall be inflicted upon them by verdict
and censure of a martiall Court: Nor shall any
officer, souldier, or Trades man, or any else of what
sort soever, members of this Colony, dare to sell any
such Toole, or instruments, necessary and usefull, for
the businesse of the Colonie, or trucke, sell, exchange, or give away his apparell, or household stuffe
of what sort soever, unto any such Seaman, either for
mony, or any such foresaid provisions, upon paine of 3
times severall whipping, for the one offender, and the
other upon perill of incurring censure, whether of
disgrace, or addition of such punishment, as shall bee
thought fit by a Court martiall.
20   Whereas sometimes heeretofore the covetous and
wide affections of some greedy and ill disposed
Seamen, Saylers, and Marriners, laying hold upon the
advantage of the present necessity, under which the
Colony sometimes suffered, have sold unto our people,
provisions of Meale, Oatmeale, Bisket, Butter, Cheese
etc., at unreasonable rates, and prises unconscion-
able: for avoiding the like to bee now put in
practise, there shall no Captain, Master, Marriner, or
Saylor, or what Officer else belonging to any ship, or
shippes, now within our river, or heereafter which
shall arrive, shall dare to bargaine, exchange,
barter, truck, trade, or sell, upon paine of death,

unto any one Landman[10] member of this present Colony,
any provisions of what kind soever, above the
determined valuations, and prises, set downe and pro-
claimed, and sent therefore unto each of your severall
ships, to bee fixed uppon your Maine mast, to the
intent that want of due notice, and ignorance in this
case, be no excuse, or plea, for any offender herein.
21   Sithence[11] we are not to bee a little carefull,
and our young Cattell, and Breeders may be cherished,
that by the preservation, and incrase of them, the
Colony heere may receive in due time assured and great
benefite, and the adventurers at home may be eased of
so great a burthen, by sending unto us yeerely
supplies of this kinde, which now heere for a while,
carefully attended, may turne their supplies unto us
into provisions of other qualities, when of these wee
shall be able to subsist our selves, and which wee may
in short time, be powerful enough to doe, if we wil
according to our owne knowledge of what is good for
our selves, forbeare to work into our own wants,
againe, by over hasty destroying, and devouring the
stockes, and authors of so profitable succeeding a
Commodity, as increase of Cattell, Kine, Hogges,
Goates, Poultrie etc. must of necessity bee granted,
in every common mans judgement, to render unto us:
Now know thee therefore, these promises carefully
considered, that it is our will and pleasure, that
every one, of what quality or condition soever hee
bee, in this present Colony, to take due notice of
this our Edict, whereby wee do strictly charge and
command, that no man shall dare to kill, or destroy
any Bull, Cow, Calfe, Mare, Horse, Colt, Goate, Swine,
Cocke, Henne, Chicken, Dogge, Turkie, or any tame
Cattel, or Poultry, of what condition soever; whether
his owne, or appertaining to another man, without
leave from the Generall, upon paine of death in the
Principall, and in the accessary, burning in the Hand,
and losse of his eares, and unto the concealer of the
same four and twenty houres of whipping, with addition
of further punishment, as shall be thought fitte by
the censure, and verdict of a Martiall Court.
22   There shall no man or woman, Launderer or
Launderesse, dare to wash any uncleane Linnen, drive
bucks,[12] or throw out the water or sudes of fowle
cloathes, in the open streete, within the

Pallizadoes, [13] or within forty foote of the same, nor
rench, [14] and make cleane, any kettle, pot, or pan, or
such like vessell within twenty foote of the olde
well, or new Pumps: nor shall any one aforesaid,
within less than a quarter of one mile from the
Pallizadoes, dare to doe the necessities of nature,
since by these unmanly, slothfull, and loathsome
immodesties, the whole Fort may bee choaked, and
poisoned with ill aires, and so corrupt (as in all
reason cannot but much infect the same) and this shall
they take notice of, and avoide, upon paine of
whipping and further punishment, as shall be thought
meete, by the censure of a martiall Court.

23   No man shall imbezell, lose, or willingly breake,
or fraudulently make away, either Spade, Shovell,
Hatchet, Axe, Mattocke, [15] or other toole or instrument
upon paine of whipping.

24   Any man that hath any edge toole, either of his
owne, or which hath heeretofore beene belonging to the
store, see that he bring it instantly to the store-
house, where he shall receive it againe by a particular note, both of the toole, and of his name taken,
that such a toole unto him appertaineth, at whose
hands, upon any necessary occasion, the said toole may
be required, and this shall he do, upon paine of
severe punishment.

25   Every man shall have an especiall and due care,
to keepe his house sweete and cleane, as also so much
of the streete, as lieth before his door, and
especially he shall so provide, and set his bedstead
whereon he lieth, that it may stand three foote at
least from the ground, as will answere the contrarie
at a martiall Court.

26   Every tradesman in their severall occupation,
trade and function, shall duly and daily attend his
worke upon his said trade or occupation, upon perill
for his first fault, and negligence therein, to have
his entertainment checkt for one moneth, for his
second fault three moneth, for his third one yeare,
and if he continue still unfaithfull and negligent
therein, to be condemned to the Gally for three yeare.

27   All overseers of workemen, shall be carefull in
seeing that performed, which is given them in charge,
upon paine of such punishment as shall be inflicted
upon him by a martiall Court.

28   No souldier or tradesman, but shall be readie,
both in the morning, and in the afternoone, upon the
beating of the Drum, to goe out unto his worke, nor
shall hee return home, or from his worke, before the
Drum beate againe, and the officer appointed for that
business, bring him of, upon perill for the first
fault to lie upon the Guard head and heeles together
all night, for the second time so faulting to be
whipt, and for the third time so offending to be
condemned to the Gallies for a yeare.

29   No man or woman, (upon paine of death)[16] shall
runne away from the Colonie, to Powhathan, or any
savage Weroance[17] else whatsoever.

30   He that shall conspire any thing against the
person of the Lord Governour, and Captaine Generall,
against the Lieutenant Generall, or against the
Marshall, or against any publike service commaunded by
them, for the dignitie, and advancement of the good of
the Colony, shall be punished with death: and he that
shall have knowledge of any such pretended act of
disloyalty or treason, and shall not reveale the same
unto his Captaine, or unto the Governour of that fort
or Towne wherein he is, within the space of one houre,
shall for the concealing of the same after that time,
be not onely held an accessary, but alike culpable as
the principall traitor or conspirer, and for the same
likewise he shall suffer death.

31   What man or woman soever, shall rob any garden,
publike or private, being set to weed the same, or
wilfully pluck up therein any roote, herbe, or flower,
to spoile and wast or steale the same, or robbe any
vineyard, or gather up the grapes, or steale any eares
of the corne growing, whether in the ground belonging
to the same fort or towne where he dwelleth, or in any
other, shallbe punished with death.

32   Whosoever Seaman, or Landman or what qualitie, or
in what place of commaund soever, shall be imployed
upon any discovery, trade, or fishing voiage into any
of the rivers within the precincts of our Colonie,
shall for the safety of those men who are committed to
his commaund, stand upon good and carefull guard, for
the prevention of any treachery in the Indian, and if
they touch upon any shore, they shal be no less
circumspect, and warie, with good and carefull guard
day and night, putting forth good Centinell, and

observing the orders and discipline of watch and ward,
and when they have finished the discovery, trade, or
fishing, they shall make hast with all speed, with
such Barke or Barkes, Pinisse, Gallie, Ship. etc. as
they shall have the commaund of, for the same purpose,
to James towne againe, not presuming to goe beyond
their commission, or to carry any such Barke or
Barkes, Gally, Pinnice, Ship. etc. for England or any
other countrey in the actual possession of any Christian Prince, upon perill to be held an enemie to this
plantation, and traitor thereunto, and accordingly to
lie liable unto such censure of punishment (if they
arrive in England) as shall be thought fit by the
Right Honourable Lords, his Majesties Councell for
this Colonie, and if it shall so happen, that he or
they shall be prevented, and brought backe hither
againe into the Colonie, their trecherous flight to be
punished with death.

33   There is not one man nor woman in this Colonie
now present, or hereafter to arrive, but shall give up
an account of his and their faith, and religion, and
repaire unto the Minister, that by his conference with
them, hee may understand, and gather, whether heretofore they have beene sufficiently instructed, and
catechised in the principles and grounds of Religion,
whose weaknesse and ignorance herein, the Minister
finding, and advising them in all love and charitie,
to repaire often unto him, to receive therein a
greater measure of knowledge, if they shal refuse so
to repaire unto him, and he the Minister give notice
thereof unto the Governour, or that chiefe officer of
that towne or fort, wherein he or she, the parties so
offending shall remaine, the Governour shall cause the
offender for his first time of refusall to be whipt,
for the second time to be whipt twice, and to acknowledge his fault upon the Saboth day, in the assembly
of the congregation, and for the third time to be
whipt every day until he heath made the same acknowledgement, and asked forgivenesse for the same, and
shall repaire unto the Minister, to be further instructed as aforesaid: and upon the Saboth when the
Minister shall catechise, and of him demaund any question concerning his faith and knowledge, he shall not
refuse to make answere upon the same perill.

34   What man or woman soever, Laundrer or Laundresse
appointed to wash the foule linnen of any one labourer
or souldier, or any one else as it is their duties so
to doe, performing little, or no other service for
their allowance out of the store, and daily provisions, and supply of other necessaries, unto the
Colonie, and shall from the said labourer or souldier,
or any one else of what qualitie whatseover, either
take any thing for washing, or withhold or steale from
him any such linnen committed to her to wash, or
change the same willingly and wittingly, with purpose
to give him worse, old and torne linnen for his good,
and proofe shall be made thereof, she shall be whipped
for the same, and lie in prison till she make restitution of such linnen, withheld or changed.
35   No Captained, Master, or Mariner, of what
condition soever, shall depart or carry out of the
river, any Ship, Barke, Barge, Gally, Pinnace etc.
Roaders[18] belonging to the Colonie, either now therein, or hither arriving, without leave and commission
from the Generall or chiefe Commaunder of the Colonie
upon paine of death.
36   No man or woman whatsoever, members of this
Colonie, shall sell or give unto any Captine, Marriner, Master, or Sailer, etc. any commoditie of this
countrey, of what quality soever, to be transported
out of the Colonie, for his or their owne private
uses, upon paine of death.
37   If any souldier indebted, shall refuse to pay his
debts unto this creditor, his creditor shall informe
his Captaine, if the Captaine cannot agree the same,
the creditor shall informe the Marshals civill and
principall officer, who shall preferre for the creditor a bill of complaint at the Marshals Court, where
the creditor shal have Justice.
    All such Bakers as are appointed to bake bread,
or what else, either for the store to be given out in
generall, or for any one in particular, shall not
steale nor imbezell, loose, or defraud any man of his
due and proper weight and measure, nor use any dishonest and deceiptfull tricke to make the bread weight
heavier, or make it courser upon purpose to keepe
backe any part or measure of the flower or meale
committed unto him, nor aske, take, or detaine any one
loafe more or lesse for his hire or paines for so

baking, since whilest he who delivered unto him such
meale or flower, being to attend the businesse of the
Colonie, such baker or bakers are imposed upon no
other service or duties, but onely so to bake for such
as do worke, and this shall hee take notice of, upon
paine for the first time offending herein of losing
his eares, and for the second time to be condemend a
yeare to the Gallies,and for the third time offending,
to be condemned to the Gallies for three yeares.[19]

    All such cookes as are appointed to seeth, bake
or dresse any manner of way, flesh, fish, or what
else, of what kind soever, either for the generall
company, or for any private man, shall not make lesse,
or cut away any part or parcel of such flesh, fish,
etc. Nor detaine or demaund any party or parcell, as
allowance or hire for his so dressing the same, since
as aforesaid of the baker, hee or they such Cooke or
Cookes, exempted from other publike works abroad, are
to attend such seething and dressing of such publike
flesh, fish, or other provisions of what kind soever,
as their service and duties expected from them by the
Colony, and this shall they take notice of, upon paine
for the first time offending herein, of losing his
eares, and for the second time to be condemned a yeare
to the Gallies: and for the third time offending to
be condemned to the Gallies for three years.

    All fishermen, dressers of Sturgeon or such like
appointed to fish, or to cure the said Sturgeon for
the use of the Colonie, shall give a just and true
account of all such fish as they shall take by day or
night, of what kinds soever, the same to bring unto
the Governour: As also of all such kegges of Sturgeon
or Caviare as they shall prepare and cure upon perill
for the first time offending heerein, of loosing his
eares, and for the second time to be condemned a yeare
to the Callies, and for the third time offending, to
be condemned to the Gallies for three yeares.
Every Minister or Preacher shall every Sabboth day
before Catechising, read all these lawes and ordinances, publikely in the assembly of the congregation
upon paine of his entertainment checkt for that weeke.

DOCUMENT 2:   Laws Engacted by the First General
                Assembly of Virginia, August 2 - 4,
                1619

Complete text taken from H. R. McIlwaine, ed., *Journals
of the House of Burgesses of Virginia,*   Vol. I, pp.
9 - 14. The text has clearly been modernized and
therefore has a number of emendations which can not be
sorted out here.

By this present General Assembly be it enacted that no
injury or oppression be wrought by the English against
the Indians whereby the present peace might be distri-
buted and ancient quarrels might be revived. And
farther be it ordained that the Chicohomini are not to
be excepted out of this law, until either that such
order come out of England or that they do provoke us
by some new injury.
    Against idleness, gaming, drunkenness, and excess
in apparel the assembly has enacted as follows.
    First, in detestation of idlers, be it enacted
that if any man be found to live as an idler or
renegade, though a freed man, it shall be lawful for
that incorporation or plantation to which he belongs
to appoint him a master to serve for wages till he
shows apparent signs of amendment.
    Against gaming at dice and cards be it ordained
by this present assembly that the winner or winners
shall lose all his or their winnings and both winners
and losers shall forfeit ten shillings a man, one ten
shillings whereof to go to the discoverer and the rest
to charitable and pious uses in the incorporation
where the faults are committed.
    Against drunkeness be it also decreed that if any
private prsons be found culpable thereof, for the
first time he is to be reproved privately by the

minister, the second time publicly, the third time to
lie in bolts 12 hours in the house of the provost
marshal and to pay his fees, and if he still continue
in that vice to undergo such severe punishment as the
Governor and Council of Estate shall thinke fit to be
inflicted on him. But if any officer offend in this
crime, the first time he shall receive a reproof from
the Governor, the second time he shall openly be
reproved in the church by the minister, and the third
time he shall first be committed and then degraded.
Provided it be understood that the Governor has always
power to restore him when he shall, in his discretion,
think fit.

Against excess of apparel, that every man be
assessed in the church for all public contributions,
if he be unmarried according to his own apparel, if he
be married, according to his own and his wife's or
either of their apparel.

As touching the instruction of drawing some of
the better disposed of the Indians to converse with
our people and to live and labor among them, the
assembly, who know well their dispositions, think it
fit to enjoin at least to counsel those of the colony
neither utterly to reject them nor yet to draw them to
come in. But in case they will of themselves come
voluntarily to places well peopled, there to do
service in killing of deer, fishing, beating corn, and
other works, that then five or six may be admitted
into every such place and no more, and that with the
consent of the Governor, provided that good guard in
the night be kept upon them, for generally, though
some among many may prove good, they are a most
treacherous people and quickly gone when they have
done a villainy. And it were fit a house were built
for them to lodge in apart by themselves, and lone
inhabitants by no means to entertain them.

Be it enacted by this present assembly that for
laying a surer foundation of the conversion of the
Indians to Christian religion, each town, city,
borough, and particular plantation do obtain unto
themselves by just means a certain number of the
native's children to be educated by them in true
religion and civil course of life. Of which children
the most towardly boys in wit and graces of nature to
be brought up by them in the first elements of

literature, so as to be fitted for the college
intended for them, that from thence they may be sent
to that work of conversion.

As touching the business of planting corn, this
present assembly does ordain that, year by year, all
and every householder and householders have in store
for every servant he or they shall keep, and also for
his or their own persons, whether they have any
servants or no, one spare barrel of corn to be delivered out yearly either upon sale or exchange, as need
shall require. For the neglect of which duty he shall
be subject to the censure of the Governor and Council
of Estate; provided always, that for the first year of
every new man this law shall not be in force.

About the plantation of mulberry trees, be it
enacted that every man, as he is seated upon his
division does, for seven years together, every year
plant and maintain in growth six mulberry trees at the
least and as many more as he shall think convenient
and as his virtue and industry shall move him to
plant; and that all such persons as shall neglect the
yearly planting and maintaining of that small proportion shall be subject to the censure of the Governor
and the Councel of Estate.

Be it further enacted, as concerning silk flax,
that those men that are upon their division or settled
habitation do this next year plant and dress 100
plants which being found a commodity may farther be
increased. And whosoever do fail in the performace of
this shall be subject to the punishment of the Govern-
or and Council of Estate.

For hemp also, both English and Indian, and for
English flax and aniseeds, we do require and enjoin
all householders of this colony, that have any of
those seeds, to make trial thereof the next season.

Moreover, be it enacted by this present assembly
that every householder does yearly plant and maintain
ten vines, until they have attained to the art and
experience of dressing a vineyard, either by their own
industry or by the instruction of some vigneron. And
that upon what penalty soever the Governor and Council
of Estate shall think fit to impose upon the neglect-
ers of this act.

Be it also enacted that all necessary tradesmen,
or so many as need shall require, such as are come

over since the departure of Sir Thomas Dale or that
shall hereafter come, shall work at their trades for
any other man; each one being paid according to the
quality of his trade and work, to be estimated, if he
shall not be contented, by the Governor and officers
of the place where he works.

Be it further ordained by this General Assembly,
and we do by these presents enact, that all contracts
made in England between the owners of land and their
tenants and servants which they shall send hither may
be caused to be duly performed and that the offenders
be punished as the Governor and Council of Estate
shall think just and convenient.

Be it established also by this present assembly
that no crafty or advantageous means be suffered to be
put in practice for the enticing away the tenants and
servants of any particular plantation from the place
where they are seated. And that it shall be the duty
of the Governor and Council of Estate most severely to
punish both the seducers and the seduced and to return
these latter into their former places.

Be it further enacted that the orders for the
magazine lately made be exactly kept and that the
magazine be preserved from wrong and sinister
practices and that, according to the orders of court
in England, all tobacco and sassafras be brought by
the planters to the cape merchant till such time as
all the goods now or heretofore sent for the magazine
be taken off their hands at the prices agreed on, that
by this means the same going for England into one hand
the price thereof may be upheld the better. And to
the end that all the whol colony may take notice of
the last order of court made in England, and all those
whom it concerns may know how to observe it, we hold
it fit to publish it here for a law among the rest of
our laws, the which orders is as follows.

Upon the 26th of October 1618, it was ordered
that the magazine should continue during the term
formerly prefixed and that certain abuses now complained of should be reformed; and that for preventing
of all impositions, save the allowance of 25 in the
hundred profit the Governor shall have an invoice as
well as the cape merchant, that if any abuse in the
sale of goods be offered, he, upon intelligence and
due examination thereof, shall see it corrected. And

for the encouragement of particular hundreds, as
Smith's hundred, Martin's hundred, Lawn's hundred and
the like, it shall be lawful for them to return the
same to their own adventurers; provided that the same
commodity be of their own growing, without trading
with any other, in one entire lump and not dispersed,
and that at the determination of the joint stock the
goods then remaining in the magazine shall be bought
by the said particular colonies before any other goods
which shall be sent by private men. And it is,
moreover, ordered that if the Lady La warre, the Lady
Dale, Captain Bargrave, and the rest would unite
themselves into a settled colony, they might be
capable of the same privileges that are granted to any
of the foresaid hundreds. Hitherto the order.

All the General Assembly by voices concluded not
only the acceptances and observation of this order,
but of the instruction also to Sir George Yeardley
next preceding the same; provided, first, that the
cape merchant do accept of the tobacco of all and
every the planters here in Virginia, either for goods
or upon bills of exchange at three shillings the pound
the best and 18 shillings the second sort; provided,
also, that the bills be duly paid in England; provided, in the third place, that if any other besides
the magazine have at any time any necessary commodity
which the magazine does want, it shall and may be
lawful for any of the colony to buy the said necessary
commodity of the said party, but upon the terms of the
magazine, viz., allowing no more gain than 25 in the
hundred, and that with the leave of the Governor;
provided, lastly, that it may be lawful for the
governor to give leave to any mariner, or any other
person that shall have any such necessary commodity
wanting to the magazine, to carry home for England so
much tobacco or other natural commodities of the
country as his customers shall pay him for the said
necessary commodity or commodities. And to the end we
may not only persuade and incite men but enforce them
also thoroughly and loyally to cure their tobacco
before they bring it to the magazine, be it enacted,
and by these presents we do enact, that if upon the
judgment of four sufficient men of any corporation
where the magazine shall reside, having first taken
their oaths to give true sentence, two whereof to be

chosen by the cape merchant and two by the incorporation, any tobacco whatsoever shall not prove vendible
at the second price, that it shall there immediately
be burned before the owner's face.

It shall be free for every man to trade with the
Indians, servants only excepted, upon pain of whipping
unless the master redeem it off with the payment of an
angel, one-fourth part whereof to go to the provost
marshal, one-fourth part to the discoverer, and the
other moiety to the public uses of the incorporation
where he dwells.

That no man do sell or give any Indians any
piece, shot, or powder, or any other arms offensive or
defensive, upon pain of being held a traitor to the
colony and of being hanged as soon as the fact is
proved, without all redemption.

That no man do sell or give any of the greater
howes to the Indians, or any English dog of quality,
as a mastive, greyhound, blood hound, land or water
spaniel, or any other dog or bitch whatsoever, of the
English race, upon pain of forfeiting five pounds
sterling to the public uses of the incorporation where
he dwells.

That no man may go above twenty miles from his
dwelling place, nor upon any voyage whatsoever shall
be absent from thence for the space of seven days together, without first having made the Governor or
commander of the same place acquainted therewith, upon
pain of paying twenty shillings to the public uses of
the same incorporation where the party delinquent
dwells.

That no man shall purposely go to any Indian
towns, habitation, or places of resort without leave
from the Governor or commander of that place where he
lives, upon pain of paying 40 shillings to public uses
as aforesaid.

That no man living in this colony but shall
between this and the first of January next ensuing
come or send to the Secretary of State to enter his
own and all his servants names and for what term or
upon what conditions they are to serve, upon penalty
of paying 40 shillings to the said Secretary of State.
Also, whatsoever masters or people do come over to
this plantation that within one month of their arrival, notice being first given them of this very law,

they shall likewise report to the Secretary of State and shall certify him upon what terms or conditions they become hither, to the end that he may record their grants and commissions and for how long time and upon what conditions their servants, in case they have any, are to serve them, and that upon pain of the penalty next above mentioned.

All ministers in the colony shall once a year, namely in the month of March, bring to the Secretary of Estate a true account of all the christenings, burials, and marriages, upon pain, if they fail, to be censured for their negligence by the Governor and Council of Estate; likewise, where there be no ministers, that the commanders of the place do supply the same duty.

No man without leave from the governor shall kill any neat cattle whatsoever, young or old, especially kine, heifers, or cow calves, and shall be careful to preserve their steers and oxen and to bring them to plough and such profitable uses, and, without having obtained leave as aforesaid, shall not kill them upon penalty of forfeiting the value of the beast so killed.

Whosoever shall take any of his neighbors boats, oars, or canoes without leave from the owner shall be held and esteemed as a felon and so proceeded against. Also, he that shall take away by violence or steals any canoes or other things from the Indians shall make valuable restitution to the said Indians and shall forfeit, if he be a freeholder, five pounds, if a servant 40 shillings, or endure a whipping; and anything under the value of 13 pence shall be accounted petty larceny.

All ministers shall duly read divine service and exercise their ministerial function according to the ecclesiastical laws and orders of the Church of England and every Sunday in the afternoon shall catechize such as are not yet ripe to come to the communion. And whosoever of them be found negligent or faulty in this kind shall be subject to the censure of the Governor and Council of Estate.

The ministers and church wardens shall seek to prevent all ungodly disorders; the committers whereof if, upon good admonitions and mild reproof, they will not forbear the said scandalous offences, as

suspicions of whoredoms, dishonest company keeping
with women, and such like, they are to be presented
and punished accordingly.

If any person, after two warnings, does not amend
his or her life in point of evident suspicion of
incontinency or of the commission of any other enor-
mous sins, that then he or she be presented by the
church wardens and suspended for a time from the
church by the minister. In which interim, if the same
person do not amend and humbly submit him or herself
to the church, he is then fully to be excommunicated
and soon after a writ or warrant to be sent from the
Governor for the apprehending of his person and
seizing all his goods. Provided always, that all the
ministers do meet once a quarter, namely at the feast
of St. Michael the Archangel, of the Nativity or our
Saviour, of the Annunciation of the Blessed Virgin,
and about mid-summer, at James City or any other place
where the Governor shall reside, to determine whom it
is fit to excommunicate, and that they first present
their opinion to the Governor ere they proceed to the
act of excommunication.

For reformation of swearing, every freeman and
master of a family after thrice admonition shall give
5 shillings of the value upon present demand to the
use of the church where he dwells, and every servant
after the like admonition, except his master discharge
the fine, shall be subject to whipping; provided, that
the payment of the fine notwithstanding, the said
servant shall acknowledge his fault publicly in the
church.

No man whatsoever coming by water from above, as
from Henrico, Charles City, or any place from the
westward of James City, and being bound for Kiccowtan
or any other part on this side of the same, shall
presume to pass by either by day or by night without
touching first here at James City, to know whether the
Governor will command him any service, and the like
shall they perform that come from Kiccowtanward or
from any place between this and that to go upward,
upon pain of forfeiting ten pounds sterling a time to
the Governor; provided, that if a servant having had
instructions from his master to observe his service
does, notwithstanding, transgress the same, that then
the said servant shall be punished at the governor's

discretion, otherwise that the master himself shall undergo the foresaid penalty.

No man shall trade into the bay either in shallop, pinnace, or ship without the Governor's license and without putting in security that neither himself nor his company shall force or wrong the Indians, upon pain that doing otherwise they shall be censured at their return by the Governor and Council of Estate.

All persons whatsoever, upon Sabbath days, shall frequent divine service and sermons both forenoon and afternoon and all such as bear arms shall bring their pieces, swords, powder and shot. And every one that shall transgress this law shall forfeit three shillings a time to the use of the church, all lawful and necessary impediments excepted. But if a servant in this case shall willfully neglect his master's command he shall suffer bodily punishment.

No maid or woman servant, either now resident in the colony or hereafter to come, shall contract herself in marriage without either the consent of her parents or her master or masters or of the magistrate and minister of the place both together. And whatsoever minister shall marry or contract any such persons without some of the aforesaid consents shall be subject to the severe censure of the Governor and Council of Estate.

Be it enacted by the present assembly that whatsoever servant has heretofore or shall hereafter contract himself in England, either by way of indenture or otherwise, to serve any master here in Virginia and shall afterward, against his said former contract, depart from his master without leave or, being once embarked, shall abandon the ship he is appointed to come in and so being left behind shall put himself into the service of any other man that will bring him hither, that then at the same servant's arrival here, he shall first serve out his time with that master that brought him hither and afterward also shall serve out his time with his former master according to his covenant.

DOCUMENT 3:   Agreement Between the Settlers at New
               Plymouth (The Mayflower Compact)
               November 11, 1620

Text taken from Benjamin Perley Poore, ed., *The
Federal and State Constitutions, Colonial Charters and
Other Organic Laws of the United States* (Washington,
D.C.: Government Printing Office, 1877). Original
spelling. Complete text. Also known as "The Plymouth
Combination," this document was usually referred to by
Plymouth inhabitants as "The Combination," and not
until 1793 was it referred to by the name "Mayflower
Compact." The historical context surrounding its
writing, as well as analysis of its contents, can be
found in Harry M. Ward, *Statism in Plymouth Colony*
Port Washington, N.Y.: Kennikat Press, 1973); and
Willmoore Kendall and George M. Carey, *The Basic
Symbols of the American Political Tradition* (Baton
Rouge: Louisiana State University Press, 1972).

Agreement Between the Settlers
At New Plymouth

     IN the Name of God, Amen. We, whose names are
underwritten, the Loyal Subjects of our dread Sove-
reign Lord King *James*, by the Grace of God, of *Great
Britain France* and *Ireland*, King, *Defender of the
Faith* &c. Having undertaken for the Glory of God, and
Advancement of the Christian Faith, and the Honour of
our King and Country, a Voyage to plant the first
Colony in the northern Parts of *Virginia* ; Do by these
Presents, solemnly and mutually, in the Presence of
God and one another, covenant and combine ourselves
together into a civil Body Politick, for our better
Ordering and Preservation, and Furtherance of the Ends
aforesaid: And by Virtue hereof do enact, constitute,

and frame, such just and equal Laws, Ordinances, Acts,
Constitutions, and Officers, from time to time, as
shall be though most meet and convenient for the
general Good of the Colony; unto which we promise all
due Submission and Obedience. IN WITNESS whereof we
have hereunto subscribed our names at *Cape-Cod* the
eleventh of *November*, in the Reign of our Sovereign
Lord King *James*, of *England*, *France*, and *Ireland*, the
eighteenth, and of *Scotland*, the fifty-fourth, *Anno
Domini*, 1620

Mr. John Carver,
Mr. William Bradford
Mr. Edward Winslow,
Mr. William Brewster,
    Isaac Allerton,
    Myles Standish,
    John Alden,
    John Turner,
    Francis Eaton,
    James Chilton,
    John Craxton,
    John Billington,
    Joses Fletcher,

    John Goodman,

Mr. Samuel Fuller,
Mr. Christopher Martin,
Mr. William Mullins,
Mr. William White,
Mr. Richard Warren,
    John Howland,
Mr. Steven Hopkins
    Digery Priest,
    Thomas Williams,
    Gilbert Winslow,
    Edmund Margesson,
    Peter Brown,
    Richard
      Britteridge,
    George Soule,

    Edward Tilly,
    John Tilly,
    Francis Cooke,
    Thomas Rogers,
    Thomas Tinker,
    John Ridgdale,
    Edward Fuller,
    Richard Clark,
    Richard Gardiner,
Mr. John Allerton,
    Thomas English,
    Edward Doten,
    Edward Liester.

DOCUMENT 4:   Laws and Orders Concluded by the
               Virginia General Assembly, March 5,
               1624

Complete text with original spelling taken from W.H.
Hening, ed., *The Statutes at Large: Being a Collection
of all the Laws of Virginia from the First Session of
the Legislature in 1619, Vol. I* (New York: R. & W. &
G. Bartow, 1823), 122 - 129.

1.   THAT there shall be in every plantation, where
      the people use to meete for the worship of God, a
      house or roome sequestred for that purpose, and
      not to be for any temporal use whatsoever, and a
      place empaled in, sequestered only to the buryal
      of the dead.
2.   That whosoever shall absent himselfe from divine
      service any Sunday without an allowable excuse
      shall forfeite a pound of tobacco, and he that
      absenteth himselfe a month shall forfeith 50lb.
      of tobacco.
3.   That there be an uniformity in our church as
      neere as may be to the canons in England; both in
      substance and circumstance, and that all persons
      yeild readie obedience unto them under paine of
      censure.
4.   That the 22nd of March be yeerly solemnized as
      holliday, and all other hollidays (except when
      they fall two together) betwixt the feast of the
      annuntiation of the blessed virgin and St.
      Michael the archangell, then only the first to be
      observed by reason of our necessities.
5.   That no minister be absent from his church above
      two months in all the yeare upon penalty of
      forfeiting halfe his means, and whosoever shall

absent above fowre months in the year shall
forfeit his whole means and cure.

6. That whosoever shall disparage a minister without
    bringing sufficient proofe to justify his reports
    whereby the mindes of his parishioners may be
    alienated from him, and his ministry prove the
    less effectual by their prejudication, shall not
    only pay 500lb. waight of tobacco but also aske
    the minister so wronged forgiveness publickly in
    the congregation.

7. That no man dispose of any of his tobacco before
    the minister be satisfied, upon pain of forfeiture
    double his part of the minister's means, and one
    man of every plantation to collect his means out
    of the first and best tobacco and corn.

8. That the Governor shall not lay any taxes or
    ympositions upon the colony their lands of como-
    dities other way than by the authority of the
    General Assembly, to be levyed and ymployed as the
    said Assembly shall appoynt.

9. The governor shall not withdraw the inhabitants
    from their private labors to any service of his
    own upon any colour whatsoever and in case the
    publick service require ymployments of many hands
    before the holding a General Assemblie to give
    order for the same, in that case the levying of
    men shall be done by order of the governor and
    whole body of the counsell and that in such sorte
    as to be least burthensome to the people and most
    free from partialitie.

10. That all the old planters that were here before or
    came in at the last coming of sir Thomas Gates
    they and their posterity shall be exempted from
    their personal service to the warrs and any
    publick charge (church duties excepted) that
    belong particularly to their persons (not exempt-
    ing their families) except such as shall be
    ymployed to command in chief.

11. That no burgesses of the General Assembly shall be
    arrested during the time of the assembly, a week
    before and a week after upon pain of the creditors
    forfeiture of his debt and such punishment upon
    the officer as the court shall award.

12. That there shall be courts kept once amonth in the
corporations of Charles City and Elizabeth Citty
for the decyding of suits and controversies not
exceeding the value of one hundred pounds of
tobacco and for punishing of petty offences, that
the commanders of the places and such others as
the governor and council shall appoint by commission shall be the judges, with reservation of
apeal after sentence to the governor and counsell
and whosoever shall appeal yf he be there cast in
suit shall pay duble damages, The commanders to be
of the quorum and sentence to be given by the
major parties.

13. That every privatt planters devident shall be
surveyed and laid out in several and the bounds
recorded by the survey; yf there by any pettie
differences betwixt neighbours about their devi-
dents to be divided by the surveyor if of much
importance to be referred to the governor and
counsell: the surveyor to have 10lbs. of tobacco
upon every hundred acres.

14. For the encouragement of men to plant store of
corne, the prise shall not be stinted, but it
shall be free for every man to sell it as deere as
he can.

15. That there shall be in every parish a bulick
granary unto which there shall be contributed for
every planter exceeding the adge of 18 years alive
at the crop after he hath been heere a year a
bushell of corne, the which shall be disposed for
the publique uses of every parish by the major
part of the freemen, the remainder yearly to be
taken out by the owners at St. Tho's his day and
the new bushell to be putt in the roome.

16. That three sufficient men of every parish shall be
sworne to see that every man shall plant and tende
sufficient of corne for his family. Those men
that have neglected so to do are to be by the said
three men presented to be censured by the governor
and counsell.

17. That all trade for corne with the salvages as well
publick as private after June next shall be pro-
hibited.

18. That every freeman shall fence in a quarter of an
acre of ground before Whitsuntide next to make a
garden for planting of vines, herbs, roots, &c.

subpoena ten pounds of tobacco a man, but that no
man for his own family shall be tyed to fence
above an acre of land and that whosoever hath
fenced a garden and [   ] of the land shall be
paid for it by the owner of the soyle; they shall
also plant Mulberry trees.

19. The proclamations for swearing and drunkenness
     sett out by the governor and counsell are con-
     firmed by this Assembly; and it is further ordered
     that the churchwardens shall be sworne to present
     them to the commanders of every plantation and
     that the forfeitures shall be collected by them to
     be for publique uses.

20. That a proclamation be read aboard every ship and
     afterwards fixed to the maste of such [   ] in,
     prohibiting them to break boulke or make privatt
     sales of any commodity until [   ] James City,
     without special order from the governor and
     counsell.

21. That the proclamation of the rates of commodities
     be still in force and that there be some men in
     every plantation to censure the tobacco.

22. That there be no weights nor measures used but
     such as shall be sealed by officers appointed for
     that purpose.

23. That every dwelling house shall be pallizaded in
     for defence against the Indians.

24. That no man go or send abroad without a sufficient
     parties well armed.

25. That men go not to worke in the ground without
     their arms (and a centinell upon them.)

26. That the inhabitants go not aboard ships or upon
     any other occasions in such numbers, as thereby to
     weaken and endanger the plantations.

27. That the commander of every plantation take care
     that there be sufficient of powder and amunition
     within the plantation under his command and their
     pieces fixt and their arms compleate.

28. That there be dew watch kept by night.

29. That no commander of any plantation do either
     himselfe or suffer others to spend powder
     unneccessarily in drinking or entertainments, &c.

30. That such persons of quality as shall be found
     delinquent in their duties being not fitt to
     undergoe corporal punishment may notwithstanding
     by ymprisoned at the discretione of the commander
     & for greater offences to be subject to a ffine

inflicted by the monthlie court, so that it exceed not the value aforesaid.

31. That every man that hath not contributed to the finding a man at the castell shall pay for himself and servants five pounds of tobacco a head, towards the discharge of such as had their servants here.

32. That at the beginning of July next the inhabitants of every corporation shall fall upon their adjoyning salvages as we did the last yeare, those that shall be hurte upon service to be cured at the publique charge; in case any be lamed to be maintained by the country according to his person and quality.

33. That for defraying of such publique debts our troubles have brought upon us. There shall be levied 10 pounds of tobacco upon every male head above sixteen years of adge now living (not including such as arrived since the beginning of July last.)

34. That no person within this colony upon the rumur of supposed changed and alteration, presume to be disobedient to the present government, nor servants to their private officers, masters or overseers at their uttermost perills.

35. That Mr. John Pountis, counsellor of state, goin to England, (being willing by our intreatie to accept of that imployment.) to solicite the general cause of the country to his majesty and the counsell, towards the charges of which voyage, the country consente to pay for every male head above sixteen years of adge then living, which have been here a yeare ffour pounds of the best merchantable tobacco, in leafe, at or before the last of October next.

Subscripts.

Sir Francis Wyatt, Knt. Governor, &c.

Capt Fran's West,   John Pott,
Sir George Yeardley   Capt. Roger Smith,
George Sandy's Trear,   Capt. Raphe Hamer.

John Pountis.

William Tucker,
Jabez Whitakers,
William Peeine,
Rauleigh Croshaw,
Richard Kingsmell,
Edward Blany,
Luke Boyse,
John Pollington.
Nath'l. Causey,
Robert Addams,
Thomas Harris,
Richard Stephens,

Nathaniel Bass,
John Willcox,
Nicho: Marten,
Clement, Dilke,
Isaeck Chaplin,
John Cew,
John Utie,
John Southerne,
Richard Bigge,
Henry Watkins,
Gabriel Holland,
Thomas Morlatt,

Copia Test,

R. HICKMAN, Cl. Sec. off.

DOCUMENT 5:   Plymouth Oath of Allegiance and
                Fidelity, 1625

Text taken from Charles Evans, "Oaths of Allegiance in
Colonial New England," *Proceedings of the American
Antiquarian Society,*   New Series, Vol. 31 (April
13, 1921 - Oct. 19, 1921), 383. Original spelling,
except for substituting "v" for "u" where appropriate
for modern usage. Text complete except for the
ellipsis inserted by Evans. The Oath of Supremacy begun
by Henry the eighth to break the power of the Roman
Catholic Church, and the Oath of Allegiance, begun by
James I in 1605 after the Gunpowder Plot, were both
required by Charles I, 1625 - 1649. The latter oath
did not refer to the king as the head of the church and
was thus more acceptable to the Puritans. The Charter
of Massachusetts Bay gave the company liberty to admit
new members on its own terms, and the colony at
Plymouth was not, strictly speaking, a colony since it
lacked a charter. Plymouth took advantage of its
position to avoid the Oaths of Supremacy and Allegiance
by writing their own, which did not mention the king
but created allegiance to the colony. The Evans
article provides historical context.

Form of Oath for All Inhabitants

     You shall sweare by the name of the great God...&
earth & in his holy fear, & presence that you shall not
speake, or doe, devise, or advise, anything or things,
acte or acts, directly, or indirectly, By land, or
water, that doth, shall, or may, tend to the
destruction or overthrowe of this present plantation,
Colonie, or Corporation of this towne Plimouth in New
England.

Neither shall you suffer the same to be spoken, or
done, but shall hinder & opposse the same, by all due
means you can.

You shall not enter into any league, treaty,
Confederace or combination, with any, within the said
Colonie or without the same that shall plote, or
contrive any thing to the hurte & ruine of the growth,
and good of the said plantation.

You shall not consente to any such confederation,
nor conceale any known unto you certainly, or by conje
but shall forthwith manifest & make knowne by same, to
the Governours of this said towne for the time being.

And this you promise & swear, simply & truly, &
faithfully to performe as a true christian [you hope
for help from God, the God of truth & punisher of
falshoode].[1]

Form of the Oath Given the Governor and
Council at Every Election

You shall swear, according to that wisdom, and
measure of discerning given unto you; faithfully,
equally & indifrently without respect of persons; to
administer Justice, in all causes coming before you.
And shall labor, to advance, & furder the good of this
Colony, & plantation, to the utmost of your power; and
oppose any thing that may hinder the same. So help you
God.

DOCUMENT 6:   The Salem Covenant of 1629

Complete text and spelling taken from Williston Walker, *The Creeds and Platforms of Congregationalism* (Boston: The Pilgrim Press, 1960). Probably the briefest covenant in American history, it nevertheless presumed that whoever owned it was in total agreement with the Puritan-Calvinistic arm of the English established church. Prospective members were subjected to a careful examination as to their knowledge, experience of grace and godly conversation. Within a few years conflict within the colonies forced the Salem community to draw up the Enlarged Covenant of 1636 which included specific articles encouraging harmony and fellowship (see Document 19).

We Covenant with the Lord and one with an other; and doe bynd our selves in the presence of God, to walke together in all his waies, according as he is pleased to reveale himselfe unto us in his Blessed word of truth.

DOCUMENT 7:   Agreement of the Massachusetts Bay
                Company at Cambridge, England, Aug. 26,
                1629

Text taken from E.S. Morgan, ed., *The Founding of
Massachusetts, The Historians and Sources*
(Indianapolis: The Bobbs-Merrill Company, Inc., 1964),
183 - 184. Original spelling of the complete text.
Although not written on American shores, the Agreement
at Cambridge was written by the colonists themselves
before embarking and not by any English authorities.
It stands, therefore, in the same category as the
Mayflower Compact, which some historians believe was
also composed in England before departure and only
brought out for signing before debarking in America.
The signatures affixed to the following document were
put there in England, however.

The true coppie of the Agreement of Cambridge,
August 26. 1629
Upon due consideracion of the state of the plantacion now in hand for New England, wherein wee (whose
names are hereunto subscribed) have ingaged ourselves:
and having weighed the greatnes of the worke in regard
of the consequences, Gods glory and the churches good:
As also in regard of the difficultyes and discourge-
ments which in all probabilityes must be forcast upon
the prosecucion of this businesse: Considering withall
that this whole adventure growes upon the joynt confi-
dence we have in each others fidelity and resolucion
herein, so as no man of us would have adventured it
without assurance of the rest: Now for the better
encourragement of ourselves and others that shall joyne
with us in this action, and to the end that every man
may without scruple dispose of his estate and afayres
as may best fitt his preparacion for this voyage, It is

fully and faithfully agreed amongst us, and every of us
doth hereby freely and sincerely promise and bynd
himselfe in the word of a Christian and in the presence
of God who is the searcher of all hearts, that we will
so really endevour the prosecucion of his worke, as by
Gods assistaunce we will be ready in our persons, and
with such of our severall familyes as are to go with us
and such provisions as we are able conveniently to
furnish ourselves withall, to embarke for the said
plantacion by the first of march next, at such port or
ports of this land as shall be agreed upon by the
Company, to the end to passe the Seas (under Gods
protection) to inhabite and continue in New England.
Provided alwayes that before the last of September next
the whole governement together with the Patent for the
said plantacion bee first by an order of Court legally
transferred and established to remayne with us and
others which shall inhabite upon the said plantacion.
And provided also that if any shall be hindered by such
just and inevitable Lett or other cause to be allowed
by 3 parts of foure of these whose names are hereunto
subscribed, then such persons for such tymes and during
such letts to be dischardged of this bond. And we do
further promise every one for himselfe that shall fayle
to be ready through his owne default by the day
appointed, to pay for every dayes defalt the summe of 3
li to the use of the rest of the Company who shall be
ready by the same day and tyme.
     This was done by order of Court the 29th day of
August. 1629.

          RICH: SALTONSTALL   ISAACK JOHNSON
          THO: DUDLEY   JOHN HUMFREY
          WILLIAM VASSALL   THO: SHARP
          NICH: WEST   INCREASE NOWELL

               JOHN WINTHROP
               WILL: PINCHON
               KELLAM BROWNE
               WILLIAM COLBRON

DOCUMENT 8:   The Watertown Covenant of July 30, 1630

Complete text with original spelling taken from *Cotton Mather, Magnalia Christi Americana* (London: 1702), Bk III, 83. For historical context one may also consult Champlin Burrage, *The Church Covenant Idea: Its Origin and Development* (Philadelphia: American Baptist Publication Society, 1904). Although strictly speaking a church covenant rather than a political one, this was the first collective document made by the Watertown colonists, and those signing it understood the document to be establishing a church-state. Comparison with the Mayflower Compact illustrates how little difference was needed to make a church covenant a true political compact, and as later compacts illustrate the move from church covenant to true political compact was a logical one.

July 30, 1630

    We whose Names are hereto subscribed, having through God's Mercy escaped out of Pollutions of the World, and been taken into the Society of his People, with all Thankfulness do hereby both with Heart and Hand acknowledge, That his Gracious Goodness, and Fatherly Care, towards us: And for further and more full Declaration thereof, to the present and future Ages, have undertaken (for the promoting of his Glory and the Churches Good, and the Honour of our Blessed Jesus, in our more full and free subjecting of our selves and ours, under his Gracious Government, in the Practice of, and Obedience unto all his Holy Ordinances and Orders, which he hath pleased to prescribe and impose upon us) a long and hazardous Voyage from East

to West, from Old England in Europe, to New England in
America that we may walk before him, and serve him,
without Fear in Holiness and Righteousness, all the
Days of our Lives: And being safely arrived here, and
thus far onwards peaceably preserved by his special
Providence, that we bring forth our Intentions into
Actions, and perfect our Resolutions, in the Beginnings
of some Just and Meet Executions; We have separated the
Day above written from all other Services, and Dedicated it wholly to the Lord in Divine Employments, for
a Day of Afflicting our Souls, and humbling our selves
before the Lord, to seek him, and at his Hands, a Way
to walk in, by Fasting and Prayer, that we might know
what was Good in his Sight: And the Lord was intreated
of us.

For in the End of the Day, after the finishing of
our publick Duties, we do all, before we depart,
solemnly and with all our Hearts, personally, Man by
Man for our selves and others (charging them before
Christ and his Elect Angels, even them that are not
here with us this Day, or are yet unborn, That they
keep the Promise unblameably and faithfully unto the
coming of our Lord Jesus) promise, and enter into a
sure Covenant with the Lord our God, and before him
with one another, by Oath and serious Protestation
made, to Renounce all Idolatry and Superstition,
Will-Worship, all Humane Traditions and Inventions
whatsoever, in the Worship of God; and forsaking all
Evil Ways, do give ourselves wholly unto the Lord
Jesus, to do him faithful Service, observing and
keeping all his Statutes, Commands, and Ordinances, in
all Matters concerning our Reformation; his Worship,
Administrations, Ministry, and Government; and in the
Carriage of our selves among our selves, and one
another towards another, as he hath prescribed in his
Holy Word. Further swearing to cleave unto that alone,
and the true Sense and meaning thereof to the utmost of
our Power, as unto the most clear Light and infallible
Rule, and All-sufficient Canon, in all things that
concern us in this our Way. In Witness of all, we do
ex Animo, and in the presence of God, hereto set our
Names, or Marks, in the Day and Year above written.

DOCUMENT 9:   Massachusetts Election Agreement, May
                18, 1631

Taken from E.S. Morgan ed., *The Founding of Massachusetts: Historians and the Sources*, p.406. The spelling and definition of the text are his. Although
elections had been held in a number of colonies prior
to this date, this is probably the oldest formal
colonial provision defining an election process. The
"commons" referred to here was essentially all freemen,
as was clarified by an agreement on May 9, 1632.

        For explanation of an order made the last general
court, held the 19th of October last, it was ordered
now, with full consent of all the commons then present,
that once in every year, at least, a general court
shall be held, at which court it shall be lawful for
the commons to propound any person or persons whom they
shall desire to be chosen assisteants, and if it be
doubtful whether it be the greater part of the commons
or not, it shall be put to the poll. The like course
to be held when they, the said commons, shall see cause
for any defect or misbehavior to remove any one or more
of the assistants. And to the end the body of the
commons may be preserved of honest and good men, it was
likewise ordered and agreed that for time to come no
man shall be admitted to the freedom of this body
politic but such as are members of some of the churches
within the limits of the same.

DOCUMENT 10:   The Oath of a Freeman, or of a Man to Be
                Made Free, 1631

Text taken from Charles Evans, "Oaths of Allegiance in
Colonial New England," *Proceedings of the American
Antiquarian Society*   New Series, Vol. 31 (April 13,
1921 - October 19, 1921), 389 and 393. The law in the
Massachusetts Bay Colony that all freemen must be
church members was modified in 1632 so that no civil
magistrate could be an elder in the church. To give
force to this new law an Oath of Freemen was developed.
Without it, those inhabitants not members of a church
would not be bound by the church covenants, and thus
not bound to the colony. In 1634 it was replaced by a
newer oath which took into account the creation of the
Massachusetts Legislature in May of 1634 (see Document
15). The replacement oath is reproduced as Document
16. The spelling is the original, and the text is
complete.

The Oath of a Freeman, or a Man to be Made FFree

        I, A.B.&c. being, by the Almighties most wise
disposicon, become a membr of this body, consisting of
the Gounr, Assistants, &
 a comnlty of the Mattachusets in Newe England, doe,
freely & sincerely acknowledge that I am iustly and
lawfully subject to the goumt of the same, & doe
accordingly submitt my pson & estate to be ptected,
ordered, & gouned by the lawes & constitucons thereof,
& doe faithfully pmise to be from time to time obedient
& conformeable thervnto, & to the authie of the said
Gounr & Assistnts & their successrs, & to all such
lawes, orders, sentences, & decrees as shalbe lawfully
made & published by them or their successors; and I

will alwaies indeavr (as in dutie I am bound) to
advance the peace & wellfaire of this bodie or comon-
wealth to my vtmost skill & abilitie; & will, to my
best power & meanes, seeke to devert & prevent whatsoeuer may tend to the ruyne or damage thereof, or of any
the said Gounr, Deputy Gounr, or Assistants, or any of
them, or their siccessrs, and will giue speedy notice
to them, or some of them, of any sedicon, violence,
treachery, or other hurt or ciuil which I shall knowe,
heare, or vehemtly suspecte to be plotted or intended
against the comonwealth, or the said goumt established;
and I will not att any time suffer or giue consent to
any counsell or attempt that shalbe offered giuen, or
attempted for the impeachmt of the said goumt, or
makeing any change or alteracon of the same, contrary
to the lawes & ordinances thereof, but shall doe my
vtmost endeavr to discover, oppose, & hinder, all & euy
such counsell & attempts.   Soe helpe me God.

DOCUMENT 11:   The Massachusetts Agreement on the
                Legislature, May 9, 1632

Text taken from Nathaniel B. Shurtleff, ed., *Records
of the Governor and Company of the Massachusetts Bay in
New England* (5 vols., Boston, 1853 - 4), I, 95 - 96.
For an introductory discussion on this and other
colonial documents concerning representation, see
Michael Kammen, *Deputyes & Libertyes: The Origins
of Representative Government in Colonial America* (New
York: Alfred A. Knopf, 1969).

A General Court, holden att Boston, May 9th, 1632
Present, The Governor,   Mr. Nowell,
Deputy Governor,   Mr. Pinchon,
Mr. Ludlowe,   S. Bradstreete

It was generally agreed upon by erection of hands,
that the Governor, Deputy Governor, & Assistants should
be chosen by the whole Court of Governor, Deputy
Governor, Assistants, & freemen, and that the Governor
shall alwaies be chosen out of the Assistants.
    John Winthrop, Esq, was chosen to the place of
Governor (by the generall consent of the whole Court,
manefested by erection of hands) for this yeare nexte
ensueing, & till a newe be chosen, & did, in presence
of the Court, take an oath to his said place belonging.
. . .
    It was ordered, that there should be two of every
plantation appointed to conferre with the Court about
raiseing of a publique stocke . . . .
    It was ordered, that the towne of Waterton shall
have that priviledge and interest in the (fish) weir
they have built upp (the) Charles Ryver, according as
the Court hereafter shall thinke meete to confirme unto
them.

DOCUMENT 12:   Cambridge Agreement, Dec. 24, 1632

Text taken from *The Records of the Town of Cambridge*
(Formerly Newtowne) Massachusetts, 1630 - 1703 (Cambridge: University Press, John Wilson and Son, 1901),
4. Text is complete and with the original spelling.
Although the institution of the town meeting, or
general meeting of the inhabitants of a colony, pre-
dates this document, and had already been adopted in a
number of colonies, this is the oldest surviving
agreement establishing the practice. In most instances
the town meeting seems to have been adopted without a
formal declaration or even a conscious decision. Even
here it seems to be not so much matter of establishing
a new procedure as it is reestablishing it in such a
way that attendance can be legally enforced.

Ann Agreement made by A Gennerall Conf for a mounthly
meeting.

     Impr that every person under subscribed shall meet
Every second Monday in Every mounth within the meeting-
house In the Afternoone within half an ouer after the
ringing of the bell and that every one that make not
his personall apearannce there and continews ther
without leave from [   ] untill the meeting bee Ended
shall for every default pay twelve pence and if it be
not paid next meeting then to dobl it and soe untill it
is paid.

DOCUMENT 13:   Dorchester Agreement, October 8, 1633

Text taken from *Dorchester Town Records: Fourth Report of the Record Commissioners* (Boston: Rockwell and Churchill, City Printers, 1880), 3.   Original spelling. The text is complete as far as the records of the town are concerned -- the ellipsis is in the original.   In addition to establishing formally a town meeting, this is the oldest surviving record of a smaller represent- ative body being selected to serve in place of the town meeting between meetings, such body usually to be called the town "selectmen."

    An agreement made by the whole consent and vote of the plantation made Mooneday 8th of October, 1633.
    Inprimus it is ordered that for the generall good and well ordering of the affayres of the Plantation their shall be every Mooneday before the Court by eight of the Clocke in the morning, and prsently upon the beating of the drum, a generall meeting of the inhabi- tants of the Plantation att the meeteing house, there to settle (and sett downe) such orders as may tend to the generall good as aforesayd; and every man to be bound thereby without gaynesaying or resistance.   It is also agreed that there shall be twelve men selected out of the Company that may or the greatest p't of them meete as aforesayd to determine as aforesayd, yet so as it is desired that the most of the Plantation will keepe the meeting constantly and all that are there although none of the Twelve shall have a free voyce as any of the 12 and that the greate[r] vote both of the 12 and the other shall be of force and efficasy as aforesayd.   And it is likewise ordered that all things concluded as aforesayd shall stand in force and be obeyed vntill the next monethly meeteing and after- wardes if it be not contradicted and otherwise ordered

upon the sayd monethly meete[ing] by the greatest p'te
of those that are prsent as aforesayd.   Moreover,
because the Court in Winter in the vacansy of the sayd
. . . . this said meeting to continue till the first
Mooneday in the moneth (7) mr Johnson, mr Eltwid
Pummery (mr. Richards), John Pearce, George Hull,
William Phelps, Thom. ffoard.

DOCUMENT 14:   Cambridge Agreement on a Town Council,
                Feb. 3, 1634

Text taken from *The Records of the Town of Cambridge*
(Formerly Newtowne) Massachusetts, 1630 - 1703 (Cambridge: University Press, John Wilson and Son, 1901),
11 - 12. Spelling is the original, and the text
complete, except for the undecipherable words which are
marked by brackets. This document was signed only
thirteen months after the town meeting was institu-
tionalized in Cambridge, indicating the difficulty that
early colonies had with involving the entire population
in day-to-day decision-making, despite their small size
(see Document 11). This move from a more or less
direct democracy to a representative system closely
watched by a town meeting was typical for the early
colonies. The degree to which the selectmen tended to
dominate the political system usually depended upon the
degree of religious fervor informing the colony. The
more tightly religious a colony was, the more likely
that the selectmen came from an oligarchy associated
with the church. The more heterogeneous and open the
social system, the more likely that the town meeting
continued to control the selectmen.

    At A Gennerall Meeting of the whole Towne Itt was
Agreed uppon by a Joynt Consent that 7 menn should be
Chossen to doe the whole bussines of the Towne and soe
to Continew untell the ffirst Monday in November next
and untell new be Chossen in their Room soe ther was
then Elected and Chossen
                    John Haynes Esqr
                    mr Symon Bradstreet
                    John Taylcott
                    Wiliam Westwood
                    John White

William Wadsworth
James Olmstead Constable

   Itt is further Ordered by a Joynt Consent that
whatsoever these Townsmen thuse Chosse [   ] shall
doe In the Compas of ther tyme shall stand in as full
force as if the whole Town did the same either for
makeing of new orders or altering of ould ones
   ffurther it is ordered that whatsoever prson they
shall send for to help anny bussness and he shall refus
to Come they shall have power to lay a fine uppon him
and to gather [   ]
   ffurther it is ordered that they shall have 0
[   ] to attent uppon them to Imploy aboute any bussines at a publik charge
   ffurther Itt is ordered that they shall meet every
first Monday in a Mounth at [   ] in the After Noone
accordinge to the former [   ]
   Also the was Chossen to Joyne [   ] James
Olmstead Constable John Beniamen Daniell Denison Andrew
Warner William Spencer which 5 acordinge to the order
of Cour[t] to survey the Towne lands and enter [   ] a
book Apointed for that purpose
   Itt is further ordered that these 5 men meet every
first Monday in the Mounth at the Constables house in
the [   ] at the Ringing of the bell

DOCUMENT 15: Massachusetts Agreement on the Legislature, May 14, 1634

From Nathaniel B. Shurtleff, ed., *Records of the Governor and Company of the Massachusetts Bay in New England* (5 vols., Boston, 1853-54), I, 116-20. In addition to Michael Kammen's book cited in the introduction to Document 11, an explanation of the events surrounding this document can be found in James K. Hosmer, ed., *Winthrop's Journal.* "History of New England" 1630 - 1649 (New York, 1908), Vol, I.

Att a General Courte, holden at Boston, May 14th, 1634 . . . it is agreed, that none but the Generall Court hath power to chuse and admitt freemen.

That none but the Generall Court hath power to make and establishe lawes, nor to elect and appoynt officers, as Governor, Deputy Governor, Assistants, Tresurer, Secretary, Captain, Leiuetenants, Ensignes, or any of like moment, or to remove such upon misdemeanor, as also to sett out the dutyes and powers of the said officers.

That none but the Generall Court hath power to rayse moneyes & taxes, & to dispose of lands, viz, to give & confirme proprietyes . . . .

It was further ordered, that the constable of every plantation shall, upon proces receaved from the Secretary, give tymely notice to the freemen of the plantation where hee dwells to send soe many of their said members as the process shall direct, to attend upon publique service; & it is agreed, that noe tryall shall passe upon any, for life or banishment, but by a jury soe summoned, or by the Generall Courte.

It is likewise ordered, that there shal be foure Generall Courts held yearely, to be summoned by the

Governor, for the tyme being, & not to be dissolved
without the consent of the major parte of the Court.

It was further ordered, that it shal be lawfull
for the freemen of every plantation to chuse two or
three of each towne before every Generall Court, to
confere of & prepare such publique busines as by them
shal be thought fitt to consider of at the nexte
Generall Court, & that such persons as shal be hereafter soe deputed by the freemen of [the] severall
plantations, to deale in their behalfe, in the publique
affayres of the commonwealth, shall have the full power
and voyces of all the said freemen, deryved to them for
the makeing & establishing of lawes, graunting of
lands, etc., & to deale in all other affaires of the
commonwealth wherein the freemen have to doe, the
matter of election of magistrates & other officers
onely excepted, wherein every freeman is to gyve his
own voyce . . . .

There is leave graunted to the inhabitants of Newe
Towne to seek out some convenient place for them, with
promise that it shal be confirmed unto them, to which
they may remove their habitations, or have as an
addition to that which already they have, provided they
doe not take it in any place to prejudice a plantation
already setled . . . .

It was further ordered, that if any Assistant, or
any man deputed by the freemen to deale in publique
occasions of the commonwealthe, doe absent himselfe
without leave in tyme of publique business, hee shal be
fined att the discretion of the Court.

It is further ordered, that in all rates &
publique charges, the townes shall have respect to levy
every man according to his estate, & with consideration
of all other his abilityes, whatsoever, & not according
to the number of his persons.

DOCUMENT 16:   The Oath of a Freeman, May 14, 1634

Text taken from Charles Evans, "Oaths of Allegiance in
Colonial New England," *Proceedings of the American
Antiquarian Society, New Series, Vol. 31* (April 13,
1921 - October 19, 1921), 394. Spelling is the original and the text is complete. This is the oath that
replaced the original, 1631 version (see Document 10),
and a comparison of the two is instructive. The former
reads as though it creates a subject, whereas this oath
reads as though it creates a citizen with political
rights and duties.

        Att a Genrall Courte, holden att Boston, May 14,
1634.
        It was agreed & ordered, that the former oath of
ffreemen shalbe revoked, soe farr as it is dissonant
from the oath of ffreemen herevnder written, & that
those that receaved the former oath shall stand bound
noe further thereby, to any intent or purpose, then
this newe oath tyes those that nowe takes ye same.

        The Oath of a Freeman

        I. A.B., being, by Gods providence, an inhabitant
& ffreeman within the jurisdiccon of this comonweale,
doe freely acknowledge my selfe to be subiect to the
govermt thereof, & therefore doe heere sweare, by the
greate & dreadfull name of the eurlyving God, that I
wilbe true & faithfull to the same, & will accordingly
yeilde assistance & support therevnto, with my pson &
estate, as in equity I am bound, & will also truely
indeavr to mainetaine & preserue all the libertyes &
previlidges thereof, submitting my selfe to the
wholesome lawes & orders made & established by the
same; and furthr, that I will not plott nor practise

any evill aginst it, nor consent to any that shall soe
doe, but will timely discovery & reveale the same to
lawfull aucthority nowe here established, for the
speedy preventing thereof. Moreouer, I doe solemnly
binde myselfe in the sight of God, that when I shalbe
called to giue my voice touching any such matter of
this state, wherein ffreemen are to deale I will giue
my vote & suffrage, as I shall iudge in myne owne
conscience may best conduce & tend to the pulique weale
of the body, without respect of psons, or favr of any
man. Soe helpe mee God in the Lord Jesus Christ.

Further, it is agreed that none but the Gen all
Court hath power to chuse and admitt freemen.

DOCUMENT 17:   Salem Oath for Residents, April 1, 1634

Text taken from Charles Evans, "Oaths of Allegiance in
Colonial New England," *Proceedings of the American
Antiquarian Society, New Series, Vol. 31*   (April 13,
1921 - October 19, 1921), 393 - 394; and Sidney Perley,

(Salem, Mass.:   1924), 195 - 196.   The text is
complete, and has the original spelling.   Although a
part of the Massachusetts Bay Colony, Salem established
its own town government early in its existence.   About
the time that the Massachusetts Bay Colony was evolving
a more liberal oath, led by Cambridge, Salem was
attempting to exert even more careful control over its
population.   Part of this attempt took the form of
requiring even those outside the franchise to take an
oath of allegiance to the colony.   The document which
follows is that oath, and should be contrasted with the
Oath of a Freeman adopted by the Bay Colony only six
weeks later (Document 16).   Generally, this Salem oath
is indistinguishable from the 1631 Oath of a Freeman
(Document 10), which implies much about the original
status of freemen in the colony if only three years
later mere inhabitants were treated almost the same.

At A Court holden att Boston, April 1th, 1634.
It was further ordered, that euy man of or above
the age of twenty yeares, whoe hath bene or shall
herefter be resident within this jurisdiccon by the
space of six monethes, as an householder or soiorner,
and not infranchised, shall take the oath herevnder
written, before the Gounr, or Deputy Gounr, or some two
of the nexte Assistants, whoe shall haue power to
convent him for that purpose, and vpon his refuseall
the second tyme, hee shalbe banished, except the Court
shall see cause to giue him further respite.

The Oath of Residents

    I doe heare sweare, and call God to witnes, that,
being nowe an inhabitant within the lymitts of this
juridiccon of the Massachusetts, I doe acknowledge
myselfe lawfully subject to the aucthoritie and gouermt
there established, and doe accordingly submitt my pson,
family, and estate, to be ptected, ordered, & gouerned
by the lawes & constitucons thereof, and doe faithfully
pmise to be from time to time obedient and conformeable
therevnto, and to the aucthoritie of the Gounr, & all
other the magistrates there, and their successrs, and
to all such lawes, orders, sentences, decrees, as nowe
are or hereafter shalbe lawfully made, decreed,
published by them or their successrs. And I will
alwayes indeavr (as in duty I am bound) to advance the
peace & wellfaire of this body pollitique, and I will
(to my best power & meanes) seeke to devert & prevent
whatsoeyer may tende to the ruine or damage thereof, or
ye Gounr, or Assistants, or any of them or their
successrs, and will giue speedy notice to them, or some
of them, of any sedicon, violence, treacherie, or othr
hurte or euill wch I shall knowe, heare, or vehemently
suspect to be plotted or intended against them or any
of them, or against the said Comon-wealth or goumt
established. Soe helpe mee God.

DOCUMENT 18:   Watertown Agreement on Civil Officers,
                August 23, 1634

Text taken from *Watertown Records: First Book, Town
Proceedings* (Watertown, Mass.: Press of Fred G.
Barker, 1894), 1. Spelling is the original, and the
text is complete. The earliest colonial records are
often quite sketchy, and there is the distinct impression given that while the colonists tried to put as
much down on paper as possible there often was time for
little else than the bare agreements. At other times,
records from the very beginning of a colony may have a
richness of expression and content that may lead one to
believe that little else was done but write such
documents. The following is an example of the former.
Typically, the first item in the records that survives
to our time is brief and quite clearly assumes the
existence of a community with a town meeting to govern
itself.

    August 23, 1634. Agreed by the consent of the
Freemen, that there shalbe Chosen three persons to be
[   ] the ordering of the civill affaires in the
Towne One of them to serve as Towne Clerk, and shall
keep the Records and acts of the Towne. The three
chosen are William Jennison,
    Briam Pembleton,
    John Eddie.

DOCUMENT 19:   The Enlarged Salem Covenant of 1636

The complete text with original spelling was taken from
Williston Walker, *The Creeds and Platforms of Congregationalism* (Boston: The Pilgrim Press, 1960), pp.
116-118.   The earlier covenant of 1629 (see Document 6)
was apparently found to be inadequate.   This "enlarged"
version probably contains the specific points of
dissension that needed to be settled, and thus provides
a"window" into their life as a people.

Gather my Saints together unto me that have made a
Covenant with me by sacrifyce.   Psa. 50:5:
Wee whose names are here under written, members of the
present Church of Christ in Salem, having found by said
experience how dangerous it is to sitt loose to the
Covenant wee make with our God: and how apt wee are to
wander into by pathes, even to the looseing of our
first aimes in entring into church fellowship: Doe
therefore solemnly in the presence of the Eternall God,
both for our own comforts, and those which shall or
maybe joyned unto us, renewe that Church Covenant we
find this Church bound unto at theire first beginning,
viz: That We Covenant with the Lord and one with an
other; and doe bynd our selves in the prsence of God,
to walke together in all his waies, according as he is
pleased to reveale himself unto us in his Blessed word
of truth.   And doe more explicitely in the name and
feare of God, profess and protest to walke as followeth
through the power and grace of our Lord Jesus.
1.   first wee avowe the Lord to be our God, and our
selves his people in the truth and simplicitie of our
spirits.
2.   Wee give our selves to the Lord Jesus Christ, and
the word of his grace, fore the teaching ruleing and
sanctifyeing of us in matters of worship, and

101

Conversation, resolveing to cleave to him alone for
life and glorie; and oppose all contrarie wayes,
cannons and constitutions of men in his worship.
3.   We promise to walk with our brethren and sisters
in this Congregation with all watchfullnes and tender-
nes, avoyding all jelousies, suspitions, backbyteings,
censurings, provoakings, secrete risings of spirite
against them; but in all offences to follow the rule of
the Lord Jesus, and to beare and forbeare, give and
forgive as he hath taught us.
4.   In publick or in private, we will willingly doe
nothing to the ofence of the Church but will be willing
to take advise for our selves and ours as acasion
shalbe presented.
5.   Wee will not in the Congregation be forward eyther
to shew our gifts or parts in speaking or scrupling, or
there discover the fayling of oure brethren or sisters
butt atend an orderly cale there unto; knowing how much
the Lord may be dishonoured, and his Gospell in the
profession of it, sleighted, by our distempers, and
weaknesses in publyck.
6.   Wee bynd our selves to studdy the advancement of
the Gospell in all truth and peace, both in regard of
those that are within, or without, noe way sleighting
our sister Churches, but useing theire Counsell as need
shalbe: nor laying a stumbling block before any, noe
not the Indians, whose good we desire to promote, and
soe to converse, as we may avoyd the verrye appearance
of evill.
7.   We hearbye promise to carre our selves in all
lawfull obedience, to those that are over us, in Church
of Commonweale, knowing how well pleasing it will be to
the Lord, that they should have incouragement in theire
places, by our not greiveing theyre spirites through
our Irregularities.
8.   Wee resolve to approve our selves to the Lord in
our perticular calings, shunning ydlesness as the bane
of any state, nor will we deale hardly, or oppressingly
with any, wherein we are the Lord's stewards.
9.   alsoe promyseing to our best abilitie to teach our
children and servants, the knowledg of God and his
will, that they may serve him also; and all this, not
by any strength of our owne, but by the Lord Christ,
whose bloud we desire may sprinckle this our Covenant
made in his name.

DOCUMENT 20:   Plymouth Agreement, November 15, 1636

Text is taken from Harry M. Ward, *Statism in Plymouth Colony* (Port Washington, N.Y.:   Kennikat Press, 1973), 17.   His text is complete, and we here use his spelling and marking.   One might compare this text with the second paragraph of the Pilgrim Code of Law (Document 21) where a version of the Plymouth Agreement was inserted as a part of the preface.   It is interesting that the paragraph in the Pilgrim Code of Law where this agreement was inserted indicates that both the Mayflower Compact (Plymouth Combination) and the original charter from King Charles (the letters-patent) comprise the legal background to what is here identified as the Plymouth Agreement of 1636.

We, the associates of New-Plymouth Coming hither as freeborn subjects of the State of England endowed with all and singular the privileges belonging to such being assembled; doe ordaine Constitute and enact that noe act imposition law or ordinance be made or imposed upon us at present, or to come but such as shall be imposed by Consent of the body of associates or their representatives legally assembled; which is according to the free liberties of England.

DOCUMENT 21:   Pilgrim Code of Law, November 15, 1636

The text of this document is taken from David Pulsifer,
ed., *Records of the Colony of New Plymouth in New
England: Vol. I, The Laws, 1623 - 1682* (Boston, the
Press of William White, 1861), pp. 6 - 12. The text is
partial and the spelling has been altered considerably.
The original is in a shorthand that is particularly
tortuous even for the times in which it was written.
Since this document is a candidate for being the first
true constitution in the English language, it was
decided to emend considerably the original so as to
make it readable. Unlike most of the documents in this
volume, The Pilgrim Code of Law has been reproduced in
its original form a number of times and is available in
most libraries. The version of the text here is
consistent with that reproduced by W. Keith Kavenagh,
ed.,
        (New York: Chelsea House, 1973), pp. 247 - 251.
Much more than a code of laws, this document lays out
the fundamental values and political institutions of
the community. It was revised in 1658, and then again
in 1671 (See Document 60).

Whereas, at his Majesty's court held the fourth and
fifth of October in the twelfth year of the reign of
our sovereign lord Charles, by the grace of God, King
of England, Scotland, France, and Ireland, Defender of
the Faith, etc., it was ordered that Major William
Brewster, Major Ralph Smith, Major John Done, and John
Jenny for the town of Plymouth, Jonathan Brewster and
Christopher Wadsworth for Duxborough, and James
Cudworth and Anthony Annable for Scittuate should be
added to the governor and assistants as committees for
the whole body of this commonweal, should meet together
the 15th of November at Plymouth, above-mentioned, and

there to peruse all the laws, orders, and constitutions
of the plantations within this government that so those
that are still fitting might be established, those that
time has made unnecessary might be rejected, and others
that were wanting might be prepared that so the next
court they might be established.

Now being assembled according to the said order,
and having read the combination made at Cape Cod the
11th of November 1620 in the year of the reign of our
late sovereign lord King James of England, France,
Ireland, the eighteenth, and of Scotland the fifty-
fourth, as also our letters patents confirmed by the
honorable council, his said Majesty established and
granted the 13th of January 1629 in the fifth year of
the reign of our sovereign lord King Charles, and
finding that, as freeborn subjects of the state of
England, we hither came endowed with all and singular
the privileges belonging to such, in the first place we
think good that it be established for an act that,
according to the . . . and due privileges of the
subject aforesaid, no imposition, law, or ordinance be
made or imposed upon us by ourselves or others at
present or to come but such as shall be made or imposed
by consent, according to the free liberties of the
state and kingdom of England and no otherwise.

That whereas, before expressed, we find a solemn
and binding combination as also letters patent deri-
vatory from his Majesty of England, our dread
sovereign, for the ordering of a body politic within
the several limits of this patent, viz., from
Cowahasset to the utmost bounds of Puckanokick
westward, and all that tract of land southward to the
southern ocean, with all and singular lands, rivers,
havens, waters, creeks, ports, fishing, fowlings, etc.,
by virtue whereof we ordain, institute, and appoint the
first Tuesday in March every year for the election of
such officers as shall be thought meet for the guiding
and government of this corporation.

This is altered afterwards to the first Tuesday in
June yearly by a general court.

That at the day and time appointed a governor and
seven assistants be chosen to rule and govern the said
plantations within the said limits for one whole year
and no more; and this election to be made only by the
freemen according to the former custom. And that then

also constables for each part and other inferior
officers be also chosen.

That in every election some one of the assistants,
or some other sufficient person, be chosen treasurer
for the year present, whose place it shall be to
receive in whatsoever sum or sums shall appertain to
the royalty of the place, either coming in by way of
fine, amercement, or otherwise, and shall improve the
same for the public benefit of this corportion by order
of the government; as also to give a just account
thereof to the ensuing treasurer and to the governor
whenever he shall demand it, or the court when they
appoint.

That a clerk of the court also be chosen for the
year.

That also one be chosen to the office of coroner
to be executed as near as may be to the laws and
practice of the kingdom of England, and to continue one
year.

The Office of the Governor

The office of the governor for the time being
consists in the execution of such laws and ordinances
as are or shall be made and established for the good of
this corporation according to the several bounds and
limits thereof; viz., in calling together or advising
with the assistants or council of the said corporation
upon such material occasions, or so seeming to him, as
time shall bring forth; in which assembly, and all
other, the governor to propound the occasion of the
assembly and have a double voice therein. If the
assistants judge the case too great to be decided by
them and refer it to the general court, then the
governor to summon a court by warning all the freemen
aforesaid that are then extant, and there also to
propound causes, and go before the assistants in the
examination of particulars, and to propound such
sentence as shall be determined. Further, it shall be
lawful for him to arrest and committ to ward any
offenders provided that with all convenient speed he
shall bring the cause to hearing either of the assistants or general court, according to the nature of the
offense. Also, it shall be lawful for him to examine
any suspicious persons for evil against the colony, as

also to intercept or oppose such as he conceives may
tend to the overthrow of the same. And that this
office continue one whole year and no more without
renewing by election.

The Oath of the Governor

You shall swear to be truly loyal; also, according
to that measure of wisdom, understanding, and discerning given unto you faithfully, equally, and
indifferently, without respect of persons, to
administer justice in all cases coming before you as
the governor of New Plymouth. You shall, in like
manner, faithfully, duly, and truly execute the laws
and ordinances of the same, and shall labor to advance
and further the good of the colonies and plantations
within the limits thereof to the utmost of your power
and oppose any thing that shall seem to hinder the
same. So help you God, who is the God of truth and
punisher of falsehood.

The Oath of a Freeman

You shall be loyal. You shall not speak or do,
devise or advise anything or things, act or acts,
directly or indirectly, by land or water, that does,
shall, or may tend to the destruction or overthrow of
this present plantation, colony, or corporation of New
Plymouth, neither shall you suffer the same to the
governor and assistants of the said colony for the time
being, or some one of them. You shall faithfully
submit to such good and wholesome laws and ordinances
as either are or shall be made for the ordering and
government of the same, and shall endeavor to advance
the growth and good of the several plantations within
the limits of this corporation by all due means and
courses. All which you promise and swear by the name
of the great God of heaven and earth, simply, truly,
and faithfully to perform as you hope for help from
God, who is the God of truth and punisher of falsehood.

The Office of an Assistant

The office of an assistant for the time being
consists in appearing at the governor's summons, and in

giving his best advice both in public court and private
council with the governor for the good of the colonies
within the limits of this government; not to disclose,
but keep secret, such things as concern the public good
and shall be thought meet to be concealed by the
governor and council of assistants in having a special
hand in the examination of public offenders and in
contriving the affairs of the colony; to have a voice
in the censuring of such offenders as shall not be
brought to public court; that if the governor has
occasion to be absent from the colony for a short time,
by the governor, with consent of the rest of the
assistants, he may be deputed to govern in the absence
of the governor. Also, it shall be lawful for him to
examine and commit to ward where any occasion arises
where the governor is absent, provided the person be
brought to further hearing with all convenient speed
before the governor or the rest of the assistants.
Also, it shall be lawful for him in his Majesty's name
to direct his warrants to any constable within the
government, who ought faithfully to execute the same
according to the nature and tenure thereof; and may
bind over persons for matters of crime to answer at the
next ensuing court of Majesty after the fact committed
or the person apprehended.

The Oath of the Assistants

You shall all swear to be truly loyal to our
sovereign lord King Charles, his heirs and successors.
Also, you shall faithfully, truly, and justly, according to that measure of discerning and discretion God
has given you, be assistant to the governor for his
present year for the execution of justice in all cases
and towards all persons coming before you without
partiality, according to the nature of the office of an
assistant read to you. Moreover, you shall diligently,
duly, and truly see that the laws and ordinances of
this corporation be faithfully executed; and shall
labor to advance the good of the several plantations
within the limits thereof and oppose anything that
shall hinder the same by all due means and courses. So
help you God, who is the God of truth and punisher of
falsehood.

The Oath of any Residing Within the Government

You shall be truly loyal to our sovereign lord
King Charles, his heirs and successors. And whereas
you make choice at present to reside within the government of New Plymouth, you shall not do, or cause to be
done, any act or acts, directly or indirectly, by land
or water, that shall or may tend to the destruction or
overthrow of the whole or any of the several colonies
within the said government that are or shall be orderly
erected and established, but shall, contrariwise,
hinder, oppose, and discover such intents and purposes
as tend thereunto to the governor for the time being,
or some one of the assistants with all convenient
speed. You shall also submit to and obey such good and
wholesome laws, ordinances, and officers as are or
shall be established within the several limits thereof.
So help you God, who is the God of truth and punisher
of falsehood.

The Oath of a Constable

You shall swear to be truly loyal to our sovereign
lord King Charles, his heirs and successors, which you
shall faithfully serve in the office of a constable in
the ward of . . . for this present year according to
that measure of wisdom and understanding and discretion
God has given you. In which time you shall diligently
see that his Majesty's peace commanded be not broken,
but shall carry the person or persons offending before
the governor of this corporation, or some one of his
assistants, and there attend the hearing of the case
and such order as shall be given you. You shall
apprehend all suspicious persons and bring them before
the said governor, or someone of his assistants, as
aforesaid. You shall duly and truly serve such
warrants and give such summons as shall be directed to
you from the governor or assistants before mentioned,
and shall labour to advance the peace and happiness of
this corporation and oppose any thing that shall seem
to annoy the same, by all due means and courses. So
help you God, who is the God of truth and punisher of
falsehood.

That the annual election of officers before
expressed be at a general court held in his Majesty's

name of England. And that the governor in due season,
by warrant directed to the several constables in his
Majesty's name aforesaid, give warning to the freemen
to make their appearance; and that all other our
courts, warrants, summons, or commands by way of
justice be all done, directed, and made in the name of
his Majesty of England aforesaid, our dread sovereign.

And for default in case of appearance at the
election before mentioned, without due excuse, each
delinquent to be amerced in three shillings sterling.

That if at any time any shall be elected to the
office of governor and will not hold according to the
election that then he be amerced in twenty pounds
sterling fine.

That if any elected to the office of assistant
refuse to hold according to election that then he be
amerced in ten pounds sterling fine.

That in case one and the same person should be
elected governor a second year, having held the place
the foregoing year, it should be lawful for him to
refuse without amercement unless they can prevail with
him by entreaty.

That the government, viz., the general courts and
courts of assistants, be held at Plymouth, and that the
governor hold his dwelling there for the present year,
except such inferior courts as for some matters shall
be allowed by this court in other places of this
government.

It is enacted that no presentment hereafter shall
be exhibited to the grand inquest to be brought to the
bench except it be done upon oath, and that it shall be
lawful for any of the assistants to administer an oath
in such case.

That the constable see the highways for man and
beast be made and kept in convenient repair, and therefore be also appointed surveyor for the liberty he is
chosen. That two surveyors in every constablerick be
chosen each year to see that the highways be mended
competently, and if it fall out that a way be wanting
upon due complaint, that then the governor panel a jury
and upon oath charge them to lay out such way as in
conscience they find most beneficial for the commonweal
and as little prejudice as may be to the particular.

That the laws and ordinances of the colony and for
the government of the same be made only by the freemen

of the corporation and no other; provided, that in such
rates and taxations as are or shall be laid upon the
whole they be without partiality so as the freemen be
not spared for his freedom, but the levy be equal. And
in case any man finds himself aggrieved that his
complaint may be heard and redressed if there be due
cause.

That an oath of allegiance to the King and fidelity to the government and the several colonies therein
be taken of every person that shall live within or
under the same.

That all trials, whether capital or between man
and man, be tried by juries according to the precedents
of the law of England, as near as may be.

That the governor and two assistants, at the
least, shall, as occasion shall be offered in time
convenient, determine in such trivial cases, viz.,
under forty shillings between man and man, as shall
come before them: as also in offense of small nature
shall determine, do, and execute as in wisdom God shall
direct them.

DOCUMENT 22:   Dedham Covenant, 1636

The text is taken from Kenneth A. Lockridge, *A New England Town: The First Hundred Years*   (New York: W.W. Norton and Company, Inc., 1970), 4 - 7; who in turn drew from *Early Records of the Town of Dedham*(6 vols., Dedham, Mass.:   1886 - 1936), III, Town and Selectmen, 1636 - 1659, 2 - 3.   Lockridge has modernized the spelling, and provides only a partial text.

One: We whose names are here unto subscribed do, in the fear and reverence of our Almighty God, mutually and severally promise amongst ourselves and each other to profess and practice one truth according to that most perfect rule, the foundation whereof is ever-lasting love.

Two: That we shall by all means labor to keep off from us all such as are contrary minded, and receive only such unto us as may be probably of one heart with us, [and such] as that we either know or may well and truly be informed to walk in a peacable conversation with all meekness of spirit, [this] for the edification of each other in the knowledge and faith of the Lord Jesus, and the mutual encouragement unto all temporal comforts in all things, seeking the good of each other out of which may be derived true peace.

Three: That if at any time differences shall rise bewteen parties of our said town, that then such party or parties shall presently refer all such differences unto some one, two, or three others of our said society to be fully accorded and determined without any further delay, if it possibly may be.

Four: That every man that . . . shall have lots [and] in our said town shall pay his share in all such . . . charges as shall be imposed on him . . . , as also become freely subject unto all such orders and

constitutions as shall be . . . made now or at any time
hereafter from this day forward, as well for loving and
comfortable society in our said town as also for the
prosperous and thriving condition of our said fellowship, especially respecting the fear of God, in which
we desire to begin and continue whatsoever we shall by
his loving favor take into hand.

Five: And for the better manifestation of our
true resolution herein, every man so received into the
town is to subscribe hereunto his name, thereby
obliging both himself and his successors after him
forever, as we have done.

DOCUMENT 23:   Providence Agreement, August 20, 1637

The complete text is taken from Charles Evans, "Oaths of Allegiance in Colonial New England," in *Proceedings of the American Antiquarian Society,* New Series, Vol. 31 (April 13, 1921 - October 19, 1921), 424. His spelling is used. The settlement of Providence by Roger Williams, who refused to take any of the oaths required by the Massachusetts Bay Colony, led to the following kind of document. Rather than being an oath, it constitutes the first expression in the new world of the separation of church and state, and of the principle of freedom of conscience. This is achieved by limiting the town meeting to "civil things." This was shortly followed by the establishing of a colony at Aquidneck (Pocasset) which did use an oath (see Document 26). From this new colony a minority withdrew, drawing up their civil compact (see Document 33). The majority that remained at Portsmouth drew up their new agreement a few days earlier (see Document 34), and it contained an oath. The Providence Agreement of 1637 was expanded upon by the Plantation Agreement of Providence, 1640 (Document 39). The bringing together of these various settlements into a unified Rhode Island can be traced through Documents 43, 50, 54, and 62.

We whose names are hereunder, desirous to inhabit in the town of Providence, do promise to subject ourselves in active and passive obedience to all such orders or agreements as shall be made for the public good of the body in an orderly way, by the major consent of present inhabitants, masters of families, incorporated together in a Towne fellowship, and others whom they shall admit unto them only in civil things.

[Signed by Richard Scott and 12 others]

DOCUMENT 24:   Orders Devised and Published by the
House of Assembly to be Observed During
the Assembly, February 25, 1638

The text is complete and with the spelling found in
William Hand Browne, ed., *Archives of Maryland:
Proceedings and Acts of the General Assembly, Jan.,
1637/8-Sept., 1664* (Baltimore: Maryland Historical
Society, 1883, pp. 32 - 33. One of the core
commitments in American political thought is to a
political process that is highly deliberative. There
is little question that deliberative processes were an
important part of the self-definition held by many of
these early communities. The document below is one of
several examples surviving from the seventeenth century
in colonial America which illustrate the concern for
orderly processes during collective decision making.

The Lieutenant General shall be called President
of the Assembly and shall appoint & direct all things
that Concern Form and decency to be used in the house
and shall Command Observance thereof as he shall see
Cause upon pain of imprisonment or fine as the house
shall take Precedence according to this Order
When any one of the house is to speak to any Bill
he shall stand up and be Bareheaded and direct his
speech to the President only and if two or more stand
up together the President shall appoint who shall
speak.

3

No man shall stand up to speak to any Bill until
the Party that last spake have sat down nor shall any
One refute another with any nipping or vncivill terms
nor shall name another but by some Circumloquation as

the Gentleman or Burgess that spake last or that argued
for or against this Bill or the Bill

4

The house shall sit every day holy days excepted
unless it be adjourned at eight of the Clock in the
morning at the furthest and at two of the Clock in the
afternoon & if any Gentlemen or Burgess not appearing
upon call at such time as the President is set at or
after either of the said hours shall be amerced 20lb of
Tobacco to be forthwth paid to the use of the house

5

After any Bill hath been once read in the house
the Bill shall be read ingrossed or utterly rejected
and upon any day or day appointed for a Session all
Bills engrossed shall be put to the question and such
as are assented to by the Greater part of the house and
if the Votes be equal that shall be judged the Greater
part which hath the Consent of the Lieutenant General
shall be undersigned by the Secretary in these words
the freemen have assented and after that the President
shall be demanded his assent in the name of the Lord
proprietary and if his asset be to the Bill, the Bill
shall be undersigned by the said Secretary in these
words the Lord Proprietary willeth that this be a Law

DOCUMENT 25:   Act for Establishing the House of
                Assembly and the Laws to Be Made
                Therein, 1638

Text, complete and with the original spelling, taken
from W.H. Brown, et. al., eds, *ARCHIVES OF MARYLAND:
VOL. I, PROCEEDINGS AND ACTS OF THE GENERAL ASSEMBLY OF
MARYLAND* (Baltimore: Maryland Historical Society,
1883), 81-82. There had been an assembly of some sort
in Maryland since 1635, but this document begins the
formal history of representative government in the
state.   The historical context can be further examined
in Michael Kammen, *DEPUTYES & LIBERTYES: THE ORIGINS
OF REPRESENTATIVE GOVERNMENT IN COLONIAL AMERICA*
New York: Alfred A. Knopf, 1972).

    Memorandum That at the first meeting of the
Assembly on the 25th day of February 1638 was Enacted
and ordeined one Act as followeth

            An Act For the Establishing the
            house of Assembly and the Laws to
                be made therein

    Whereas the Kings Majestie by his Letters pattents
hath given and granted full free and absolute power and
authority to the Lord Proprietary of this province to
make and ordeine any laws apperteining to the state of
this Province by and with the advice assent and
approbation of the freemen of the same or of the
greater part of them or of their Deligates or deputies
in such sort and forme as to the said Lord proprietarie
should seem best.   By Vertue Whereof Severall writts or
Summons have been directed to certain Gentlemen to
appear personally at this Assembly and to the rest of
the free men inhabiting within the Severall hundreds of

                                            119

this Colony and the Isle of Kent to elect their
delegates or deputies in their names and steeds to be
present at the same and accordingly all the freemen of
the said severall hundreds and of the Isle of Kent
(some few excepted) have elected certain persons to
that end and the same their Election have subscribed
and returned upon record and their said Dellegates and
Deputies are now assembled accordingly. Be it
therefore Enacted and ordeined by the said Lord
Proprietarie of and with the advice assent and
approbation of the Freemen and of the delegates and
deputies assembled at this present Assembly that the
said Severall Persons so elected and returned as
aforesaid shall be and be called Burgesses and shall
supply the places of all the freemen consenting or
subscribing to such their election in the same manner
and to all the same intents and purposes as the
Burgesses of any burrough in England in the Parliament
of England useth to Supply the place of the Inhabitants
of the Burroughe whereof he is Elected Burges and that
the said Gentlemen and Burgesses and such other Freemen
(not having Consented to any the Elections as
aforesaid) as now are or shall be at any time Assembled
or any twelve or more of them whereof the Lieutenant
Generall and Secretary of the Province to be allwaies
two shall be called the house of Assembly; and that all
Acts and ordinances assented unto and approved by the
said house or by the Major part of the Persons
assembled and afterward assented unto by the Lieutenant
Generall in the name of the said Lord proprietarie and
shall be adjudged and established for laws to all the
same force and effect as if the said Lord proprietary
and all the freemen of this Province were personally
present and did assent to and approve of the same

[Approved by the freemen, and the Lieutenant
General in behalf of the Lord Proprietor, March 12,
1638.]

DOCUMENT 26:   Government of Pocasset, March 7, 1638

Complete text with the original spelling taken from
John Russell Bartlett, ed., *Records of the Colony of
Rhode Island and Providence Plantations in New England:
Vol I, 1636 to 1663* (Providence, R.I.:   A. Crawford
Greene and Brother, State Printers, 1856), 52-53.
Consult the comments accompanying Document 23 for the
historical setting of this document.   One part passed
before lunch, the other after.

            The 7th day of the first month,1638

    We whose names are underwritten do here solemnly
in the presence of Jehovah incorporate ourselves into a
Bodie Politick and as he shall help, will submit our
persons, lives and estates unto our Lord Jesus Christ,
the King of Kings and Lord of Lords and to all those
perfect and most absolute laws of his given us in his
holy word of truth, to be guided and judged thereby.

        Exod. 24. 3, 4.
        2 Cron. 11. 3
        2 Kings. 11. 17

[Signed by William Coddington and eighteen others]

            The 7th of the first month, 1638.

    We that are Freemen Incorporate of this Bodie
Politick do Elect and Constitute William Coddington,
Esquire, a Judge amongst us, and so covenant to yield
all due honour unto him according to the lawes of God,
and so far as in us lyes to maintaine the honour and
privileges of his place which shall hereafter be

ratifyed according unto God, the Lord helping us so to do. William Aspinwall, Sec'ry

I, William Coddington, Esquire, being called and chosen by the Freemen Incorporate of this Bodie Politick, to be a Judge amongst them, do covenant to do justice and Judgment impartially according to the lawes of God, and to maintaine the Fundamentall Rights and Privileges of this Body Politick, which shall hereafter be ratifyed according unto God, the Lord helping us to do so.

Wm. Coddington

William Aspinwall is appointed Secretary.

It is agreed that William Dyre shall be Clarke[1] of this Body.

DOCUMENT 27:   Plantation Covenant at Quinnipiack,
                   April, 1638

Although the framers used the above title, it is more
frequently referred to in the history books as the "New
Haven Plantation Covenant." The text is taken from
Isabel Macbeath Calder, *The New Haven Colony* (New
Haven: Yale University Press, 1934), p. 51, who in
turn cites the New Haven Colonial Records, 1638-1649,
p. 12. The first part of the first sentence in
brackets has been added by this editor on the basis of
information found in Calder and elsewhere. The
spelling and punctuation is Calder's. This document
was adopted shortly after the group arrived from
Boston, and at the end of a day of prayer and fasting.
It was adopted as a general agreement until the people
could become familiar enough with each other's
religious views, sentiments, and moral conduct to adopt
a definite and written frame of government and code of
laws. This was passed 14 months later and is known as
the Fundamental Articles of New Haven (see Document
37). The earlier document, reproduced below, was not a
true church covenant and was thus termed by the authors
a "plantation covenant" to indicate its lesser status.

[We the assembly of free planters do solemnly
covenant] thatt as [in] matters thatt Concerne the
gathering and ordering of a Chur. so Likewise in all
publique offices wch concerne Cuill orders as Choyce of
magistrates and officers makeing and repealing of Lawes
devideing allotmts of Inheritance and all things of
Like nature we would all of vs be ordered by those
Rules wch the scripture holds forth to vs.

DOCUMENT 28:   An Act for Church Liberties, 1638

Text complete as found in W.H. Browne, ed., *Archives of
Maryland: Proceedings and Acts of the General Assembly
Jan. 1637/8-Sept., 1664* (Baltimore: Maryland Historical Society, 1883), p. 40. One of the first colonial
statements on religious freedom, it is notable for
extending the rights to Catholics. Later in the
century a Protestant majority would temporarily rescind
the right for Catholics, but a few years later include
them again.

     Be it enacted by the Lord Proprietarie of this
Province by and with the Advice and approbation of the
ffreemen of the same that Holy Church within this
Province shall have all her rights liberties and
immunities safe whole and inviolable in all things This
act to continue till the end of the next Generall
Assembly and then with the Consent of the Lord Proprietarie to be perpetuall.

DOCUMENT 29:   An Act for Swearing Allegeance, 1638

The complete text with original spelling is from W.H.
Browne, ed., *Archives of Maryland: January, 1637/8-
September, 1664* (Baltimore: Mayland Historical Society, 1883), pp. 40-41. The problem of political
obligation was handlily solved in this era not by some
formal theory of consent, but rather by the expedient
of having all inhabitants take an oath if they wished
to remain inhabitants. Colonists were supposedly
required to take an oath of fidelity to the king of
England, a requirement that engendered some controversy
among the colonists. The source of the controversy lay
not in swearing allegiance to the king, but rather in
the genesis of such oaths which originally were instituted to recognize the monarch as head of the Church.
The Catholics in Maryland were no less hesitant about
such matters than the radical Protestant dissenters in
New England who had left England primarily to escape
the established Church. This oath should be compared
with those contained in Documents 5, 10, 16, 17, and
40. Comparison with oaths internal to longer documents
such as the Pilgrim Code of Law (Document 21) should
also prove instructive.

    Be it Enacted and ordeined by the Lord Propri-
etarie of this Province by and with the Consent and
approbation of the ffreemen of the same that all and
every person or persons of the age of eighteen years
and upwards Inhabitants or that Shall come hereafter to
Inhabite within this Province shall within one month
next after this present Assembly shall be dissolved or
within one month after such person or persons shall
land or come into this Province take an oath to our
Soveraigne Lord King Charles his heirs and Successors
in these words following (I: A B doe truely

acknowledge professe testifie and declare in my
concience before God and the World that our Soveraigne
Lord King Charles is lawfull and rightfull King of
England and of all other his Majesties Dominions and
Countries and I will bear true faith and allegeance to
his Majestie his heirs and lawfull Successors and him
and them will defend to the uttermost of my power
against all conspiracies and such attempts whatsoever
which shall be made against his or their Crowne or
dignity and shall and will doe my best endeavour to
disclose and make known to his Majestie his heirs and
lawfull Successors all Treasons and traiterous
consperacies which I shall know or heare to be intended
against his Majestie his heirs and lawfull Successors
And I doe make this recognition and acknowledgement
heartily willingly and truely upon the faith of a
Christian So help me God) And Be it further Enacted
By the authority aforesaid that if any person or
persons to whom the Said oaths Shall be tendred by
Virtue of this present act Shall willfully refuse to
take the same that then Upon such tender and refusall
the said person or persons so refuseing to take the
said Oath shall be imprisoned till the next County
Court or hundred Court of Kent and if at such Court
such partie shall upon, the Second tender refuse again
to take the said oath the partie or parties so
refuseing shall forfeit and lose all his Lands goods
and Chattells within this Province to the Lord
Proprietarie and his heirs and Shall be banished the
said Province for ever (except women covert who Shall
be committed only to prison untill such time as they
will take the same oath.)

     To which end Be it further Enacted by the autho-
rity aforesaid that the Lieutent Generall or other
officer Governour or Governours (for the time being) of
this Province or two of the Councill or the Secretary
of the Province for the time being or any Judge sitting
in Court or the Commander of the Isle of Kent for
persons being or that Shall be in the Ile of Kent Shall
have full power to administer the said oath in manner
aforesaid according to the intention of this present
act This Act to continue till the end of the next
assembly

DOCUMENT 30: An Act What Persons Shall Be Called to
Every General Assembly and an Act Con-
cerning the Calling of General
Assemblies, 1638

The text, complete and with the original spelling, is
taken from W.H. Browne, ed., *Archives of Maryland:
January, 1537/8 -September, 1664* (Baltimore: Maryland
Historical Society, 1883), pp. 74 - 75. This simple
act comes close to defining the entire form of
government in Maryland at the time. The nature and
role of the legislature, the process of elections, the
definition of the suffrage, the process of passing
legislation -- all are here established. The result is
one of the earliest representative assemblies to be
established in America.

Be in enacted by the Lord Proprietary of this province,
of and with the advice and approbation of the freemen
of the same, that, from henceforth, everyone being of
the council of this province and any other gentlemen of
able judgment and quality summoned by writ and the lord
of every manor within this province after manors be
erected shall or may have his voice, seat, and place in
every General Assembly to be hereafter called in this
province and shall be called by summons or writ unto
the same. And also be it further enacted, by the
authority aforesaid, that, from henceforth forever,
after such time that any summons or writ shall issue
for the calling or summoning a General Assembly of the
freemen of this province, the commander or, in defect
of a commander, the high constable of every hundred
within this province or, in defect of a constable, the
sheriff of the county, shall within every hundred
summon all the freemen inhabiting within every hundred,
as soon as conveniently may be, to assemble at a

certain place and time to be by him appointed and
prefixed. Which freemen so assembled, or the major
part of them, shall elect and chose some one, two, or
more able and sufficient men for the hundred, as the
said freemen or the major part of them so assembled
shall think good, to come to every such General
Assembly at the time and place in such writ or summons
limited and appointed, then and there, for him or
themselves and all the freemen of the hundred and in
their names and stead, to consult concerning the
affairs of this province; and shall make a return in
writing of the name or names of the persons so to be
from time to time elected and chosen, and such person
and persons so to be from time to time elected and
chosen shall and may have a voice, place, and seat in
every such General Assembly. And from henceforth such
person or persons only so elected and chosen out of and
for every hundred within this province, and such
persons as shall be personally called by writ as afore,
shall have a place, voice, and seat in all or any
General Assembly hereafter to be held within this
province. And every act and ordinance made in such
General Assemblies by persons so called, elected, and
chosen as aforsaid, or the major part of them, and
assented to by the Lord Proprietary or his heirs, lords
and proprietaries of this province, or by his or their
lieutenant-general thereunto authorized by special
warrant from the said Lord Proprietary or his heirs,
shall be judged, deemed, and taken to be of as good
force and strength and as effectual to all intents and
purposes as if the Lord Proprietary himself and all the
freemen within the said province had been personally
present at such General Assemblies and had consented to
and approved of the making and enacting of such laws
and ordinances. Provided, that all acts approved by
the freemen and by the Lieutenant-General in the name
of the Lord Proprietary, as aforesaid, shall be of
force until the Lord Proprietary shall signify his
disassent to the same under the great seal, and no
further or longer.

An Act Concerning the calling of General
Assemblies, 1638.

Be it enacted by the Lord Proprietary of this
province, of and with the assent and approbation of the
freemen of the same, that from and after this General

Assembly shall be dissolved, a General Assembly of the
freemen of this province shall be called and summoned
once in every three years at the least to consult of
the affairs and public good of this province and for
the enacting of laws and ordinances for the better
government of the same. And that the said freemen so
assembled shall, from and after the summoning of such
assembly and assemblies until the dissolution of the
same, have the like power, privileges, authority, and
jurisdiction in all causes and matters arising or to
arise or happen within this province as the House of
Commons within the realm of England at any time
heretofore assembled in that kingdom have had, used, or
enjoyed or of right ought to have, use, or enjoy in,
about, or concerning any matters, things, and causes
whatsoever which have at any time happened or risen
within the realm of England. This act to continue till
the end of the next General Assembly.

DOCUMENT 31:   An Act for the Liberties of the People,
                1638

Taken from W.H. Browne, ed., *Archives of Maryland: January, 1637/8 - September, 1664* (Baltimore: Maryland Historical Society, 1883), p. 41. Along with the Pilgrim Code of Law (Document 21) and the Massachusetts Body of Liberties (Document 41), this is one of the earliest attempts to specify and protect the rights of citizens inhabiting a colony as distinct from rights of proprietors. Each of these three documents takes a different approach to the problem. This document, as well as the others from colonial Maryland reproduced in this volume, is notable for placing a time limit on the duration of rights. The implication is quite straightforward that the rights being protected, far from being inalienable, result from action by the body politic and can be rescinded for reasons acceptable to the legislature.

 Be it Enacted By the Lord Proprietarie of this Province of and with the advice and approbation of the ffreemen of the same that all the Inhabitants of this Province being Christians (Slaves excepted) Shall have and enjoy all such rights liberties immunities priviledges and free customs within this Province as any naturall born subject of England hath or ought to have or enjoy in the Realm of England by force or vertue of the common law or Statute Law of England (saveing in such Cases as the same are or may be altered or changed by the Laws and ordinances of this Province)
 And Shall not be imprisoned nor disseissed or dispossessed of their freehold goods or Chattels or be out Lawed Exiled or otherwise destroyed fore judged or punished then according to the Laws of this province

saveing to the Lord proprietarie and his heirs all his
rights and prerogatives by reason of his domination and
Seigniory over this Province and the people of the same
This Act to Continue till the end of the next Generall
Assembly

DOCUMENT 32:   Fundamental Orders of Connecticut, 1639

Text, complete and with the original spelling, is taken
from Francis N. Thorpe, ed., *The Federal and State Con-*
stitutions, Colonial Charters, and Other Organic Laws
of the United States   (Washington, D.C.:
Government Printing Office, 1907), pp. 519 - 523. This
document, along with the Pilgrim Code of Law (Document
21), and the New Haven Fundamentals (Document 46), is a
candidate for the earliest written constitution in
America. It describes itself internally as a
"combination" and "confederation", although one could
with equal truth call it a compact. As such, it bears
the same pedigree as Documents 3, 13, 22, 26, 27, 33,
34, 35, 38, and 39, to name just a few. The
similarities among these documents raises the
possibility of calling these earlier covenants and
compacts "proto-constitutions" or "partial
constitutions." It should be noted that this document,
as well as the Pilgrim Code of Law, prominently
displays oaths as an essential part. This highlights
the role of the other oaths reproduced in this volume
in establishing government.

    FORASMUCH as it hath pleased the Allmighty God by
the wise disposition of his diuyne pruidence so to
Order and dispose of things that we the Inhabitants and
Residents of Windsor, Harteford and Wethersfield are
now cohabiting and dwelling in and vppon the River of
Conectecotte and the Lands thereunto adioyneing; and
Well knowning where a people are gathered togather the
word of God requires that to mayntayne the peace and
vnion of such a people there should be an orderly and
decent Gouerment established according to God, to order
and dispose of the affayres of the people at all
seasons as occation shall require; doe therefore

assotiate and conioyne our selues to be as one Publike
State or Commonwelth; and doe, for our selues and our
Successors and such as shall be adioyned to vs att any
tyme hereafter, enter into Combination and Confederation togather, to mayntayne and prsearue the liberty
and purity of the gospell of our Lord Jesus wch we now
prfesse, as also the disciplyne of the Churches, wch
according to the truth of the said gospell is now
practised amongst vs; As also in or Cieuell Affaires to
be guided and gouerned according to such Lawes, Rules,
Orders and decrees as shall be made, ordered & decreed,
as followeth: --
    1.   It is Ordered, sentenced and decreed, that
there shall be yerely two generall Assemblies or
Courts, the on the second thursday in Aprill, the
other the second thursday in September, following; the
first shall be called the Courte of Election, wherein
shall be yerely Chosen from tyme to tyme soe many
Magestrats and other publike Oficers as shall be found
requisitte: Whereof one to be chosen Gouernour for the
yeare ensueing and vntill another be chosen, and noe
other Magestrate to be chosen for more then one yeare;
pruided allwayes there be sixe chosen besids the
Gouernour; wch being chosen and sworne according to an
Oath recorded for that purpose shall haue power to
administer iustice according to the Lawes here
established, and for want thereof according to the rule
of the word of God, wch choise shall be made by all
that are admitted freemen and haue taken the Oath of
Fidellity, and doe cohabitte wthin this Jurisdiction,
(Hauing been admitted Inhabitants by the major prt of
the Towne wherein they liue,) or the mayor prte of such
as shall be then prsent.
    2.   It is Ordered, sentensed and decreed, that
the Election of the aforesaid Magestrats shall be on
this manner: euery prson prsent and quallified for
choyse shall bring in (to the prsons deputed to receaue
them) one single papr wth the name of him written in yt
whome he desires to haue Gouernour, and he that hath
the greatest number of papers shall be Gouernor for
that yeare. And the rest of the Magestrats or publike
Officers to be chosen in this manner: The Secrtary for
the tyme being shall first read the names of all that
are to be put to choise and then shall first read the
names of all that are to be put to choise and then

shall seuerally nominate them distinctly, and euery one
that would haue the prson nominated to be chosen shall
bring in one single paper written vppon, and he that
would not haue him chosen shall bring in a blanke: and
euery one that hath more written papers than blanks
shall be a Magistrat for that yeare; wch papers shall
be receaued and told by one or more that shall be then
chosen by the court and sworne to be faythfull therein;
but in case there should not be sixe chosen as
aforesaid, besids the Gouernor, out of those wch are
nominated, then he or they wch haue the most written
paprs shall be a Magestrate or Magestrats for the
ensueing yeare, to make vp the aforesaid number.

    3.   It is Ordered, sentenced and decreed, that
the Secretary shall not nominate any prson, nor shall
any prson be chosen newly into the Magestracy wch was
not prpownded in some Generall Courte before, to be
nominated the next Election; and to that end yt shall
be lawfull for ech of the Townes aforesaid by their
deputyes to nominate any two who they conceaue fitte to
be put to election; and the Courte may ad so many more
as they iudge requisitt.

    4.   It is Ordered, sentenced and decreed that noe
prson be chosen Gouernor aboue once in two years, and
that the Gouernor be always a member of some approved
congregation, and formerly of the Magestracy wthin this
Jurisdiction; and all the Magestrats Freemen of this
Comonwelth: and that no Magestrate or other publike
officer shall execute any prte of his or their Office
before they are seuerally sworne, wch shall be done in
the face of the Courte if they be prsent, and in case
of absence by some deputed for that purpose.

    5.   It is Ordered, sentenced and decreed, that to
the aforesaid Courte of Election the seurall Townes
shall send their deputyes, and when the Elections are
ended they may prceed in any publike searuice as at
other Courts. Also the other Generall Courte in
September shall be for makeing of lawes, and any other
publike occation, wch conserns the good of the
Comonwealth.

    6.   It is Ordered, sentenced and decreed, that
the Gournor shall, ether by himselfe or by the
secretary, send out summons to the Constables of enr
Towne for the cauleing of these two standing Courts, on
month at lest before their seurall tymes: And also if

the Gournor and the gretest prte of the Magestrats see
cause vppon any spetiall occation to call a generall
Courte, they may giue order to the secretary soe to do
wthin fowerteene dayes warneing; and if vrgent
necessity so require, vppon a shorter notice, giueing
sufficient grownds for yt to the deputyes when they
meete, or else be questioned for the same; And if the
Gournor and Mayor prte of Magestrats shall ether
neglect or refuse to call the two Generall standing
Courts or ether of them, as also at other tymes when to
occations of the Commonwelth require, the Freemen
thereof, or the Mayor prte of them, shall petition to
them soe to doe: if then yt be ether denyed or
neglected the said Freemen or the Mayor prte of them
shall haue power to giue order to the Constables of the
seuerall Townes to doe the same, and so may meete
togather, and chuse to themselues a Moderator, and may
prceed to do any Acte of power, wch any other Generall
Courte may.
      7.   It is Ordered, sentenced and decreed that
after there are warrants giuen out for any of the said
Generall Courts, the Constable or Constables of ech
Towne shall forthwth give notice distinctly to the
inhabitants of the same, in some Publike Assembly or by
goeing or sending from howse to howse, that at a place
and tyme by him or them lymited and sett, they meet and
assemble themselues togather to elect and chuse certen
deputyes to be att the Generall Courte then following
to agitate the afayres of the comonwelth; wch said
Deputyes shall be chosen by all that are admitted
Inhabitants in the seurall Townes and haue taken the
oath of fidellity; pruided that non be chosen a Deputy
for any Generall Courte wch is not a Freeman of this
Commonwelth.
      The a-foresaid deputyes shall be chosen in manner
following: euery prson that is prsent and quallified
as before exprssed, shall bring the names of such,
written in seurall papers, as they desire to haue
chosen for that Imployment, and these 3 or 4, more or
lesse, being the number agreed on to be chosen for that
tyme, that haue greatest number of papers written for
them shall be dputyes for that Courte; whose names
shall be endorsed on the backe side of the warrant and
returned into the Courte, wth the Constable or
Constables hand vnto the same.

8.   It is Ordered, sentenced and decreed, that
Wyndsor, Hartford and Wethersfield shall haue power,
ech Towne, to send fower of their freemen as deputyes
to euery Generall Courte; and whatsoeuer other Townes
shall be hereafter added to this Jurisdiction, they
shall send so many deputyes as the Courte shall judge
meete, a resonable prportion to the number of Freemen
that are in the said Townes being to be attended
therein; wch deputyes shall have the power of the whole
Towne to giue their voats and alowance to all such
lawes and orders as may be for the publike good, and
unto wch the said Townes are to be bownd.
9.   It is ordered and decreed, that the deputyes
thus chosen shall haue power and liberty to appoynt a
tyme and a place of meeting togather before any
Generall Courte to aduise and consult of all such
things as may concerne the good of the publike, as also
to examine their owne Elections, whether according to
the order, and if they or the gretest prte of them find
any election to be illegall they may seclud such for
prsent from their meeting, and returne the same and
their resons to the Courte; and if yt proue true, the
Courte may fyne the prty or prtyes so intruding and the
Towne, if they see cause, and giue out a warrant to goe
to a newe election in a legall way, either whole or in
prte.   Also the said deputyes shall haue power to fyne
any that shall be disorderly at their meetings, or for
not coming in due tyme or place according to
appoyntment; and they may return the said fynes into
the Courte if yt be refused to be paid, and the
tresurer to take notice of yt, and to estreete or levy
the same as he doth other fynes.
10.   It is Ordered, sentenced and decreed, that
euery Generall Courte, except such as through neglecte
of the Gournor and the greatest prte of Magestrats the
Freemen themselves doe call, shall consist of the
Gouernor, or some one chosen to moderate the Court, and
fower other Magestrats at lest, wth the mayor prte of
the deputyes of the seuerall Townes legally chosen; and
in case the Freemen or mayor prte of them through
neglect or refusall of the Gouernor and mayor prte of
the magestrats, shall call a Courte, that yt shall
consist of the mayor prte of Freemen that are prsent or
their deputyes, wth a Moderator chosen by the: *In wch
said Generall Courts shall consist the supreme power of*

the Commonwelth, and they only shall haue power to make laws or repeale them, to graunt leuyes, to admitt of Freemen, dispose of lands vndisposed of, to seuerall Townes or prsons, and also shall haue power to call ether Courte or Magestrate or any other prson whatsoeuer into question for any misdemeanour, and may for just causes displace or deale otherwise according to the nature of the offence; and also may deale in any other matter that concerns the good of this common welth, excepte election of Magestrats, wch shall be done by the whole boddy of Freemen: In wch Courte the Gouernour or Moderator shall haue power to order the Courte to giue liberty of spech, and silence vnceasonable and disorderly speakeings, to put all things to voate, and in case the vote be equall to haue the casting voice. But non of these Courts shall be adiorned or dissolued wthout the consent of the major prte of the Court.

    11. It is ordered, sentenced and decreed, that when any Generall Courte vppon the occations of the Commonwelth haue agreed vppon any sume or somes of mony to be leuyed vppon the seuerall Townes wthin this Jurisdiction, that a Committee be chosen to sett out and appoynt wt shall be the prportion of euery Towne to pay of the said leuy, prvided the Committes be made vp of an equall number out of each Towne.

    14th January, 1638,[1] the 11 Orders abouesaid are voted.

The Oath of the Gournor, for the (Prsent)

    I N.W. being now chosen to be Gournor wthin this Jurisdiction, for the yeare ensueing, and vntil a new be chosen, doe sweare by the greate and dreadful name of the everliueing God, to prmote the publicke good and peace of the same, according to the best of my skill; as also will mayntayne all lawfull priuiledges of this Commonwealth: as also that all wholsome lawes that are or shall be made by lawfull authority here established, be duly executed; and will further the execution of Justice according to the rule of Gods word; so helpe me God, in the name of the Lo: Jesus Christ.

The Oath of a Magestrate, for the Prsent

I, N.W. being chosen a Magestrate wthin this Jurisdiction for the yeare ensueing, doe sweare by the great and dreadful name of the euerliueing God, to prmote the publike good and peace of the same, according to the best of my skill, and that I will mayntayne all the lawfull priuiledges threof according to my vnderstanding, as also assist in the execution of all such wholsome lawes as are made or shall be made by lawfull authority heare established, and will further the execution of Justice for the tyme aforesaid according to the righteous rule of Gods word; so helpe me God, etc.

DOCUMENT 33:   Newport Agreement, April 28, 1639

The complete text with the original spelling is taken from John Russell Bartlett, ed., *Records of the Colony of Rhode Island and Providence Plantations in New England: Vol. I, 1636 to 1663*   (Providence, R.I.:   A. Crawford Greene and Brother, State Printers, 1856), 69. This is the document drawn up by the dissenting minority that withdrew from the settlement at Pocasset (See the discussion of Document 23).   It is not an oath but rests upon the agreement among the people, implying popular sovereignty.

Pocasset.   On the 28th of the 2d [month], 1639

It is agreed.

By vs whose hands are underwritten, to propagate a Plantation in the midst of the Island or elsewhere; And doe engage ourselves to bear equall charges, answerable to our strength and estates in common; and that our determinations shall be by major voice of judge and elders; the Judge to have a double voice.

[William Coddington and eight others.]

DOCUMENT 34:   The Government of Portsmouth, April 30,
                1639

The complete text with original spelling is taken from
John Russell Bartlett, ed., *Records of the Colony of
Rhode Island and Providence Plantations in New England:
Vol. I, 1636 to 1663*   (Providence, R.I.:   A. Crawford
Greene and Brother, State Printers, 1856), 70 - 71.
See Documents 23, 26, and 33 for events leading up to
this agreement, and Documents 43, 51, 52, 55, and 63
for subsequent events.   The gaps are in the original,
and words in brackets indicate illegible words that
have been supplied on the basis of context.

                    Aprill the 30th, 1639

     We, whose names are under[written doe acknowledge]
ourselves the legall subjects of [his Majestie] King
Charles, and in his name [doe hereby binde] ourselves
into a civill body politicke, unto his lawes according
to matters of justice.

     [Signed by William Hutchinson and thirty
     associates.]

     According to the true intent of the [foregoing
instrument, wee] whose names are above particularly
[recorded, do agree] joyntly or by the major voice to
g[overne ourselves by the] ruler or judge amongst us in
all [transactions] for the space and tearme of one
[yeare,   he] behaving himselfe according to the t[enor
of the same.]
     We have freely made choice of [   ] to be ruler
or judge among us.
     We have also, for the help and ease [of the
conducting of] public business and affairs for [the

                                              145

colonies] for one yeare, allso chosen unto him William
Ballston, William Freeborne, John Porter, John [   ],
John Wall, Philip Sherman, as allso William Aspinwall
to lay out lands as they shall be disposed.

We have also made choice of [   ] amongst
us for this yeare ensuing.

It is appoynted that there shall be [a court held
every] yeare, every quarter, one for [   ]
to doe right betwixt man and [man--a] jury of twelve
men; as also it is [ordered, that] the eight men chosen
unto him [shall hold a] meeting amongst themselves, to
consult [together]; as also to put an end to any
controverzy, if it amount not to the value of fortie
[shillings.] The Judge, with the rest of the eight men
[shall decide it] if brought to ye publicke Court.

DOCUMENT 35:   Guilford Covenant, June 1, 1639

Text complete with spelling as found in Champlin
Burrage, *The Church Covenant Idea: Its Origin and
Development* (Philadelphia: American Baptist
Publication Society, 1904), 94. Not, strictly
speaking, a true covenant, this agreement was made
aboard ship before the colonists reached America.
Guilford was part of the New Haven colony, being just a
few miles to the east. The same law prevailed in the
New Haven colony that had been passed in Massachusetts
Bay Colony in 1631. This law limited the franchise to
church members, a restriction not found in Plymouth
Colony or the Colony of Connecticut. The rather vague,
non-oath form used in the Guilford document of 1639,
was replaced in 1643 by a more suitable agreement (see
Document 45).

June 1.   Individuals who, the next September, purchase
Menunkatuck, afterwards Guilford, enter into the
following covenant: We whose names are hereunder
written, intending by God's gracious permission to
plant ourselves in New England, and, if it may be, in
the southerly part about Quinnipiack, we do faithfully
promise each to each, for ourselves and our families,
and those that belong to us, that we will, the Lord
assisting us, sit down and join ourselves together in
one entire plantation, and to be helpful each to the
other in any common work, according to every man's
ability, and as need shall require; . . . As for our
gathering together in a church way, and the choice of
officers and members to be joined together in that way,
we do refer ourselves until such time as it shall
please God to settle us in our plantation.

      [Signed by Henry Whitfield and twenty-four
            others]

DOCUMENT 36:   Structure of Town Governments, October
                 10, 1639

Based upon the text in J. H. Trumbull and C. J.
Hoadley, eds., *The Public Records of the Colony of
Connecticut, 1636 - 1776,*   Vol. I, pp. 36 - 39. The
spelling is without emendation. Most of the so-called
colonies were actually collections of towns, each of
which had established its own form of self-government.
The establishment of a colony wide government, usually
a legislature in which each town was represented, in
effect created what we would now recognize as a federal
system. The Fundamental Orders of Connecticut should
be viewed in this light (Document 32), since it
established the "confederation" that is acting in this
document. The Structure of Town Governments amplifies
and clarifies the nature of the relationship between
the town and colony-wide governments, mainly by
focusing upon respective jursdictions. The
Organization of the Government of Rhode Island
(Document 43), and the New Haven Fundamentals (Document
46) similarly relate to confederacies of towns.

      The Townes of Hartford, Windsore and Wethersfield,
or any other of the Townes within this jurisdiction,
shall each of them haue power to dispose of their owne
lands vndisposed of, and all other comodityes arysing
out of their owne lymitts bounded out by the Court, the
libertyes of the great River excepted, as also to
choose their owne officers, and make such orders as may
be for the well ordering of their owne Townes, being
not repugnant to any law here established, as also to
impose penaltyes for the breach of the same, and to
estreat and levy the same, and for non-payment to
distrayne, and yf there be noe personall estate, to sue
to the Court to sell his or their house or land, for
making satisfaction. Also each of the aforesayd Townes

shall haue power by a generall consent once every yeare
to choose out 3, 5, or 7 of their cheefe Inhabitants,
whereof one to be chosen moderator, who having taken an
oath prouided in that case, shall haue a casting voice
in case they be equall, wch sayd prsons shall meett
once in every 2 monthes & being mett together, or the
major part of them, whereof the moderator to be one,
they shall haue power to heare, end and determine all
controversies, eyther trespasses or debts not exceeding
40s. provided both partyes live in the same Towne; also
any two of them or the moderator may graunt out summons
to the party or partyes to come to their meetings to
answere the actions; also to administer oath to any
witnesses for the clearing of the cause, and to giue
judgment and execution against the party offending.
But yf eyther party be grieved att the sentence, he
shall haue liberty to appeale to a higher Court,
prvided it be before judgment and execution be
graunted. But yf it fall out there be noe ground for
the appeale, the Court to confirme the judgment and
giue good costs, and fine or punish the prty appealing.
    The Townes aforesayd shall each of them prvide a
Ledger Booke, with an Index or alphabett vnto the same:
Also shall choose one who shall be a Towne Clerke or
Register, who shall before the Generall Court in Aprill
next, record every man's house and land already
graunted and measured out to him, with the bounds &
quantity of the same, and whosoever shall neglect 3
monthes after notice given to bring into the sayd Towne
Clerke or Register a note of his house and land, with
the bounds and quantity of the same, by the nearest
estimacion, shall forfeit 10s. and soe 10s. a month for
ever month he shall soe neglect. The like to be done
for all land hereafter graunted and measured to any;
and all bargaines or morgages of land whatsoever shall
be accounted of noe value vntill they be recorded, for
wch entry the Register shall receaue 6d. for every
parcell, delivering every owner a coppy of the same
vnder his hand, whereof 4d. shall be for himselfe and
2d. for the Secretary of the Court. And the sayd
Register shall, every Generall Court, in Aprill and
September, deliver into the same a transcript fayrely
written of all such graunts, bargaines or ingagements
recorded by him in the Towne Booke, and the Secretary
of the Court shall record it in a booke fayrely written

prvided for that purpose, and shall preserue the coppy
brought in vnder the hand of the Town Clerke. Also the
sayd Towne Clerke shall haue for every serch of a
parcell ld. and for every coppy of a parcell id.; and a
coppy of the same vnder the hands of the sayd Register
or Towne Clerk and two of the men chosen to governe the
Towne, shall be a sufficient evidence to all that haue
the same.

   After the death and decease of any person
possessed of any estate, be it more or lesse, and who
maketh a will in writing or by word of mouth, those men
wch are appointed to order the affayres of the Towne
where any such person deceaseth, shall within one month
after the same, at furthest, cause a true Inventory to
be taken of the sayd estate in writing, as also take a
coppy of the sayd will or testament and enter it into a
booke or keepe the coppy in safe custody, as also enter
the names vppon record of the Children and Legatees of
the Testator or deceased prson, and the sayd orderers
of the Affayres of the Towne are to see every such will
and Inventory to be exhibited into the publique Court,
within one quarter of a yeare, where the same is to be
registered; and the sayd orderers of the affayres of
the Towne shall doe their indeauour in seeing that the
estate of the Testator be not wasted nor spoyled, but
improved for the best advantage of the Children or
Legatees of the Testator, according to the mind of the
Testator, for their and euery of their use, by their
and every of their allowance and approbacion. But when
any prson dyeth intestate, the sayd orderers of the
affayres of the Townes shall cause an Inventory to be
taken, and then the publique Court may graunt the
administracion of the goodes and Chattells to the next
of kin, jointly or severally, and divide the estate to
the wiefe (yf any be,) children or kindred, as in
equity they shall see meet; and yf noe kindred be
found, the Court to administer for the publique good of
the Common, prvided there be an Inventory registered,
that yf any of the kindred in future tyme appeare they
may haue justice and equity done vnto them; and all
charges that the publique Court or the orderers of the
affayres of the Townes are att about the trust
committed to them, eyther for writing or otherwise, it
is to be payd out of the estate.

Within 20 days after the end of this Court, the
Secretary shall provide a coppy of all the penall lawes
or orders standing in force, and all other that are of
generall concernement for the governement of the
Commonwealth, and shall giue direction to the
Constables of every Towne to publish the same within 4
dayes more, att some publique meeting in their severall
Townes, and then shall cause the sayd lawes and orders
to be written into a booke in their severall Townes,
and kept for the use of the Towne, and soe for future
tyme for all lawes or orders that are made as
aforesayd, each session of the Generall Courts; and
once every yeare the Constables, in their severall
Townes, shall read or cause to be read in some publique
meeting all such lawes as then stand in force and are
not repealed; and the Secretary of the Court shallhaue
12d. for the coppy of the orders of each session of
every generall Court, from each of the Townes.

Also, the Secretary of the Court shall have xid.
for every action that is entred, to be payed by him
that enters the action, and he that is cast in the suit
to allow it in costs.

DOCUMENT 37:   Fundamental Articles of New Haven
                June 4/14, 1639

Text in *New Haven Colonial Records* (1638 - 1649), pp.
11 - 17. It is reproduced here completely and with the
original spelling. Having originally organized
themselves under the Plantation Covenant at Quinnipiack
(Document 27) written about a year earlier, the
settlers had cause to reconsider the nature of their
government. Specifically, they considered whether full
citizenship should be limited to members of the church.
Carefully going over the commitments embodied in the
earlier document, they concluded in the affirmative.
This document is notable for the careful deliberation
it records, as well as the careful attention to
biblical precedent.

The 4th day of the 4th moneth called June 1639,
all the free planters assembled together in a ge[neral]
meetinge to consult about settling civill Government
according to God, and about the nomination of persons
thatt might be founde by consent of all fittest in all
respects for the foundation worke of a church w[hich]
was intend to be gathered in Quinipieck. After solemne
invocation of the name of God in prayer [for] the
presence and help of his speritt, and grace in those
weighty businesses, they were reminded of t[he] busines
whereabout they mett [viz] for the establishment of
such civill order as might be most p[leas]ing unto God,
and for the chuseing the fittest men for the foundation
worke of a church to be gather[ed]. For the better
inableing them to discerne the minde of God and to
agree accordingly concerning the establishment of
civill order, Mr. John Davenport propounded divers
quaeres to them publiquely praying them to consider
seriously in the presence and feare of God the weight

of the busines they met about, and nott to be rash or
sleight in giveing their votes to things they
understoode nott, butt to digest fully and thoroughly
whatt should be propounded to them, and without respect
to men as they should be satisfied and perswaded in
their owne mindes to give their answers in such sort as
they would be willing they should stand upon recorde
for posterity.

This being earnestly pressed by Mr. Davenport, Mr.
Robt. Newman was intreated to write in carracters and
to read distinctly and audibly in the hearing of all
the people whatt was propounded and accorded on that
itt might appeare thatt all consented to matters
propounded according to words written by him.

QUAER. I. Whether the Scripturs doe holde forth a
perfect rule for the direction and government of all
men in all duet[ies] which they are to performe to God
and men as well in the government of famyles and
commonwealths as in matters of the chur.

This was assented unto by all, no man dissenting
as was expressed by holding up of hands. Afterward itt
was read over to them thatt they might see in whatt
words their vote was expressed: They againe expressed
their consent thereto by holdeing up their hands, no
man dissenting.

QUAER. 2. Whereas there was a covenant solemnly
made by the whole assembly of free-planters of this
plantation the first day of extraordenary humiliation
which wee had after wee came together, thatt as in
matters thatt concerne the gathering and ordering of a
chur. so likewise in all publique offices which
concerne civill order, as choyce of magistrates and
officers, makeing and repealing of lawes, devideing
allottments of inheritance and all things of like
nature we would all of us be ordered by those rules
which the scripture holds forth to us. This covenant
was called a plantation covenant to distinguish itt
from [a] chur. covenant which could nott att thatt time
be made, a chur. nott being then gathered, butt was
deferred till a chur. might be gathered according to
God: Itt was demaunded, whether all the free planters
doe holde themselves bound by thatt covenant in all
businesses of thatt nature which are expressed in the
covenant to submitt themselves to be ordered by the
rules held forth in the scripture.

This also was assented unto by all, and no man
gainsaid itt, and they did testefie the same by
holde[ing] up their hands both when itt was first
propounded, and confirmed the same by holdeing up their
hands when itt was read unto them in publique . . . .
QUAER. 3. Those who have desired to be received
as free planters, and are settled in the plantation
with a purp[ose,] resolution and desire thatt they may
be admitted into a chur. fellowship according to Christ
as soone [as] God shall fitt them thereunto: were
desired to express itt by holdeing up of hands:
Accordingly a[ll] did expresse this to be their desire
and purpose by holdeing up their hands twice, [vix]
both att the [pro]posall of itt, and after when these
written words were read unto them.
QUAER. 4. All the free planters were called upon
to expresse whether they held themselves bound to
esta[blish] such civill order as might best conduce to
the secureing of the purity and peace of the
ordina[nces] to themselves and their posterity
according to God. In answer hereunto they expressed by
hold[ing] up their hands twice as before, thatt they
held them selves bound to establish such [civil order]
as might best conduce to the ends aforesaid.
Then Mr. Davenport declared unto them by the
scripture whatt kinde of persons might best be trusted
with matters of government, and by sundry arguments
from scripture proved that such men as were discrib[ed]
in Exod. 18.2. Deut. 1.13, with Deut 17.15, and 1. Cor.
6: 1 to 7, ought to be intrusted by them, seeing [they]
were free to cast themselves into thatt mould and forme
of common wealth which appeareth best for them in
referrence to the secureing of the pure and peaceable
injoyment of all Christ his ordinances [in] the church
according to God, whereunto they have bound themselves
as hath beene acknowledged. Having thus said he satt
downe, praying the company freely to consider whether
they would have [it] voted att this time or nott:
After some space of silence Mr. Theophilus Eaton
answered itt mi[ght] be voted, and some other allso
spake to the same purpose, none att all opposeing itt.
Then itt was propounded to vote.
QUAER. 5. Whether Free Burgesses shalbe chosen
out of chur. members they thatt are in the foundat[ion]
worke of the church being actually free burgesses, and

to chuse to themselves out of the li[ke] estate of
church fellowship and the power of chuseing magistrates
and officers from among themselves and the power off
makeing and repealing lawes according to the worde, and
the devideing of inheritances and decideing of
differences thatt may arise, and all the businesses of
like nature are to be transacted by those free
burgesses.

This was putt to vote and agreed unto by the
lifting up of hands twice as in the former itt was
done. Then one man stood up after the vote was past,
and expressing his dissenting from the rest in part
yett grantinge I. That magistrates should be men
fearing God. 2. Thatt the church is the company
whence ordenaryly such men be expected. 3. Thatt they
that chuse them ought to be men fearing God: onely att
this he stuck, That free planters ought nott to given
this power out of their hands: Another stood up and
answered that in this case nothing was done but with
their consent. The former answered thatt all the free
planters ought to resume this power into their owne
hands againe if things were not orderly carryed. Mr.
Theophilus Eaton answered thatt in all places they
chuse committyes, in like manner the companyes of
London chuse the liveryes by whom the publique
magistrates are chosen. In this the rest are not
wronged because they expect in time to be of the livery
themselves, and to have the same power. Some other
intreated the former to give his arguments and reasons
whereupon he dissented. He refused to doe itt and said
they might nott rationally demaund itt, seeing he lett
the vote passe on freely and did nott speake till after
itt was past, because he would nott hinder whatt they
agreed upon. Then Mr. Davenport, after a short
relation of some former passages betweene them two
about this quest. prayed the company thatt nothing
might be concluded by them in this weighty quest. butt
whatt themselves were perswaded to be agreeing with the
minde of God and they had heard whatt had beene said
since the voteing, intreated them againe to consider of
itt, and putt itt againe to vote as before. --Againe
all of them by holding up their hands did shew their
consent as before, And some of them professed that
whereas they did waver before they came to the assembly
they were now fully convinced thatt itt is the minde of

God. One of them said that in the morning, before he
came, reading Deut. 17.15. he was convinced att home,
another said thatt he came doubting to the assembly
butt he blessed God by whatt had beene saide he was now
fully satisfied thatt the choyce of burgesses out of
chur. members, and to intrust those with the power
before spoken off is according to the minde of God
revealed in the scriptures. All haveing spoken their
apprehensions, itt was agreed upon, and Mr. Robert
Newman was desired to write itt as an order whereunto
every one that hereafter should be admitted here as
planters should submitt and testefie the same by
subscribeing their names to the order, namely that
church members onely shall be free burgesses, and that
they onely shall chuse magistrates & officers among
themselves to have the power of transacting all the
publique civill affayres of this Plantation, of makeing
and repealing lawes, devideing of inheritances,
decideing of differences thatt may arise and doeing all
things or businesses of like nature.

    This being thus settled as a foundamentall
agreement concerning civill government: Mr. Davenport
proceeded to propound some things to consideration
aboute the gathering of a chur. And to prevent the
blemishing of the first beginnings of the chur. worke,
Mr. Davenport advised thatt the names of such as were
to be admitted might be publiquely propounded, to the
end thatt they who were most approved might be chosen,
for the towne being cast into severall private meetings
wherein they thatt dwelt nearest together gave their
accounts one to another of Gods gracious worke upon
them, and prayed together and conferred to their
mutuall ediffication, sundry of them had knowledg one
of another, and in every meeting some one was more
approved of all then any other, For this reason, and to
prevent scandalls, the whole company was intreated to
consider whom they found fittest to nominate for this
worke.

    QUAER. 6. Whether are you all willing and doe
agree in this thatt twelve men be chosen that their
fitnesse for the foundation worke may be tried, however
there may be more named yett itt may be in their power
who are chosen to reduce them to twelve, and itt be in
the power of those twelve to chuse out of themselves

seaven that shall be most approved of the major part to
begin the church.

This was agreed upon by consent of all as was
expressed by holdeing up of hands, and thatt so many as
should be thought fitt for the foundation worke of the
church shall be propounded by the plantation, and
written downe and passe without exception unlesse they
had given publique scandall or offence, yett so as in
case of publique scandall or offence, every one should
have liberty to propound their exception att thatt time
publiquely against any man that should be nominated
when all their names should be writt downe butt if the
offence were private, thatt mens names might be
tendered, so many as were offended were intreated to
deale with the offender privately, and if he gave nott
satisfaction, to bring the matter to the twelve thatt
they might consider of itt impartially and in the feare
of God.   The names of the persons nominated and agreed
upon were Mr. Theoph. Eaton, Mr. John Davenport. Mr.
Robert Newman, Mr. Math. Gilbert, Mr. Richard Malbon,
Mr. Nath: Turner, Eze: Chevers, Thomas Fugill, John
Ponderson, William Andrewes, and Jer. Dixon.   Noe
exception was brought against any of those in publique,
except one about takeing an excessive rate for meale
which he sould to one of Pequanack in his need, which
he confessed with griefe and declared thatt haveing
beene smitten in heart and troubled in his conscience,
he restored such a part of the price back againe with
confession of his sin to the party as he thought
himselfe bound to doe.   And itt being feared thatt the
report of the sin was heard farther th[an] the report
of his satisfaction, a course was concluded on to make
the satisfaction known to as many as heard of the sinn.
Itt was also agreed upon att the said meeting thatt if
the persons above named did finde themselves straitened
in the number of fitt men for the seaven, thatt itt
should be free for them to take into tryal of fitnes
such other as they should thinke meete, provided thatt
it should be signified to the towne upon the Lords day
who they take in, thatt every man may be satisfied of
them according to the course formerly taken.

DOCUMENT 38:   Agreement of the Settlers at Exeter in
                 New Hampshire, July 5, 1639

Complete text and spelling taken from Isaac W. Hammond,
ed., *Documents Relating to Towns in New Hampshire*
(Concord, N.H.: Parsons B. Cogswell, 1882), 132 - 134.
Many editors, including Francis N. Thorpe, reproduce
only the agreement above the 35 signatures, whereas the
oaths immediately following in the town records are
also reproduced here since they are clearly part of the
founding act. Hammond notes that the document is
apparently in the handwriting of John Whelewright.
There is some disagreement with respect to the date of
its writing. Thorpe transcribes it as "mo. 8. D. 4.
1639," whereas Hammond transcribes it as "Mon., 5th d.
4th, 1639." For reasons internal to the two versions
it appears that Hammond has done the more careful job,
so his transcription is used here, along with his
rendering of the date.

        Whereas it hath pleased the Lord to moue the heart
of our Dread Soveraigne Charles, by the grace of God,
King of England, Scotland, France & Ireland, to grant
license & liberty to sundry of his subjects to plant
themselves in the westerne partes of America: Wee, his
loyall subjects, brethren of the church of Exeter,
situate & lying upon the river of Piscataquacke, wh
other inhabitants there, considering wth ourselves the
holy will of god and our owne necessity, that we should
not live whout wholsome lawes & government amongst us,
of wch we are altogether destitute; doe in the name of
Christ & in the sight of God combine ourselves
together, to erect & set up amongst us such government
as shall be to our best discerning, agreeable to the
will of god, professing ourselves subjects to our
Sovereign Lord King Charles, according to the libertys

of our English Colony of the Massachusetts & binding
ourselves solemnely by the grace & helpe of Christ & in
his name & fear to submit ourselves to such godly &
christian laws as are established in the realme of
England to our best knowledge, & to all other such
lawes wch shall upon good grounds, be made & inacted
amongst us according to God, yt we may live quietly &
peaceablely together, in all godliness and honesty.

Mon., 5th d., 4th, 1639.

[Signed by John Whelewright and 34 others.]

The Elders or Rulers Oath

You shall swear by the great and dreadful Name of
the High God, Maker and Governor of Heaven and earth
and by the Lord Jesus Christ, the Prince of the Kings
and rulers of the earth, that in his Name and fear you
will rule and govern his people according to the
righteous will of God, ministering justice and judgment
on the workers of iniquite, and ministering due
incouragement and countenance to well doers, protecting
of the people so far as in you lieth, by the help of
God from foreigne annoyance and inward desturbance,
that they may live a quiet and peacabble life in all
godliness and honesty. So God be helpful and gracious
to you and yours in Christ Jesus.

The Oath of the People

We do swear by the Great and dreadful Name of the
High God, Maker and Governor of heaven and earth, and
by the Lord Jesus Christ, the King and Saviour of his
people, that in his Name and fear, we will submit
ourselves to be ruled and governed according to the
will and word of God, and such wholsome laws and
ordinances as shall be derived[1] therefrom by our
honored Rulers and the lawful assistants, with the
consent of the people, and that we will be ready to
assist them by the help of God, in the administration
of justice and preservation of the peace, with our
bodies and goods and best endeavors according to God.
So God protect and save us and ours in Jesus Christ.

DOCUMENT 39:   Plantation Agreement at Providence,
                August 27, 1640

Taken from J.R. Bartlett, ed., *Records of the Colony
of Rhode Island and Providence Plantations in New England: Vol. I, 1636 to 1663* (Providence, R.I.:   A.
Crawford Greene and Brother, State Printers, 1856), 27
- 31. The text is complete with the original spelling.
See Document 23.

           Report of Arbitrators at Providence,
         containing proposals for a form of government

         Providence the 27th of the 5th mo. in the yeare
         (so called) 1640.

         Wee, Robert Coles, Chad Browne, William Harris,
and John Warner, being freely chosen by the consent of
our louing friends and neighbours the Inhabitants of
this Towne of Providence, having many differences
amongst us, they being freely willing and also bound
themselves to stand to our Arbitration in all
differences amongst us to rest contented in our
determination, being so betrusted we have seriously and
carefully indeavoured to weigh and consider all those
differences, being desirous to bringe vnity and peace,
although our abilities are farr short in the due
examination of such weighty things, yet so farre as we
conceive in laying all things together we have gone the
fairest and equallest way to produce our peace.
         I. Agreed, We have with one consent agreed that
in parting those particler properties which some of our
friends and neighbours have in Patuxit, from the
general Common of our towne of Providence, to run vppon
a streight line from a fresh spring being in the
Gulley, at the head of that cove running by that point

of land called Saxafras vnto the town of Mashipawog, to
an oake tree standing neere vnto the corne field, being
at this time the neerest corne field vnto Patuxit, the
oake tree having four marks with an axe, till some
other land marke be set for a certaine bound. Also, we
agree that if any meadow ground lyeing and joineing to
that Meadow, that borders uppon the River of Patuxit
come within the aforesaid line, which will not come
within a streight line from long Cove to the marked
tree, then for that meadow to belong to Pawtuxit, and
so beyond the towne of Mashipawog from the oake tree
between the two fresh Rivers Pawtuxit and
Wanasquatucket of an even Distance.
         2.   Agreed. We have with one consent agreed that
for the disposeing, of those lands that shall be
disposed belonging to this towne of Providence to be in
the whole Inhabitants be the choise of five men for
generall disposeall, to be betrusted with disposeall of
lands and also of the townes Stocke, and all Generall
things and not to receive in any six dayes as
townesmen, but first to give the Inhabitants notice to
consider if any have just cause to shew against the
receiving of him as you can apprehend, and to receive
none but such as subscribe to this our determination.
Also, we agree that if any of our neighbours doe
apprehend himselfe wronged by these or any of these 5
disposers, that at the General towne meeting he may
have a tryall.
         Alsoe wee agree for the towne to choose beside the
other five men one or more to keepe Record of all
things belonging to the towne and lying in Common.
         Wee agree, as formerly hath bin the liberties of
the town, so still, to hould forth liberty of
Conscience.
         III. Agreed, that after many Considerations and
Consultations of our owne State and alsoe of States
abroad in way of government, we apprehend, no way so
suitable to our Condition as government by way of
arbitration. But if men agree themselves by
arbitration, no State we know of disallows that,
neither doe we: But if men refuse that which is but
common humanity betweene man and man, then to compel
such vnreasonable persons to a reasonable way, we agree
that the 5 disposers shall have power to compell him
either to choose two men himselfe, or if he refuse, for

them to choose two men to arbitrate his cause, and if
these foure men chosen by every partie do end the
cause, then to see theire determination performed and
the faultive to pay the Arbitrators for theire time
spent in it: But if those foure men doe not end it,
then for the 5 disposers to choose the 3 men, and for
the certainty hereof, wee agree the major part of the 5
disposers to choose the 3 men, and the major part of
the 3 men to end the cause hauing power from the 5
disposers by a note under theire hand to performe it,
and the faultive not agreeing in the first to pay the
charge of the last, and for the Arbitrators to follow
no imployment till the cause be ended without consent
of the whole that have to doe with the cause.

Instance. In the first Arbitration the offendor
may offer reasonable terms of peace, and the offended
may exact upon him and refuse and trouble men beyond
reasonable satisfaction; so for the last arbitrators to
judge where the fault was, in not agreeing in the
first, to pay the charge of the last.

IV.. Agreed, that if any person damnify any man,
either in goods or good name, and the person offended
follow not the cause vppon the offendor, that if any
person giue notice to the 5 Disposers, they shall call
the party delinquent to answer by Arbitration.

Instance. Thus, if any person abuse an other in
person or goods, may be for peace sake, a man will at
present put it vp, and it may so be resolue to revenge:
therefore, for the peace of the state, the disposers
are to look to it in the first place.

V.   Agreed, for all the whole Inhabitants to
combine ourselves to assist any man in the pursuit of
any party delinquent, with all our best endeavours to
attack him: but if any man raise a hubbub, and there
be no just cause, then for the party that raised the
hubbub to satisfy men for their time lost in it.

VI. Agreed, that if any man have a difference
with any of the 5 Disposers which cannot be deferred
till general neeting of the towne, then he may have the
Clerk call the towne together at his [discretion] for a
tryall.

Instance. It may be, a man may be to depart the
land, or to a farr parte of the land; or his estate may
lye vppon a speedy tryall or the like case may fall
out.

VII. Agreed, that the towne, by the five men shall give every man a deed of all his lands lying within the bounds of the Plantation, to hould it by for after ages.

VIII. Agreed, that the 5 disposers shall from the date hereof, meete every month-day vppon General things and at the quarter-day to yeeld a new choise and give vp theire old Accounts.

IX. Agreed, that the Clerke shall call the 5 Disposers together at the month-day, and the generall towne together every quarter, to meete vppon general occassions from the date hereof.

X.   Agreed, that the Clerke is to receive for every cause that comes to the towne for a tryall 4d.[1] for making each deed 12d. and to give vp the booke to the towne at the yeeres end, and yeeld to a new choice.

XI. Agreed, that all acts of disposall on both sides to stand the difference.

XII. Agreed, that every man that hath not paid in his purchase money for his Plantation shall make vp his 10s. to be 30s. eqval with the first purchasers: and for all that are received townsmen hereafter, to pay the like summe of money to the town stocke.

These being those things wee have generally concluded on, for our peace, we desireing our loveing friends to receive as our absolute determination, laying ourselves downe as subjects to it.

[Signed by the four writers in the document plus thirty-five others.]

DOCUMENT 40:   Connecticut Oath of Fidelity, 1640

Text taken in full, and with the original spelling,
from J. Hammond Trumbull, ed., *The Public Records of
the Colony of Connecticut Prior to the Union With New
Haven Colony* (Hartford: Brown & Parsons, 1850), 54.
This document is sometimes referred to as The
Connecticut Oath of Agreement.

An Oath for Paqua' and the Plantations There:

I A.B. being by the Pruidence of God an inhabitant
wthin the Jurisdiction of Conectecotte, doe acknowledge
my selfe to be subject to the gourment thereof, and doe
sweare by the great and dreadfull name of the eur
liueing God to be true and faythfull vnto the same, and
doe submitt boath my Prson & estate thereunto,
according to all the holsome lawes & orders that ether
are or hereafter shall be there made by lawfull
authority: And that I will nether plott nor practice
any euell agaynst the same, nor consent to any that
shall so doe, but will tymely discour the same to
lawfull authority established there; and that I will
maynetayne, as in duty I am bownd, the honor of the
same & of the lawfull Magestrats thereof, promoteing
the publike good thereof, whilst I shall so continue an
Inhabitant there, and whensour I shall give my vote,
suffrage or prxy, being cauled thereunto touching any
matter wch conserns this Commonwelth, I will giue yt as
in my conscience may conduce to the best good of the
same, wch out of respect of prson or favor of any man;
So helpe me God in the Lo: Jesus Christ.

DOCUMENT 41:   Massachusetts Body of Liberties
                December, 1641

Original spelling with the complete text.   Taken from
S. Whitmore, *Bibliographical Sketch of the Laws of
Massachusetts Colony, 1889* pp. 32 - 60.   Probably the
first true bill of rights written in America, the
Massachusetts Body of Liberties looks very restrictive
to our eyes today.   It is difficult to find any rights
that were treated as if they were inalienable.   In
addition, the document is more a statement of fundamental values than a set of limits on government.   In
this regard, it bears a kinship with Documents 1, 2, 4,
44, 52, 58, 60, 68, and 71 reproduced in this volume.
It is difficult to think of a colonial document that is
better at revealing the fundamental value commitments
of a community.

        A Coppie of the Liberties of the Massachusets
                Collonie in New England

        The free fruition of such liberties Immunities and
priveledges as humanitie, Civilitie, and Christianitie
call for as due to every man in his place and
proportion; without impeachment and Infringement hath
ever bene and ever will be the tranquillitie and
Stabilitie of Churches and Commonwealths.   And the
deniall or deprivall thereof, the disturbance if not
the ruine of both.
        We hould it therefore our dutie and safetie whilst
we are about the further establishing of this
Government to collect and expresse all such freedomes
as for present we foresee may concerne us, and our
posteritie after us, And to ratify them with our
sollemne consent.

Wee doe therefore this day religiously and unanimously decree and confirme these following Rites, liberties, and priveledges concerneing our Churches, and Civill State to be respectively impartiallie and inviolably enjoyed and observed throughout our Jursidiction for ever.

I.   No mans life shall be taken away, no mans honour or good name shall be stayned, no mans person shall be arested, restrayned, banished, dismembred, nor any wayes punished, no man shall be deprived of his wife or children, no mans goods or estaite shall be taken away from him, nor any way indammaged under Coulor of law, or Countenance of Authoritie, unlesse it be by vertue or equitie of some expresse law of the Country warranting the same, established by a generall Court and sufficiently published, or in case of the defect of a law in any partecular case by the word of god.   And in Capitall cases, or in cases concerning dismembring or banishment, according to that word to be judged by the Generall Court.

2.   Every person within Jurisdiction, whether Inhabitant or forreiner shall enjoy the same justice and law, that is generall for the plantation, which we constitute and execute one towards another, without partialitie or delay.

3.   No man shall be urged to take any oath or subscribe any articles, covenants or remonstrance, of a publique and Civill nature, but such as the Generall Court hath considered, allowed, and required.

4.   No man shall be punished for not appearing at or before any Civill Assembly, Court, Councell, Magistrate, or officer, nor for the omission of any office or service, if he shall be necessarily hindred, by any apparent Act or providenc of god, which he coule neither foresee nor avoid.   Provided that this law shall not prejudice any person of his just cost or damage in any civill action.

5.   No man shall be compelled to any publique worke or service unlesse the presse be grounded upon some act of the generall Court, and have reasonable allowance therefore.

6.   No man shall be pressed in person to any office, worke, warres, or other publique service, that is necessarily and suffitiently exempted by any naturall or personall impediment, as by want of yeares

greatnes of age, defect of minde, fayling of sences, or
impotencie of Lymbes.

7. No man shall be compelled to goe out of the
limits of this plantation upon any offensive warres
which this Commonwealth or any of our freinds or
confederats shall volentarily undertake. But onely
upon such vindictive and defensive warres in our owne
behalfe, or the behalfe of our freinds, and confederats
as shall be enterprized by the Counsell and consent of
a Court generall, or by Authority derived from the
same.

8. No mans Cattell or goods of what kinde soever
shall be pressed or taken for any publique use or
service, unlesse it be by warrant grounded upon some
act of the generall Court, nor without such reasonable
prices and hire as the ordinarie rates of the Countrie
do afford. And if his Cattle or goods shall perish or
suffer damage in such service, the owner shall be
suffitiently recompenced

9. No monoplies shall be granted or allowed
amongst us, but of such new Inventions that are
profitable to the Countrie, and that for a short time.

10. All our lands and heritages shall be free
from all finds and licences upon Alienations, and from
all hariotts[1], wardships, Liveries,[2] Primerseisens,[3]
yeare day and wast, Escheates,[4] and forfeitures, upon
the deaths of parents, or Ancestors, be they naturall,
casuall, or Juditiall.

11. All persons which are of the age of 21
yeares, and of right understanding and meamories,
whether excommunicate or condemned shall have full
power and libertie to make there wills and testaments,
and other lawfull alienations of theire lands and
estates.

12. Every man whether Inhabitant or fforreiner,
free or not free shall have libertie to come to any
publique Court, Councell, or Towne meeting, and either
by speech or writeing to move any lawful, seasonable,
and materiall question, or to present any necessary
motion, complaint, petition, Bill or information,
whereof that meeting hath proper cognizance, so it be
done in convenient time, due order, and respective
manner.

[13.]   No man shall be rated here for any estaite or revenue he hath in England, or in any forreine parties till it be transported hither.

[14.]   Any conveyance or Alienation of land or other estaite what so ever, made by any woman that is married, any childe under age, Ideott, or distracted person, shall be good, if it be passed and ratified by the consent of a generall Court.

15.   All Covenous or fraudulent Alienations or Conveyances of lands, tenements, or any hereditaments, shall be of no validitie to defeate any man from due debts or legacies, or from any just title, clame or possession, of that which is so fradulently conveyed.

16.   Every Inhabitant that is an howse holder shall have free fishing and fowling in any great ponds and Bayes, Coves and Rivers, so farre as the sea ebbes and flowes within the presincts of the towne where they dwell, unlesse the freemen of the same Towne or the Generall Court have otherwise appropriated them, provided that this shall not be extended to give leave to any man to come upon other proprietie without there leave.

17.   Every man of or within this Jurisdiction shall have free libertie, not with standing any Civill power to remove both himselfe, and his familie at their pleasure out of the same, provided there be no legall impediment to the contrarie.

18.   No mans person shall be restrained or imprisoned by any Authority what so ever, before the law hath sentenced him thereto, If he can put in sufficient securitie, bayle, or mainprise, for his appearance, and good behaviour in the meane time, unlesse it be in Crimes Capitall, and Contempts in open Court, and in such cases where some expresse act of Court doth allow it.

19.   If in a generall Court any miscariage shall be amongst the Assistants when they are by themselves that may deserve an Admonition or fine under 20 sh, it shall be examined and sentenced amongst themselves, If amongst the Deputies when they are by themselves, It shall be examined and sentenced amongst themselves, If it be when the whole Court is togeather, it shall be judged by the whole Court, and not severallie as before.

20. If any which are to sit as Judges in any
other Court shall demeane themselves offensively in the
Court, the rest of the Judges present shall have power
to censure him for it, if the cause be of a high nature
it shall be presented to and censured at the next
superior Court

21. In all cases where the first summons are not
served six dayes before the Court, and the cause
briefly specified in the warrant, where appearance is
to be made by the partie summoned, it shall be at his
libertie whether he will appeare or not, except all
cases that are to be handled in Courts suddainly called
upon extraordinary occasions, In all cases where there
appeares present and urgent cause Any Assistant or
officer apointed shal have power to make out
Attaichments for the first summons.

22. No man in any suit or action against an other
shall falsely pretend great debts or damages to vex his
Adversary, if it shall appeare any doth so, The Court
shall have power to set a reasonable fine on his head.

23. No man shall be adjudged to pay for detaining
any Debt from any Crediter above eight pounds in the
hundred for one yeare, And not above that rate
proportionable for all somes what so ever, neither
shall this be a coulour or countenance to allow any
usurie amongst us contrarie to the law of god.

24. In all Trespasses or damages done to any man
or men, If it can be proved to be done by the meere
default of him or them to whome the trespasse is done,
It shall be judged no trespasse, nor any damage given
for it.

25. No Summons pleading Judgement, or any kinde
of proceeding in Court or course of Justice shall be
abated, arested, or reversed, upon any kinde of
cercumstantiall errors or mistakes, If the person and
cause be rightly understood and intended by the Court.

26. Every man that findeth himselfe unfit to
plead his owne cause in any Court, shall have Libertie
to imploy any man against whom the Court doth not
except, to helpe him, Provided he give him noe fee, or
reward for his paines. This shall not exempt the
partie him selfe from Answering such Questions in
person as the Court shall thinke meete to demand of
him.

27. If any plaintife shall give into any Court a declaration of his cause in writeing, The defendant shall also have libertie and time to give in his answer in writeing, And so in all further proceedings betwene partie and partie, So it doth not further hinder the dispach of Justice then the Court shall be willing unto.

28. The plaintife in all Actions brought in any Court shall have libertie to withdraw his Action, or to be nonsuited before the Jurie hath given in their verdict, in which case he shall alwaies pay full cost and chardges to the defendant, and may afterwards renew his suite at an other Court if he please.

29. In all Actions at law it shall be the libertie of the plaintife and defendant by mutual consent to choose whether they will be tryed by the Bench or by a Jurie, unlesse it be where the law upon just reason hath otherwise determined. The like libertie shall be granted to all persons in Criminall cases.

30. It shall be in the libertie both of plaintife and defendant, and likewise every delinquent (to be judged by a Jurie) to challenge any of the Jurors. And if his challenge be found just and reasonable by the Bench, or the rest of the Jurie, as the challenger shall choose it shall be allowed him, and tales de cercumstantibus impaneled in their room.

31. In all cases where evidence is so obscure or defective that the Jurie cannot clearly and safely give a positive verdict, whether it be a grand or petit Jurie, It shall have libertie to give a non Liquit, or a spetiall verdict, in which last, that is in a spetiall veredict, the Judgement of the cause shall be left to the Court, and all Jurors shall have libertie in matters of fact if they cannot finde the maine issue, yet to finde and present in their verdict so much as they can, If the Bench and Jurors shall so differ at any time about their verdict that either of them can not proceed with peace of conscience the case shall be referred to the Generall Court, who shall take the question from both and determine it.

32. Every man shall have libertie to replevy his Cattell or goods impounded, distreined, seised, or

extended, unless it be upon execution after Judgement, and in paiment of fines. Provided he puts in good securitie to prosecute his replevin, And to satisfie such demands as his Adversary shall recover against him in Law.

33. No mans person shall be Arrested, or imprisoned upon execution or judgment for any debt or fine, if the law can finde competent meanes of satisfaction otherwise from his estaite, And if not his person may be arrested and imprisoned where he shall be kept at his owne charge, not the plaintife's till satisfaction be made: unlesse the Court that had cognizance of the cause or some superior Court shall otherwise provide.

34. If any man shall be proved and Judged a common Barrator vexing others with unjust frequent and endlesse suites, It shall be in the power of Courts both to denie him the benefit of the law, and to punish him for his Barratry.

35. No mans Corne nor hay that is in the field or upon the Cart, nor his garden stuffe, nor any thing subject to present decay, shall be taken in any distresse, unles he that takes it doth presently bestow it where it may not be imbesled nor suffer spoile or decay, or give securitie to satisfie the worth thereof if it comes to any harme.

36. It shall be in the libertie of every man cast condemned or sentenced in any cause in any Inferior Court, to make their Appeale to the Court of Assistants, provided they tender their appeale and put in securitie to prosecute it before the Court be ended wherein they were condemned, And within six dayes next ensuing put in good securitie before some Assistant to satisfie what his Adversarie shall recover against him; And if the cause be of a Criminall nature, for his good behaviour and appearance, And everie man shall have libertie to complaine to the Generall Court of any Injustice done him in any Court of Assistants or other

37. In all cases where it appeares to the Court that the plaintife hath willingly and witingly done wronge to the defendant in commenceing and prosecuting any action or complaint against him, They shall have power to impose upon him a proportionable fine to the use of the defendant, or accused person, for his false complaint or clamor.

38. Everie man shall have libertie to Record in the publique Rolles of any Court any Testimony give[n] upon oath in the same Court, or before two Assistants, or any Deede or evidence legally confirmed there to remaine in perpetuam rei memoriam, that is for perpetuall memoriall or evidence upon occasion.

39. In all Actions both reall and personall betweene partie and partie, the Court shall have power to respite execution for a convenient time, when in their prudence they see just cause so to doe.

40. No Conveyance, Deede, or promise what so ever shall be of validitie, If it be gotten by Illegal violence, imprisonment, threatenings, or any kinde of forcible compulsion called Dures.

41. Everie man that is to Answere for any Criminall cause, whether he be in prison or under bayle, his cause shall be heard and determined at the next Court that hath proper Cognizance thereof, And may be done without prejudice of Justice.

42. No man shall be twise sentenced by Civill Justice for one and the same Crime, offence, or Trespasse.

43. No man shall be beaten with above 40 stripes, nor shall any true gentleman, nor any man equall to a gentleman be punished with whipping, unless his crime be very shamefull, and his course of life vitious and profligate.

44. No man condemned to dye shall be put to death within fower dayes next after his condemnation, unles the Court see spetiall cause to the contrary, or in case of martiall law, nor shall the body of any man so put to death be unburied 12 howers, unlesse it be in case of Anatomie.

45. No man shall be forced by Torture to confesse any Crime against himselfe nor any other unlesse it be in some Capitall case where he is first fullie convicted by cleare and suffitient evidence to be guilty, After which if the cause be of that nature, That it is very apparent there be other conspiratours, or confederates with him, Then he may be tortured, yet not with such Tortures as be Barbarous and inhumane.

46. For bodilie punishments we allow amongst us none that are inhumane Barbarous or cruell

47. No man shall be put to death without the testimony of two or three witnesses, or that which is equivalent there unto.

48. Every Inhabitant of the Countrie shall have free libertie to search and veewe any Rooles, Records, or Regesters of any Court or office except the Councell, And to have a transcript or exemplification thereof written examined, and signed by the hand of the officer of the office paying the appointed fees therefore.

49. No free man shall be compelled to serve upon Juries above two Courts in a yeare, except grand Jurie men, who shall hould two Courts together at the least.

50. All Jurors shall be chosen continuallie by the freemen of the Towne where they dwell.

51. All Associates selected at any time to Assist the Assistants in Inferior Courts, shall be nominated by the Townes belonging to that Court, by orderly agreement amonge themselves.

52. Children, Idiots, Distracted persons, and all that are strangers, or new commers to our plantation, shall have such allowances and dispensations in any cause whether Criminall or other as religion and reason require.

53. The age of discretion of passing away of lands or such kinde of herediments, or for giveing of votes, verdicts or Sentence in any Civill Courts or causes, shall be one and twentie yeares.

54. When so ever anything is to be put to vote, any sentence to be pronounced, or any other matter to be proposed, or read in any Court or Assembly, If the president or moderator thereof shall refuse to performe it, the Major parte of the members of that Court or Assembly shall have power to appoint any other meete man of them to do it, And if there be just cause to punish him that should and would not.

55. In all suites or Actions in any Court, the Plaintife shall have libertie to make all the titles and claims to that he sues for he can. And the Defendant shall have libertie to plead all the pleas he can in answere to them, and the Court shall judge according to the intire evidence of all.

56. If any man shall behave himselfe offensively at any Towne meeting, the rest of the freemen then present, shall have power to sentence him for his

offence, So be it the mulct or penaltie exceed not twentie shilings.

57. When so ever any person shall come to any very suddaine untimely and unnaturall death, Some Assistant, or the Constables of that Towne shall forthwith sumon a Jury of twelve free men to inquire of the cause and manner of their death, and shall present a true verdict thereof to some neere Assistant, or the next Court to be helde for that Towne upon their oath.

Liberties More Peculiarlie Concerning the Free Men.

58. Civill Authoritie hath more power and libertie to see the peace, ordinances and Rules of Christ observed in every church according to his word, so it be done in a Civill and not in an Ecclesiastical way.

59. Civill Authoritie hath power and libertie to deale with any Church member in a way of Civill Justice, notwithstanding any Church relation, office, or interest.

60. No church censure shall degrade or depose any man from any Civill dignitie, office, or Authoritie he shall have in the Commonwealth.

61. No Magestrate, Juror, Officer, or other man shall be bound to informe present or reveale any private crim or offence, wherein there is no perill or danger to this plantation or any member thereof, when any necessarietye of conscience binds him to secresie grounded upon the word of god, unlesse it be in case of testimony lawfully required.

62. Any Shire or Towne shall have libertie to choose their Deputies whom and where they please for the General Court, So be it they be free men, and have taken there oath of fealtie, and Inhabiting in this Jurisdiction.

63. No Governor, Deputie Governor, Assistant, Associate, or grand Jury man at any Court, nor any Deputie for the Generall Court, shall at any time bear his owne chardges at any Court, but their necessary expences shall be defrayed either by the Towne, or Shire on whose service they are, or by the Country in generall.

64. Everie Action betweene partie and partie, and proceedings against delinquents in Criminall causes

shall be briefly and destinctly entered in the Rolles of every Court by the Recorder thereof. That such actions be not afterwards brought againe to the vexation of any man.

65. No custome or prescription shall ever prevaile amongst us in any morall cause, our meaneing is maintaine anythinge that can be proved to bee morrallie sinfull by the word of god.

66. The Freemen of everie Towneship shall have power to make such by laws and constitutions as may concerne the wellfare of their Towne, provided they be not of a Criminall, but onely of a prudentiall nature. And that their penalties exceede not 20 sh. for one offence. And that they be not repugnant to the publique laws and orders of the Countrie. And if any Inhabitant shall neglect or refuse to observe them, they shall have power to levy the appointed penalties by distresse.

67. It is the constant libertie of the freemen of this plantation to choose yearly at the Court of Election out of the freemen all the Generall officers of this Jurisdiction. If they please to dischardge them at the day of Election by way of vote. They may do it without shewing cause. But if at any other generall Court, he hould it due justice, that the reasons thereof be alleadged and proved. By Generall officers we meane, our Governor, Deputie Governor, Assistants, Treasurer, Generall of our warres. And our Admirall at Sea, and such as are or hereafter may be of the like generall nature.

68. It is the libertie of the freemen to choose such deputies for the Generall Court out of themselves, either in their owne Townes or elsewhere as they judge fittest, And because we cannot foresee what varietie and weight of occasions may fall into future consideration, And what counsells we may stand in neede of, we decree. That the Deputies (to attend the Generall Court in the behalfe of the Countrie) shall not any time be stated or inacted, but from Court to Court, or at the most but for one yeare. that the Countrie may have an Annuall libertie to do in that case what is most behoofefull for the best welfaire thereof.

69. No Generall Court shall be desolved or
adjourned without the consent of the Major parte
thereof.

70. All Freemen called to give any advise, vote,
verdict, or sentence in any Court, Counsell, or Civill
Assembly, shall have full freedome to doe it according
to their true Judgments and Consciences, So it be done
orderly and inofensively for the manner.

71. The Governor shall have a casting voice
whensoever an Equi vote shall fall out of the Court of
Assistants, or generall assembly, So shall the
presendent or moderator have in all Civill Courts or
Assemblies.

72. The Governor and Deputie Governor Joyntly
consenting or any three Assistants concurring in
consent shall have power out of Court to reprive a
condemned malefactour, till the next quarter or
generall Court. The generall Court onely shall have
power to pardon a condemned malefactor.

73. The Generall Court hath libertie and
Authoritie to send out any member of the Comanwealth of
what qualitie, condition or office whatsoever into
forreine parts about any publique message or
Negotiation. Provided the partie sent be acquainted
with the affaire he goeth about, and be willing to
undertake the service.

74. The freemen of every Towne or Towneship,
shall have full power to choose yearly or for lesse
time out of themselves a convenient number of fitt men
to order the planting or prudential occasions of that
Towne, according to Instructions given them in
writeing, Provided nothing be done by them contrary to
the publique laws and orders of the Countrie, provided
also the number of such select persons be not above
nine.

75. It is and shall be the libertie of any member
or members of any Court, Councell or Civill Assembly in
cases of makeing or executing any order or law, that
properlie concerne religion, or any cause capitall or
warres, or Subscription to any publique Articles or
Remonstrance, in case they cannot in Judgement and
conscience consent to that way the Major vote or
suffrage goes, to make their contra Remonstrance or
protestation in speech or writeing, and upon request to
have their dissent recorded in the Rolles of that

Court. So it be done Christianlie and respectively for the manner. And their dissent onely be entered without the reasons thereof, for the avoiding of tediousness.

76. When so ever any Jurie of trialls or Jurours are not cleare in their Judgments or consciences conserneing any cause wherein they are to give their verdict, They shall have libertie in open Court to advise with any man they thinke fitt to resolve or direct them, before they give in their verdict.

77. In all cases wherein any freeman is to give his vote, be it in point of Election, makeing constitutions and orders, or passing sentence in any case of Judicature or the like, if he cannot see reason to give it positively one way or an other, he shall have libertie to be silent, and not pressed to a determined vote.

78. The Generall or publique Treasure or any parte thereof shall never be exspended but by the appointment of a Generall Court, nor any Shire Treasure, but by the appointment of the freemen thereof, nor any Towne Treasurie but by freemen of that Towneship.

Liberties of Woemen

79. If any man at his death shall not leave his wife a competent portion of his estaite, upon just complaint made to the Generall Court she shall be relieved.

80. Everie marryed woeman shall be free from bodilie correction or stripes by her husband, unlesse it be in his owne defence upon her assault. If there be any just cause of correction complaint shall be made to Authoritie assembled in some Court, from which onely she shall receive it.

Liberties of Children

81. When parents dye intestate, the Elder sonne shall have a doble portion of his whole estate reall and personall, unlesse the Generall Court upon just cause alleadged shall Judge otherwise.

82. When parents dye intestate, haveing noe heires males of their bodies their Daughters shall

inherit as Copartners, unles the Generall Court upon just reason shall judge otherwise.

83. If any parents shall wilfullie and unreasonably deny any childe timely or convenient mariage, or shall exercise any unnaturall severitie towards them, Such children shall have free libertie to complain to Authoritie for redresse.

84. No Orphan dureing their minoritie which was not committed to tuition or service by the parents in their life time, shall afterwards be absolutely disposed of by any kindred, friend, Executor, Towneship, or Church, nor by themselves without the consent of some Court, wherein two Assistants at least shall be present.

Liberties of Servants

85. If any servants shall flee from the Tiranny and crueltie of their masters to the howse of any freeman of the same Towne, they shall be there protected and susteyned till due order be taken for their relife. Provided due notice thereof be speedily given to their masters from whom they fled. And the next Assistant or Constable where the partie flying is harboured.

86. No servant shall be put of for above a yeare to any other neither in the life of their master nor after their death by their Executors or Administrators unlesse it be by consent of Authoritie assembled in some Court, or two Assistants.

87. If any man smite out the eye or tooth of his man servant, or maid servant, or otherwise mayme or much disfigure him, unlesse it be by meere casualtie, he shall let them goe free from his service. And shall have such further recompense as the Court shall allow him.

88. Servants that have served diligentlie and faithfully to the benefitt of their maisters seaven yeares, shall not be sent away emptie. And if any have bene unfaithfull, negligent or unprofitable in their service, notwithstanding the good usage of their maisters, they shall not be dismissed till they have made satisfaction according to the Judgement of Authoritie.

Liberties of Forreiners and Strangers

89.   If any people of other Nations professing the
true Christian Religion shall flee to us from the
Tiranny or oppression of their persecutors, or from
famyne, warres, or the like necessary and compulsarie
cause, They shall be entertayned and succoured amongst
us, according to that power and prudence god shall give
us.
90.   If any ships or other vessels, be it freind
or enemy, shall suffer shipwrack upon our Coast, there
shall be no violence or wrong offered to their persons
or goods.   But their persons shall be harboured, and
relieved, and their goods preserved in safety till
Authoritie may be certified thereof, and shall take
further order therein.
91.   There shall never be any bond slaverie
villinage or Captivitie amongst us, unles it be lawfull
Captives taken in just warres, and such strangers as
willingly selle themselves or are sold to us.   And
these shall have all the liberties and Christian usages
which the law of god established in Israell concerning
such persons doeth morally require.   This exempts none
from servitude who shall be Judged thereto by
Authoritie.

Off the Bruite Creature

92.   No man shall exercise any Tirranny or
Crueltie towards any bruite Creature which are usuallie
kept for mans use.
93.   If any man shall have occasion to leade or
drive Cattel from place to place that is far of, So
that they be weary, or hungry, or fall sick, or lambe,
It shall be lawful to rest or refresh them, for a
competent time, in any open place that is not Corne,
meadow, or inclosed for some peculiar use.

94.
I.

Dut. 13.6.10
Dut. 17.2.6.
Ex. 22.20

If any man after legall conviction shall have or worship any other god, but the lord god, he shall be put to death.

2.

Ex. 22.18
Lev. 20.27
Dut. 18.10

If any man or woeman be a witch, (that is hath or consulteth with a familiar spirit,) They shall be put to death.

3.

Lev. 24.15.16

If any person shall Blaspheme the name of God, the father, Sonne, or Holie ghost, with direct expresse, presumptuous or high handed blasphemie, or shall curse god in the like manner, he shall be put to death.

4.

Ex. 21.12
Numb. 35.13.14
30.31

If any person committ any wilfull murther, which is manslaughter, committed upon premeditated mallice, hatred, or Crueltie, not in a mans necessarie and just defence, nor by meere casualtie against his will, he shall be put to death.

5.

Numb. 25.20.21
Lev. 24.17

If any person slayeth an other suddainely in his anger or Crueltie of passion, he shall be put to death.

6.

Ex. 21.14

If any person shall slay an other through guile, either by poysoning or other such divelish practice, he shall be put to death.

7.

Lev. 19.23   If any man or woman shall lye with
                      any beast or brute creature by Carnall
                      Copulation, They shall surely be put to
                      death. And the beast shall be slaine
                      and buried and not eaten.

8.

Lev. 19.22   If any man lyeth with mankinde as
                      he lyeth with a woeman, both of them
                      have committed abhomination, they both
                      shall surely be put to death.

9.

Ex. 20.14   If any person committeth Adultery
                      with a married or espoused wife, the
                      Adulterer and Adulteresse shall surely
                      be put to death.

10.

Ex. 21.16   If any man stealeth a man or
                      mankinde, he shall surely be put to
                      death.

11.

Dut. 19.16.   If any man rise up by false witnes,
   18.19   wittingly and of purpose to take away
                      any man's life, he shall be put to
                      death.

12.

  If any man shall conspire and attempt any
invation, insurrection, or publique rebellion against
our commonwealth, or shall indeavour to surprize any
Towne or Townes, fort or forts therein, or shall
treacherously and perfediouslie attempt the alteration
and subversion of our frame of politie or Government
fundamentallie, he shall be put to death.

95. A declaration of the Liberties the Lord Jesus
hath given to the Churches.

I.   All the people of god within this
Jurisdiction who are not in a church way, and be
orthodox in Judgement, and not scandalous in life,
shall have full libertie to gather themselves into a
Church Estaite. Provided they doe it in a Christian
way, with due observation of the rules of Christ
revealed in his word.
2.   Every Church hath full libertie to exercise
all the ordinances of god, according to the rules of
Scripture.
3.   Every Church hath free libertie of Election
and ordination of all their officers from time to time,
provided they be able pious and orthodox.
4.   Every Church hath free libertie of Admission,
Recommendation, Dismission, and Expulsion, or deposall
of their officers, and members, upon due cause, with
free exercise of the Discipline and Censures of Christ
according to the rules of his word.
5.   No Injunctions are to be put upon any Church,
Church Officers or member in point of Doctrine, worship
or Discipline, whether for substance or cercumstance
besides the Institutions of the lord.
6.   Every Church of Christ hath freedome to
celebrate dayes of fasting and prayer, and of
thanksgiveing according to the word of god.
7.   The Elders of Churches have free libertie to
meete monthly, Quarterly, or otherwise, in convenient
numbers and places, for conferences, and consultations
about Christian and Church questions and occasions.
8.   All Churches have libertie to deale with any
of their members in a church way that are in the hand
of Justice. So it be not to retard or hinder the
course thereof.
9.   Every Church hath libertie to deal with any
magestrate, Deputie of Court or other officer what soe
ever that is a member in a church way in case of
apparent and just offence given in their places. so it
be done with due observance and respect.
10.   Wee allowe private meetings for edification
in religion amongst Christians of all sortes of people.
So it be without just offence both for number, time,
place, and other cercumstances.

11. For the preventing and removeing of errour
and offence that may grow and spread in any of the
Churches in this Jurisdiction. And for the preserveing
of trueith and peace in the several churches within
them selves, and for the maintenance and exercise of
brotherly communion, amongst all the churches in the
Countrie, It is allowed and ratified, by the Authoritie
of this Generall Court as a lawfull libertie of the
Churches of Christ. That once in every month of the
yeare (when the season will beare it) It shall be
lawfull for the minesters and Elders, of the Churches
neere adjoyneing together, with any other of the
breetheren with the consent of the churches to assemble
by course in each severall Church one after an other.
To the intent after the preaching of the word by such a
minister as shall be requested thereto by the Elders of
the church where the Assembly is held, The rest of the
day may be spent in publique Christian Conference about
the discussing and resolveing of any such doubts and
cases of conscience concerning matter of doctrine or
worship or government of the church as shall be
propounded by any of the Breetheren of that church,
with leave also to any other Brother to propound his
objections or answeres for further satisfaction
according to the word of god. Provided that the whole
action be guided and moderated by the Elders of the
Church where the Assemblie is helde, or by such others
as they shall appoint. And that no thing be concluded
and imposed by way of Authoritie from one or more
Churches upon an other, but onely by way of Brotherly
conference and consultations. That the trueth may be
searched out to the satisfying of every man's
Conscience in the sight of god according to his worde.
And because such an Assembly and the worke their of car
not be duely attended to if other lectures be held in
the same weeke. It is therefore agreed with the
consent of the Churches. That in that weeke when such
an Assembly is held. All the lectures in all the
neighbouring Churches for the weeke shall be forborne.
That so the publique service of Christ in this more
solemne Assembly may be transacted with greater
deligence and attention.
96. How so ever these above specified rites,
freedomes, Immunities, Authorities and priveledges,
both Civill and Ecclesiasticall are expressed onely

under the name and title of Liberties, and not in the
exact forme of Laws, or Statutes, yet we do with one
consent fullie Authorise, and earnestly intreate all
that are and shall be in Authoritie to consider them as
laws, and not to faile to inflict condigne and
proportionable punishments upon every man impartiallie,
that shall infringe or violate any of them.

97. Wee likewise give full power and libertie to
any person that shall at any time be denied or deprived
of any of them, to commence and prosecute their suite,
Complaint, or action against any man that shall so doe,
in any Court that hath proper Cognizance or judicature
thereof.

98. Lastly because our dutie and desire is to do
nothing suddainlie which fundamentally concerne us, we
decree that these rites and liberties, shall be Audably
read and deliberately weighed at ever Generall Court
that shall be held, within three yeares next insueing,
And such of them as shall not be altered or repealed
they shall stand so ratified, That no man shall
infringe them without due punishment.

And if any Generall Court within these next thre
yeares shall faile or forget to reade and consider them
as abovesaid. The Governor and Deputie Governor for
the time being, and every Assistant present at such
Courts shall forfeite 20 sh. a man, and everie Deputie
10 sh. a man for each neglect, which shall be paid out
of their proper estate, and not by the Country or the
Townes which choose them. And when so ever there shall
arise any question in any Court amonge the Assistants
and Associates thereof about the explanation of these
Rites and liberties, The Generall Court onely shall
have power to interprett them.

DOCUMENT 42:   The Combination of the Inhabitants Upon
                 the Piscataqua River for Government
                            Oct. 22, 1641

Text taken from Francis N. Thorpe, ed., *The Federal
and State Constitutions, Colonial Charters, and Other
Organic Laws of the United States* (Washington, D.C.:
Government Printing Office, 1907). The text is
complete, and the spelling is as found in Thorpe.

   Whereas sundry Mischiefs and Inconveniences have
befallen us, and more and greater may, in regard of
want of Civill Government, his gracious Majesty haveing
settled no order for us, to our knowledge, we whose
names are underwritten, being Inhabitants upon the
River of Pascataqua have voluntarily agreed to combine
ourselves into a body Politick, that wee may the more
comfortably enjoy the Benefit of his Majesties Laws,
and doe hereby actually engage ourselves to submit to
his Royall Majesties Laws, together with all such Laws
as shall be concluded by a major part of the Freemen of
our Society, in Case they be not repugnant to the laws
of England, and administered in behalf of his Majestie
And this wee have mutually promised, and engaged to
doe, and so to continue till his excellent Majestie
shall give other orders concerning us. In witness
whereof Wee have hereunto set our hands, October 22.
In the 16 year of the Reigne of our Sovereigne Lord,
Charles by the grace of God, King of Great Brittaine,
France and Ireland, Defender of the Faith, &c.

       Subscribed by   Thomas Larkham,
                                 Richard Waldrene,
                                 William Ealdrene, with
                                    38 more.

                                                 187

DOCUMENT 43:   Organization of The Government of Rhode
                Island, March 16-19, 1642

Complete text with the original spelling taken from
John Russell Bartlett, ed., *Records of Rhode Island
and Providence Plantations in New England, Vol. I*
(Providence, R.I.: A Crawford Greene and Brother,
State Printers, 1856), pp. 111-115.

The Generall Court of Election began and held at
Portsmouth, from the 16th of March, to the 19th of the
same no., 1641.
        1.   It was ordered and agreed, before the Elec-
tion, that an Ingagement by oath should be taken of
all the officers of this Body now to be elected, as
likewise for the time to come; the ingagement which
the severall officers of the State shall give is this;
To the Execution of this office, I Judge myself bound
before God to walk faithfully and this I profess in ye
presence of God.

BY ELECTION.

        2.   Mr. Will'm Coddington is chosen Governour
for one whole yeare, or till a new be chosen.
        Mr. Wm. Brenton is chosen Dep'ty Governour, for
one whole yeare, or, &c.
        Mr. John Coggshall is chosen Assistant for one
whole yeare, or, &c.
        Mr. Rob't Harding is chosen Assistant for one
whole yeare, or, &c.
        Mr. Wm. Balston is chosen Assistant and Treasurer
for one whole yeare, etc.
        Mr. John Porter is chosen Assistant forone whole
yeare, or until, &c.

Wm. Dyre is chosen Secretary for one whole yeare, or until, &c.

Mr. Rob't Jeoffreys is chosen Treasurer for one whole yeare, or, &c.

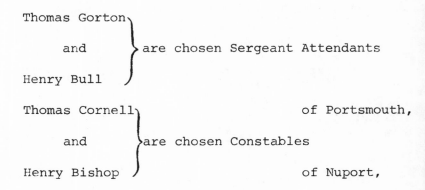

Thomas Gorton

and   are chosen Sergeant Attendants

Henry Bull

Thomas Cornell   of Portsmouth,

and   are chosen Constables

Henry Bishop   of Nuport,

for one yeare, or till a new be chosen.

3.   It is ordered and unanimously agreed upon, that the Government which this Bodie Politick doth attend vnto in this Island, and the Jurisdiction thereof, in favour of our Prince is a DEMOCRACIE, or Popular Government; that is to say, It is in the Powre of the Body of Freemen orderly assembled, or the major part of them, to make or constitue Just Lawes, by which they will be regulated, and to depute from among themselves such Ministers as shall see them faithfully executed between Man and Man.

4.   It was further ordered, by the authority of this present Courte, that none bee accounted a Delinquent for Doctrine: Provided, it be not directly repugnant to ye Government or Lawes established.

5.   It was further ordered, that all such who shall kill a Fox shall have six shillings and eight pence, for his paines, duly paid vnto him by the Treasurer of ye Towne in which lands it was killed: Provided, that he bring the Head thereof to said Treasurer; and this order shall be of sufficient authority to the Treasurer to pay and discharge the said summ.

6.   It is further ordered, that all Men who shall kill any Deare (except it be upon his own proper Land), shall bring and deliver half the said Deare into the Treasurie, or pay Forty shillings; and further it is ordered, that the Governour and Deputy

Governour shall have authority to give forth a Warrant to some one deputed of each Towne to kill some against the Court times for the Countries use, who shall by his Warrant have Libertie to kill wherever he find; Provided, it be not within any man's enclosure, and to be paid by the Treasurer: Provided, also, that no Indian shall be suffered to kill or destroy at any time or any where.

7. It is ordered from henceforth, that the Quarter Session Courts shall alway be kept the first, the first Tuesday in March; the second, the first Tuesday in June; the third, the first Tuesday in September; the last, the first Tuesday in December.

8. It is ordered, that Eight Gunns and their furniture with two corsletts, now in the hands of Mr. Willbore, shall be taken off by the Threasurie Jointlie, as part of satisfaction for what debts from him in now dew therto: and that the said Armes be equally divided to each Towne.

9. It is ordered, that the Deputie Governour and Mr. Willbore, and Mr. Coggshall, and Mr. Jeremy Clarke, shall be joyned in commission with the Two Treasurers that now bee, to examine the Treasurie, and to even the accounts, and then to present them so rectified to the next Generall Court; and what oneveness there is found to bee, the one Treasurer shall make payment to the other Treasurer within twentie dayes after the period of their commission: the limits which are set for the performance of this, shall be three weeks from the date hereof.

10. It is ordered, that Mr. Porter, Mr. Balston, Mr. Easton, and Mr. Jeoffreys shall runn the line between the two Towns within twentie dayes after the date hereof, or else shall forfeit a Mark a peece; and performing it within the (time or) tearme they shall hav a Mark a peace for their Labour.

11. It is ordered, that each Towne shall provide a Towne Book, wherein they shall Record the Evidences of the Land by them impropriated; and shall also have Powre to give forth a Coppie thereof, which shall be a clear evidence for them and theirs, to whom it is so granted.

12. It is ordered, that the Officers of Justice of the Peace is confirmed to the Magistrates.

13. It is ordered, that no Fiers shall be
kindled by any whatsoever to runn at randome, eyther
in Medows or Woods; but what by him that so kindled it
shall forthwith be put out, that it damnifie none.
And that if damage shall accrew, satisfaction to the
utmost shall be awarded.

14. It is ordered, that a Booke shall be provided, wherein the Secretary shall write all such Lawes
and Acts, as are made and constituted by the Body, to
be left alway in that Towne where the said Secretary
is not resident; and also that coppies of such Acts as
shall be made now or hereafter, at the Generall Courts
concerning necessary uses and ordinances to be observed, shall be fixed upon some public place where all
men may see and take notice of them; or that coppies
thereof be given to the Clerks of the Bank, who shall
read them at the head of the Companie.

15. It is ordered, that a Manual Seale shall be
provided for the State, and that the Signett or En-
graving thereof, shall be a sheafe of Arrows bound up,
and in the liess or Bond, this motto indented: Amor
vincent omnia..

16. It is ordered, that Ingagement shall be
taken by the Justice of the Peace in their Quarter
Sessions of all men or youth above fifteen years of
age, eyther by the oath of Fidelity, or some other
strong cognizance.

17. It is ordered, that a Line be drawen and a
way be cleared between the Townes of Nuport and Portsmouth, by removing of the wood and mowing it; that
drift Cattle may sufficiently pass; and for the
performance thereof, Capt. Morris, of the one Towne,
and Mr. Jeoffreys of the other, are appointed to draw
the Line, and to be paid therefore, and the Townes to
perform the rest.

18. It is ordered, that the Traine Bands shall
choose among the Freemen, one or more such as shall be
for their commanders, and present them to the Towne.
The Major vote of the Towne, by the Authority of this
Court, shall have the negative voice for the Establishment of them, and shall order their Powre till
the next Generall Courte.

19. It is ordered, that the major part of the
Courts, being lawfully assembled at the place and
houre appointed, shall have full Powre to transact the

business that shall be Presented: Provided, it be the
Major part of the Body entire, if it be the Generall
Court (present) or the Major part of the Magistrates,
with the Jury in the inferior Courts; and that such
acts concluded and issued be of as full authority as
if there were all present. Provided, there be due and
seasonable notice given of every such Court.

DOCUMENT 44:   Capitall Lawes of Connecticut,
                Established by the Generall Court the
                First of December, 1642.

The text is taken from *The Blue Laws of New Haven Colony*, compiled by "An Antiquarian" (Hartford: Case, Tiffany & Co., 1838), pp. 102-104; who in turn drew upon the *Public Records of the Colony of Connecticut*. The spelling is the original. The text is a portion of a longer ordinance passed on that day by the legislature. This document should be compared with the equivalent section in Document 41.

1.   Yf any man after legall conviction, shall have or worship any other God but the Lord God, he shall be put to death. Deu. 13; 6, and 17. 2 Ex. 22; 20.

2.   Yf any man or woman be a Witch, (that is) hath or consulteth w'th a familliar spirit, they shall be put to death. Ex. 22; 18. Lev. 20; 27. Deu. 18;10,11.

3.   If any p'son shall blaspheme the name of God the ffather, Son or Holy Goste w'th direct, expres pr'sumptuous or highanded blasphemy, or shall curse God in the like manner, he shall be put to death. Lev. 24; 15, 16.

4.   Yf any p'son shall comitt any willfull murther, w'ch is manslaughter comitted vppon mallice, hatred or cruelty, not in a mans necessary and just defence, nor by mere casualty against his will, he shall be put to death. Ex. 21; 12, 13, 14. Num. 35; 30, 31.

5.   Yf any person shall slay another through guile, ether by poysonings or other such Diuilish (Devlish) practices, he shall be put to death. Ex. 21;14.

6.   Yf any man or woman shall ly w'th any Beast
or brut creature by carnall copulation, they shall
surely be put to death, and the Beast shall be slayne
and buried. Lev. 20; 15, 16.

7.   Yf any man lye w'th mankind as he lyeth w'th
a woman, both of them have comitted abomination, they
both shall surely be put to Death. Lev. 20;13.

8.   Yf any p'son comiteth Adultery w'th a
married or espoused wife, the Adulterer and the
Adulteres shall surely be put to Death. Lev. 20; 10
and 18, 20. Deu. 22; 23, 24.

9.   Yf any man shall forcibly and w'thout
consent rauishe any mayd or Woman that is lawfull
married or contracted, he shall be put to Death. Deu.
22;25.

10.   Yf any man stealeth a man or mankind, he
shall be put to Death. Ex. 21; 16.

11.   Yf any man rise vp by false witness,
wittingly and of purpose to take away any man's life,
he shall be put to Death. Deu 19; 16, 18, 19.

12.   Yf any man shall conspire or attempte any
Inuasion, Insurrection or Rebellion against the comon
welth, he shall be put to Deth.

13.   Yf any childe or children aboue sixteene
yeers old, and of sufficient understanding, shall
curse or smite their natural father or mother, hee or
they shall bee put to Death; unlesse it can bee
sufficiently testified that the parents have been very
vnchristianly negligent in the education of such
children, or so provoake them by extreme and cruel
correction that they have beene foreced thereunto to
preserve themselues from Death or maiming. Ex. 21;
17. Lev. 20. Ex. 20; 15.

14.   Yf any man have a stubborne and rebellious
sonne, of sufficient yeares and vnderstanding, viz.,
sixteene yeares of age, which will not obey the voice
of his father or the voice of his mother, and that
when they haue chastened him, will not hearken vnto
them; then may his father and mother, being his
naturall parents, lay hold on him and bring him to the
Magestrates assembled in courte, and testify vnto
them, that theire sonne is stubborne and rebellious,
and will not obey their voyce and chastisement, but
lives in sundry notorious crimes, such a sonne shall
bee put to Death. Deu. 21; 20, 21.

DOCUMENT 45:　　The Government of Guilford, June 19,
　　　　　　　　1643

The text, complete and with the original spelling, is
taken from Bernard Christian Steiner, *A History of
the Plantation of Menunkatuck and of the Original Town
of Guilford, Connecticut* (Baltimore:　The Friedenwald
Company, 1897), 35 - 37.　Until this time the government of Guilford had been in conformity with the grant
from Lord Say and Brook to Theophilus Eaton.　As a
part of New Haven Colony, they were entitled to one
Magistrate in whom was invested the entire executive
and judicial powers.　The settlers were either freemen
or planters.　Freemen were restricted to church
members, and from their ranks were chosen all public
officers, including the Magistrate and the three or
four deputies chosen to sit with the Magistrate in
General Courts.　The planters were all those inhabitants above the age of twenty-one, with a certain
estate, which qualified them to vote in town meetings.
This unusually strict division into classes helps
explain some of the strong language in this document,
as well as why the town meeting is relatively unimpor-
tant compared with the General Court.　See Document 35
for an earlier agreement.

　　　A church was here gathered at Guilford consisting
of these 7 persons:-Mr. Henry Whitfield, Mr. John
Higginson, Mr. Samuel Desborow, Mr. William Leete, Mr.
Jacob Sheaffe, John Mepham and John Hoadley.
　　　The nineteenth day of the fourth moneth, 1643,
the ffeoffeesl in trust for purchasing the plantation
resigned up their right into the hands of the church,
and these foure of them, also wch were chosen to the
exercise of civil power, did also expresse that their
right and power for that worke was now terminated and

ended, whereof notice being taken at the public
meeting, it was further prpounded, agreed and concluded, that whereas, for the time past (while as yet
there was no church gathered amongst us) we did choose
out foure men to wit Robert Kitchel, William Chitten-
den, John Bishop and William Leete, into whose hands
we did put full power and authority to act, order and
dispatch all matters, respecting the publicke weale
and civill government of this plantation, until a
church was gathered amongst us, wch the Lord in mercy
having now done, according to the desire of or hearts,
and the said foure men at this publicke meeting,
having resigned up their trust, and power to the
intent that all power and authority might be rightly
settled within the church, as most safe and suitable
for securing of those mayne ends wch wee prpounded to
orselves in or coming hither and sitting downe together, namely, that wee might settle and uphold all
the ordinances of God in an explicit congregational
church way, wth most purity, peace and liberty, for
the benefit both of orselves and our posterities after
us. We do now therefore, all and every of us agree,
order and conclude that only such planters, as are
also members of the church   shall bee, and be
called freemen, and that such freemen only shall have
power to elect magistrates, Deputies and all other
officers of public trust or authority in matters of
importance, concerning either the *civill officers or
government here, from amongst themselves and not
elsewhere,*   and to take an account of all such officers, for the honest and faithful discharge of their
several places respectively, and to deale with and
prceed against them for all misdemeanors and delin-
quencies in their several places according to rule,
unto which Magistrates Deputies or officers we doe
freely subject orselves in all lawfull commands,
prvided that they bee yearly chosen, from time to
time, and prvided also that no lawes nor orders bee by
them made, but before all the planters, then and there
inhabiting and residing have had due warning and
notice of their meeting, or of what is to bee done so
that all weighty objections may be duly attended,
considered and according to righteousness, satis-
fyingly removed.

It is since further agreed and ordered, that in all general courts (consisting of the Magistrates and Deputies who are also appointed to keep particular courts) all orders shall be made, in general courts by the major part of the ffreemen, and all actions in particular courts, sustained by the major vote of the Magistrates and Deputies,   it provided for issue sake that when the votes fall equall in either of those courts, then the magistrate shall have a double or casting vote.

Also it is agreed that there shall bee one fixed genrall Court yearly for election of officers &c when shall be chosen the Deputies for the particular court, Treasurer, Secretary, Sureveyors of highways, Marshall, Viewers of fences, &c.

It is ordered that there shall be foure fixed prticulr Courts every yeare (viz.) the first Thursdays in ffebruary, May, September and December, when and where all the members of the Court are to attend, from time to time, at eight o'clock in the forenoon upon the penalty of five shillings for every such default.

It was further ordered that all the freemen and planters should attend each and all of these courts, and remain to their close -- unless dismissed -- under suitable but severe penalties.

And it was further ordered that whosoever so appearing and attending shall have just cause to speake to or transact any business wth the Court or company, or to or with any person or persons in their presence, they shall both in expressions and in all other manner of their behavyor, so comely and respectfully demeane themselves, as may hold forth an honorable esteem of the Authority then present, and a due attendance to peace, not speaking untill called or allowed to speake, nor addressing their speech to any but the Court, or Magistrate, or such as they shall allow him or them to speake unto, nor continuing by impertinencies, needless repetitions or multiplicatons of words, wch rather tends to darken than cleare the truth, or right of the matter upon such penalty as the Court, considering the fact or carriage wth the aggravating circumstances adjoyned shall see cause to impose and inflict.

DOCUMENT 46: New Haven Fundamentals, October 27, 1643

The text is reproduced from Francis N. Thorpe, ed., *The Federal and State Constitutions* (Washington, D. C.: Government Printing Office, 1907), pp. 526-529. He in turn drew upon the *New Haven Colonial Records, 1638-1649,* pp. 112-116. While not as well known as the Fundamental Orders of Connecticut (Document 32), the New Haven Fundamentals is every bit as interesting and important. Both should be seen as the primary constitutional precursors to the 1662 Connecticut Charter when the colonies of Connecticut and New Haven were incorporated into a royal colony. That 1662 charter was effectively written by the combined citizens of the two older colonies, or written to satisfy them.

It was agreed and concluded as a fundamental order not to be disputed or questioned hereafter that none shall be admitted to be free burghesses in any of the plantations within this jurisdiction for the future but such planters as are members of some or other of the approved churches of New England; nor shall any but such free burghesses have any vote in any election, the six present freemen at Milford enjoying the liberty with the cautions agreed; nor shall any power or trust church members as before, to be the ordinary judges to hear and determine all inferior cases, whether civil or criminal, provided that no civil cause to be tried in any of these plantation courts in value exceed 20; and that the punishment in such criminals, according to the mind of God revealed in his word touching such offenses, do not exceed stocking and whipping, or, if the fine be pecuniary, that

it exceed not five pounds. In which court, the
magistrate or magistrates, if any be chosen by the
free burghesses or the jurisdiction for that plantation, shall sit and assist, with due respect to their
place, and sentence shall be according to the vote of
the major part of each such court. Only if the
parties, or any of them, be not satisfied with the
justice of such sentences or executions, appeals or
complaints may be made from and against these courts
to the court of magistrates for the whole jurisdiction.
          3.   All such free burghesses through the whole
jurisdiction shall have vote in the election of all
magistrates, whether governor, deputy-governor, or
other magistrates, with a treasurer, a secretary, and
a marshal, etc., for the jurisdiction. And for the
ease of those free burghesses, especially in the more
remote plantations, they may by proxy vote in these
elections, though absent, their votes being sealed up
in the presence of the free burghesses themselves,
that their several liberties may be preserved and
their votes directed according to their own particular
light, and these free burghesses may, at every election, choose so many magistrates for each plantation
as the weight of affairs may require, and as they
shall find fit men for that trust. But it is provided
and agreed that no plantation shall at any election be
left destitute of a magistrate if they desire one to
be chosen out of those in church fellowship with them.
          4.   All the magistrates for the whole juris-
diction shall meet twice a year at New Haven, namely
the Monday immediately before the sitting of the two
fixed general courts hereafter mentioned, to keep a
court called the Court of Magistrates for the trial of
weighty and capital cases, whether civil or criminal,
above those limited to the ordinary judges in the
particular plantations; and to receive and try all
appeals brought to them from the aforesaid plantation
courts; and to call all the inhabitants, whether free
burghesses, free planters, or others, to account for
the breach of any laws established, and for other
misdemeanors, and to censure them according to the
quality of the offense. In which meetings of magistrates less than four shall not be accounted a court,
nor shall they carry on any business as a court. But

it is expected and required that all the magistrates
in this jurisdiction do constantly attend the public
service at the times before mentioned, and if any of
them be absent at one of the clock in the afternoon on
Monday aforesaid when the court shall sit, or if any
of them depart the town without leave while the court
sits, he or they shall pay for any such default twenty
shilings fine, unless some providence of God occasion
the same, which the court of magistrates shall judge
of from time to time. And all sentences in this court
shall pass by the vote of the major part of the
magistrates therein. But from this court of magistrates appeals and complaints may be made and brought
to the general court as the last and highest of this
jurisdiction. But in all appeals or complaints from
or to what court soever due costs and damages shall be
paid by him or them that make appeal or complaint
without just cause.

    5.   Besides the plantation courts and court of
magistrates, there shall be a general court for the
jurisdiction which shall consist of the governor,
deputy-governor, and all the magistrates within the
jurisdiction, and two deputies for every plantation in
the jurisdiction, which deputies shall from time to
time be chosen against the approach of any such
general court by the aforesaid free burghesses, and
sent with due certificate to assist in the same. All
which, both governor and deputy-governor, magistrates
and deputies, shall have their vote in the said court.
This general court shall always sit at New Haven,
unless upon weighty occasion the general court see
cause for a time to sit elsewhere, and shall assemble
twice every year, namely the first Wednesday in April
and the last Wednesday in October. In the latter of
which courts the governor, deputy-governor, and all
the magistrates for the whole jurisdiction, with a
treasurer, a secretary, and marshal, shall yearly be
chosen by all the free burghesses before mentioned.
Besides which two fixed courts, the governor, or in
his absence the deputy-governor, shall have power to
summon a general court at any other time as the urgent
and extraordinary occasions of the jurisdiction may
require. And at all general courts, whether ordinary
or extraordinary, the governor and deputy-governor,
and all the rest of the magistrates for the

jurisdiction with the deputies for the several
plantations, shall sit together til the affairs of the
jurisdiction be dispatched or may safely be respited.
And if any of the said magistrates or deputies shall
either be absent at the first sitting of the said
general court, unless some providence of God, hinder,
which the said court shall judge of, or depart or
absent at the first sitting of the said general court,
unless some providence of God, hinder, which the said
court shall judge of, or depart or absent themselves
disorderly before the court be finished, he or they
shall each of them pay twenty shillings fine, with due
considerations of further aggravations if there shall
be cause. Which general court shall, with all care
and diligence, provide for the maintenance of the
purity of religion and suppress the contrary,
according to their best light from the word of God and
all wholesome and sound advice which shall be given by
the elders and churches in the jurisdiction so far as
may concern their civil power to deal therein.

Secondly, they shall have power to make and
repeal laws and, while they are in force, to require
execution of them in all the several plantations.

Thirdly, to impose an oath upon all the magistrates for the faithful discharge of the trust committed to them according to their best abilities, and
to call them to account for the breach of any laws
established or for other misdemeanors and to censure
them as the quality of the offense shall require.

Fourthly, to impose an oath of fidelity and due
subjection to the laws upon all the free burghesses,
free planters, and other inhabitants within the whole
jurisdiction.

Fifthly, to settle and levy rate and contributions upon all the several plantations for the public
service of the jurisdiction.

Sixthly, to hear and determine all causes,
whether civil or criminal, which by appeal or complaint shall be orderly brought to them from any of
the other courts or from any of the other plantations.
In all which, with whatsoever else shall fall within
their cognizance or judicature, they shall,proceed
according to the scriptures, which is the rule of all
righteous laws and sentences. And nothing shall pass
an act of the general court but by the consent of the

major part of the magistrates and the greater part of the deputies.

These generals being thus laid and settled, though with purpose that the circumstntials such as the value of the causes to be tried in the plantations courts, the ordinary and fixed times of meetings both for the general courts, the ordinary and fixed times of meetings both for the general courts and courts of magistrates, how often and when they shall sit, with the fines for absences or default, be hereafter considered of, continued, or altered as may best and most advance the course of justice and best suit the occasions of the plantations, the court proceed to present particular business of the jurisdiction.

DOCUMENT 47:   The New England Confederation, 1643

Text taken from *The Annals of America, Vol. I,*
(Chicago: William Benton, Publisher). These twelve
articles drawn up and approved by the four colonies of
Massachusetts, Plymouth, Connecticut, and New Haven
constitute the first major attempt at federalism in
America. The federation lasted formally until 1684,
although in fact it ceased effectively functioning in
1664.

ARTICLES OF CONFEDERATION between the plantations
under the government of the Massachusetts, the plantations under the government of New Plymouth, the
plantations under the government of Connecticut, and
the government of New Haven with the plantations in
combination therewith:
   WHEREAS we all came into these parts of America
with one and the same end and aim, namely, to advance
the kingdom of our Lord Jesus Christ and to enjoy the
liberties of the Gospel in purity with peace; *and
whereas* in our settling (by a wise providence of God)
we are further dispersed upon the seacoasts and rivers
than was at first intended, so that we cannot according to our desire with convenience communicate in
one government and jurisdiction; *and whereas* we live
encompassed with people of several nations and strange
languages which hereafter may prove injurious to us or
our posterity; and forasmuch as the natives have
formerly committed sundry insolences and outrages upon
several plantations of the English and have of late
combined themselves against us; and seeing by reason
of those sad distractions in England which they have
heard of, and by which they know we are hindered from
that humble way of seeking advice, or reaping those
comfortable fruits of protection, which at other times

we might well expect, we, therefore, do conceive it
our bounden duty, without delay, to enter into a
present consociation among ourselves, for mutual help
and strength in all our future concernments.

That, as in nation and religion, so in other
respects, we be and continue one according to the
tenor and true meaning of the ensuing articles.
Wherefore it is fully agreed and concluded by and
between the parties of jurisdictions above named, and
they jointly and severally do by these presents agree
and conclude that they all be and henceforth be called
by the name of the United Colonies of New England.

2.   The said United Colonies, for themselves and
their posterities, do jointly and severally hereby
enter into a firm and perpetual league of friendship
and amity for offense and defense, mutual advice and
succor upon all just occasions, both for preserving
and propogating the truth and liberties of the Gospel
and for their own mutual safety and welfare.

3.   It is further agreed that the plantations
which at present are, or herefter shall be, settled
within the limits of the Massachusetts shall be
forever under the Massachusetts, and shall have
particular jurisdiction among themselves in all cases
as an entire body; and that Plymouth, Connecticut, and
New Haven shall each of them have like particular
jurisdiction and government within their limits, and
in reference to the plantations which already are
settled, or shall hereafter be erected, or shall
settle within their limits respectively; provided that
no other jurisdiction shall hereafter be taken in as a
distinct head or member of this confederation, nor
shall any other plantation or jurisdiction in present
being, and not already in combination or under the
jurisdiction of any of these confederates, be received
by any of them; nor shall any two of the confederates
join in one jurisdction without consent of the rest,
which consent to be interpreted as is expresed in the
6th article ensuing.

4.   It is by these confederates agreed that the
charge of all just wars, whether offensive or defensive, upon what part or member of this confederation
soever they fall, shall both in men and provisions and
all other disbursements be borne by all the parts of
this confederation in different proportions according

to their different ability in manner following, namely, that the commissioners for each jurisdiction, from time to time as there shall be occasion, bring a true account and number of all the males in every plantation or any way belonging to or under their federal jurisdictions of what quality or condition soever they be from sixteen years old to threescore being inhabitants there. And that according to the different numbers which from time to time shall be found in each jurisdiction, upon a true and just account, the service of men and all charges of the war be borne by the poll; each jurisdiction or plantation being left to their own course and custom of rating themselves and people according to their different estates with due respects to their qualities and exemptions among themselves though the confederation take no notice of any such privilege; and that according to their different charge of each jurisdiction and plantation, the whole advantage of the war (if it please God to bless their endeavors), whether it be in lands, goods, or persons, shall be proportionately divided among the said confederates.

5. It is further agreed that, if any of these jurisdictions or any plantation under or in combination with them be invaded by any enemy whatsoever, upon notice and request of any three magistreates of that jurisdiction so invaded, the rest of the confederates, without any further meeting or expostulation, shall forthwith send aid to the confederate in danger but in different proportions; namely, the Massachusetts, 100 men sufficiently armed and provided for such a service and journey, and each of the rest, 45 so armed and provided, or any less number, if less be required according to this proportion . . . But in any such case of sending men for present aid, whether before or after such order or alteration, it is agreed that at the meeting of the commissioners for this confederation the cause of such war or invasion be duly considered; and if it appear that the fault lay in the parties so invaded that then that jurisdiction or plantation make just satisfaction, both to the invaders whom they have injured, and bear all the charges of the war themselves, without requiring any allowance from the rest of the confederates toward the same. And,

further, that if any jurisdiction see any danger of
any invasion approaching, and there be time for a
meeting, that in such case three magistreates of that
jurisdiction may summon a meeting at such convenient
place as themselves shall think meet, to consider and
provide against the threatened danger; provided when
they are met they may remove to what place they
please. Only while any of these four confederates
have but three magistrates in their jurisdiction,
their request or summons from any two of them shall be
accounted of equal force with the three mentioned in
both the clauses of this article, till there be an
increase of magistrates there.

    6.   It is also agreed that for the managing and
concluding of all affairs proper and concerning the
whole confederation, two commissioners shall be chosen
by and out of each of these four jurisdictions;
namely, two for the Massachusetts, two for Plymouth,
two for Connecticut, and two for New Haven, being all
in church fellowship with us, which shall bring full
power from their several General Courts respectively
to hear, examine, weigh, and determine all affairs of
our war or peace leagues, aids, charges, and numbers
of men for war, division of spoils and whatsoever is
gotten by conquest, receiving of more confederates for
plantations into combination with any of the confederates, and all things of like nature, which are the
proper concommitants or consequents of such a confederation for amity, offense, and defense, not inter-
meddling with the government of any of the jurisdictions, which by the 3rd article is preserved entirely
to themselves . . . It is further agreed that these
eight commissioners shall meet once every year,
besides extraordinary meetings (according to the 5th
article), to consider, treat, and conclude of all
affairs belonging to this confederation . . .

    8.   It is also agreed that the commissioners for
this confederation hereafter at their meetings,
whether ordinary or extraordinary, as they may have
commission or opportunity, do endeavor to frame and
establish agreements and orders in general cases of a
civil nature, wherein all the plantations are interested, for preserving peace among themselves and
preventing as much as may be all occasion of war or
difference with others, as about the free and speedy

passage of justice in every jurisdiction, to all the
confederates equally as to their own, receiving those
that remove from one plantation to another without due
certificates; how all the jurisidictions may carry it
toward the Indians, that they neither grown insolent
nor be injured without due satisfaction, lest war
break in upon the confederates through such miscarriage.

It is agreed that if any servant run away from
his master into any other of these confederated
jurisdictions, that in such case, upon the certificate
of one magistrate in the jurisdiction out of which the
said servant shall be delivered either to his master
or any other that pursues and brings such certificate
of proof. And that upon the escape of any prisoner
whatsoever, or fugitive for any criminal cause,
whether breaking prison, or getting away from the
officer, or otherwise escaping, upon the certificate
of two magistrates of the jurisdiction out of which
the escape is made, that he was a prisoner, or such an
offender at the time of the escape, the magistreates,
or some of them of that jurisdiction where for the
present the said prisoner or fugitive abides, shall
forthwith grant such a warrant as the case will bear
for the apprehending of any such person, and the
delivery of him into the hands of the officer or other
person who pursues him. And if there be help required
for the safe returning of any such offender, then it
shall be granted to him that craves the same, he
paying the charges thereof.

9.   And for that the justest wars may be of
dangerous consequence, especially to the smaller
plantations in these United Colonies, it is agreed
that neither the Massachusetts, Plymouth, Connecticut,
nor New Haven, nor any of the members of them, shall
at any time hereafter begin, undertake, or engage
themselves, or this confederation, or any part thereof
in any war whatsoever (sudden exigents with the
necessary consequents thereof excepted which are also
to be moderated as much as the case will permit)
without the consent and agreement of the forenamed
eight commissioners, or at least six of them, as in
the 6th article is provided; and that no charge be
required of any of the confederates in case of a
defensive war till the aid commissioners have met and

approved the justice of the war, and have agreed upon
the sum of money to be levied, which sum is then to be
paid by the several confederates in proportion according to the 4th article . . .

11. It is further agreed that if any of the
confederates shall hereafter break any of these
present articles, or be any other ways injurious to
any one of the other jurisdictions, that both peace
and this present confederation may be entirely preserved without violation.

DOCUMENT 48:   Massachusetts Bicameral Ordinance,
                March 7, 1644

Complete text with original spelling taken from N.B.
Shurtleff, ed., *Massachusetts Colonial Records: Vol.
II, Records of the Governor and Company of the
Massachusetts Bay Colony* (Boston: 1853-54), 58-59.
Discussions of the historical context, as well as
examples of related documents can be found in Michael
Kammen, *Deputyes and Libertyes: The Origins of
Representative Government in America*   (New York:
Alfred A. Knopf, 1969). See Document 49.

        Forasmuch as, after long experience, wee find
divers inconveniences in the manner of our proceeding
in Courts by magistrates & deputies siting together, &
accounting it wisdome to follow the laudable practice
of other states who have layd groundworks for government & order in the issuing of business of greatest &
highest consequence,-
        It is therefore ordered, first, that the magis-
trates may sit & act busines by themselves, by drawing
up bills & orders which they shall see good in their
wisdome, which haveing agreed upon, they may present
them to the deputies to bee considered of, how good &
wholesome such orders are for the country, & accordingly to give their assent or dissent, the deputies in
like manner siting apart by themselves, & consulting
about such orders & lawes as they in their discretion
& experience shall find meete for common good, which
agreed upon by them they may present to the magistrates, who, according to their wisdome, haveing
seriously considered of them, may consent unto them or
disalow them; & when any orders have passed the
approbation of both magistrates & deputies, then such
orders to bee ingrossed, & in the last day of the

Court to bee read deliberately, & full assent to bee
given; provided, also, that all matters of judicature
which this Court shall take cognisance of shal bee
issued in like manner.

DOCUMENT 49:   Massachusetts Ordinance on the
              Legislature, November 13, 1644

The complete and original text is taken from N.B.
Shurtleff, ed., *Records of the Governor and Company
of the Massachusetts Bay Colony.*   See Document 48
for related information. This is a comprehensive
ordinance altering the size and mode of electing the
legislature. See Document 15 for the original formation of this legislature.

    It is ordered, that the freemen of this jurisdic-
tion shall meete in their severall townes within two
months after the date hereof, to consider of whom they
would nominate to be put to vote upon the day of
election of newe magistrates, to the number of seaven,
at which meeting every freeman shall have liberty to
put in his vote for whom hee thinketh fit, all which
votes votes shal be sealed up at that meeting, & sent
by some one or two (whom they shall choose) to the
sheire townes in each sheire,1 upon the last 5th day
of the last month, at which meeting the said selectmen
of every towne (by whom the votes being brought) shall
not have power to open them, being sealed up, as
before, but shall choose one or two from amongst
themselves, by whom they shall send the aforesaid
votes, being all sealed up in one paper, unto Boston,
on the last third day of the first month, at which
meeting there shal be two magistrates, before whom the
proxies shal be opened & sorted; & those persons
nominated for magistrates that have most votes, to the
number of seaven, shal be they that shal be put to
vote at the day of election; & that such as have most
votes to be first nominated & put to election, that
the freemen may know for whom to send in their proxies.   The select men of every sheire, being at this

meeting, shall take care to send to the aforesaid
selectmen of every towne whom they be that are to be
put to vote, which select men of every towne shall
call a meeting of their townes, & acquaint them whom
they are, that so the freemen may have time to consider of them, & send in their proxies accordingly; & no
other shal be put to vote but such as are agreed upon,
as before.

Whereas wee haveing found by experience that the
charge of this Generall Court groweth very great &
burthensome, in regard of the continuall increase of
deputies sent unto the same, & further forseeing that
as townes increase the number wil be still augmented,
to the unsupportable burthen of this common wealth; as
also it being thought a matter worthy the triall,
dureing the standing of this order, to have the use of
the negative vote forborne, both by magistrates &
deputies, the premisses considered, it is declared by
the Court, (if the freemen shall accept thereof,) that
a tryall shal be made for one yeare ensuing the day of
election next, by choyce of twenty deputies out of the
severall sheires to equall the number of magistrates
chosen upon the day of election, the choyce of them to
be thus divided: Suffolke chall choose sixe, Middlesex sixe, & essex & Norfolk, being joyned in one,
shall chose eight; and further, to the end the ablest
gifted men may be made use of in so weighty a worke,
it shal be at the liberty of the freemen to choose
them, in their own sheires, or elsewhere, as they
shall see best, the choyce to be after this manner:
the freemen of each shire, meeting in their owne
severall townes together within two months next
following, shall there give in their severall votes
for so many deputies as belong unto their sheire to
choose, which votes shal be forthwith sealed up, & one
or two chosen to carry them sealed to their sheire
town the last 5th day of the last month following,
where, in the presence of one magistrate, they shal be
opened & conferd togeather, & so many as shall have
the major vote of the sheire are chosen, not exceeding
the number aforesaid; & such as are so chosen shall
assemble themselves at the next Court of Election,
presented under the hands of those which were sent
from the townes to the sheire meetings aforesaid, the
names & severall number of vote they there had, from

which assembly those onely that had the greatest
number of votes, to equall the number of magistrates
then chosen, shal be confirmed, & the rest dismissed
from the present sevice, from every sheire a like
number, so neare as may be; the magistrates & deputies
thus chosen shall sit togeather as a full & sufficient
Generall Court, to act in al things by the major vote
of the whole Court; and further, it is declared, that
every towne shall fourthwith, namely, by the last of
the next month, send in under the hands of their late
deputies their vote, assenting or dissenting to this
proposition, to the house of Mr. Nowell, who, together
with one of the late deputies of Charlestowne, one of
Cambridge, & one of Boston, shall have power to peruse
the said votes, & if they shall find that the greater
number of the townes shall agree that this may be
propounded to them shall proceed, they shall thereupon
fourthwith certify the Governor thereof, who shall
thereupon give speedy notice to every towne that they
may proceed according to this declaration; & whereas
it may fall out that two or more sheires may make
choyce of one & the same men, it is therefore provided, that Suffolk shall begin makeing knowne to
Middlesex whom they have chosen, who the next 4th day
following shall make their choyce, & send word to
Essex & Norfolke whom Suffolk & themselves have
chosen; then the next 4th day shall Essex and Norfolke
make their choyce.

DOCUMENT 50:   Majority Vote of Deputies and
              Magistrates Required for the Passage
              of Laws in Connecticut, February 5,
              1645

Text taken from J. H. Trumbull and C. J. Hoadly, eds.,
*The Public Records of the Colony of Connecticut, 1636
- 1776* (Hartford, Conn.: Brown and Parsons, 1850),
Vol. I, 356. Text is complete, and the spelling is
unaltered. The Fundamental Orders referred to in this
text is reproduced as Document 32. Once again, the
date is confused because at the time the new year
began in March, making January and February part of
the old year in their calendar system. In our calendar system the date of this document should place it
in 1645.

     Whereas it is said in the Fundamental Orders that
the general court shall consist of the governor or
some one chosen to moderate and four other magistrates
at least, it is now ordered and adjudged to be a
lawful corut if the governor or deputy with other
magistreates be present in court with the major part
of deputies lawfully chosen. But no act shall pass or
stand for a law which is not confirmed both by the
major part of the said magistrates, and by the major
part of the deputies there present in court, both
magistrates and deputies being allowed, either of
them, a negative vote. Also the particular court may
be kept by the governor or deputy with [3] other
magistrates.

DOCUMENT 51:   Warwick Agreement, August 8, 1647

Complete text with the original spelling taken from J.
R. Bartlett, ed., *Records of the Colony of Rhode
Island and Providence Plantations in New England:
Vol. I, 1636 - 1663*   (Providence: A. Crawford Greene
and Brother, State Printers, 1856), 134-35.   Unlike
Providence, Portsmouth, and Newport, Warwick did not
write its own founding document prior to the granting
of an official charter in 1644.   The settlers here did
not feel it lawful to erect their own government
without explicit authority from England.   Three years
after Rhode Island was chartered as a colony, this
document was finally written.

      KNOW ALL MEN, Colonies, Peoples, and Nations,
unto whom the same hereof shall come; that wee, the
chiefe Sachems, Princes or Governours of the Nanhigan-
sets (in the part of America, now called New-England),
together with the joynt and unanimous consent of all
our people and subjects, inhabitants thereof, do upon
serious consideration, mature and deliberate advise
and counsell, great and weighty grounds and reasons
moving us thereunto, whereof one most effectual unto
us, is, that noble fame we have heard of that Great
and mighty Prince, Charles, King of Great Britaine, in
that honorable and princely care he hath all his
servants, and true and loyall subjects, the consideration whereof moveth and bendeth our hearts with one

consent, freely, voluntarily, and most humbly to
submit, subject, and give over ourselves, peoples,
lands, rights, inheritances, and possessions whatsoever, in ourselves and our heires successively for
ever, unto the protection, care and government of that
worthy and royal Prince, Charles, King of Great
Britaine and Ireland, his heires and successors
forever, to be ruled and governed according to the
ancient and honorable lawes and customes, established
in that so renowned realme and kingdome of Old England; we do, therefore, by these presents, confesse,
and most willingly and submissively acknowledge
ourselves to be the humble, loving and obedient
servants and subjects of his Majestie; to be ruled,
ordered, and disposed of, in ourselves and ours,
according to his princely wisdome, counsell and lawes
of that honorable State of Old England;
                                        and wrighting us
of what wrong is, or may be done unto us, according to
his honorable lawes and customes, exercised amongst
his subjects, in their preservation and safety, and in
the defeating and overthrow of his, and their enemies;
not that we find ourselves necessitated hereunto, in
repect of our relation, or occasion we have, or may
have, with any of the natives in these parts, knowing
ourselves sufficient defence, and able to judge in any
matter or cause in that respect; but have just cause
of jealousy and suspicion of some of His Majesty's
pretended subjects. Therefore our desire is, to have
our matters and causes heard and tried according to
his just and equall lawes, in that way and order His
Highness shall please to appoint:

                having ourselves been the chief Sachems,
or Princes successively, of the country, time out of
mind; and for our present and lawfull enacting hereof,
being so farre remote from His Majestie, wee have, by
joynt consent, made choice of foure of his loyall and
loving subjects, our trusty and well-beloved friends,
Samuel Gorton, John Wickes, Randall Houlden and John
Warner, whom we have deputed, and made our lawful
Attornies or Commissioners, not only for the acting
and performing of this our Deed, in the behalfe of his
Highnesse, but also for the safe custody, careful
conveyance, and declaration hereof unto his grace:

being done upon the lands of the Nanhigansett, at a
Court or Generall Assembly called and assembled together, of purpose, for the publick enacting, and
manifestation hereof.

And for the further confirmation, and establishing
of this our Act and Deed, wee, the abovesaid Sachems or
Princes, have, according to that commendable custome of
Englishmen, subscribed our names and sett our seals
hereunto, as so many testimonies of our fayth and
truth, our love and loyalty to that our dread Sove-
raighne, and that according to the Englishmen's account.

DOCUMENT 52:   Acts and Orders of 1647

Spelling is as appears in John Russell Bartlett, ed.,
*Records of the Colony of Rhode Island and Providence
Plantations in New England* (Providence: A. Crawford
Greene and Brother, State Printers, 1856). The text is
quite lengthy and is here reproduced only in part.
Sections excluded deal with more standard or mundane
aspects of law such as fraud, forgery, trespassing,
larceny, assault, robbery, burglary, etc. Although
having every appearance of being simply a code of law,
careful reading indicates that the Acts and Orders of
1647, like the Pilgrim Code of Law (Document 21), is an
almost complete document of foundation and qualifies as
one of the early constitutions.

Acts and Orders

Made and agreed upon at the Generall Court of Election,
held at Portsmouth, in Rhode Island, the 19, 20, 21 of
May, Anno. 1647, for the Colonie and Province of
Providence.
    Mr. John Coggeshall is chosen Moderator of the
present Assembly.
    2.   It was Voted and found, that the major part
of the Colonie was present at this Assemblie, whereby
there was full power to transact.
    3.   It was further agreed, that in case the
Assemblie departe unto the number of Fortie; those
fortie shall stay and act as if the whole were present,
and be of as full authoritie.
    4.   It was agreed, that all should set their
hands to an engagement to the Charter.
    5.   It was agreed and ordered, that a week before
any General Courte, notice should be given to every

Towne by the head officer, that they chuse a Committee
for the Transaction of the affaires there, except it
bee for the Election of Generall Officers; and such as
go not, may send their votes sealed.

6.   It was ordered, upon the request of the
Commissioners of the Towne of Providence, that their
second instruction should be granted and established
unto the, Vidg't. Wee do voluntarily assent, and are
freely willing to receive and to be governed by the
Lawes of England, together with the way of the Administration of them, soe far as the nature and constitution
of this Plantation will admit, desiring (soe far as
possible may be), to hold a correspondence with the
whole Colonie in the modell that hath been latelie
shewn vnto us by our worthy Friends of the Island, if
the Generall Court shall compleate and confirm the
same, or any other Modell as the Generall Courte shall
agree vpon according to our Charter.

7.   It was unanimously agreed, That we do all
owne and submit to the Lawes, as they are contracted in
the Bulke with the Administration of Justice, according
thereto, which are to stand in force till the next
Generall Courte of Election, and every Towne to have a
Coppie of them, and then to present what shall appeare
therein not to be suitable to the Constitution of the
place, and then to amend it.

8.   It was agreed, that Warwick should have the
same priviledges as Providence.

9.   It was agreed, that the Generall Courte of
Tryall should be held at Newport vpon the second
Tuesday of June next ensuing.

10.   It was agreed, that the Election of Offices
should be by papers.

Mr. John Coggeshall is chosen President of this
Province, or Colonie.

Mr. Roger Williams is chosen Assistant of
         Providence,
Mr. John Samford is chosen Assistant of
         Portsmouth,
Mr. Wm. Coddington is chosen Assistant of
         Newport,
Mr. Randall Holden is chosen Assistant of
         Warwick,
William Dyre is chosen Gen. Recorder,
Mr. Jeremy Clerke is chosen Treasurer.

11. It is ordered, that all cases presented,
concerning General Matters for the Colony, shall be
first stated in the Townes, Vigd't, That is, when a
case is propounded, The Towne where it is propounded,
shall agitate and fully discuss the matter in their
Towne Meetings and conclude by Vote; and then shal the
Recorder of the Towne, or Towne Clerk, send a coppy of
the agreement to every of the other three Townes, who
shall agitate the case likewise in each Towne and vote
it, and collect the votes. Then shall they commend it
to the Committee for the General Courte (then a meeting
called), who being assembled and finding the Major
parte of the Colonie concurring in the case, it shall
stand for a Law till the next Generall Assembly of all
the people, then and there to be considered, whether
any longer to stand yea or no; Further it is agreed,
that six men of each Towne shall be the number of the
Committe premised, and to be freely chosen. And
further it is agreed, that when the General Courte thus
assembled, shall determine the cases before hand thus
presented, It shall also be lawful for the said General
Court, and hereby are they authorized, that if vnto
them or any of them some case or cases shall be presented that may be deemed necessary for the public
weale and good of the whole, they shall fully debate,
discuss and determine ye matter among themselves; and
then shall each Committee returning to their Towne
declare what they have done in the case or cases
premised. The Townes then debating and concluding, the
votes shall be collected and sealed up, and then by the
Towne Clarke of each Towne shall be sent with speed to
the General Recorder, who, in the presence of the
President shall open the votes; and if the major vote
determine the case, it shall stand as a Law till the
next General Assemblie then or there to be confirmed or
nullified.
12. It is ordered, that the Courte of Election
shall alway be held upon the first Tuesday after the
15th of May, annually, if wind or weather hinder not.
Then the General Court of Tyrall immediately to succeed
vpon the dissolving of the said General Court, Vidg't:
the next day; and that the next General Court of

Election shall be held at Providence Towne. Further,
it is agreed, that forasmuch as many may be necessarily
detained, that they cannot come to the General Court of
Election, that then they shall send their votes sealed
upon unto the said Court, which shall be as effectual
as their personal appearances.

13. It is ordered, that each Towne shall choose
and order ye authoritie of two Surveyors for the
Highways, and appoint time to mend them; also that they
are to have notice of all cattle that shall be exported, and returne the marks of them unto the Towne;
and if any shall presume to export any without giving
notice of it to the men appointed, or their Deputies he
shall forfeit all such Cattle so exported, or the worth
of them.

14. It is ordered, that the Inhabitants of
Portsmouth and Newport here present doe presently
choose their officers of the Island; but that this act
shall be not precedent for the future, but that the
constant course of choosing shall be hereafter, when as
the year is out, as the Major votes of the Townes of
Portsmouth and Newport shall order it sometimes before
the year is out, in some peaceable and moderate way
which they shall agree upon.

The Engagement of the Officers

You. A. B_____, being called and chosen
vnto public employment, and the office of _____,
by the free vote and consent of ye Inhabitants of the
Province of Providence Plantations (now orderly met),
do, in the present Assemblie, engage yourself faithfully and truly to the utmost of your power to execute
the commission committed vnto you; and do hereby
promise to do neither more nor less in that respect
than that which the Colonie [authorized] you to do
according to the best of your understanding.

We, the Inhabitants of the Province of Providence
Plantations being here orderly met, and having by free
vote chosen you _____, to public office and
officers for the due administration of Justice and the
execution thereof throughout the whole Colonie, do

hereby engage ourselves to the utmost of our power to suport and vphold you in your faithful performance thereof.

15. It is ordered, that the Councills of Newport and Portsmouth, shall consult and agree how and in what manner (within these thirtie dayes) the monthly and quarterly Courts shall be ordered, and who shall sit therein; further, it is agreed, that all cases depending shall be heard and issued at the next Generall Court of Tryall.

16. It is ordered, that the Townes shall appoint men to view all Goates and Swine killed or to be killed, and shew the eare markes of them unto the said persons or one of them, whereby it may appeare to be their own; and if any shall presume to conceale eyther Swine or Goats so killed or to be killed, shall forfeit five pounds; one half to the State, the other to him that will sue for it, eyther by action or bill. It shall be lawfull also, for those that are appointed to the service being necessarily detayned, to make, constitute, and appoint a Deputie.

17. It is ordered, that John Cooke and Thomas Brownell, are chosen Water Bailies for the Colonie.

18. It is ordered, that the Seale of the Province   shall be an Anchor.

19. It is ordered, that the Councils of the Townes consisting of six men shall be chosen at their next Towne Meetings.

20. It is ordered, that the Sea Lawes, otherwise called the Lawes of Oleron, shall be in force among us for the benefit of Seamen (vpon ye Island), and the Chief Officers in the Towne shall have power to summon the Court and determine the cause or causes presented.

21. It is ordered, that none shall goe out of the Court without leave; or if any do depart, he shall leve his vote behind him, that his power remain, though his person be absent.

22. It is ordered, forasmuch as Mr. Roger Williams hath taken great paines and expended much time in the obtayning of the Charter for this Province of Noble Lords and Governors; be it enacted and established, that in regard of his so great travaile, charges and good endeavours, we do freely give and grant to the said Roger Williams one hundred pounds, to be levied

out of the three townes, Vidg't: Fifty pounds out of
Newport, thirtie pounds out of Portsmouth, and twentie
pounds out of Providence, which rate is to be levied
and paid in by the last of November next.

23. It is ordered, that forasmuch as there are
some remote places inhabited and possessed within our
Charter, and it is found necessary that a vigilant eye
be had over them, it is ordered, that Newport shall
take into their custody the Trading house or houses of
the Narragansett Bay; Portsmouth to take in Prudence;
and Patuxet shall be left to their choice, whether they
will have Providence, Portsmouth or Newport over them.
And it is ordered, that the officers of each Towne
shall have full power and authoritie in them or eyther
of them, according to their precincts, by this present
Court assyned.

24. It is ordered, that there is free Libertie
granted for the free Inhabitants of ye Province (if
they will) to erect an Artillery Garden, and those that
are desirous to advance the Art Military, shall have
freedom to exercise themselves therein, and to agree of
their forme, and choose their officers, as they shall
agree among themselves.

25.   Provided,   shall
choose their officers   after the 15th of
June next, vpon paine of forfeiting Tenn pounds a Town,
if neglected.

26. It is ordered, that in cases of necessity
without the bounds of the Townes, a special officer for
ye execution of Justice, may be authorized by any of
the Generall Officers for a general case.

27. It is ordered, that ye General Officers shall
write to the Bay about Patuxet Inhabitants; and also
write to the Inhabitants thereof to owne and choose the
Government of the Province.

28. It is ordered, that the Dutch, French or
other Alliants, or any Englishman inhabiting among
them, shall pay the like customs and duties, as we doe
among them for all such goods as shall be imported for
the English, excepting beaver. Also, we do absolutely
prohibit them or any of them to trade or barter with
the Indians within our Jurisdiction, upon paine of
forfeiture of Shipp and Goods; and this to take effect
after due notice given. The Generall Officers are

ordered to write to the Dutch Governor, and upon the
returne of the answer it shall be commended to the
Townes to consider of.

29. It is ordered, that all ye Inhabitants in
each Towne shall choose their Military Officers from
among themselves on the first Tuesday after the 12th of
March; and that eight sevarall times in the yeare, the
Bands of each plantation or Towne, shall, openlie in
the field, be exercised and disciplined by their
Commanders and Officers, in the months of May, August,
January and February excepted; and on the first Monday
of ye other months, all the Train Bands to make their
personal appearances completely armed, to attend their
colors, by 8 o'clock in the morning, at the second
beate of ye Drum; and if any appear not, they shall
forfeit and pay five shillings into the hands of the
Clarke of ye Band; and if any shall come defective in
his Armes or furniture, he shall forfeit and pay ye sum
of twelve pence, after the Town Council have caused
them to be supplied; and that all men who shall come
and remaine ye space of twenty days, shall be liable to
ye injunction of this order; Provided, herdsmen,
fighter-men and such as be left of necessity at Farmes,
shall pay two shilings and sixpence for every dayes
absence: And that the two Chief officers in each
Towne, to witt: one of the Commonweale, the other of
the Band, upon the exhibition of the complaint by ye
Clark (which shall be within three dayes after the
fault committed), shall judge and determine of ye
reasons of the excuses, who, upon the hearing thereof,
shall determine whether every such person shall pay
five shillings, two shillings and sixpence, or nothing;
and according as they find any defective, shall give
their warrants to ye Clark to distraine their Goods if
they shall refuse to pay what is ordered. And if the
Clarke shall neglect to gather up what is ordered, he
shall forfeit and pay so much into the hands of the
Captain, the next training day; And that all the fines
and forfeitures shall be imployed to the use and
service of the Band. And the Towne Councils shall have
power to cause those which are defective in armes, to
be supplied in an equal way according to Estate and
strength. And if any of ye Traine Band after his
appearance shall refuse or neglect the command of his

Captain, to be exercised and disciplined, he shall
forfeit as much as if he had not appeared: And that
the Town Council shall order the power of the Military
Officers within the Towne, and in all caes that concerne ye whole, the President and ye foure assistants,
and ye Captains of every Band shall be the Councill of
Warr; that if any of the Officers of ye Band be at any
time left out, they shall beare Armes again, for ye
Constitution of our place will not beare the contrary:
that every Inhabitant of the Island above sixteen or
under sixty yeares of age, shall alwayes be provided of
a Musket, one pound of powder, twenty bullets, and two
fadom of Match, with sword, rest, bandaleers all
completely furnished.

    30. It is ordered, that in regard of ye many
incursions that we are subjected vnto, and that an
Alarum for ye giving of notice thereof is necessary
when occasion is offered. It is agreed, that this form
be observed. Vidg't: Three Muskets distinctly discharged, and a Herauld appointed to go speedilie threw
the Towne, and crie, Alarum! Alarum! ! and the Drum to
beate incessantly; upon which, all to repair (upon
forfeiture and the Town Councill shall order) unto the
Town House, there to receive information of the Town
Councill what is farther to be done.

    31. It is ordered and agreed, that if any person
or persons, shall sell, give deliver, or any otherwayes
convey any powder, shott, lead, gunn, pistoll, sword,
dagger, halberd or pike to the Indians that are or may
prove offensive to this Colonie, or any member thereof,
he or they, for the first offence, shall forfeit ye sum
of five pounds; and for his second offence, offending
in the same kind, and being lawfully convicted, shall
forfeit ten pounds; half to the State, and half tohim
that will sew for it, and no wager of Law by any means
to be allowed to the offender. And, it is further
ordered, that if any person shall mend or repaire their
Guns, or _____ he shall forfeit the same penaltie.

    32. It is ordered, that the Towne Officers shall
given their enagagements in their severall Townes to ye
General Officer in that Towne, before they execute
their office.

33. It is ordered, that if the Indians shall offer to putt away upon exchange or barter, their false peag for good, and warrant it so to be, and it be found otherwise, it shall be confiscated to the Public Treasury.

34. It is ordered, that every Towne shall have a coppy of the Lawes and Orders, and that each Towne shall pay for their coppy; and also, that the Councell for the Townes shall order the fees for their Officers, and the Generall Officers shall order the fees of the General Officers: Provided, that nothing already concluded in the Bulck of Lawes be any wayes crossed or envaded.

For the Province of Providence.

Forasmuch as we have received from our Noble Lords and Honored Governours, and that by virtue of an ordinance of the Parliament of Engalnd, a free and absolute Charter of Civill incorporation, &c. Wee do joyntlie agree to incorporate ourselves, and soe to remaine a Body Politicke by the authoritie thereof, and therefore do declare to own ourselves and one another to be Members of the same Body, and to have right to the Freedome and priviledges thereof by subscribing our names to thess words, following: vidg't.

Wee, whose names are here vnder written, doe engage ourselves to the vttmost of our Estates and Strength, to mainteyne the authority and to enjoy the Libertie granted to vs by our Charter, in the extent of itt according to the Letter, and to mainteyne each other by the same authoritie, in his lawfull right and Libertie.

And with this our Charter gives vs powre to governe ourselves and such other as come among vs, and by such a forme of Civill Government as by the Voluntarie consent, &c., shall be found most suitable to our Estate and condition,

It is agreed, by this present Assembly thus incorporate, and by this present act declared, that the forme of Government established in is DEMOCRATICALL; that is to say, a Government held by ye free and voluntarie consent of all, or the greater parte of the free Inhabitants.

And now to the end that we may give, each to
other, (notwithstanding our different consciences,
touching the truth as it is in Jesus, whereof, upon the
point we all make mention), as good and hopeful assurance as we are able, touching each man's peaceable and
quiett enjoyment of his lawfull right and Libertie, we
doe agree vnto, and by the authoritie above said,
Inact, establish, and confirme these orders following.

Touching Lawes.

That no person, in this Colonie, shall be taken or
imprisoned, or be disseized of his Lands or Liberties,
or be Exiled, or any other otherwise molested or
destroyed, but by the Lawfull judgment of his Peeres,
or by some known Law, and according to the Letter of
it, Ratified and confirmed by the major part ofthe
Generall Assembly lawfully met and orderly managed.
       2.   That no person shall (but at his great
perill), presume to beare or execute any office, that
is not lawfuly called to it, and confirmed in it; nor
though he be lawfully called and confirmed, presume to
doe more or less than those that had powre to call him,
or did authorize him to doe.
       3.   That no Assembly shall have powre to consti-
tute any Lawes for the binding of others, or to ordaine
Officers for the execution thereof, but such as are
founded upon the Charter and rightlie derived from the
General Assemblie, lawfully met and orderly managed.
       4.   That no person be employed in any service for
the Publick Administration of Justice and Judgment vpon
offenders, or between Man and Man, without good encouragement, and due satisfaction from the Publick,
eyther out of the common stock, or out of the stocks of
those that have occasioned his service; that so, those
that are able to serve, may not be unwilling, and those
that are able and willing, may not be disabled by being
overburthened. And then, in case a man be called vnto
Office by a lawfull Assemble, and refuse to beare
office, or be alled by an officer to assist in the
execution of his office, and refuse to assist him, he
shall forfeit as much again as his wages would have
amounted unto, or be otherwise fined by the judgment of
his Peers, and to pay his fine or forfeiture, unless

the Colony, or that lawful Assembly release him.   But
in case of eminent danger, no man shall refuse.

And now, forasmuch as our Charter gives us powre
to make such Lawes, Constitutions, Penalties, and
Officers of Justice for the execution thereof as we, or
the greater part of vs shall, by free consent, agree
vnto, and yet does premise that those Lawes, Constitutions, and Penalties soe made shall be conformable to
the Lawes of England, soe far as the nature and constitution of our place will admit, to the end that we may
show ourselves not only unwilling that our popularity
should prove (as some conjecture it will,) an Anarchie,
and so a common Tyranny, but willing and exceedingly
desirous to preserve every man safe in his person, name
and estate; and to show ourselves, in soe doing, to be
also vnder authoritie, by keeping within the verge and
limitts prescribed us in our Charter, by which we have
Authoritie in this respect to act; Wee do agree and by
this present act determine, to make such Lawes and
Constitutions soe conformable, &c., or rather to make
those Lawes ours, and better known among us; that is to
say, such of them, and so farr, as the nature and
constitution of our place will admit.

Touching the Common Law.

It being the common right among common men, and is
profitable eyther to direct or correct all, without
exception; and it being true, which that Great Doctor
of the Gentiles once said, that the Law is made or
brought to light, not for a righteous man, who is a Law
vnto himselfe, but for the Lawless and disobedient in
the Generall, but more particularly for murderers of
Fathers and Mothers; for Manslayers, for whoremongers,
and those that defile themselves with mankind; for
Menstealers, for Lyars and perjured persons, vnto
which, vpon the point, may be reduced the common Law of
the Realme of England, the end of which is, as is
propounded, to preserve every man safe in his own
person, name and estate; Wee doe agree to make, or
rather to bring such Lawes to light for the direction
or correction of such lawless persons, and for their
memories sake to reduce them to these five generall
Lawes or Heads; viz.:

    1.   Under that head of murdering Fathers and Mothers, being ye highest and most unnatural, are comprehended those Lawes that concerne High Treason, Pettie Treason, Rebellion, Misbehaviour, and their accessaries.

    2.   Under the Law for Manslayers, are comprehended those Lawes that concerne Self-murder, Murder, Homicide, Misadventure, casual death, cutting out the Tongue or Eyes, Witchcraft, Burglarie, Robberie, Burning of Houses, Forcible entryes, Rescuos and Escape, Riotts, Routs and Unlawfull Assemblies, Batteries, Assaults and Threats and their accessaries.

    3.   Under the Law for Whoremongers, and those that defile themselves with mankind, being the chief of that nature, are comprehended those Lawes that concerne Sodomie, Buggerie, Rape, Adulterie, Fornication, and their Accessaries.

    4.   Under the Law for Menstealers, being the chief of that nature, are comprehended those Lawes that concern Theft of men, Larcenie, Trespasses by Men or beasts, Fraudulent dealing by deceitfull bargaine, Covenants, Conveyances by Barratrie, Conspiracie, Champertie and Maintenance, by forging or rasing records, Writs, Deeds, Leases, Bills, &c., and by using fallse weights and measures and their accessaries.

    5.   Under the Law for Lyars and perjured persons, being the chiefe of that nature, are comprehended such as concerne perjurie itselfe, breach of covenant, Slander, False witnesse-bearing, and their accessories.

    And as necessary concomitants hereof, to prevent Murder, Theft and Perjury, We do joyntlie agree in this present Assemblie, to make or produce such Laws as concerne provision for the poore, soe that the impotent shall be mainteyned and the able employed. And to prevent Poverties, it is agreed, that such Lawes be made and produced as concernes ye ordering of Alehouses, and Taverns, Drunkenness and unlawfull gaming therein; and instead of such to propagate Archerie, which is both man-like and profitable; and to prevent whoredom and those evils before mentioned, it is agreed by this present Assemble to constitute and establish some ordinance touching Marriage, Probate of Wills, and Intestates . . . .

Rebellion.

It is agreed and enacted by this present Assemblie, that no inferiour shall rise up or rebell against his superiour, especially such to whom he more directlie owes faith, dutie, and ready obedience; it being altogether unsuitable to civill order, which by the authoritie of our Charter we purpose to propagate; wherefore, we doe declare that we counte it a kind of Rebellion for a servant to threat, assault, or strike his master; and the penaltie for a threat or assault shall be, to be bound to his good behaviour; for striking especially if it be malitiouslie, to be sent to the House of Correction, there to remaine for six months, or to satisfie his master. It is allso Rebellion for a child to threat, assault, or strike his Parents, and his Penaltie shall be, to be sent to the House of Correciton, there to remaine a twelve-month, or to humble himslef to his parents' satisfaction. It is allso Rebellion to threat, assault or strike a Judge of Recrod; and the penaltie to be bound to his good behaviour, and further fined by his Peers. it is also a kind of Rebellion to withstand an arrest, and the execution of Judgment; the penaltie to be bound to his good behaviour, and to be judged by his Peers.

Misbehaviour.

It is agreed by this present Assemblie, and by this act declared, that for any man to sue words of contempt against a chief officer, especially in the execution of his office, is against good manners, and misbehaviour; and his penaltie shall be, to be bound to appeare at the next Court, where such matters are to be Tryed: where, being lawfully convict by his Peers, he shall be bound to his good behaviour, so to remaine for three months space, or till the next Court following .
. . .

Touching Whoremongers.

First of Sodomie, which is forbidden by this present Assemblie threwout the whole Colonie, and by Sundry Statutes of England. 25 IIen. viii. 6; 5 Eliz.

xvii. It is a vile affection, whereby men given up
thereto, leave the natural use of woman, and burne in
their lusts, one toward another; and so men with men
worke that which is vnseemly, as that Doctor of the
Gentiles in his letter to the Romans once spake, i. 27;
The Penaltie concluded by that State under whose
authoritie we are, is Felonie of death, without
remedye. See 5 Eliz. 17.

Buggerie.

Buggerie is forbidden by this present Assembly
threwout the whole Colonie, and also strengthened by
the same Statute of England. It is a most filthy lying
with a beast as with a woman, and is abominatio and
confusion; the just reward whereof prepared to our
hands, is Felonie of death, without remedie. See 5
Eliz. 17.

Rape.

Rape is forbidden by this present Assembly threwout the whole Colonie; and we do hereby declare, that
it is when a man through his vile and unbridled affection, lyeth with, forceth a woman against her will;
like hereunto is the knowing of a maid carnally who is
vnder ye age of Tenn yeares, though it be with her
consent. The penaltie we do declare to be Felonie of
death. See, for confirmation, 13 Edw. i. 34; and if
the Woman consent after, she loseth her dowre of Lands.
See 6 Rich. ii. 6. And so doth a married wife that
elopeth with her adventurer. 13 #dw. i. 34.

Adulterie and Fornication.

Is forbidden by this present Assembliy threwout
the Colonie, with this memento, that the Most High will
judge them. 13 IIen. iv. Adultery is declared to be a
vile affection, whereby men do turn aside from ye
naturall use of their own wives, and do burn in their
lusts towards strange flesh; and we do agree, that what
penaltie the Wisdome of the State of England have or
shall appoint touching these transgressions, the

accessarie and effects shall stand in force threwout the whole Colonie.

Touching Menstealers.

It is agreed, and by this present Assembly enacted, that the taking away, deflouring or contracting in marriage a maid under sixteen yeares of age, against the will of, or vnknown to the Father or Mother of the Maid, is a kind of stealing of her; and that the penaltie shall be eyther five years' imprisonment or satisfaction of her parents. 4 Will. and Mary, 8 . . .

Touching Liars and Perjured Persons.

Forasmuch as the consciences of sundry men, truly conscienable, may scruple the giving or taking of an oath, and it would be noways suitable to the nature and constitution of our place (who professeth ourselves to be men of different consciences, and no one wiling to force another) to Debar such as cannot do so, eyther from bearing office amongst vs, or from giving in testimony in a case depending.

Be it enacted by the authority of this present Assembly, that a solemn profession or Testimony in a Court of Record, or before a Judge of Record, shall be accounted, threwout the whole Colonie of as full force as an oath; and because many, in giving engagement or testimony, are usually more over awed with the Penaltie which is known, than with the most High, who is little known in the Kingdoms of men.

It is, therefore, further agreed and ordered, that he that falsifieth such a solemn profession or testimony, shall be accounted among vs as a perjured person, and his penaltie shall be that, looke what detriment is or might be brought vpon others by falsifying his engagement or testimony, the same shall fall upon himself. He shall also forfeit five pounds, and be disenabled eyther to beare office, or to give in Testimony in any Court of Record, vntill the Colonie release him; and this forfeiture and determinet, (the

partie being lawfully convicted,) shall be, one halfe
to the King's Custome, and the other shall go to the
partie grieved that sues for it, by action of debt or
bill: but in case the partie be not worth so much,
then shall he be imprisoned in the House of Correction
till it be wrought out, or else sett in the Pillory in
some open place, and have his Eares nayled thereto; and
then may the partie grieved receive his dammages; and
the procurer shall have the like penaltie.   See 5 Eliz.
9.

Breach of Covenant.

Breach of Covenant is by the present Assembly,
forbidden threwout the whole Colonie.

It is enacted, and agreed, that they that perform
not their Covenants made eyther by word or writing,
(excepting those before excepted,) shall be liable to
satisfie what the other can prove he is damnified by
reason of the non-performance thereof, which he may
recover upon an action of the case.

And be it further enacted, that no person re-
tayning a servant, shall putt their servant away, nor
no person retayned shall depart from their master,
mistress or dame, untill the end of the term covenanted
for, vss it be for some reasonable and sufficient
cause, witnessed before and allowed by the Head Officer
or Officers of the Towne, and three or foure able and
discreet men of the Comon Councill or Towne appointed
thereto, vnder their hands in writing, for the discharge eyther of Master or Servant.

And be it enacted further, that that Master,
Mistress or Dame, that putts away their servant without
sufficient cause, and so allowed with such a discharge,
shall forfeit the sum of forty shillings; and if any
servant departe from his or her Master, Mistress or
Dame's service before the end of the Terme covenanted
for, vnless it be for some sufficient cause allowed of
as before, or not serve according to the Tenure of the
promise or covenant, vpon complaint vnto the Head
Officers of the Towne and their associates, the matter

being fully proved, he shall be committed to Ward
without Baile or Mainprize, vntill by sufficient
sureties he be bound to his Master, Mistress or Dame,
to perform the engagement.

Be it enacted, by the authoritie above said, that
he that shall retaine a Servant now lawfully dismissed
and sett at liberty from his Master, shall forfeit for
every such offence five pounds, which the Master may
recover by an action of Debt. See 5 Eliz. 4 . . . .

Slaunder.

Forasmuch as a good name is better than precious
ointment, and Slaunderers are worser than dead flies to
corrupt and alter the savour thereof, it is agreed, by
this present Assembly, to prohibitt the raysing or
spreading of false reports, Slaunderers and Libells
throwout the whole Colonie; and we further declare that
the partie offended or grieved by such False reports,
Slaunders, and Libells as hereafter followeth, may
bring his action of slaunder aginst the reporter and
speaker thereof, in case vpon demand he reaveale not
the author, but if revealed, then against the Author,
and shall recover sufficient damages. The cases
actionable are these; for a man to say eyther by word
or writing, and yet not able to prove it, that another
is a Traytor, a Fellon, a Thiefe, a Cutt-purse, or hath
stole something; a perjured person, or hath forsworn
himselfe in any man's case; a Bankrupt, a Cheater, or
one that lives by cheating; to call and be not able to
prove it, an unmarried woman a whore; a young man
unmarried, a whoremaster; to say a young man keepeth a
House of Bawdery; or that a Tradesman maketh nothing
but bad wares; or that a Merchant or shop-keeper hath
nothing but rotten, bad and vnsound wares in his house
or shopp, or to speak any thing in the dispragement of
a Man's goods that he putts to sale whereby he may be
damnified.

Poore.

It is agreed and ordered, by this present Assembly, that each Towne shall provide carefully for the

reliefe of the poore, to maintaiyne the impotent, and
to employ the able, and shall appoint an overseer for
the same purpose. See 43 Eliz. 2.

Scoulds.

It is ordered, Common Scoulds shall be punished
with the Ducking Stoole.

Ale Houses.

It is ordered, by the authority of this present
Assembly, that no Taverne, Alehouse or Victualling
House, shall be kept threwout the whole Colonie without
Licence or Allowance; and whosoever shall keep Taverne
or Alehouse, or Victualling house without licence,
shall forfeit twenty shillings, which shall be levied
to the vse of the poore, and shall by the head officer
of the Towne be forthwith discharged. See 3 Car. 3.

Licenses.

Be it also encated by the authority of this
present Assembly, that each Towne shall have power to
allow Tavernes, Alehouses, and Victualling houses
within its own precincts; and the Head officer of the
Towne shall binde by Recognizance every such Taverne,
Alehouse keeper and Victualler so allowed, with two
such sufficient sureties to keep good order in his
house, and not to vse such games as are judged by the
Lawes of England to be vnlawfull in such Common houses,
as Carding, Dicing, Slide, Groat, &c., and not to
suffer any Townsmen to remeine tipling therein for one
hours space, vnder the penaltie of ten shillings for
every such default, vpon the view of the head officers,
or vpon the information of sufficient witnesses vpon
their solemn testimony, or by his owne confession; And
every Townsman so taken, shall forfeit for every time,
three shillings and four pence; which forfeitures shall
be taken by distreint and given to the overseer for the
use of the Poore.

Drunkenness.

Drunkenness is forbidden throwout this whole
Colonie; and it is further agreed, that the head
officer of each Towne, or any other Magistrate shall
have powre upon his owne view, confession of the partie
or proof vpon one witness his Testimony, to convict a
person of drunkenness, who shall be by him enjoyned to
pay five shillings, for that fact into the hands of the
overseer for the vse of the poore, within one week
after the same conviction; and in case the partie
refuse so to do or be not able; then shall he be sett
in the Stocks, and there remaine for the space of six
houres;and for the second offence, being convicted as
aforesaid, he shall forfeit ten shillings, to be paid
as before; and shall be bound by the head officer or
magistrate before whom he is convicted, to his good
behaviour, with two sufficient sureties in the summe of
tenpounds. 21 Jac. 7 . . . .

Marriage.

It is agreed, and ordered by this present Assemblie, for the preventing of many evills and mischiefs
that may follow thereon, that no contract or agreement
between a Man and a Woman to owne each other as Man and
Wife, shall be owned from henceforth threwout the Whole
Colonie as a lawfull marriage, nor their Children or
Issue so coming together to be legitimate or lawfullie
begotten, but such as are, in the first place, with the
parents, then orderly published in two severall meetings of the Townsmen, and lastly confirmed before the
head officer of the Towne, and entered into the Towne
clerk's Booke. And that man that goes contrarie to
this present Ordinance established, shall forfeit five
pounds to the parents of the Maid, and be bound to his
good behaivor; and all the accessories shall forfeit
five pounds a man, halfe whereof shall go to the
grieved parents and the other halfe of the Towne . . .

Touching the Public Administration of
Justice According to the Lawes Agreed
Upon and Established Throwout the Whole Colonie.

Be it enacted by this present Assemblie, that for
matters of greater weight and moment, there shall be
erected a Generall Court of Tryalls for the whole
Colonie, and Generall Officers for the Administration
of Justice therein.

The Court shall be held twice in the yeare, in
case there be matters that are then and there to be
Tryed, Sci: upon the next day after the dissolving of
the Court of Election held in May, and the other upon
the last Tewsday of the eighth moneth, commonly called
October, and these Courts to be held at _____

It is further agreed, that to these Colonie Courts
of Tryall, shall appertaine the Tryall of such Crimes
as may hazard Life, Limbe, Disfranchisement or Bannishment; and such Trespasses, Debts, and differences (as
by the Common Councill eyther of Towne or Townes shall
be judged too weightie for a more private determining).
Also, such matters of difference as fall out betweene
Towne and Towne, or between parties dwelling in two
Townes more remote, or in the case of an arrest of a
man belonging to a neighbour Colonie, or, in cases of
great importance; also, attaints of Inquests, and
Tryalls of perjuries, and finally all such matters as
are not referred, by any charter or order, vnto any
Towne apart, or to the Island, or two Townes joyntlie.

Be it enacted further by the authority of this
present Assemblie, that the Generall Officer for the
whole Colonie shall be these, Sci: One President,
foure Assistants, in every Towne one, one General
Recorder, one Publick Treasurer, and a General Sargent;
which Officers shall be chosen every yeare in the
General Assembly, and towards the latter end of that
Session. They shall also be chosen after this matter:
for President, Recorder, Treasurer and Serjant each
Towne shall present one; and he which the major part of
the General Assembly pitcheth upon by paper, shall
stand and be confirmed in his Office for that yeare;
and for Assistant, each Towne shall present two, and he
which the vote by paper pitcheth upon, shall be the
Assistant in that Towne.

Be it further enacted, that the President and
Assistants shall have such a Commission by which they
shall be conservators of the peace in the same Towne
where they live and throwout the whole Colony. By this
Commission, they shall keep the peace, and in case it
be broke by threats, assaults, or affrayes, eyther
before any of them or vpon lawfull complaint, he or
they shall bind the parties by recognizance with two
sufficient sureties vnto the peace, and to prepare at
that Court where such matters are to be tryed, and soe
to remaine, vntill by proclamation in open Court he
shall be acquitted . . . .

President's Commission.

By a speciall commission, the President shall sitt
as Chief Judge in the Colonie Courts of Tryall, to see
that order and course of Law appointed thereto be dulie
observed, and the verdict being given in, he is to
pronounce the sentence.

In case it be a matter of Felonie, to deliver vp
to the Generall Sargent to the execution, or see it
done and performed.

In case it be a matter of Trespass, debt or any
other difference betweene Man and Man; he is, together
with the Assistants, to tax the costs and to send forth
a Writ of Execution unto the Generall Sargant at least
tenn dayes before, to give the whole Colonie notice, to
the end they may prepare for the Generall Assemblie.

Assistants.

By a speciall commission, all the assistants, if
not necessarily deteyned, shall sit with the President
in ye Generall Courts of Tryall, and shall supply the
roome of a Coroner in each Towne where they dwell.

Touching the Generall Recorder.

Be it enacted by this present Assemblie, that the
Generall Recorder's Office shall be in the generall, to
keep a Coppie of all the Records or Acts of the Gene-
rall Assemblie, Generall and particular Courts of
Judicature, Rolles of the Freemen of the Colonie,
Records, Evidences, Sales and Bargaines of Land, Wills

and Testaments of the Testators, and orders of the Townsmen touching the Intestate, Records of the Limitts and Bounds of Townes, their Highways, Driftwayes, Commons and Fencings, Priviledges and Liberties. And forasmuch as matters of greatest concernement ought to be kept and preserved with the greatest vigilance: Be it enacted, that the Generall purchases, (which are all we can shew for our right to our Lands, and the Charter which is that which gives vs who are Subjects right to exercise authority one over another,) be kept in a strong chest, having foure severall Locks annexed thereto, and that each Towne keep a key thereof, that soe, as there is a common right and interest therein, there may be no access vnto them in a divided way, (lest also, they be divided) but with a common consent. And let it be further enacted, that this chest be placed in the safest place of the Colonies; and the Generall Recorder, also, shall have the key to the Roome in which it is placed.

Be it also enacted, that he that is Generall Recorder, shall supply the roome of the Clerke of the peace or assizes, in the Generall Court of Tryall, as it is a Court of Assize or Goale delivery. And as Clark of assize, his office shall be to receive examination, information, recognizances and bailments, presented by the Officer who committed the Felon to prison. He shall also receive the bill of indictments presented by him who was bound to prosecute the prisoner; he shall read the indictments and enroll the acts of the Court itself, the indictment, the process, the answer, the traverse itself, the verdict, the judgment thereupon, and the execution. And as this Court is a Court of Common Please, soe he shall supply the roome of the master of the office, and in that regard his office shall be, vpon the request of the plaintiff or his Attorney, (in matters that clearly appertaine vnto that Court,) to direct a Writ to the General Sargant to arrest the defendant, in such an action, of such a man, and to take baile for his appearance by such a day as the writ makes mention to be returnable; and in case the General Sargant returne ye defendants Bond by the day appointed, then shall he enter into his appearance, and in case they proceed, his office shall be, to file such declarations and answers. But in case after a declaration is filed in

expectation of an answer, or to make his defence, and
he doth not, then the plaintiff taketh him by fault,
which is called confessing the action; and then the
Recorders office shall be, to enter and record a nihil
dicit (id est,) he saith nothing thereon, and so shall
be send out a writ of enquiry of dammages vnto the
Towne where the defendant lives. And the head officer
of the Towne, at the next Towne Court, shall enquire of
damages, and by a writ of destringes to the Sargant,
shall cause the defendant for that purpose to come to
the Court, and in case he appeare not, he shall forfeit
the distraint, and the head officer of the Towne may
distraine again and again. The matter being issued in
the Towne, it shall be returned into the office, and
the Recorder shall then enter the postia returne, and
give forth to the General Sargent a writ of Execution.

Touching the Publick Treasurer.

Be it enacted, that the Publick Treasurer shall
only receive such finds, forfeitures, amercements and
taxes, as fall vpon such as are not within the liberties of the three Townes specified in the Charter;
and Warwick, that is invested with the like priviledges
and powre; and that the Townes mentioned shall receive
and keep safe in their custody all finds, forfeitures
and amercements that shall be levied upon the Inhabitants thereof vntill they be called for by the authority from England; but if vpon our humble petition, they
be granted to the Colony, then shall they enjoy them as
a helpe in their Government as their custom forever.
Moreover, looke what comes into the Publick Treasury by
that way, he shall give account of in the Generall
Assembly.

Touching the Generall Sargant.

Be it enacted by this present Assemblie, that he
that is chosen Generall Sargant shall be an able man of
Estate, for so ought a Sheriff to be, whose place he
supplies; whose office shall be to attend all Colonye
Courts of Tryall, and to serve eyther by himselfe or
the Serjants of each Towne, all Writts originall or
judiciall; who having arrested a man for that which he
is bailable, he shall take baile by an obligation to

himselfe, with sufficient sureties; the condition of
which shall be, to make appearance in the place, and at
the time, the bill, writt, or warrant specifies. He
shall also gather vp all fines, forfeitures and amercements, that are made at the Colonie Courts of Tryall,
and shall returne them faithfully unto the Treasurie to
which they appertaine. When he is chosen, he shall be
solemnly engaged to exact no more than his wages, and
to take no more than is forfeited; for not serving
writts and warrants, he shall lose to the party
grieved, treble damages, forfeit Forty Pounds; twentie
whereof is the King's Custome, and twentie shall be to
the party that sueth. And he that summons or doth
arrest without warrant, shall be imprisoned till he pay
to the party grieved ten pounds, his costs and damages,
and twentie pounds to the King. See the 43 Eliz. 6.
He shall also have the charge of the prison for the
Colony, and the prisoners therein.

But forasmuch as Justice cannot be had in the
general Court of Judicature, notwithstanding these
Officers, without Pleaders and Tryars, be it enacted,
that there shall be both, and rules given for their
orderly proceedings.

Touching the Inquest for Tryars.

To save needless expenses and travailes, be it
enacted, by the authority of this present Assemblie,
that all Traitors, Felons, and such as are suspected
thereof shall be indicted by twelve or sixteen honest
and lawful men of, and also in the Towne where the
person was taken, or of, and in the Towne where his
Tryall shall be, and at the Court of Tryall. And that
three of the most sufficient and least suspicious
persons in each Towne bee chosen by the Townsmen tenn
days before, and sent to that Court to attend the
Tryall of such matters as shall be presented, and that
these be returned and arrayed by the General Sargent,
so that the parties may have knowledge of them foure
dayes before the Sessions of the Justices upon paine of
ten pounds; and that they be chosen by neyther old men
above seventy yeares, nor mean men, nor such as have a
charter of exemption, nor an indictor, nor interested
in the deliverance of an indictee. See 42 Edw. iii.

11; 13 Edw. i. 37; 25 Edw. iii. 3; 3 Hen. v. 3; 23 Hen.
vi. 9.

And be it further enacted, that no man shall pass
vpon the Life of a Man in this Colonie, nor in plea
real, no, nor personal in any issue joyned, that
amounts in the dammage to the value of forty marks, nor
touching forcible entry, nor touching Riotts, who is
not clear worth forty pounds, nor in smaller matters in
the Towne that is not clearly worth twenty pounds.

And be it further enacted, that men have their
peremptory and other challenges, to the full, as they
have them in England, where for petty Treason, Murder
and Felony, they may challenge to the number of twentie. See 32 Hen. viii. 3.

And be it enacted, that the inquest upon the
Tryall of persons indicted of Felonie, shall eyther
allow of, or reject the witnesses according to their
consciences, of all or the major part of them. 4 Jac.
3.

And be it further enacted, that the inquest being
thus chosen by the Townes, and summoned by the Sargant,
in case any of them appeare not, their roome shall be
supplied by such among those that stand about, or that
live in the same Towne (and they refusing, the same
fine,) where the Colonie Court of Tryall is held, and
every man soe chosen and summoned, if he appeares not,
shall lose and forfeit five shillings and ten pence; or
what he might have gott if he had attended the service
which the Court shall determine, which, by a distringas
from the Court, the Serjant shall require, and levie
and deliver into the Treasury to which it belongs.

And be it further enacted by the authority of this
present Assemblie, that if any false verdict be given
in any action, suit, or demand, either in this or in
any other Court of the Colonie, in any thing personall,
as Trespass, Debt, Difference, &c.; the party grieved
shall have a writ of attaint out of this Court of the
Colonie, putting in sufficient security against each
partie giving in such an untrue verdict, whereby yee
parties shall be summoned by great distresses; and in
case the thing in demand and the verdict surmounts
forty pounds, to the three able men of each Towne shall
be added twelve of the same Towne, where the Colonie
Court of Tryall shall be, being worth three score

pounds a piece, if such and so many are to be had, and
in case these find they gaven an vntrue verdict, every
one of the former inquest shall forfeit twenty pounds,
ten whereof is the King's custome, and ten pounds shall
go to the partie grieved, that sues for it; he shall be
also not of credence, neither shall his solemn testimony be taken in any Court, vntill the Colonie release
him. But if, eyther the demand or verdict be vnder
forty pounds, then shall the inquest be worth fifty
pounds a man; and every one of the petty inquest being
found guilty, shall forfeit five pounds, the like
punishment as is before specified. See 23 IIen. viii.
3; 37 Hen. viii. 5. And in case he that sues for the
writ of attaint makes it not good, every party attainted may have his action against him, and recover
sufficient dammages.

Touching Pleaders.

Be it enacted by the authority of this present
Assembly, that any man may plead his own case in any
Court, or before any Judge of Record Throwout the whole
Colonie, or may make his Attorney to plead for him, or
may vse the Attorney that belongs to the Court which
may be two in a Towne, to wit; discreet, honest and
able men for understanding, chosen by the Townsmen of
the same Towne, and solemnly engaged by the head
officer thereof, not to vse any manner of deceit to
beguile eyther Court or partie. And these being thus
chosen and confirmed, shall be authorized, being
entertayned, to plead to any Court in the Colonie; but
in case such pleader or Attorney shall vse any manner
of deceit as is aforesaid, and be thereof attainted, or
that shall be notoriously in any default of record, he
shall forfeit his place, and never more be admitted to
plead in any Court of the Colonie. See 3 Edw. 1, 28; 4
Hen. iv. 18.

Be it also further enacted, that in matters of
oversie betweene partie and partie, or Towne and Towne,
that belongs to the hearing and determination of the
Colony Court of Tryall, the partie complaining, or his
attorney, shall goe to the General Record, and in his
office shall enter his action; then shall he request a
writ to arrest the defendant as is abovesaid,

returnable at least twenty dayes before the Court; the
bond of the defendant being returned into the
Recorder's Office, the plaintiff or his Attorney,
shall, within foure dayes after, file his declaration
in the Recorder's Office (or he shall be non-suited)
where the defendant or his Attorney may see it and take
forth a coppie thereof; then shall the defendant or his
Attorney, file the answer eight dayes before the Court.
And so shall they join issue, that Court, and proceed
to Tryall, where the witnesses to prove or disprove the
issue being produced, the plaintiff and defendant may
plead their own cause, or have their Attorneys plead
for them before ye Bench, and the inquest; and the
verdict and judgment being given, the Recorder shall
enter it. But in case the defendant puts in his
answer, and at the Court makes his demurr, then shall
the Court judge of the sufficiency thereof, and so
shall accept the demurr, or proceed; but in case he
neyther puts in his answer, nor demurr, or gives in his
answer, but puts not in his demurr, and yet appeares
not, then shall be entered, he saith nothing; and so
shall it be taken for granted he confesseth the action,
and then shall go forth a writ from the Court vnto the
Towne in which he lives, to enquire of dammages, which
being returned to the Recorder, a process or writ shall
go forth for Execution.

And now forasmuch as we have prescribed Rules and
orders, whereby are declared both the authoritie,
office and duty of every person that shall be employed
about this Colonie Court of Tryall, and have likewise
declared, that the President's and foure assistants'
office (among other things that belong to their care)
is to see that order and course of Law appointed to
this Court be dewly observed.

It is agreed, and by the authority of this present
Assemblie enacted, that as the former Lawes are committed to their custodie to see them observed or
executed, soe are these constitutions, so farr, as they
have a respect vnto an orderly finding out of Justice
and the administration thereof, committed to their
charge, to see them observed.

And furthermore be it enacted, as that which adds
to the comely and commendable order of this Court of
Judicature, that at eight of the clock in the morning

of those dayes vpon which the Court is appointed at the
farthest, the President, the Towne Assistants, and the
Head Officers of the same Towne where the Court shall
be kept, (for their Councill and helpe,) shall sit in
the publicke Sessions house, and also the Generall
Recorder, where shall attend those that seeke for
justice, their pleaders, witnesses, Tryars and the
Generall Sarjant with his prisoners ready either to rid
his hands of them, or else to doe execution vpon them
or others as Justice shall require.

In the first place, the Recorder shall present,
and if there be time read over the bills of indictment;
and if, in case they have been examined or presented by
an inquest before, then shall he pass them over; if
not, then shall the President sett apart the honest and
lawfull men prepared for that purpose, by a solemn
engagement, faithfully to enquire touching the bills,
and soe shall send them forth with the same.

Then, in case there be any controversies or
difficulties between partie and partie that are lawfully and orderly presented to that Court for Tryall,
the Recorder shall read them over in the open Courte,
and that which was first joyned for issue, shall come
first to the hearing. And because the twelve men are
to have the hearing and determining of all controversies and differences depending between partie and
partie, they shall be first called forth by the President and placed in order before those that are to be
judged, from whom they shall receive a solemn charge
vpon the perill and penaltie the law hath provided, to
do justice between the parties contending, according to
evidence. This done, then shall the parties, (having
first had their lawfull challenges,) or their Attornies
plead their cases before them, produced their witnesses
for what they affirme, which shall be taken upon the
like perill. When they have sufficiently discussed the
difference, then shall the President or any other of
the Assistants mind the inquest of the most material
passages and arguments that are brought by one and
other for the case and against it, without alteration
or leaning to one party or another, (which is too
commonly seene,) and soe shall the President advise the
inquest to goe forth and do justice and right between
their neighbours, according to the evidence that has

been brought, for what has been pleaded. These being
gone forth, then may the Court proceed to deale with
such as are bound by recognizance eyther to release
them or to continue their Bonds, according as there is
just cause, and may read over the Indictments that have
been enquired into before, and are now presented as
true bills, or that were committed to the inquest in
the beginning of the Court and are returned true bills,
The twelve men returning with a verdict it shall be
recorded, and soe shall they be employed, vntill all
the differences be ended.

And forasmuch as it belongs to the Justices to
taes the costs, lett the vacant times be so employed.

These controversies, differences and demands being
thus all issued, then let the Recorder call to ye
Sarjant to bring forth ye Prisoners. Before each
prisoner lett his inductment be read, and he demanded
what he saieth to the indictment, whether Guilty or
not. If he answer Guilty, his confession shall be
recorded. If he sayeth not Guilty, then lett him be
demanded if he will be tryed by God and the Country,
sci: his countrymen. If he consents, the President
shall call forth the twelve men before him, wish him to
look upon them, and ask if he have any thing against
them; if not, then he shall charge them vpon the former
perill, to deale faithfully and truly in the matter; it
being a matter of consequence and moment, and to
proceed to determine according to the light of their
consciences, vpon the evidence given in, and if any be
found Guilty of death, to be reprieved to the next
Court. And thus having issued all matters depending,
the President with the assistants and councellors shall
give forth writs vnto the Generall Sarjant for the
severall executions, and so break vp the Court for that
time and sitting.

And be it further enacted, by the authoritie of
this present Assemblie, that the perill that any
officer shall susteyne, for going without, besides, or
beyond his Commission, shall be first lawfuly and
orerly judged. And that no officer employed in this
Colonie shall think it strange or hard dealing to be
brought to his faire Tryall, and Judgment for what he
hath done amiss.

    Be it enacted, that the Cheife Officers of the
Colonie, Island, or Townes, shall be tryed and judgedin
the Generall Assembly be a committe of the most able
and impartiall men, chosen out from among them, against
whom they may have also their lawfull challenges: and
that all other officers abusing their offices, shall be
tryed and judged eyther in the Towne by which they were
chosen; or, if the Towne please, or if not chosen by
the Towne, then shall they be tryed and judged by the
Colonie Courts of Tryalls, And in case any man sues for
Justice against an officer or other, and he cannot be
heard, or is heard and cannot be righted by any Law
extant among vs, then shall the partie grieved petition
to the Generall or Law making Assemblie, and shall be
relieved.
    And now forasmuch as the choice of all the offi-
cers that are to be employed in this Colonie, like the
Colonies about vs, once a year, whereby it may be
easily collected, that he that hath an office or charge
this yeare, may have none another; and it would be too
prejudicial to the peace of the place or quiet Government thereof, for a man out of a discontented self-
will, or other pretence, not to resigne, together with
his office, belonging to the Colonie, Island or Towne,
to him that is chosen and appointed thereto . . . .

DOCUMENT 53:   The Laws and Liberties of Massachusetts,
                1647

Only about thirty per cent of the original text is
reproduced here. It is based on the copy of the 1648
edition in the Henry E. Huntington Library as reproduced in the volume *The Laws and Liberties of
Massachusetts*   (Cambridge: Harvard University Press,
1929). The volume has an introduction by Max Farrand
but no listed editor. The sections of the text here
omitted contain the more mundane provisions concerning
such things as the rates of cattle, viewers of pipestaves, the salting of fish, surveying, etc. Essentially a codification of laws passed over a number of
years, this organic act contains everything we might
today expect to find in a constitution, and functioned
much as a constitution for the colony. The spelling of
the original has been retained, except for replacing
the use of the German "s" with the standard English
form.

THE BOOK OF THE GENERAL

LAUUES AND LIBERTYES

CONCERNING THE INHABITANTS OF THE MASSACHUSETS

COLLECTED OUT OF THE RECORDS OF THE GENERAL
COURT

FOR THE SEVERAL YEARS WHEREIN THEY WERE MADE

AND ESTABLISHED,

And now revised by the same Court and desposed into an

Alphabetical order and published by the same Authoritie in the

General Court held at Boston the fourteenth of the

first month Anno 1647.

TO OUR BELOVED BRETHREN AND NEIGHBOURS

The Inhabitants of the Massachusets, the Governour, Assistants

and Deputies assembled in the Generall Court of that

Jurisdiction with grace and peace in our

Lord Jesus Christ.

So soon as God had set up Politicall Government among his people Israel hee gave them a body of lawes of judgement both in civil and criminal causes. These were brief and fundamental principles, yet withall so full and comprehensive as out of them clear deductions were to be drawne to all particular cases in future times. For a Common-wealth without lawes is like a Ship without rigging and steeradge. Nor is it sufficient to have principles or fundamentalls, but these are to be drawn out into so many of their deductions as the time and condition of that people may have use of. And it is very unsafe & injurious to the body of the people to put them to learn their duty and libertie from generall rules, nor is it enough to have lawes except they be also just. Therefore among other priviledges which the Lord bestowed upon his peculiar people, these he calls them specially to consider of, that God was neerer to them and their lawes were more righteous then other nations. God was sayd to be amongst them or neer to them because of his Ordnances established by himselfe, and their lawes righteous

because himselfe was their Law-giver: yet in the
comparison are implyed two things, first that other
nations had something of Gods presence amongst them.
Secondly that there was also somwhat of equitie in
their lawes, for it pleased the Father (upon the
Covenant of Redemption with his Son) to restore so
much of his Image to lost man as whereby all nations
are disposed to worship God, and to advance righteousnes: Which appears in that of the Apostle Rom. I. 21.
They knew God &c: and in the 2. 14. They did by
nature the things conteined in the law of God. But the
nations corrupting his ordinances (both of Religion,
and Justice) God withdrew his presence from them
proportionably whereby they were given up to abominable
lusts Rom. 2.21. Wheras if they had walked according
to that light & law of nature might have been preserved
from such moral evils and might have injoyed a common
belssing in all their natural and civil Ordinances:
now, if it might have been so with the nations who were
so much strangers to the Covenant of Grace, what
advantage have they who have interest in this Covenant,
and may injoye the special presence of God in the
puritie and native simplicitie of all his Ordinances by
which he is so neer to his owne people. This hath been
no small priviledge, and advantage to us in New-England
that our Churches, and civil State have been planted,
and growne up (like two twwinnes) together like that of
Israel in the wilderness by which wee were put in minde
(and had opportunitie put into our hands) not only to
gather our Churches, and set up the Ordinances of
Christ Jesus in them according to the Apostolick
patterne by such light as the Lord graciously afforded
us: but also withall to frame our civil Politie, and
lawes according to the rules of his most holy word
whereby each do help and strengthen other (the Churches
the civil Authoritie, and the civil Authoritie the
Churches) and so both prosper the better without such
emulation, and contention for priviledges or priority
as have proved the misery (if not ruine) of both in
some other places.

For this end about nine years wee used the help of
some of the Elders of our Churches to compose a modell
of the Judiciall lawes of Moses with such other cases
as might be referred to them, with intent to make sure

of them in composing our lawes, but not to have them
published as the lawes of this Jurisdiction: nor were
they voted in Court. For that book intitled The
Liberties &c: published about seven years since (which
conteines also many lawes and orders both for civil &
criminal causes, and is commonly [though without
ground] reported to be our Fundamentalls that wee owne
as established by Authoritie of this Court, and that
after three years experience & generall approbation:
and accordingly we have inserted them into this volume
under the severall heads to which they belong yet not
as fundamentalls, for divers of them have since been
repealed, or altered, and more may justly be (at least)
amended heerafter as further experience shall discover
defects or inconveniences for *Ninil simul natum
et perfectum.*   The same must we lay of this present
Volume, we have not published it as a perfect body of
laws sufficient to carry on the Government established
for future times, nor could it be expected that we
should promise such a thing. For if it be no disparagement to the wisedome of that High Court of Parliament in England that in four hundred years they could
not so compile their lawes, and regulate proceedings in
Courts of justice &c: but that they had still new work
to do of the same kinde almost every Parliament: there
can be no just cause to blame a poor Colonie (being
unfurnished of Lawyers and Statemen) that in eighteen
years hath produced no more, nor better rules for a
good, and setled Government then this Book holds forth:
nor have you (our Bretheren and Neighbours) any cause,
whether you look back upon our Native Country, or take
your observation by other States, & Commonwealths in
Europe) to complaine of such as you have imployed in
this service; for the time which hath been spent in
making laws, and repealing and altering them so often,
nor of the charge which the Country hath been put to
for those occasions, the Civilian gives you a satis-
factorie reason of such continuall alterations addi-
tiona &c: *Crescit in Orbe dolus.*
    These Lawes which were made successively in divers
former years, we have reduced under severall heads in
an alphabetical method, that so they might the more
readily ye be found, & that the divers lawes concerning
one matter being placed together the scope and intent

of the whole and of every of them might the more easily
be apprehended: we must confesse we have not been so
exact in placing every law under its most proper title
as we might, and would have been: the reason was our
hasty indeavour to satisfie your longing expectation,
and frequent complaints for want of such a volume to be
published in print: wherin (upon every occasion) you
might readily see the rule which you ought to walke by.
And in this (we hope) you will finde satisfastion, by
the help of the references under the several heads, and
the Table which we have added in the end. For such
lawes and orders as are not of generall concernment we
have not put them into this booke, but they remain
still in force, and are to be seen in the booke of the
Records of the Court, but all generall laws not heer
inserted nor mentioned to be still of force are to be
accounted repealed.

You have called us from amongst the rest of our
Bretheren and given us power to make these lawes: we
must now call upon you to see them executed: remem-
bring that old & true proverb, The execution of the law
is the life of the law. If one sort of you viz:
non-Freemen should object that you had no hand in
calling us to this worke, and therefore think yourselvs
not bound to obedience &c. Wee answer that a subsequent, or implicit consent is of like force in this
case, as an expresse precedent power: for in putting
your persons and estates into the protection and way of
subsistance held forth and exercised within this
jurisdiction, you doe tacitly submit to this Government
and to all the wholesome lawes thereof, and so is the
common repute in all nations and that upon this Maxim.

If any of you meet with some law that seemes not
to tend to your particular benefit, you must consider
that lawes are made with respect to the whole people,
and not to each particular person: and obedience to
them must be yeilded with respect to the common welfare, not to thy private advantage, and as thou yeil-
dest obedience to the law for comon good, but to thy
disadvantage: so another must observe some other law
for them good, though to his own damage; thus must we
be content to bear one anothers burden and so fullfill
the Law of Christ.

That distinction which is put between the Lawes of
God and the laws of men, becomes a snare to many as it
is mis-applyed in the ordering of their obedience to
civil Authoritie; for when the Authoritie is of God and
that in way of an Ordinance Rom. 13. I. and when the
administration of it is according to deductions, and
rules gathered from the word of God, and the clear
light of nature in civil nations, surely there is no
humane law that tendeth to common good (according to
those principles) but the same is mediately a law of
God, and that in way of an Ordinance which all are to
submit unto and that for conscience sake.   Rom. 13. 5.

By order of the General Court.

INCREASE NOWEL, SECR.

The Book of the General Lauues and
Libertyes Concerning &c:

FORASMUCH as the free fruition of such Liberties,
    Immunities, priviledges as humanitie, civilitie &
    christianity call for as due to everie man in his
    place, & proportion, without impeachment &
    infringement hath ever been, & ever will be the
    tranquility & stability of Churches &
    Comon-wealthes; & the deniall or deprivall thereof
    the disturbance, if not ruine of both:

It is therefore ordered by this Court, & Authority
thereof, That no mans life shall be taken away; no mans
honour or good name shall be stayned; no mans person
shall be arrested, restrained, bannished, dismembred
nor any wayes punished; no man shall be deprived of his
wife of children; no mans goods or estate shall be
taken away from him; nor any wayes indamaged under
colour of law or countenance of Authoritie unles it be
by the vertue or equity of some expresse law of the
Country warranting the same established by a General
Court & sufficiently published; or in case of the
defect of a law in any particular case by the word of
God.   And in capital cases, or in cases concerning

dismembring or banishment according to that word to be
judged by the General Court [1641]

Abilitie.

All persons of the age of twenty one years, and of
right understanding & memorie whether excommunicate,
condemned or other, shall have full power and libertie
to make their Wills & Testaments & other lawfull
Alientations of their lands and estates. [1641]

Actions.

All Action of debt, accounts, slaunder, and
Actions of the case concerning debts and accounts shall
henceforth be tryed where the Plantiffe pleaseth; so it
be in the jurisdiction of that Court where the Plantiffe, or Defendant dwelleth: unles by consent under
both their hands it appeare they would have the case
tryed in any other Court. All other Actions shal be
tryed within that jurisdiction where the cause of
Action doth arise. [1642]
      2.   It is ordered by this Court & Authoritie
thereof, That every person impleading another in any
court of Assistants, or County court shal pay the sum
of ten shillings before his case be entred, unless the
court fee cause to admit any to sue in
[1642]
      3.   It is ordered by the Authority aforesayd,
That where the debt or damage recovered shall amount to
ten pounds in every such case to pay five shillings
more, and where it shall amount to twenty pounds or
upward there to pay ten shillings more then the first
ten shillings, which sayd additions shall be put to the
Judgement and Execution to be levied by the Marshall
and accounted for to the Treasurer. [1647]
      4.   In all actions brought to any court the
Plantiffe shall have liberty to withdraw his action or
to be non-suted before the Jurie have given in their
verdict; in which case he shall alwayes pay full cost
and charges to the Defendant, and may afterward renew
his sute at another Court. [1641]

Age.

It is ordered by this Court & the Authoritie thereof, that the age for passing away of lands, or such kinde of hereditaments, or for giving of votes, verdicts or sentences in any civil courts or causes, shall be twenty and one years: but in case of chusing of Guardions, fourteen years [1641 1647]

Ana-Baptists.

Forasmuch as experience hath plentifully & often proved that since the first arising of the Ana-baptists about a hundred years past they have been the Incendiaries of Common-Wealths & the Infectors of persons in main matters of Religion, & the Troublers of Churches in most places where they have been, & that they who have held the baptizing of Infants unlawful, have usually held other errors or heresies together therwith (though as hereticks used to doe they have concealed the same untill they espied a fit advantage and opportunity to vent them by way of question or scruple) and wheras divers of this kinde have since our coming into New-England appeared amongst our selvs, some whereof as others before them have denied the Ordinance of Magistracy, and the lawfulnes of making warre, others the lawfulnes of Magistrates, and their Inspection into any breach of the first Table: which opinions is conived at by us are like to be increased among us & so necessarily bring guilt up us, infection, & trouble to the Churches & hazzard to the whole Common-wealth:
It is therfore ordered by this Court & Authoritie therof, that if any person or persons within this Jurisdiction shall either openly condemn or oppose the baptizing of Infants, or goe about secretly to reduce others from the approbation or use thereof, or shall purposely depart the Congregation at the administration of that Ordinance; or shall deny the Ordinance of Magistracy, or their lawfull right or authoritie to make war, or to punish the outward breaches of the first Table, and shall appear to the Court wilfully and obstinately to continue therin, after due means of conviction, everie such person or persons shall be sentenced to Banishment. [1644] . . . .

Arrests.

It is ordered and decreed by this Court & Authoritie thereof, That no mans person shall be arrested or
imprisoned for any debt or fine if the law can finde
any competent meanes of satisfaction otherwise from his
estate. And if not this person may be arrested and
imprisoned, where he shall be kept at his own charge,
not the Plaintiffs, till satisfaction be made; unles
the Court that had cognisance of the cause or some
superiour Court shall otherwise determine: provided
neverthelesse that no mans person shall be kept in
prison for debt but when there appears some estate
which he will not produce, to which end any Court or
Commissioners authorized by the General Court may
administer an oath to the partie or any others suspected to be privie in concealing his estate, but shall
satisfie by service if the Creditor require it but
shall not be solde to any but of the English nation.
[1641: 1647] . . . .

Bond-slavery.

It is ordered by this Court and authoritie thereof, that there shall never be any bond-slavery, ville-
nage or captivitie amongst us; unless it be lawfull
captives, taken in just warrs, and such strangers as
willingly sell themselves, or are solde to us: and
such shall have the libertyes and christian usages
which the law of God established in Israell concerning
such persons doth morally require, provided, this
exempts none from servitude who shall be judged thereto
by Authoritie. [1641] . . . .

CAPITAL LAWES.

If any man after legal conviction shall HAVE OR
WORSHIP any other God, but the LORD GOD: he shall be
put to death. Exod. 22. 20. Deut. 13.6. & 10. Deut.
17. 2. 6.
    2.   If any man or woman be a WITCH, that is, hath
or consulteth with a familiar spirit, they shall be put
to death. Exod. 22. 18. Levit. 20. 27. Deut. 18. 10.
11.

3.   If any person within this Jurisdiction
whether Christian or Pagan shall wittingly and willingly presume to BLASPHEME the holy Name of God, Father,
Son or Holy-Ghost, with direct, expresse, presumptuous,
or highhanded blasphemy, either by wilfull or obstinate
denying the true God, or his Creation, or Government of
the world: or shall curse God in like manner, or
reproach the holy religion of God as if it were but a
politick device to keep ignorant men in awe; or shal
utter any other kinde of Blasphemy of the like nature &
degree they shall be put to death. Levit. 24. 15. 16.
        4.   If any person shall commit any wilfull
MURTHER, which is Man slaughter, committed upon pre-
meditate malice, hatred, or crueltie not in a mans
necessary and just defence, nor by meer casualty
against his will, he shall be put to death. Exod. 21.
12. 13. Numb. 35. 31.
        5.   If any person slayeth another suddenly in his
ANGER, or CRUELTY of passion, he shall be put to death.
Levit. 24. 17. Numb. 35. 20. 21.
        6.   If any person shall slay another through
guile, either by POYSONING, or other such devilish
practice, he shall be put to death. Exod. 21. 14.
        7.   If any man or woman shall LYE WITH ANY BEAST,
or bruit creature, by carnall copulation; they shall
surely be put to death: and the beast shall be slain,
& buried, and not eaten. Lev. 20. 15. 16.
        8.   If any man LYETH WITH MAN-KINDE as he lieth
with a woman, both of them have committed abomination,
they both shal surely be put to death: unles the one
partie were forced (or be under fourteen years of age
in which case he shall be severely punished) Levit. 20.
13.
        9.   If any person commit ADULTERIE with a married
or espoused wifed; the Adulterer & Adulteresse shall
surely be put to death. Lev. 20. 19. & 18. 20 Deu. 22.
23. 27.
        10.   If any man STEALETH A MAN, or Man-kinde, he
shall surely be put to death Exodus 21. 16.
        11.   If any man rise up by FALSE-WITNES wittingly,
and of purpose to take away any mans life: he shal be
put to death. Deut. 19. 16. 18. 16.
        12.   If any man shall CONSPIRE, and attempt any
Invasion, Insurrection, or publick Rebellion against

our Common-Wealth: or shall indeavour to surprize any
Town, or Townes, Fort, or Forts therin; or shall
treacherously, & perfidiously attempt the Alteration
and Subversion of our frame of Politie, or Government
fundamentally he shall be put to death. Numb. 16. 2
Sam. 3. 2 Sam. 18. 2 Sam. 20.

     13. If any child, or children, above sixteen
years old, and of sufficient understanding, shall
CURSE, or SMITE their natural FATHER, or MOTHER; he or
they shall be put to death: unles it can be sufficiently testified that the Parents have been very
unchristianly negligent in the education of such
children; or so provoked them by extream, and cruel
correction: that they have been forced therunto to
preserve themselves from death or maiming. Exod. 21.
17. Lev. 20. 9. Exod 21. 15.

     14. If a man have a stubborn or REBELLIOUS SON,
of sufficient years & uderstanding (viz) sixteen years
of age, which will not obey the voice of his Father, or
the voice of his Mother, and that when they have
chastened him will not harken unto them: then shal his
Father & Mother being his natural parents, lay hold on
him, & bring him to the Magistrates assembled in Court
& testifie unto them, that their Son is stubborn &
rebellious & will not obey their voice and chastisement, but lives in sundry notorious crimes, such a son
shal be put to death. Deut. 21. 20. 21.

     15. If any man shal RAVISH any maid or single
woman, comitting carnal copulation with her by force,
against her own will; that is above the age of ten
years he shal be punished either with death, or with
some other greivous punishment according to circumstances as the Judges, or General court shal determin.
[1641] . . . .

Charges Publick.

     . . . And it is further ordered that the Comis-
sioners for the severall towns in everie Shire shall
yearly upon the first fourth day of the week in the
seventh month, assemble at their shire Town: & bring
with them fairly written the just number of males
listed as aforesaid, and the assessments of estates
made in their several towns according to the rules &

directions in this present order expressed, and the
said Comissioners being so assembled shall duly and
carefully examin all the said lists and assessments of
the severall towns in that Shire, and shall correct &
perfect the same according to the true intent of this
order, as they or the major part of them shall determine, & the same so perfected they shal speedily
transmit to the Treasurer under their hands or the
hands of the major part of them and therupon the
Treasurer shal give warrants to the Constables to
collect & levie the same; so as the whole assessment
both for persons & estates may be payd in unto the
Treasurer before the twentith day of the ninth month,
yearly, & everie one shal pay their rate to the Constable in the same town where it shal be assessed. No
shall any land or estate be rated in any other town bu
where the same shal lye, is, or was improved to the
owners, reputed, owners or other propietors use or
behoof if it be within this Jurisdiction. And if the
Treasurer canot dispose of it there, the Constable
shall send it to such place in Boston, or elswhere as
the Treasurer shall appoint at the charge of the
Countrie to be allowed the Constable upon his accout
with the Treasurer. And for all peculiars viz: such
places as are not yet layd within the bounds of any
town the same lands with the persons and estates
therupon shall be assessed by the rates of the town
next unto it, the measure or estimation shall be by th
distance of the Meeting houses . . . .

Children.

For as much as the good education of children is
of singular behoof and benefit to any Common-wealth;
and wher as many parents & masters are too indulgent
and negligent of their duty in that kinde. It is
therefore ordered that the Selectmen of every town, in
the severall precincts and quarters where they dwell,
shall have a vigilant eye over their brethren & neighbours, to see, first that none of them shall suffer so
much barbarism in any of their families as not to
indeavour to teach by themselves or others, their
children & apprentices so much learning as may inable
them perfectly to read the english tongue, & knowledge

of the Capital laws: upon penaltie of twentie shillings for each neglect therin. Also that all masters
of families doe once a week (at the least) catechize
their children and servants in the grounds & principles
of Religion, & if any be unable to doe so much: that
then at the least they procure such children or apprentices to learn some short orthodox catechism without
book, that they may be able to answer unto the questions that shall be propounded to them out of such
catechism by their parents or masters or any of the
Selectmen when they shall call them to a tryall of what
they have learned in this kinde. And further that all
parents and masters do breed & bring up their children
& apprentices in some honest lawful calling, labour or
imploymet, either in husbandry, or some other trade
profitable for themselves, and the Common-wealth if
they will not or cannot train them up in learning to
fit them for higher imployments. And if any of the
Selectmen after admonition by them given such masters
of families shal finde them still negligent of their
dutie in the particulars aforementioned, wherby children and servants become rude, stubborn & unruly; the
said Selectmen with the help of two Magistrates, or the
next County court for that Shire, shall take such
children or apprentices from them & place them with
some masters for years (boyes till they come to twenty-
one, and girls eighteen years of age compleat) which
will more strictly look unto, and force them to submit
unto government according to the rules of this order,
if by fair means and former instructions they will not
be drawn unto it. [1642]

2.   Wheras sundry gentlemen of qualitie, and
others oft times send over their children into this
country unto some freinds heer, hoping at the least
therby to prevent their extravagant and riotous courses, who not with standing by means of some unadvised
and ill-affected persons, which give them credit, in
expectation their freinds, either in favour to them or
prevention of blemish to themselves, will discharge
what ever is done that way, they are no lesse lavish &
profuse heer to the great greif of their freinds,
dishonour of God & reproach of the Countrie.

It is therefore ordered by this Court & authoritie
thereof; That if any person after publication heerof

shall any way give credit to any such youth, or other
person under twentie one years of age, without order
from such their freinds, heer, or elswhere, under their
hands in writing they shall lose their debt whatever it
be. And further if such youth or other person incur
any penalty by such means and have not wherwith to pay,
such person, or persons, as are occasions therof shall
pay it as delinquents in the like case should doe.
[1647]

3.   If any parents shall wilfully, and unreasonably deny any childe timely or convenient marriage, or
shall exercise any unnaturall severeitie towards them
such children shal have libertie to complain to Authoritie for redresse in such cases.   [1641]

4.   No Orphan during their minority which was not
committed to tuition, or service by their parents in
their life time, shall afterward be absolutely disposed
of by any without the consent of some Court wherin two
Assistants (at least) shall be present, except in case
of marriage, in which the approbation of the major part
of the Selectmen, in that town or any one of the next
Assistants shall be sufficient. And the minoritie of
women in case of marriage shall be till sixteen years.
[1646] . . . .

Councill.

This Court considering how the weighty affairs of
this Jurisdiction whether they concern this peculiarly
or have reference to the rest of our confederated
Colonies may be duly and speedily transacted in the
vacancy of the Generall Court for the satisfaction of
the Comissioners, in respect of the weighty and sodain
occasions which may be then in hand, doth heerby
expresse and declare,   That the General Court ough
to be called by the Governour, when the importancy of
the busines doth require it, and that time and opportunitie will safely admit the same, and that all other
necessary matters are to be ordered and dispatched by
the major part of the Council of the Common-wealth, &
therfore to that end letters signifying, breifly, the
busines and the time and place of meeting for consul-
tation ought to be sent unto the Assistants. Also it
is heerby declared, that seven of the said Assistants

meeting, the Governour or Deputy Governour being one is
a sufficient Assembly to act, by impressing of soldiers
or otherwise as need shall be. And in case of extream
and urgent necessitie, when indeavours are reasonably
used to call together the Assistants and the busines
will not admit deay, then the acts of so many as do
assemble are to be accounted, and are accounted valid,
& sufficient. Also it is intended that the generall
words aforementioned contein in them power to impresse
& send forth soldiers, and all manner of victuails,
vessels at sea, carriages and all other necessaries,
and to send warrants to the Treasurer to pay for them.
[1645]

Courts.

For the better administration of justice and
easing the Countrie of unnecessary charge and travells:
it is ordered by this Court and Authoritie thereof;
That there shal be four Quarter Courts of Assistants yearly kept by the Governour, or Deputy Gover:
and the rest of the Magistrates, the first of them on
the first third day (viz: tuisday) in the fourth month
called June: the second on the first third day of the
seventh month: the third on the first third day of the
tenth moth: the fourth on the first third day of the
first month called March. Also there be four County
Courts held at Boston, by such of the Magistrates as
shall reside in, or neer the same, viz: by any five,
four or three of them, who shall have pwoer to assemble
together upo the last fift day ofthe eight, eleventh,
second & fift months everie year, and there to hear &
determin all civil causes & criminal, not extending
tolife, member or banishment according to the course of
the court of Assistnts, & to summon Juries out of the
neighbour towns, & the Marshall & other Officers shall
give attendance there as at other Courts.   And it is
further ordered that tehre shall be four Quarter Courts
kept yearly by the Magistrates of Essex, with such
other persons of worth as shall fro time totime be
apointed by the General Court; at the nominatio of the
towns in that Shrie by orderly agreemet amog theselves,
to be joyned in Commission with them so that with them
so that with the Magistrates they be five in all and so

that no Court be kept without one Magistrate at the
least: and so any three of the Commissioners aforesaid
may keep Court in the absence of the rest: yet none of
all the Magistrates are excluded from any of these
Courts who can, and please to attend the same. And the
General Court to appoint from time to time, which of
the said Magistrates shall specially belong to everie
of the said Courts. Two of these Quarter Courts shall
be kept at Salem, the other at Ipswitch. The first,
the last third day of the week in the seventh month at
Ipswitch. The second at Salem the last third day of
the tenth month. The third at Ipswitch the last third
day of the first month. The fourth the last third day
of the fourth month at Salem. All and every which
Courts shall be holden by the Magistrates of Salem and
Ipswitch with the rest of that County or so many of
them shall attend the same; but no Jurie men shal be
warned from Ipswitch to Salem nor from Salem to Ipswitch. Also there shall be a Grand Jurie at either
place, once a year. Which Courts shall have the same
power in civil and criminal causes as the courts of
Assistants have (at Boston) except tryalls for life,
lims or banishment, which are wholy reserved unto the
courts of Assistants. The like libertie for County
courts and tryall of causes is graunted to the Shire
town of Cambridge for the County of Midlesex, as Essex
hath, to be holden by the Magistrates of Midlesex &
Suffolk & such other men of worth as shall be nominated
and chosen as aforesaid, one of which Courts shall be
holden on the last third day of the eight month, and
another on the last third day of the second month from
year to year. And the like libertie for County Courts
and tryall of causes is graunted to the County of
Norfolk to be holden at Salisburie on the last third
day of the second month; and another at Hampton on such
day as the General Court shall appoint to be kept in
each place from time to time. And if any shal finde
himselfe greived with the sentence of any the said
County courts he may appeal to the next court of
Assistants. Provided he put in sufficient caution
according to law. Lastly, it is ordered by the Authoritie aforesaid that all causes brought to the courts of
Assistants by way of appeal, and other causes specially
belonging to the said courts, shall be first determined

from time to time: & that causes of divorce shall be tryed only in the said court of Assistants. [1635 1636 1639 1641 1642]

2.   For the more speedy dispatch of all causes which shall concern Strangers, who cannot stay to attend the ordinary Courts of justice, It is ordered by this Court and Authoritie therof;

That the Governour or Deputy Governour with any two other Magistrates, or when the Governour or Deputy Governour cannot attend it, that any three Magistrates shall have power to hear and determin by a Jurie of twelve men, or otherwise as is used in other Courts, all causes civil and criminal triable in County Courts, which shall arise between such Strangers, or wherin any such Stranger shall be a partie. And all records of such proceedings shall be transmitted to the Records of the Court of Assistants, to be entered as tryalls in other Courts, all which shall be at the charge of the parties, as the Court shall determin, so as the Country be no wayes charged by such courts. [1639]

3.   For the electing of our Governour, Deputy Governor, Assistants and other general Officers upon the day or dayes appointed by our Pattent to hold our yearly Court being the last fourth day of the week (viz: Wednesday) of every Easter Term; it is solemnly and unanimously decreed and established,

That henceforth the Freemen of this Jurisdiction shal either in person or by proxie without any Summons attend & consummate the Elections, at which time also they shal send their Deputies with full power to consult of and determin such matters as concern the welfare of this Common-wealth; from which General Court no Magistrates or Deputy shall depart or be discharged without the consent of the major part both of Magistrates and Deputies, during the first four dayes of the first Session therof, under the penaltie of one hundred pounds for everie such default on either part. And for the after Sessions, if any be, the Deputies for Dover are at libertie whether to atted or not. [1643]

4.   Forasmuch as after long experience wee finde divers inconveniences in the manner of our proceeding in Courts by Magistrates and Deputies sitting together, and account it wisedome to follow the laudable practice of other States, who have layd ground works for

government and order for issuing busines of greatest
and highest consequence: it is therfore ordered by
this Court and Authoritie therof,

   That henceforth the Magistrates may sit and act
busines by themselves, by drawing up Bills and Orders
which they shall see good in their wisdom, which having
agreed upon, they may present them to the Deputies to
be considered of, how good and wholesom such orders are
for the Countrie & accordingly to give their assent or
dissent. The Deputies in like manner sitting apart by
themselves and consulting about such orders and laws as
they in their discretion and experience shall finde
meet for the common good: which agreed upon by them
they may present to the Magistrates who having seriously considered of them may manifest their consent or
dissent thereto. And when any Orders have passed the
approbation of both Magistrates and Deputies, then to
be ingrossed: which in the last day of this Court or
Sessions shal be deliberately read over. Provided also
that all matters of Judicature which this Court shall
take cognisance of, shall be issued in like manner
(unles the Court upon some particular occasion or
busines agree otherwise). [1644] . . . .

Deputies for the Generall Court.

   For easing the body of Freemen now increasing, and
better dispatching the busines of General Courts, It is
ordered and by this Court declared;

   That henceforth it shall be lawfull for the
Freemen of everie Plantation to choose their Deputies
before every Generall Court, to confer of, and prepare
such publick busines as by them shall be thought fit to
consider of at the next General court. And that such
persons as shall be heerafter so deputed by the Freemen
of the several Plantations to deal on their behalfe in
the publick affairs of the Common-wealth, shall have
the full power and voices of all the said Freemen
derived to them for the making and establishing of
Laws, graunting of lands, and to deal in all other
affairs of the Comon-wealth wherin the Freemen have to
doe: the matter of election of Magistrates and other
officers only excepted wherin every Freeman is to give
his own voice. [1634]

2.   Forasmuch as through the blessing of God the
number of towns are much increased, It is therfore
ordered and by this Court enacted;

That henceforth no town shall send more then two
Deputies to the General Court; though the number of
Freemen in any town be more then twenty. And that all
towns which have not to the number of twenty Freemen
shall send but one Deputy, & such towns as have not ten
Freemen shall send none, but such Freemen shall vote
with the next town in the choice of their Deputie or
Deputies til this Court take further order. [1636
1638]

3.   It is ordered by this Court and Authoritie
therof, That when the Deputyes for severall towns are
met together before, or at any General court, it shall
be lawfull for them or the major part of them to hear
and determin any difference that may arise about the
election of any of their members, and to order things
amongst themselves that may concern the well ordering
of their body. And that heerafter the Deputies for the
General court shall be elected by papers as the Governour is chosen. [1634 1635]

4.   It is ordered by this Court and Authoritie
therof; That the Freemen of any Shire or town have
liberty to choose such Deputies for the General court
either in their own Shire, Town, or elsewhere, as they
judge fittest, so be it they be Freemen and inhabiting
within this Jurisidction. And because wee cannot
foresee what variety and weight of occasions may fall
into future consideration, & what counsells we may
stand in need of: wee decree that the Deputies to
attend the General court in behalfe of the Coutry shall
not at any time be stated and enacted but from court to
court, or at the most but for one year, that the
Countrie may have an annual liberty to doe in what case
what is most behoofefull for the best welfare therof.
[1641] . . . . .

Ecclesiasticall:

I.   All the people of God within this Jurisdiction who are not in a Church way and be orthodox in
judgement and not scandalous in life shall have full
libertie to gather themselves into a Church estate,

provided they doe it in a christian way with due
observation of the rules of Christ revealed in his
word. Provided also that the General Court doth not,
nor will heerafter approve of any such companyes of men
as shall joyne in any pretended way of Church fellowship unles they shall acquaint the Magistrates and the
Elders of the neighbour Churches where they intend to
joyn, & have their approbation therin.
    2.   And it is farther ordered, that no person
being a member of any Church which shal be gathered
without the approbation of the Magistrates and the said
Churches shal be admitted to the Freedom of this
Common-wealth.
    3.   Everie Church hath free liberty to exercise
all the Ordinances of God according to the rules of the
Scripture.
    4.   Everie Church hath free libertie of election
and ordination of all her Officers from time to time.
Provided they be able, pious and orthodox.
    5.   Everie Church hath also free libertie of
admission, recommendation, dismission & expulsion or
deposall of their Officers and members upon due cause,
with free exercise of the disciplin and censures of
Christ according to the rules of his word.
    6.   No injuction shall be put upon any Church,
church Officer or member in point of doctrine, worship
or disciplin, whether for substance or circumstance
besides the institutions of the Lord.
    7.   Everie Church of Christ hath freedom to
celebrate dayes of Fasting and prayer and of Thanksgiving according to the word of God.
    8.   The Elders of churches also have libertie to
meet monthly, quarterly or otherwise in convenient
numbers and places, for conference and consultations
about christian and church questions and occasions.
    9.   All Churches also have libertie to deal with
any their members in a church way that are in the hands
of justice, so it be not to retard and hinder the
course therof.
    10. Everie Church hath libertie to deal with any
Magistrate, Deputy of court, or other Officer whatsoever that is a member of theirs, in a church way in
case of apparent and just offence, given in their
places, so it be done with due observance and respect.

11. Wee also allow private meetings for edification in Religion amongst christians of all sorts of
people so it be without just offence, both for number,
time, place and other circumstances.

12. For the preventing and removing of errour and
offence that may grow and spread in any of the Churches
in this jurisdiction, and for the preserving of truth &
peace in the severall Churches within themselves, and
for the maintainance and exercise of brotherly comunion
amongst all the Churches in the country.

It is allowed and ratified by the authoritie of
this Court, as a lawfull libertie of the Churches of
Christ, that once in every month of the year (when the
season will bear it) it shall be lawfull for the
Ministers and Elders of the Churches neer adjoyning,
together with any other of the Brethren, with the
consent of the Churches, to assemble by course in
everie several church one after another, to the intent,
that after the preaching of the word, by such a Minister as shal be requested therto, by the Elders of the
Church where the Assemby is held, the rest of the day
may be spent in public christian conference, about the
discussing and resolving of any such doubts & cases of
consciences concerning matter of doctrine, or worship,
or government of the Church as shall be propounded by
any of the Brethren of that Church; with leave also to
any other Brother to propound his objections, or
answers, for further satisfaction according to the word
of God. Provided that the whole action be guided and
moderated by the Elders of the Church where the Assembly is held, or by such others as they shall appoint.
And that nothing be concluded and imposed by way of
Authoritie from one, or more Churches, upon another,
but only by way of brotherly conference & consultations, that the truth may be searched out to the
satisfying of every mans conscience in the sight of God
according to his word. And because such an Assemblie
and the work therof cannot be duly attended if other
Lectures be held the same week, it is therfore agreed
with the consent of the Churches, that in what week
such an Assembly is held all the Lectures in all the
neighbouring Churches for the week dayes shall be
forborne, that so the publick service of Christ in this

Assembly may be transacted with greater diligence &
attention. [1641]

   13. Forasmuch as the open contempt of Gods word
and Messengers therof is the desolating sinne of civil
States and Churches and that the preaching of the word
by those whom God doth send, is the chief ordinary
means ordained of God for the converting, edifying and
saving the souls of the Elect through the presence and
power of the Holy-Ghost, therunto promised: and that
the ministry of the word, is set up by God in his
Churches, for those holy ends: and according to the
respect or contempt of the same and of those whom God
hath set apart for his own work & imployment, the weal
or woe of all Christian States is much furthered and
promoted; it is therefore ordered and decreed,
   That if any christian (so called) within this
Jurisdiction shall contemptuously behave himselfe
toward the Word preached or the Messengers therof
called to dispense the same in any Congregation; when
he doth faithfully execute his Service and Office
therin, according to the will and word of God, either
by interrupting him in his preaching, or by charging
him falsely with any errour which he hath not taught in
the open face of the Church: or like a son of Korah
cast upon his true doctrine or himselfe any reproach,
to the dishonour of the Lord Jesus who hath sent him
and to the disparagement of that his holy Ordinance,
and making Gods wayes contemptible and ridiculous:
that everie such person or persons (whatsoever censure
the Church may passe) shall for the first scandall be
convented and reproved openly by the Magistrate at some
Lecture, and bound to their good behaviour. And if a
second time they break forth into the like contemptuous
carriages, they shall either pay five pounds to the
publick Treasurie; or stand two hours openly upon a
block or stool, four foot high on a lecture day with a
paper fixed on his breast, written in Capital letters
[AN OPEN AND OBSTINATE CONTEMNER OF GODS HOLY ORDINAN-
CES] that others may fear and be ashamed of breaking
out into the like wickednes. [1646]
   14. It is ordered and decreed by this Court and
Authoritie thereof; That wheresoever the ministry of
the word is established according to the order of the
Gospell throughout this Jurisidiction every person

shall duly resort and attend therunto respectively upon
the Lords days & upon such publick Fast dayes & dayes
of Thanksgiving as are to be generally kept by the
appointmet of Authoritie: & if any person within this
Jurisidiction shal without just and necessarie cause
withdraw himselfe from hearing the publick ministry of
the word after due meanes of conviction used, he shall
forfeit for his absence from everie such publick
meeting five shillings. All such offences to be heard
and determined by any one Magistrate or more from time
to time. [1646]

15. Forasmuch as the peace and prosperity of
Churches and members therof as well as civil Rights &
Liberties are carefully to be maintained, it is ordered
by this Court & decreed, That the civil Authoritie heer
established hath power and liberty to see the peace,
ordinances and rules of Christ be observed in everie
Church according to his word. As also to deal with any
church-member in a way of civil justice notwithstanding
any church relation, office, or interest; so it be done
in a civil and not in an ecclesiastical way. Nor shall
any church censure degrade or depose any man from any
civil dignity, office or authoritie he shall have in
the Commonwealth. [1641]

16. Forasmuch as there are many Inhabitants in
divers towns, who leave their several habitations and
therby draw much of the in-come of their estates into
other towns wherby the ministry is much neglected, it
is therfore ordered by this Court and the authoritie
therof; That from henceforth all lands, cattle and
other estates of any kinde whatsoever, shall be lyable
to be rated to all common charges whatsoever, either
for the Church, Town or Comon-wealth in the same place
where the estate is from time to time. And to the end
there may be a convenient habitation for the use of the
ministry in everie town in this Jurisdiction to remain
to posterity. It is decreed by the authoritie of this
Court that where the major part of the Inhabitants
(according to the order of regulating valid town acts)
shall graunt, build, or purchase such habitation it
shall be good in law, and the particular sum upon each
person assessed by just rate, shal be duly paid according as in other cases of town rates. Provided alwayes
that such graunt, deed of purchase and the deed of gift

therupon to the use of a present preaching Elder and
his next successour and so from time to time to his
successors: be entred in the town book and acknowledged before a Magistrate, and recorded in the Shire
court. [1647]

Elections.

It is ordered by this Court and Authoritie therof:
That for the yearly choosing of Assistants for the time
to come instead of papers the Freemen shall use indian
corn and beans. The indian corn to manifest election,
the beans for blanks. And that if any Freeman shall
put in more then one indian corn or bean for the choise
or refusal of any publick Officer, he shall forfeit for
everie such offence ten pounds. And that any man that
is not free or otherwise hath not libertie of voting,
putting in any vote shal forfeit the like sum of ten
pounds. [1643]

2. For the preventing of many inconveniences
that otherwise may arise upon the yearly day of Election, and that the work of that day may be the more
orderly, easily and speedily issued, it is ordered by
this Court and the authoritie thereof.

That the Freemen in the several towns and villages
within this Jurisdiction, shall this next year from
time to time either in person or by proxie sealed up,
make all their elections,by papers, indian corn and
beans as heerafter is expressed, to be taken, sealed up
& sent to the court of Election as this order appoints,
the Governour, Deputie Governour, Major Generall,
Treasurer, Secretary and Comissioners for the united
Colonies to be chosen by writing, open or once folded,
not twisted or rolled up, that so they may be the
sooner and surer perused: and all the Assistants to be
chosen by indian corn and beans, the indian corn to
manifest election as in Sect: I; and for such small
villages as come not in person and that send no Deputies to the Court, the Constable of the said village,
together with two or three of the chiefe Freemen shall
receive the votes of the rest of their Freemen, and
deliver them together with their own sealed up to the
Deputie or Deputies for the next town, who shall

carefully convey the same unto the said Court of
Election. [1647]

3. For asmuch as the choice of Assistants in
case of supply is of great concernment, and with all
care and circumspection to be attended; It is therfore
ordered by this Court and Authoritie therof,

That when any Assistants are to be supplyed, the
Deputies for the General Court shall give notice to
their Constables or Selectmen to call together their
freemen in their severall towns: to give in their
votes unto the number of seven persons, or as the
General Court shall direct, who shall then and there
appoint one to carrie them sealed up unto their Shire
towns upon the last fourth day of the week in the first
month from time to time; which persons for each town so
assembled shall appoint one for each Shire to carrie
them unto Boston the second third day of the second
month there to be opened before two Magistrates. And
those seven or other number agreed upon as aforesaid,
that have most votes shall be the men which shall be
nominated at the court of Election for Assistants as
aforesaid. Which persons the Agents for each Shire
shall forthwith signifie to the Constables of all their
several towns in writing under their hands with the
number of votes for each person: all which the said
Constables shall forthwith signifie to their Freemen.
And as any hath more votes then other so shall they be
put to vote. [1647]

4. It is decreed and by this Court declared That
it is the constant libertie of the Freemen of this
Jurisdiction to choose yearly at the court of Election
out of the Freemen, all the general Officers of this
Jurisdiction, and if they please to discharge them at
the court of Election by way of vote they may doe it
without shewing cause. But if at any other General
Court, we hold it due justice that the reason therof be
alledged and proved. By general Officers we mean our
Governour, Deputy Governour, Assistants, Treasurer,
General of our wars, our Admirall at sea, Commissioners
for the united-Colonies and such others as are, or
heerafter may be of the like general nature. [1641]

Sect: <u>3</u> . . . .

Fornication

It is ordered by this Court and Authoritie therof,
That if any man shall commit Fornication with any
single woman, they shall be punished either by en-
joyning to Marriage, or Fine, or corporall punishment,
or all or any of these as the Judges in the courts of
Assistants shall appoint most agreeble to the word of
God. And this Order to continue till the Court take
further order. [1642]

Freemen, Non-Freemen.

WHERAS there are within this jurisdiction many
members of churches who to exempt themselves from all
publick service in the Common-wealth will not come in,
to be made Freemen, it is therfore ordered by this
Court and the Authoritie therof,
That all such members of Churches in the severall
towns within this Jurisidction shall not be exempted
from such publick service as they are from time to time
chosen to by the Freemen of the severall towns: as
Constables, Jurors, Select-men and Surveyors of high-
wayes. And if any such person shall refuse to serve
in, or take upon him any such Office being legally
chosen therunto, he shall pay for every such refusall
such Fine as the town shall impose, not exceeding
twenty shilings as Freemen are lyable to in such cases.
[1647]

Fugitives, Strangers.

It is ordered by this Court and Authoritie therof,
That if any people of other nations prosessing the true
Christian Religion shall flee to us from the tyranie or
oppression of their persecutors, or from Famine, Wars,
or the like necessarie and compulsarie cause, they
shall be entertained and succoured amongst us according
to that power and prudence God shall give us.   [1641]

Gaming.

UPON Complaint of great disorder by the use of the
game called Shuffle-board, in houses of common
entertainment, wherby much pretious time is spent

unfruitfully and much wast of wine and beer occasioned; it is therfore ordered and enacted by the Authoritie of this Court;

That no person shall henceforth use the said game of Shuffle-board in any such house, nor in any other house used as common for such purpose, upon payn for every Keeper of such house to forfeit for everie such offence five shillings: Nor shall any person at any time play or game for any monie, or mony-worth upon penalty of forefeiting treble the value therof: one half to the partie informing, the other half to the Treasurie. And any Magistrate may hear and detrmin any offence against this Law. [1646 1647]

General Court.

It is ordered, and by this Court declared that the Governour and Deputie Governour joyntly consenting, or any three Assistants concurring in consent shall have power out of Court to reprieve a condemned malefactor till the next Court of Assistants: or General Court. And that the General Court only shall have power to pardon a condemned malefactor.

Also it is declared that the General Court hath libertie and Authoritie to send forth any member of this Common-wealth, of what qualitie and condition or office whatsoever into forrein parts, about any publick Message or negociation: notwithstanding any office or relation whatsoever. Provided the partie so sent be acquainted with the affairs he goeth about, and be willing to undertake the service.

Nor shall any General Court be dissolved or adjourned without the consent of the major part therof. [1641]

Governour.

It is ordered, and by this Court declared that the Governour shall have a casting vote whensoever an equivote shall fall out in the Court of Assistants, or general Assemblie: so shall the President or Moderatour have in all civil Courts or Assemblies   [1641]

Heresie.

ALTHOUGH no humane power be Lord over the Faith &
Consciences of men, and therfore may not constrein them
to beleive or professe against their Consciences: yet
because such as bring in damnable heresies, tending to
the subversion of the Christian Faith, and destruction
of the soules of men, ought duly to be restreined from
such notorious impiety, it is therfore ordered and
decreed by this Court;
     That if any Christian within this Jurisdiction
shall go about to subvert and destroy the christian
Faith and Religion, by broaching or mainteining any
damnable heresie; as denying the immortalitie of the
Soul, or the resurrection of the body, or any sin to be
repented of in the Regenerate, or any evil done by the
outward man to be accounted sin: or denying that
Christ gave himself a Ransom for our sins, or shal
affirm that wee are not justified by his Death and
Righteousnes, but by the perfection of our own works;
or shall deny the moralitie of the fourth commandement,
or shall indeavour to seduce others to any the herisies
aforementioned, everie such person continuing obstinate
therin after due means of conviction shall be sentenced
to Banishment. [1646] . . . .

Idlenes.

It is ordered by this Court and Authoritie therof,
that no person, Housholder or other shall spend his
time idlely or unproffitably under pain of such punishment as the Court of Assistants or County Court shall
think meet to inflict. And for this end it is ordered
that the Constable of everie place shall use speciall
care and diligence to take knowledge of offenders in
this kinde, especially of common coasters, unproffit-
able fowlers and tobacco takers, and present the same
unto the two next Assistants, who shall have power to
hear and determin the cause, or transfer it to the next
Court. [1633]

Jesuits.

THIS court taking into consideration the great
wars, combustions and divisions which are this day in

Europe: and that the same are observed to be raysed
and fomented chiefly by the secret underminings, and
solicitations of those of the Jesuiticall Order, men
brought up and devoted to the religion and court of
Rome; which hath occasioned divers States to expell
them their territories; for prevention wherof among our
selves, It is ordered and enacted by Authoritie of this
Court,

That no Jesuit, or spiritual or ecclesiastical
person [as they are termed] ordained by the authoritie
of the Pope, or Sea of Rome shall henceforth at any
time repair to, or come within this Jurisdiction: And
if any person shal give just cause of suspicion that he
is one of such Societie or Order he shall be brought
before some of the Magistrates, and if he cannot free
himselfe of such suspicion he shall be committed to
prison, or bound over to the next Court of Assistants,
to be tryed and proceeded with by Banishment or otherwise as the Court shall see cause: and if any person
so banished shall be taken the second time within this
Jurisdiction upon lawfull tryall and conviction he
shall be put to death. Provided this Law shall not
extend to any such Jesuit, spiritual or ecclesiasticall
person as shall be cast upon our shoars, by ship-wrack
or other accident, so as he continue no longer then
till he may have opportunitie of passage for his
departure; nor to any such as shall come in company
with any Messenger hither upon publick occasions, or
any Merchant or Master of any ship, belonging to any
place not in emnitie with the State of England, or our
selves, so as they depart again with the same Messenger, Master or Merchant, and behave themselves inoffensively during their abode heer. [1647] . . . .

Impresses.

It is ordered, and by this Court declared, that no
man shall be compelled to any publick work, or service,
unlesse the Presse be grounded upon some act of the
General Court; and have reasonable allowance therfore:
nor shall any man be compelled in person to any office,
work, wars, or other publick service that is necessarily and sufficiently exempted, by any natural or
personal impediment; as by want of years, greatnes of
age, defect of minde, failing of senses, or impotencye

of lims. Nor shall any man be compelled to go out of
this Jurisdiction upon any offensive wars, which this
Common-wealth, or any of our freinds or confoederates
shall voluntarily undertake; but only upon such vindictive and defensive wars, in our own behalf, or the
behalf of our freinds and confoederates; as shall be
enterprized by the counsell, and consent of a General
Court, or by Authoritie derived from the same. Nor
shall any mans cattle or goods of what kinde soever be
pressed, or taken for any publick use or service; unles
it be by Warrant grounded upon some act of the General
Court: nor without such reasonable prizes and hire as
the ordinarie rates of the Countrie doe afford. And if
his cattle or goods shall perish, or suffer damage in
such service, the Owner shall be sufficiently recompenced. [1641]

Imprisonment.

It is ordered, and by this Court declared; that no
mans person shall be restreined or imprisoned by any
authoritie whatsoever before the Law hath sentenced him
therto: if he can put in sufficient securitie, Bayle
or Mainprize for his appearance, and good behaviour in
the mean time: unles it be in crimes Capital, and
contempt in open Court, and in such cases where some
expresse Act of Court doth allow it. [1641]

Indians

It is ordered by Authoritie of this Court; that no
person whatsoever shall henceforth buy land of any
Indian, without license first had & obtained of the
General Court: and if any shall offend heerin, such
land so bought shall be forfeited to the Countrie.
Nor shall any man within this Jurisidiction
directly or indirectly amend, repair, or cause to be
amended or repaired any gun, small or great, belonging
to any Indian, nor shall indeavour the same. Nor shall
sell or give to any Indian, directly or indirectly any
such gun, or any gun-powder, shot or lead, or shot-
mould, or any militarie weapons or armour: upon payn
of ten pounds fine, at the least for everie such
offence: and that the court of Assistants shall have

power to increase the Fine; or to impose corporall
punishment (where a Fine cannot be had) at their
discretion.
     It is ordered by the Authoritie aforesaid that
everie town shall have power to restrein all Indians
from profaning the Lords day. [1633 1637 1641]
     2.   Wheras it appeareth to this Court that
notwithstanding the former Laws, made against selling
of guns, powder and Ammunition to the Indians, they are
yet supplyed by indirect means, it is thefore ordered
by this Court and Authoritie therof;
     That if any person after publication heerof, shall
sell, give or barter any or barter any gun or guns,
powder, bullets, shot or lead to any Indian whatsoever,
or unto any person inhabiting out of this Jurisdiction
without license of this Court, or the court of Assistants, or some two Magistrates, he shall forfeith for
everie gun so sold, given or bartered ten pounds: and
for everie pound of powder five pounds: and for everie
pound of bullets, shot or lead fourty shillings: and
so proportionably for any greater or lesser quantitie.
[1642]
     3.   It is ordered by this Court and Authoritie
therof, that in all places, the English and such others
as co-inhabit within our Jurisidiction shall keep their
cattle from destroying the Indians corn, in any ground
where they have right to plant; and if any of their
corn be destroyed for want of fencing, or herding; the
town shall make satisfaction, and shall have power
among themselves to lay the charge where the occasion
of the damage did arise. Provided that the Indians
shall make proof that the cattle of such a town, farm,
or person did the damage. And for encouragement of the
Indians toward the fencing in their corn fields, such
towns, farms or persons, whose cattle may annoy them
that way, shall direct, assist and help them in felling
of trees, ryving, and sharpening of rayls, & holing of
posts: allowing one English-man to three or more
Indians. And shall also draw the fencing into place
for them, and allow one man a day or two toward the
setting up the same, and either lend or sell them tools
to finish it. Provided that such Indians, to whom the
Countrie, or any town hath given, or shall give ground
to plant upon, or that shall purchase ground of the

English shall fence such their corn fields or ground at
their own charge as the English doe or should doe; and
if any Indians refuse to fence their corn ground (being
tendred help as aforesaid) in the presence and hearing
of any Magistrate or selected Townsmen being met
together they shall keep off all cattle or lose one
half of their damages.

And it is also ordered that if any harm be done at
any time by the Indians unto the English in their
cattle; the Governour or Deputie Governour with two of
the Assistants or any three Magistrates or any County
Court may order satisfaction according to law and
justice. [1640   1648]

4.   Considering that one end in planting these
parts was to propagate the true Religion unto the
Indians: and that divers of them are become subjects
to the English and have ingaged themselves to be
willing and ready to understand the Law of God, it is
therfore ordered and decreed,

That such necessary and wholsom Laws, which are in
force, and may be made from time to time, to reduce
them to civilitie of life shall be once in the year (if
the times be safe) made known to them, by such fit
persons as the General Court shall nominate, having the
help of some able Interpreter with them.

Considering also that interpretation of tongues is
appointed of God for propagating the Truth: and may
therfore have a blessed successe in the hearts of
others in due season, it is therfore farther ordered
and decreed,

That two Ministers shall be chosen by the Elders
of the Churches everie year at the Court of Election,
and so be sent with the consent of their Churches (with
whomsoever will freely offer themselves to accompany
them in that service) to make known the heavenly
counsell of God among the Indians in most familiar
manner, by the help of some able Interpreter; as may be
most available to bring them unto the knowledge of the
truth, and their conversation to the Rules of Jesus
Christ. And for that end that something be allowed
them by the General Court, to give away freely unto
those Indians whom they shall perceive most willing &
ready to be instructed by them.

And it is farther ordered and decreed by this
Court; that no Indian shall at any time powaw, or
performe outward worship to their false gods: or to
the devil in any part of our Jurisdiction; whether they
be such as shall dwell heer, or shall come hither: and
if any shall transgresse this Law, the Powawer shall
pay five pounds; the Procurer five pounds; and every
other countenancing by his presence or otherwise being
of age of discretion twenty shillings. [1646]

Inditements.

If any person shall be indicted of any capital
crime (who is not then in durance) & shall refuse to
render his person to some Magistrates within one month
after three Proclaimations publickly made in the town
where he usually abides, there being a month betwixt
Proclaimation and Proclaimation, his lands and goods
shall be seized to the use of the common Treasurie,
till he make his lawfull appearance. And such with-
drawing of himselfe shall stand in stead of one wittnes
to prove his crime, unles he can make it appear to the
Court that he was necessarily hindred. [1646]

In-keepers, Tippling, Drunkenes.

FORASMUCH as there is a necessary use of houses of
common entertainment in every Common-wealth, and of
such as retail wine, beer and victuals; yet because
there are so many abuses of that lawfull libertie, both
by persons entertaining and persons entertained, there
is also need of strict Laws and rules to regulate such
an employment: It is therfore ordered by this Court
and Authoritie therof;
That no person or persons shall at any time under
any pretence or colour whasoever undertake to be a
common Victuailer, Keeper of a Cooks shop, or house for
common entertainment, Taverner, or publick seller of
wine, ale, beer or strong-water (by re-tale), nor shall
any sell wine privately in his house or out of doors by
a lesse quantitie, or under a quarter cask: without
approbation of the selected Townsmen and Licence of the
Shire Court where they dwell: upon pain of forfeiture
of five pounds for everie such offence, or imprisonment

at pleasure of the Court, where satisfaction cannot be had.

And every person so licenced for common entertainment shall have some inoffensive Signe obvious for strangers direction, and such as have no such Signe after three months so licensed from time to time shall lose their license: and others allowed in their stead. Any licensed person that selleth beer shall not sell any above two-pence the ale-quart: upon penaltie of three shillings four pence for everie such offence. And it is permiteed to any that will to sell beer out of doors at a pennie the ale-quart and under.

Neither shall any such licenced person aforesaid suffer any to be drunken, or drink excessively viz: above half a pinte of wine for one person at one time; or to continue tippling above the space of half an hour, or at unreasonable times, or after nine of the clock at night in, or about any of their houses on penaltie of five shillings for everie such offence.

And everie person found drunken viz: so that he be therby bereaved or disabled in the use of his understanding, appearing in his speech or gesture in any the said houses or elsewhere shall forfeith ten shillings. And for excessive drinking three shillings four pence. And for continuing above half an hour tippling two shillings six pence. And for tippling at unreasonable times, or after nine a clock at night five shillings: for everie offence in these particulars being lawfully convict therof. And for want of payment such shall be imprisoned untill they pay: or be set in the Stocks one hour or more [in some open place] as the weather will permit not exceeding three hours at one time . . . .

Juries, Jurors.

It is ordered by this Court and Authoritie therof, that the Constable of everie town upon Proces from the Recorder of each Court, shall give timely notice to the Freemen of their town, to choos so many able discreet men as the Proces shal direct which men so chosen he shall warn to attend the Court wherto they are appointed, and shall make return of the Proces unto the Recorder aforesaid: which men so chosen shall be

impannelled and sworn truly to try betwixt partie and
partie, who shall finde the matter of fact with the
damages and costs according to their evidence, and the
Judges shall declare the Sentence (or direct the Jurie
to finde) according to the law. And if there be any
matter of apparent equitie as upon the forfeiture of an
Obligation, breach of covenant without damage, or the
like, the Bench shall determin such matter of equitie.

 2. Nor shall any tryall passe upon any for life
or bannishment but by a special Jurie so summoned for
that purpose, or by the General Court.

 3. It is also ordered by the Authoritie aforesaid that there shall be Grand-Juries summoned everie
year unto the several Courts, in each Jurisdiction; to
inform the Court of any misdemeanours that they shall
know or hear to be committed by any person or persons
whatsoever within this Jurisdiction. And to doe any
other service of the Common-wealth, that according to
law they shall be injoyned to by the said Court; and in
all cases wherin evidence is so obscure or defective
that the Jurie cannot clearly and safely give a positive verdict, whether it be Grand, or Petty Jurie, it
shall have libertie to give a   or a
special verdict, in which last, that is, a special
verdict the judgement of the Cause shall be left unto
the Bench. And all jurors shall have libertie in
matters of fact if they cannot finde the main issue yet
to finde and present in their verdict so much as they
can.

 4. And if the Bench and Jurors shall so differ
at any time about their verdict that either of them
cannot proceed with peace of conscience, the Case shall
be referred to the General Court who shall take the
question from both and determin it.

 5. And it is farther ordered that whensoever any
Jurie of tryalls, or Jurors are not clear in their
judgements or consciences, concerning any Case wherin
they are to give their verdict, they shall have libertie, in open court to advise with any man they shall
think fit to resolve or direct them, before they give
in their verdict. And no Freeman shall be compelled to
serve upon Juries above one ordinary Court in a year:
except Grand-jurie men, who shall hold two Courts
together at the least, and such others as shall be
summoned to serve in case of life and death or bannishment. [1634 1641 1642]

Justice.

It is ordered, and by this Court declared; that
every person within this Jurisdiction, whether Inhabitant or other shall enjoy the same justice and law that
is general for this Jurisdiction which wee constitute
and execute one towards another, in all cases proper to
our cognisance without partialitie or delay. [1641] .
. . .

Liberties Common

It is ordered by this Court, decreed and declared;
that everie man whether Inhabitant or Forreiner, Free
or not Free shall have libertie to come to any publick
Court, Counsell, or Town-meeting; and either by speech
or writing, to move any lawfull, reasonable, or material question; or to present any necessarie motion,
complaint, petition, bill or information wherof that
Meeting hath proper cognisance, so it be done in
convenient time, due order and respective manner.
[1641]
     2.   Everie Inhabitant who is an hous-holder shall
have free fishing and fowling, in any great Ponds,
Bayes, Coves and Rivers so far as the Sea ebs and
flows, within the precincts of the town where they
dwell, unles the Freemen of the same town, or the
General Court have otherwise appropriated them.
Provided that no town shall appropriate to any particular person or persons, any great Pond conteining more
then ten acres of land: and that no man shall come
upon anothers proprietie without their leave otherwise
then as heerafter expressed; the which clearly to
determin, it is declared that in all creeks, coves and
other places, about and upon salt water where the Sea
ebs and flows, the Proprietor of the land adjoyning
shall have proprietie to the low water mark where the
Sea doth not ebb above a hundred rods, and not more
wheresoever it ebs farther. Provided that such
Proprietor shall not by this libertie have power to
stop or hinder the passage of boats or other vessels
in, or through any sea creeks, or coves to other mens
houses or lands. And for great Ponds lying in common
though within the bounds of some town, it shall be free

for any man to fish and fowl there, and may passe and
repasse on foot through any mans proprietie for that
end, so they trespasse not upon any mans corn or
meadow. [1641 1647]

   3.   Every man of, or within this Jurisdiction
shall have free libertie, (notwithstanding any civil
power) to remove both himself and his familie at their
pleasure out of the same. Provided there be no legal
impediment to the contrary. [1641]

Lying.

WHERAS truth in words as well as in actions is
required of all men, especially of Christians who are
the professed Servants of the God of Truth; and wheras
all lying is contrary to truth, and some sorts of lyes
are not only sinfull (as all lyes are) but also perni-
cious to the Publick-weal, and injurious to particular
persons; it is therfore ordered by this Court and
Authoritie therof,

   That everie person of the age of discretion [which
is accounted fourteen years] who shall wittingly and
willingly make, or publish any Lye which may be perni-
cious to the publick weal, or tending to the damage or
injurie of any particular person, or with intent to
deceive and abouse the people with false news or
reports: and the same duly proved in any Court or
before any one Magistrate (who hath heerby power
graunted to hear, and determin all offences against
this Law) such person shall be fined for the first
offence ten shillings, or if the partie be unable to
pay the same then to be set in the stocks so long as
the said Court of Magistrate shall appoint, in some
open place, not exceeding two hours. For the second
offence in that kinde wherof any shall be legally
convicted the sum of twenty shillings, or be whipped
upon the naked body not exceeding ten stripes. And for
the third offence that way fourty shillings, or if the
partie be unable to pay, then to be whipped with more
stripes, not exceeding fifteen. And if yet any shall
offend in the like kinde, and be legally convicted
therof, such person, male or female, shall be fined ten
shillings a time more then formerly: or if the partie
so offending be unable to pay, then to be whipped with

five, or six more stripes then formerly not exceeding
fourty at any time.

The aforesaid fines shall be levied, or stripes
inflicted either by the Marshal of that Jurisdiction,
or Constable of the Town where the offence is committed
according as the Court or Magistrate shall direct. And
such fines so levied shall be paid to the Treasurie of
that Shire where the Cause is tried.

And if any person shall finde himselfe greived witl
the sentence of any such Magistrate out of Court, he
may appeal to the next Court of the same Shire, giving
sufficient securitie to prosecute his appeal and abide
the Order of the Court. And if the said Court shall
judge his appeal causlesse, he shall be double fined
and pay the charges of the Court during his Action, or
corrected by whipping as aforesaid not exceeding
fourtie stripes; and pay the costs of Court and partie
complaining or informing, and of Wittnesses in Case.

And for all such as being under age of discretion
that shall offend in lying contrary to this Order their
Parents or Masters shall give them due correction, and
that in the presence of some Officer if any Magistrate
shall so appoint. Provided also that no person shall
be barred of his just Action of Slaunder, or otherwise
by an proceeding upon this Order. [1645]

Magistrates.

THIS court being sensible of the great disorder
growing in this Commonwealth through the contempts cast
upon the civil Authoritie, which willing to prevent,
doe order and decree;

That whosoever shall henceforth openly or willingl
defame any Court of justice, or the Sentences or
proceedings of the same, or any of the Magistrates or
other Judges of any such Court in respect of any Act or
Sentence therin passed, and being therof lawfully
convict in any General Court or Court of Assistants
shall be punished for the same by Fine, Imprisonment,
Disfranchisement or Bannishment as the qualitie and
measure of the offence shall deserve.

And if any Magistrate or other member of any court
shall use any reproachfull, or un-beseeming speeches,
or behaviour towards any Magistrate, Judge, or member
of the Court in the face of the said Court he shall be

sharply reproved, by the Governour, or other principal
Judge of the same Court for the time being. And if the
qualitie of the offence be such as shall deserve a
farther censure, or if the person so reproved shall
reply again without leave, the same Court may proceed
to punish any such offender by Fine, or Imprisonment,
or it shall be presented to, and censured at the next
superiour Court.

2.   If in a General Court any miscarriage shall be
amongst the Magistrates when they are by themselves, it
shall be examined, and sentenced amongst themselves.
If amongst the Deputies when they are by themselves, it
shall be examined, and sentenced amongst themselves.
If it be when the whole Court is together, it shall be
judged by the whole Court, and not severall as before.
[1637 1641]

3.   And it is ordered by the Authoritie of this
Court that the Governour, Deputie Governour, or greater
part of the Assistants may upon urgent occasion call a
General Court at any time. [1647]

4.   And wheras there may arise some difference of
judgement in doubtfull cases, it is therfore farther
ordered;

That no Law, Order, or Sentence shall passe as an
Act of the Court without the consent of the greater
part of the Magistrates on the one partie, and the
greater number of the Deputies on the other part.

5.   And for preventing all occasions of partial
and undue proceeding in Courts of justice, and avoyding
of jealousies which may be taken up against Judges in
that kinde, it is farther ordered,

That in everie Case of civil nature between partie
and partie where there shall fall out so neer relation
between any Judge and any of the parties as between
Father and Son, either by nature or marriage, Brother
and Brother; in like kinde Uncle and Nephew, Land-lord
and Tenent in matter of considerable value, such Judge
though he may have libertie to be present in the Court
at the time of the tryall, and give reasonable advice
in the Case, yet shall have no power to vote or give
sentence therin, neither shall Sit as Judge, but
beneath the Bench when he shall so plead or give advice
in the Case.   [1635]

Monopolies.

It is ordered, decreed and by this Court declared; that there shall be no Monopolies graunted or allowed amongst us, but of such new inventions that are profitable for the Countrie, and that for a short time. [1641]

Oaths, Subscription

It is ordered and decreed, and by this Court declared; that no man shall be urged to take any oath, or subscribe any Articles, Covenants, or remonstrance of publick and civil nature but such as the General Court hath considered, allowed and required. And that no oath of Magistrate, counceller or any other Officer shall binde him any farther, or longer then he is resident, or reputed an Inhabitant of this Jurisdictio [1641]

Oppression

For avoyding such mischeifs as may follow by such illdisposed persons as may take libertie to oppresse and wrong their neighbours, by taking excessive wages for work, or unreasonable prizes for such necessarie merchandizes or other commodities as shall passe from man to man, it is ordered, That if any man shall offend in any of the said cases he shall be punished by Fine, or Imprisonment according to the qualitie of the offence, as the Court to which he is presented upon lawfull tryall & conviction shall adjudge. [1635] . . . .

Profane Swearing.

It is ordered, and by this Court decreed, that if any person within this Jurisdiction shall swear rashly and vainly either by the holy Name of God, or any other oath, he shall forfeit to the common Treasurie for everie such severall offence ten shillings. And it shall be in the power of any Magistrate by Warrant to the Constable to call such person before him, and upon

sufficient proof to passe sentence, and levie the said
penaltie according to the usuall order of Justice. And
if such person be not able, or shall utterly refuse to
pay the aforesaid Fine, he shall be committed to the
Stocks there to continue, not exceeding three hours,
and not lesse then one hour. [1646] . . . .

Punishment

It is ordered, decreed, and by this Court declared;
that no man shall be twice sentenced by civil Justice
for one and the same Crime, offence or Trespasse. And
for bodily punishments, wee allow amongst us none that
are in-humane, barbarous or cruel. [1641]

Schools.

It being one chief project of that old deluder,
Satan, to keep men from the knowledge of the Scriptures, as in former times keeping them in an unknown
tongue, so in these later times by perswading from the
use of Tongues, that so at least the true sense and
meaning of the Original might be clowded with false
glosses of Saint-seeming-deceivers; and that Learning
may not be buried in the graves of our fore-fathers in
Church and Commonwealth, the Lord assisting our indeavours: it is therfore ordered by this Court and
Authoritie therof;
    That everie Township in this Jurisdiction, after
the Lord hath increased them to the number of fifty
Householders shall then forthwith appoint one within
their Town to teach all such children as shall resort
to him to write and read, whose wages shall be paid
either by the Parents or Masters of such children, or
by the Inhabitants in general by way of supply, as the
major part of those that order the prudentials of the
Town shall appoint. Provided that those which send
their children be not oppressed by paying much more
then they can have them taught for in other Towns.
    2. And it is farther ordered, that where any Tow:
shall increase to the number of one hundred Families or
Householders they shall set upon a Grammar-School, the
Masters therof being able to instruct youth so far as
they may be fitted for the Universitie. And if any

Town neglect the performance heerof above one year then
everie such town shall pay five pounds per annum to the
next such School, till they shall perform this Order.
[1647] . . . .

Strangers.

It is ordered by this Court and the Authoritie
therof; that no Town or person shal receive any stranger resorting hither with intent to reside in this
Jurisdiction, nor shall allow any Lot or Habitation to
any, or entertain any such above three weeks, except
such person shall have allowance under the hand of some
one Magistrate, upon pain of everie Town that shall
give, or sell any Lot or Habitation to any not so
licenced such Fine to the Countrie as the County Court
shall impose, not exceeding fifty pounds, nor lesse
then ten pounds. And of everie person receiving any
such for longer time then is heer expressed or allowed,
in some special cases as before, or in case of
entertainment of friends resorting from other parts of
this Country in amitie with us, shall forfeit as
aforesaid, not exceeding twenty pounds, nor lesse then
four pounds: and for everie month after so offending,
shal forfeit, as aforesaid not exceeding ten pounds,
nor lesse then fourty shillings. Also, that all
Constables shall inform the Courts of new commers which
they know to be admitted without licence, from time to
time. [1637 1638 1647]

Summons.

It is ordered, and by this Court declared; that no
Summons, Pleading, Judgement or any kinde of proceeding
in Court or course of justice shall be abated, arested
or reversed upon any kinde of circumstantial errors or
mistakes, if the person and the Cause be rightly
understood and intended by the Court.
2.   And that in all cases where the first Summons
are not served six dayes before the Court, and the Case
briefly specified in the Warrant where appearance is to
be made by the partie summoned; it shall be at his
libertie whether he will appear, or not, except all
Cases that are to be handled in Courts suddenly called

upon extraordinarie occasions. And that in all cases
where there appears present and urgent cause any
Assistant or Officer appointed shall have power to make
out Attachments for the first Summons. Also, it is
declared that the day of Summons or Attachment served,
and the day of appearance shall be taken inclusively as
part of the six dayes. [1641 1647]

Suits, vexatious Suits.

It is ordered and decreed, and by this Court
declared; that in all Cases where it appears to the
Court that the Plaintiffe hath willingly & wittingly
done wrong to the Defendant in commencing and prosecuting any Action, Suit, Complaint or Indictment in his
own name or in the name of others, he shall pay treble
damages to the partie greived, and be fined fourty
shillings to the Common Treasurie. [1641 1646] . . .

Tobacco.

This Court finding that since the repealing of the
former Laws against Tobacco, the same is more abused
then before doth therfore order,
That no man shall take any tobacco within twenty
poles of any house, or so neer as may indanger the
same, or neer any Barn, corn, or hay-cock as may
occasion the fyring therof, upon pain of ten shillings
for everie such offence, besides full recompence of all
damages done by means therof. Nor shall any take
tobacco in any Inne or common Victualing-house, except
in a private room there, so as neither the Master of
the said house nor any other Guests there shall take
offence therat, which if any doe, then such person
shall forthwith forbear, upon pain of two shillings
sixpence for everie such offence. And for all Fines
incurred by this Law, one half part shall be to the
Informer the other to the poor of the town where the
offence is done. [1638 1647]

Torture.

It is ordered, decreed, and by this Court declared;
that no man shall be forced by torture to confesse any

crime against himselfe or any other, unles it be in
some Capital where he is first fully convicted by
clear and sufficient evidence to be guilty. After
which, if the Case be of that nature that it is very
apparent there be other Conspirators or Confoederates
with him; then he may be tortured, yet not with such
tortures as be barbarous and inhumane.

    2.   And that no man shal be beaten with above
fourty stripes for one Fact at one time. Nor shall any
man be punished with whipping, except he have not
otherwise to answer the Law, unles his crime be very
shamefull, and his course of life vitious and profligate. [1641]

Townships.

    It is ordered, decreed, and by this Court declared
that if any man shall behave himselfe offensively at
any Town-meeting, the rest then present shall have
power to sentence him for such offence, so be it the
mulct or penalty exceed not twety shillings.

    2.   and that the Freemen of everie Township, and
others authorized by law, shall have power to make such
Laws and Constitutions as may concern the welfare of
their Town. Provided they be not repugnant to the
publick Laws and Orders of the Countrie. And if any
Inhabitant shall neglect or refuse to observe them,
they shall have power to levie the appointed penalties
by distresse.

    3.   Also that the Freemen of everie town or
Township, with such other the Inhabitats as have taken
the Oath of fidelitie shall have full power to choos
yearly, or for lesse time, within each Township a
convenient number of fit men to order the planting and
prudential occasions of that Town, according to
instructions given them in writing.

    Provided, nothing be done by them contrary to the
publick Laws and Orders of the Countrie. Provided also
that the number of such Select persons be not aboue
nine.

    4.   Farther, it is ordered by the Authoritie
aforesayd, that all Towns shall take care from time to
time to order and dispose of all single persons, and
In-mates within their Towns to service, or otherwise.
And if any be greived at such order or dispose, they
have libertie to appeal to the next County Court.

5.   This Court taking into considerattion the
usefull Parts and abilities of divers Inhabitants
amongst us, which are not Freemen, which if improved to
publick use, the affairs of this Common-wealth may be
the easier caried an end in the severall Towns of this
Jurisdiction doth order, and heerby declare;

That henceforth it shall may be lawfull for the
Freemen within any of the said Towns, to make choice of
such Inhabitants (though non-Freemen) who have taken,
or shall take the Oath of fidelitie to this Government
to be Jurie-men, and to have their Vote in the choice
of the Select-men for the town Affairs, Assessements of
Rates, and other Prudentials proper to the Select-men
of the several Towns. Provided still that the major
part of all companyes of Select-men be Free-men from
time to time that shall make any valid Act. As also,
where no Select-men are, to have their Vote in ordering
of Schools, hearing of cattle, laying out of High-wayes
and distributing of Lands; any Law, Use or Custom to
the contrary notwithstanding. Provided also that no
non-Freeman shall have his Vote, untill he have
attained the age of twenty one years. [1636 1641
1647]

Tryalls.

Wheras this Court is often taken up in hearing and
deciding particular Cases, between partie and partie,
which more properly belong to other inferiour Court.
And that if the partie against whom the Judgment shall
have any new evidence, or other new matter to plead, he
may desire a new Tryall in the same Court upon a Bill
or review. And if justice shall not be done him upon
that Tryall he may then come to this Court for releif.
[1642]

2.   it is ordered, and by this Court declared,
that in all Actions of Law it shall be the libertie of
the Plaintiffe and Defendant by mutuall consent to
choos whether they will be tryed by the Bench or a
Jurie, unles it be where the Law upon just reason hath
otherwise determined. The like libertie shall be
graunted to all persons in any criminal Cases.

3.   Also it shall be in the libertie both of
Plaintiffe and Defendant, & likewise everie delinquent
to be judged by a Jurie, to challenge any of the

Jurors, & if the challenge be found just and reasonable, by the Bench or the rest of the Jurie as the
Challenger shall choos, it shall be allowed him, &
                                impannelled in their room.
     4.   Also, children, Ideots, distracted persons ar
all that are strangers or new comers to our Plantation
shall have such allowances, and dispensations in any
Case, whether criminal or others, as Religion and
reason require.   [1641]

Votes.

     It is ordered, decreed and by this Court declared;
that all, and everie Freeman, and others authorized by
Law, called to give any Advice, Vote, Verdict or
Sentence in any Court, Council or civil Assemblie,
shall have full freedom to doe it according to their
true judgements and consciences, so it be done orderly
and inoffensively, for the manner.   And that in all
cases wherin any Freeman or other is to give his Vote
be it in point of Election, making Constitutions and
Orders or passing Sentence in any case of Judicature or
the like, if he cannot see light or reason to give it
positively, one way or other, he shall have libertie to
be silent, and not pressed to a determinate vote.   And
farther that whensoever any thing is to be put to vote,
and Sentence to be pronounced or any other matter to be
proposed, or read in any Court or Assemblie, if the
President or Moderator shall refuse to perform it, the
major part of the members of that Court or Assemblie
shall have power to appoint any other meet man of them
to doe it.   And if there be just cause, to punish him
that should, and would not.   [1641]

Userie.

     It is ordered, decreed & by this Court declared,
that no man shall be adjudged for the meer forbearance
of any debt, above eight pounds in the hundred for one
year, and not above that rate proportionably for all
sums whatsoever, Bills of Exchange excepted, neither
shall this be a colour or countenance to allow any
usurie amongst us contrary to the Law of God.   [1641
1643] . . . .

Witnesses.

It is ordered, decreed, and by this Court declared, that no man shall be put to death without the testimonie of two or three witnesses, or that which is equivalent therunto.   [1641]

2.   And it is ordered by this Court and the Authoritie therof, that any one Magistrate, or Commissioner authorized therunto by the General Court may take the Testimonie of any person of fourteen years of age, or above, of sound understanding and reputation, in any Case civil or criminal; and shall keep the same in his own hands till the Court, or deliver it to the Recorder, publick Notarie or Clerk of the writs to be recorded, that so nothing may be altered in it. Provided, that where any such witnesse shall have his abode within ten miles of the Court, and there living and not disabled by sicknes, or other infirmitie, the said Testimonie so taken out of court shall not be received, or made use of in the Court, except the witnes be also present to be farther examined about it. Provided also, that in all capital cases all witnesses shall be present wheresoever they dwell.

3.   And it is farther ordered by the Authoritie aforesaid, that any person summoned to appear as a witnes in any civil Court between partie and partie, shall not be compellable to travell to any Court or place where he is to give his Testimonie, except he who shall so summon him shall lay down or give him satisfaction for his travell and expences, out-ward and home-ward; and for such time as he shall spend in attendance in such case when he is at such Court or place, the Court shall award due recompence. And it is ordered that two shillings a day shall be accounted due satisfaction to any Witnes for travell and expences: and that when the Witnes dwelleth within three miles, and is not at charge to passe over any other Ferrie than betwixt Charlstown and Boston then one shilling six pence per diem shall be accounted sufficient. And if any Witnes after such payment or satisfaction shall fail to appear to give his Testimonie he shall be lyable to pay the parties damages upon an action of the Case. And all Witnesses in criminal cases shall have suitable satisfaction, payd by the Treasurer upon

Warrant from the Court or Judge before whom the case is
tryed. And for a general rule to be observed in all
criminal causes, both where the Fines are put in
certain, and also where they are otherwise, it is
farther ordered by the Authoritie aforesayd, that the
charges of Witnesses in all such cases shall be borne
by the parties delinquent, and shall be added to the
Fines imposed; that so the Treasurer having upon
Warrant from the Court or other Judge satisfied such
Witnesses, it may be repayd him with the Fine: that so
the Witness may be timely satisfied, and the countrie
not damnified. [1647] . . . .

DOCUMENT 54:   Massachusetts Ordinance on Legislative
Procedure, October 18, 1648

Text taken from N. B. Shurtleff, ed., *Records of the Governor and Company of the Massachusetts Bay Colony.*   See Documents 15, 47, and 48 for related information. Text is complete with the original spelling.

For the better carrying on the occassions of the Generall Court, & to the end that the records of the same, together with what shall be presented by way of petition, etc., or passes by way of vote, either amongst the magistrates or deputies, may hereafter be more exactly recorded, & kept for public use,-
It is hereby ordered, that as there is a secretary amongst the magistrates, (who is the generall officer of the common wealth, for the keeping the publike records of the same,) so there shall be a clarke amongst the deputies, to be chosen by them, from time to time; that (by the Court of Elections, and then the officers to begin their entryes, their recompence accordingly) there be provided, by the auditor, four large paper books, in folio, bound up with velum & pastboard, two whereof to be delivered to the secretary, & two to the clarke of the House of Deputies, one to be a journall to each of them, the other for the faire entry of all lawes, acts, & orders, etc., that shall passe the magistrates and deputies, that of the secretaries to be the publike record of the country, that of the clarkes to be a book onely of coppies.
That the secretary & clarke for the deputies shall briefly enter into their journals, respectively, the title of all bills, orders, lawes, petitions, etc., which shal be presented & read amongst them, what are

referd to committees, & what are voted negatively or
affirmatively, & so for any addition or alteration.

That all bills, lawes, petitions, etc, which shal
be last concluded amongst the magistrates, shall
remaine with the Governor till the latter end of that
session, & such as are last assented to by the deputies
shall remaine with the speaker till the said time, when
the whole Courte shall meete together, or a committee
of magistrates & deputies, to consider what hath passed
that session, where the secretary & clarke shall be
present, & by their journals call for such bils, etc,
as hath passed either house, & such as shall appeare to
have passed the magistrates & deputies shall be delivered to the secretary to record, who shall record the
same within one month after every session, which being
done, the clarke of the deputies shall have liberty,
for one month after, to transcribe the same into his
booke; & such bills, orders, etc, that hath onely
passed the magistrates, shall be delivered to the
secretary to keepe upon file, & such as have onely
passed the deputies shal be delivered to their clarke
to be kept upon file, in like manner, or otherwise
disposed of, as the whole Court shall appoint; that all
lawes, orders, & acts of Courte, contained in the ould
bookes, that are of force, & not ordered to be printed,
be transcribed in some alphabeticall or methodicall
way, by direction of some committee that this Courte
shall please to appoint, & delivered to the secreary to
record in the first place, in the said booke of records, & then the acts of the other sessions in order
accordingly, & a coppy of all to be transcribed by the
clarke of the deputies, as aforesaid.

DOCUMENT 55:   Charter of Providence, March 14, 1649

Taken from J.R. Bartlett, ed., *Records of the Colony of Rhode Island and Providence Plantation in New England: Vol. I, 1636 - 1663.* (Providence, R.I.: A. Crawford Greene and Brother, State Printers, 1856), 214-216. The text is complete with the original spelling. This is not a true charter insofar as it does not proceed from the king. Rather, it is typical of many early colonial documents in that it proceeds from powers of self-government frequently granted in the original charters from England. In effect it is one of the earliest examples of a town charter being granted form what we would today consider the state level. It is equivalent to the state of Texas granting Houston a city charter. Note that since the inhabitants are taking it upon themselves to form a charter, they are careful to cite their authority to do so under the charter granted by the king, implying that the king is sanctioning this docuemnt and thus justifying the use of the word "charter" to describe its legal status.

Charter of Providence

Whereas, by virtue of a free and absolute charter of civill incorporation, granted to the free inhabitants of the colonie of Providence, by the Right Honorable Robert, Earl of Warwick, Governor in chiefe with the rest of the Honorable Commoners, bearing the date the 7th day of March, Anno 1643, givinge and grantinge full power and authoritie vnto the said inhabitants to governe themselves and such others as shall come among them, as also to make, constitute and ordaine such lawes, orders and constitutions, and to inflict such punishments and penalties as is conformable to the lawes of England, so neare as the nature

and constitution of the place will admit, and which may
best suite the estate and condition thereof, and
whereas the said towns of Providence, Portsmouth,
Newport and Warwick are far remote from each other,
whereby so often and free intercourse of help, in
decidinge of differences and trying of causes and the
like, cannot easilie and at all times be had and
procured of that kind is requisite; therefore, upon the
petition and humble request of the freemen of the Town
of Providence, exhibited unto this present session of
the General Assembly, wherein they desire freedome and
libertie to incorporate themselves into a body politicke, and we, the said Assembly, having duly weighed
and seriously considered the premises, and being
willing and ready to provide for the ease and lbiertie
of the people, have thought fit, and by the authoritie
aforesaid, and by these presents, do give, grant and
confirme unto the free Inhabitants of the towne of
Providence, a free and absolute charter of civill
incorporation and government, to be knowne by the
Incorporation of Providence Plantation in the Narrangansett Bay, in New-England, together with full power
and authoritie to governe and rule themselves, and such
others as shall hereafter inhabit within any part of
the said Plantation, by such a form of civill government, as by voluntarie consent of all, or the greater
part of them, shall be found most suitable unto their
estate and condition; and, to that end, to make and
ordaine such civill orders and constitutions, to
inflict such punishments upon transgressors, and for
execution thereof, and of the common statute lawes of
the colonye agreed unto, and the penalties and so many
of them as are not annexed already unto the colonye
court of trialls, so to place and displace officers of
justice, as they or the greater parte of them shall, by
one consent, agree unto. Provided, nevertheless, that
the said lawes, constitutions and punishments, for the
civill government of the said plantation, be conformable to the lawes of England, so far as the nature and
constitution of the place will admit, yet, always
reserving to the aforesaid General Assemblie power and
authoritie so to dispose the generall governmente of
that plantation as it stands in reference to the rest
of the plantations, as they shall conceive, from time
to time, most conducing to the generall good of the

said plantations. And we the said Assemblie, do
further authorise the aforesaid inhabitants to elect
and engage such aforesaide officers upon the first
second day of June, annually. And, moreover, we
authorize the said inhabitants, for the better
transacting of their publicke affaires, to make and use
a publicke seal as the knowne seale of Providence
Plantation, in the Narrangansett Bay, in New-England.
    In testimonie whereof, we the said Generall Assem-
blie, have hereunto sett oure handes and seales the
14th of March, anno 1648.

                            John Warner
                            Clerk of the Assemblie.

DOCUMENT 56: Maryland Toleration Act, April 21, 1649

Text, complete and with original spelling, taken from
William Hand Browne, ed., *The Archives of Maryland: Vol.
I, Proceedings and Acts of the General Assembly of
Maryland, January 1637/8 - September 1664*   (Baltimore: Maryland Historical Society, 1883), 244-247.
Passed in accordance with instructions from Lord
Baltimore, this document protected Maryland from the
charge of intolerance toward Protestants. When the
Protestants were in charge of the colony for a time
after 1654, Catholics were not protected in their
faith, but this document was reinstated with the
restoration of Lord Baltimore. As such, it constitutes
the broadest definition of religious freedom during the
seventeenth century and an important step toward true
freedom of religion. The harsh blasphemy provisions
were never enforced.

Acts and Orders of Assembly assented vnto

Enacted and made at a Generall Sessions of the said
Assembly held at St Maries on the one and twentieth day
of Aprill Anno Domini 1649 as followeth viz:

An Act Concerning Religion

fforasmuch as in a well governed and Xpian[1] Common
Weath[2] matters concerning Religion and the honor of God
ought in the first place to bee taken, into serious
consideracion and endeavoured to bee settled. Be it
therefore ordered and enacted by the Right Noble
Cecilius Lord Baron of Baltemore absolute Lord and
Proprietary of this Province with the advise and
consent of this Generall Assembly. That whatsoever
pson or psons within this Province and the Islands

thereunto belonging shall from henceforth blaspheme
God, that is Curse him, or deny our Saviour Jesus
Christ to bee the sonne of God, or shall deny the holy
Trinity the ffather sonne and holy Ghost, or the
Godhead of any of the said Three psons of the Trinity
or the Vnity of this Godhead, or shall use or utter any
reproachfull Speeches, words or language concerning the
said Holy Trinity, or any of the said three psons
thereof, shalbe punished with death and confiscation or
forfeiture of all his or her lands and goods to the
Lord Proprietary and his heires, And bee it also
Enacted by the Authority and with the advise and assent
aforesaid. That whatsoever pson or psons shall from
henceforth use or utter any reproachfull words or
Speeches concerning the blessed Virgin Mary the Mother
of our Saviour or the holy Apostles or Evangelists or
any of them shall in such case for the first offence
forfeit to the said Lord Proprietary and his heirs
Lords and Proprietaries of this Province the sume of
ffive pound Sterling or the value thereof to be Levyed
on the goods and chattells of every such pson soe
offending, but in case such Offender or Offenders,
shall not then have such goods and chattells sufficient
for the satisfyeing of such forfeiture, or that the
same bee not otherwise speedily satisfyed that then
such Offender or Offenders shalbe publiquely whipt and
bee ymprisoned during the pleasure of the Lord Proprietary or the Leivet³ or cheife Governor of this
Province for the time being. And that every such
Offender or Offenders for every second offence shall
forfeit tenne pound sterling or the value thereof to
bee levyed as aforesaid, or in case such offender of
Offenders shall not then haue goods and chattells
within this Province sufficient for that purpose then
to be publiquely and severly whipt and imprisoned as
before is expressed. And that every pson or psons
before mentioned offending herein the third time, shall
for such third Offence forfeit all his lands and Goods
and bee for ever banished and expelled out of this
Province. And be it also further Enacted by the same
authority advise and assent that whatsoever pson or
psons shall from henceforth vppon any occasion or
otherwise in a reproachful manner or Way declare call
or denominate any pson or psons whatsoever inhabiting
residing traffiqueing trading or comerceing within this

Province or within any the Ports, Harbors, Creeks or
Havens to the same belonging to an heritick, Scis-
matick, Idolator, puritan, Independent, Prespiterian
popish prest, Jesuite, Jesuited papist, Lutheran,
Calvenist, Anabaptist, Brownist, Antinomian, Barrowist,
Roundhead, Sepatist, or any other name or terme in a
reproachfull manner relating to matter of Religion
shall for every such Offence forfeit and loose the some
fr tenne shillings sterling or the value thereof to bee
levyed on the goods and chattells of ever such Offender
and offenders, the one half thereof to be forfeited and
paid unto the person and persons of whom such reproachfull words are or shalbe spoken or vttered, and the
other half thereof to the Lord Proprietary and his
heires Lords and Proprietries of this Province, But if
such psons or psons who shall at any time vtter or
speake any such reproachful words or Language shall not
have Goods or Chattells sufficient and overt within
this Province to bee taken to satisfie the penalty
aforesaid or that the same bee not otherwise speedily
satisfied, that then the pson or psons soe offending
shalbe publickly whipt, and shall suffer imprisonmt
without baile or maineprise vntill hee shee or they
respectively shall satisfy the party soe offended or
grieved by such reproachfull Language by asking him or
her respectively forgivenes publiquely for such his
Offence before the Magistrate or chiefe Officer or
Officers of the Towne or place where such Offence
shalbe given. And be it further likewise Enacted by
the Authority and consent aforesaid That every person
and persons within this Province that shall at any time
hereafter prophane the Sabbath or Lords day called
sunday by frequent swearing, drunkennes or by any
uncivill or disorderly recreacion, or by working on
that day when absolute necessity doth not require it
shall for every such first offence forfeit 2s. 6d 4
sterling or the value thereof, and for the second
offence 5s sterling or the value thereof, and for the
third offence and soe for every time as shall offend in
like manner afterwards 10s sterling or the value
thereof. And in case such offender and offenders shall
not have sufficient goods or chattels within this
Province to satisfy any of the said Penalties respectively hereby imposed for prophaning the Sabbath or
Lords day called Sunday as aforesaid, That in Every

such case the partie soe offending shall for the first
and second offence in that kinde be imprisoned till hee
or shee shall publickly in open court before the chiefe
Commander Judge or Magistrate, or that County Towne or
precinct where such offence shalbe committed acknowledge the Scandall and offence he hath in that respect
given against God and the good and civill Governemt of
this Province And for the third offence and for every
time after shall also bee publickly whipt. And whereas
the inforceing of the conscience in matters of Religion
hath frequently fallen out to be of dangerous Consequence in those commonwealthes where it hath been
practised,And for the more quiett and peaceable government of this Province, and the better to preserve
mutuall Love and amity amongst the Inhabitants thereof.
Be it Therefore also by the Lo: Proprietary with the
advise and consent of this Assembly Ordeyned & enacted
(except as in this psent Act is before Declared and
sett forth) that noe person or psons whatsoever within
this Province, or the Islands, Ports, Harbors, Creekes,
or havens thereunto belonging professing to beleive in
Jesus Christ, shall from henceforth bee any waies
troubled, Molested or discountenanced for or in respect
of his or her religion not in the free exercise thereof
within this Province or the Islands thereunto belonging
nor any way compelled to the beliefe or exercise of any
other Religion against his or her consent, soe as they
be not unfaithfull to the Lord Proprietary, or molest
or conspire against the civill Governemt established or
to bee established in this Province vnder him or his
heires. And that all & every pson and psons that shall
presume contrary to this Act and the true intent and
meaning thereof directly or indirectly either in person
or estate willfully to wrong disturbe trouble or molest
any person whatsoever within this Province professing
to believe in Jesus Christ for or in respect of his or
her religion or the free exercise thereof within this
Province other than is provided for in this Act that
such pson or psons soe offending, shalbe compelled to
pay trebble damages to the party soe wronged or molested, and for every such offence shall also forfeit 20s
sterling in money or the value thereof, half thereof
for the vse of the Lo: Proprietary, and his heires
Lords and Propietaries of this Province, and the other
half for the vse of the party soe wronged or molested

as aforesaid, Or if the ptie soe offending as aforesaid shall refuse or bee vnable to recompense the party soe wronged, or to satisfy such ffyne or forfeiture, then such Offender shalbe severely punished by publick whipping & imprisonmt during the pleasure of the Lord Proprietary, or his Leivetenant or cheife Governor of this Province for the tyme being without baile or maineprise And bee it further alsoe Enacted by the authority and consent aforesaid That the Sheriff or other Officer of Officers from time to time to bee appoitned & authorized for that purpose, of the County Towne or precinct where every particular offence in this psent Act conteyned shall happen at any time to bee committed and wherevppon there is hereby a fforfeiture ffyne or penalty imposed shall from time to time distraine and seise the goods and estate of every such pson soe offending as aforesaid against this psent Act or any part thereof, and sell the same or any part thereof for the full satisfaccion of such forfeiture, ffine, or penalty as aforesaid, Restoring vnto the ptie soe offending the Remainder or overplus of the said goods or estate after such satisfaccion soe made as aforesaid

The freemen haue assented. Tho: Hatton

Enacted by Governor Wllm Stone

DOCUMENT 57:   Towns of Wells, Gorgiana, and Piscataqua
              Form an Independent Government, July,
              1649

Text is complete and taken from W. Keith Kavenagh, ed.,
Foundations of Colonial America: A Documentary History
(New York: Chelsea House, 1973), 263-264.   Spelling is
his.   Kavenagh takes his text from J. P. Baxter and M.
F. Farnham, eds., *Documentary History of the State of
Maine*, 2nd. Series, Vol. VII, 266.   This document is
typical of those written during the Cromwellian era
when the interruption of the monarchy cast into doubt
the continued legality of the charters written earlier
in the century, and coherent instructions from England
were not forthcoming.   While many colonies continued
under their former organic documents, others like this
one felt compelled to refound themselves.

    Whereas the inhabitants of Piscataqua, Gorgiana,
and Wells in the province of Maine, have here begun to
propogate and populate these parts of the country, did
formerly by power derivative from Sir Ferdinando
Gorges, Knight, exercise the regulating the affairs of
the country as nigh as we could according to the laws
of England, and such other ordinances as was thought
meet and requisite for the better regulating thereof.
Now, forasmuch as Sir Ferdinando Gorges is dead, the
country by their general letters sent to his heirs in
June 1647 and 48, but by the said distractions in
England no return is yet come to hand, and command from
the Parliament not to meddle in so much as was granted
to Mr. Rigley, most of the commissioners being departed
the privince, the inhabitants are for present in some
distraction about the regulating of the affairs of
these sites.   For the better ordering whereof, till
further order, power, and authority shall come out of

England, the inhabitants with one free and univeranimus
consent do bind themselves in a body politic, a combination to see these parts of the country and province
regulated according to such laws as formerly have been
exercised and such others as shall be thought meet, not
repugnant to the fundamental laws of our native
country, and to make choice of such governor or
governess and magistrates as by most voices they shall
think meet. Dated in Gorgiana, alias Accomenticus, the
[   ] day of July 1649. The privileges of
Accomenticus' charter excepted.

DOCUMENT 58:   Connecticut Code of Laws, 1650

Partial text with the original spelling taken from J.
Hammond Trumbull, ed., *The Public Records of the Colony
of Connecticut, Vol. II*   (Hartford: Brown and Parsons,
1850).   This Code, sometimes cited as "Mr. Ludlow's
code" after the man who drew it up, or "The Code of
1650," appears at the end of Volume II with its own
pagination.   It is immediately preceeded by the Fundamental Orders of Connecticut (see Document 32), which
is termed the "Constitution of 1639," and serves as a
preface to this text.   The document is fifty-four pages
long, and is here reproduced only in part.   Too long to
reproduce in full, it is hoped that these selections
from it will establish its rightful place as a foundation document.   The portions not produced deal with the
more mundane aspects of law such as penalties for
burglary and theft, weights and measures, heights of
fences, fines, the militia, swearing, murder, the
keeping of records, etc.   The portions reproduced deal
more directly with rights, values, and other aspects of
self-definition a people might engage in.

ESTABLISHED BY THE GENERAL COURT, MAY, 1650

Forasmuch as the free fruition of such Libberties,
Immunities, Privileges, as Humanity, Civillity and
Christianity, call for, as due to euery man in his
place and proportion, without Impeachmt and infringement, hath euer beene and euer will bee the Tranquil-
lity and Stabillity of Churches and Common wealths, and
the denyall or deprivall thereof, the disturbance if
not ruine of both:
It is therefore ordered by this Courte and Authority thereof, that no mans life shall bee taken away, no
mans honor or good name shall bee stained, no mans

person shall be arrested, restrained, banished, dismem-
bered nor any way punished; no man shall bee deprived
of his wife or children, no mans goods or estate shall
bee taken away from him, nor any wayes indamaged, vnder
colour of Law or countenance of Authority, vnless it be
by the vertue or equity of some express Law of the
Country warranting the same, established by a Generall
Courte, and sufficiently published, or in case of the
defect of a Law in any perticular case, by the word of
God . . .

CAPITALL LAWES

[N.B. The first twelve laws in this section are word
for word the same as those adopted in December of 1642
-- see Document 44 -- and are thus not reproduced
here.]

13. If any Childe or Children aboue sixteene
yeares old and of sufficient vnderstanding, shall Curse
or smite theire naturall father or mother, hee or they
shall bee put to death, vnless it can bee sufficiently
testified that the Parents haue beene very vnchristianly negligent in the education of such Children, or
so prouoake them by extreme and cruell correction that
they haue beene forced thervnto to preserue themselves
from death [or] maiming. Exo. xxi: 17; Levit: xx. [9];
Exo: xxi. 15.

14. If a man haue a stubborne and rebellious sonne
of sufficient yeares and vnderstanding, viz: sixteene
yeares of age, wch will not obey the voice of his
father or the voice of his mother, and that when they
haue chastened him, will not hearken vnto them, then
may his Father and Mother, being his naturall parents,
lay hold on him and bring him to the Magistrates
assembled in Courte, and testifie vnto them that theire
Sonne is stubborne and rebelious and will not obey
theire voice and chastisement, but liues in sundry
notorioug crimes, such a Sonne shall bee put to death.
Deut: xxi. 20, 21 . . .

CHILDREN

Forasmuch as the good Education of Children is of
singular behoofe and benefit to any Common wealth, and
whereas many parents and masters are too indulgent and
negligent of theire duty in that kinde; --
It is therefore ordered by this Courte and Authority thereof, that the Select men of euery Towne, in the
seuuerall precincts and quarters where they dwell,
shall haue a vigilant eye ouer their brethren and
neighbors, to see first, that none of them shall suffer
so much Barbarisme in any of theire familyes as not to
indeauer to teach by themselues or others theire
Children and Apprentices so much learning as may inable
them perfectly to read the Inglish tounge, and knowledge of the Capitall Lawes, vppon penalty of twenty
shillings for each neglect therein. Allso, that all
Masters of familyes doe once a weeke at least, catechise theire children and servants in the grounds and
principles of religion; and if any bee vnable to doe so
much, that then at the least they procure such Children
or Apprentices to learne some shorte orthodox Cate-
chisme, without booke, that they may bee able to answer
to the questions that shall bee propounded to them out
of such Catechismes by theire parents or Masters or any
of the Select men, when they shall call them to a
tryall of what they haue learned in this kinde. And
further, that all Parents and Masters doe breed and
bring vp theire Children and Apprentices in some honest
lawfull [calling,] labour or imployment, either in
husbandry, or some other trade proffitable for themselues and the Common wealth, if they will not nor
cannott traine them vp in Learning to fitt them for
higher imployments. And if any of the Select men,
after Admonition by them giuen to such Masters of
familyes, shall finde them still negligent of theire
duty in the perticulars aforementioned, wherby Children
and Seruants become rude, stubborne and vnruly, the
said Select men with the helpe of two Magistrates shall
take such Children or Apprentices from them, and place
them with some masters for yeares, boyes till they come
to twenty one and girles to eighteene yeares of age
compleat, wch will more stricly looke vnto, and force
them to submitt vnto gouernemt, according to the rules
of this order, if by faire means and former instructions they will not bee drawne vnto it . . .

ECLESEASTICALL

Forasmuch as the open contempt of Gods word, and
messenger thereof, is the desolating sinne of Ciuill
States and Churches, and that the preaching of the Word
by those whome God doth send is the chiefe ordinary
meanes ordained by God for the converting, edefying and
sauing the soules of the elect, through the presence
and power of the Holy Ghost therevnto promised; and
that the ministry of the Word is sett vp by God in his
Churches for those holy ends, and according to the
respect or contempt of the same and of those whome God
hath set aparte for his owne worke and imployment, the
weale or woe of all Christian States it much furthered
and promoated: --
It is therfore ordered and decreed, that if any
Christian (so called,) within this Jurissdiction shall
contemptuously [behave] himselfe towards the word
preached or the messengers th[ereof,] called to dis-
pence the same in any Congregation, when hee faithfully
execute his serviue and office therein according to the
will and word of God, either by interrupting him in his
preaching, or by charging him falsely with an error wch
hee hath not taught in the open face of the Church, or
like a sonne of Korah, cast vppon his true doctrine or
himselfe any reproach, to the dishonor of the Lord
Jesus whoe hath sent him, and to the disparagement of
that his holy ordinance, and making God's wayes
contemptible or ridiculous, that euery such person or
persons, (whatsoeuer censure the Church may passe,)
shall for the first scandall, bee convented and
reproved openly by the Magistrate, at some Lecture, and
bound to theire good behauiour: And if a second time
they breake forth into the like contemptuous carraiges,
they shall either pay fiue pounds to the publique
Treasure, or stand two houres openly vppon a block or
stoole foure foott high, vppon a Lecture day, with a
paper fixed on this breast written with Capital
Letters, AN OPEN AND OBSTINATE CONTEMNER OF GODS HOLY
ORDINANCES, that others may feare and bee ashamed of
breaking out into like wickedness.
It is ordered and decreed by this Court and Authority thereof, that wheresoeuer the ministry of the word
is established according to the order of the Gospell
throughout this Jurissdiction, euery person shall duely

resorte and attend therevnto respectiuely vppon the
Lords day, and vppon such publique fast dayes and dayes
of Thanksgiuing as are to bee generally kept by the
appointment of Authority. And if any person within
this Jurissdiction shall without just and necessary
cause withdraw himselfe from hearing the publique
ministry of the word, after due meanes of conviction
vsed, he shall forfeit for his absence from euery such
publique meeting, fiue shillings: All such offences to
bee heard and determined by any one Magistrate or more,
from time to time.

Forasmuch as the peace and prosperity of Churches
and members thereof, as well as Ciuill rights and
Libberties are carefuly to bee maintained, - It is
ordered by this Courte and decreed, that the Civill
Authority heere established hath power and libberty to
see the peace, ordinances and rules of Christe bee
obserued in euery Church according to his word; as
allso to deale with any Church member in a way of
Ciuill [justice] notwithstanding any church relation,
office or interest, so it bee done in a Ciuill and not
in an Eclesiasticall way; nor shall any church censure
degrade or depose any man from any Ciuill dignitye,
office or authority hee shall haue in the Commonwealth
. . .

FORNICATION

It is ordered by this Courte and Authority thereof,
that if any man shall committ fornication with any
single woman, they shall bee punished either by inioyn-
ing to marriage, or fyne, or corporall punishment, or
all or any of these, as the Courte or Magistrates shall
appoint, most agreeable to the word of God.

GAMING

Vppon complaint of great disorder by the vse of the
Game called Shuffle Board, in howses of Common interteinement, whereby much precious time is spent vnfruit-
fully and much waste of Wyne and Beare occasioned, --

It is therefore ordered and enacted by the Authority of this Courte, that no person shall henceforth vse
the said game of Shuffle Board, in any such howse, nor
in any other howse vsed as Common for such purpose,

vppon payne for euery keeper of such howse to forfeitt
for euery such offence twenty shillings; and for euery
person playing at the said Game in any such howse to
forfetitt for euery such offense fiue shillings. The
like penalty shall bee for playing in any place at any
vnlawfull game . . .

IDLENESS

It is ordered by this Courte and Authority thereof,
that no person, howseholder or other, shall spend his
time idlely or unprofitably, under paine of such
punishment as the Courte shall thinke meet to inflict:
and for this end, It is ordered, that the Constable of
euery place shall vse speciall care and diligence to
take knowledge of offendors in this kinde, especially
of common Coasters, vnprofitable fowlers, and Tobacko
takers, and present the same vnto any Magistrate, who
shall hauepower to heare and determine the case or
transferr it to the [next] Courte.

INDIANS

It is ordered and decreed, that where any company
of Indians doe sitt downe neare any English plantations, that they shall declare whoe is their Sachem or
Chiefe, and that the said Chiefe or Sachem shall pay to
the saide English such tresspasses as shall be comitted
by any Indian in the said plantation adioyning, either
by spoyling or killing any Cattle or Swyne, either with
trapps, doggs or arrowes; And they were not to pleade
that it was done by strangers, vnless they can produce
the prtye and deliuer him or his goods into the custody
of the english: And they shall pay the double dammage
if it were done voluntarily. The like ingagement this
Courte all so makes to them in case of wrong or iniury
done to them by the English, wch shall bee paid by the
prty by whome it was done, if hee can bee made to
appeare, or otherwise by the Towne in whose limmitts
such facts are committed.

Forasmuich as or lenity and gentlnes towards
Indians hath made them growe bold and insolent, to
enter into Englishmens howses, and vnadvisedly handle
swords and peeces and other instruments, many times to
the hazzard of limbs or liues of English or Indians,

and allso oft steale diuerse goods out of such howses
where they resorte; for the preventing whereof, It is
ordered, that whatsoeuer Indian shall hereafter meddle
with or handle any English mans weapons, of any sorte,
either in theire howses or in the fields, they shall
forfeitt for euery such defaulte halfe a fathom of
wampum; and if any hurte or injurye shall therevppon
follow to any persons life or limbe, wound for wound,
and shall pay for the healing such wounds and other
dammages. And for anythinge they steale, they shall
pay double, and suffer such further punnishment as the
Magistrates shall adiudge them. The Constable of any
Towne may attache and arrest any Indian that shall
transgress in any such kinde before mentioned; and
bring them before some Magistrate, whoe may execute the
penalty of this order vppon offendors in any kinde
beforementioned; and bring them before some Magistrate,
whoe may execute the penalty of this order vppon
offendors in any kinde except life or limbe, and any
person that doth see such defaults may prosecute, and
shall haue halfe the forfeiture.

It is ordered by this Courte and Authority thereof,
that no man within this Jurissdiction shall, directly
or indirectly, amend, repaire, or cause to bee amended
or repaired, any gunn, small or great, belonging to any
Indian, nor shall indeauor the same; nor shall sell nor
giue to any Indian, directly or indirectly, any such
gunn, nor any gunpowder, or shott, or lead, or shott
mould, or any military weapon or weapons, armor, or
arrowe heads; nor sell nor barter nor giue any dogg or
doggs, small or great; vppon paine of ten pounds fyne
for euery offence, at least in any one of the aforementioned perticulars; and the Courte shall haue power
to increase the fyne, or to impose corporall punnishment where a fyne cannott bee had, at theire discretion.

And it is allso ordered, that no person nor persons
shall trade with them at or about theire wigwams, but
in there vessells or pinnaces, or at theire owne
howses, vnderpenalty of twenty shillings for each
default . . .

Whereas diuerse persons departe from amongst vs,
and take vp theire aboade with the Indians, in a
prophane course of life; for the preventing whereof,

It is ordered that whatsoeuer person or persons
that now inhabiteth, or shall inhabitt within this
Jurissdiction, and shall departe from vs and settle or
joine with the Indians, that they shall suffer three
yeares imprisonment at least, in the Howse of Correction, and vndergoe such further censure, by fyne or
corporall punishment, the perticular Courte shall judge
meet to inflict in such cases . . .

This Courte, judging it necessary that some meanes
should bee vsed to conuey the lighte and knowledge of
God and of his Worde to the Indians and Natiues amongst
vs, doe order that one of the teaching Elders of the
Churches in this Jurissdiction, with the helpe of
Thomas Stanton, shall bee desired, twise at least in
every yeare to goe amongst the neighbouring Indians and
indeauor to make knowne to them the Councells of the
Lord, and thereby to draw and stirr them vp to direct
and order all theire wayes and coversations according
to the rule of his Worde; And Mr. Gouernor and Mr.
Deputy, and the other Magistrates are desired to take
care to see the things attended, and with theire owne
presence so farr as may bee convenient, incourage the
same.

This Courte hauing duly weighed the joint determination and argument of the Commissioners of the
United English Colonyes at New Hauen, in Anno 1646, in
reference to the Indians, and judging it to bee both
according to rules of prudence and righteousness, doe
fully assent thervnto, and order, that it bee recorded
amongst the Acts of this Courte, and attended in future
practice as occasions may present and require: The
said conclusion is as followeth; -- The Commissioners
seriously considering the many willfull wrongs and
hostile practices of the Indians against the English,
together with theire interteining, protecting and
rescuing of offenders, as late our experience showeth,
(wch if suffered, the peace of the Colonyes cannot bee
secured,) It is therefore concluded, that in such cases
the Magistrates of any of the Jurissdictions may, at
the charge of the Plaintiff, send some convenient
strength of English, and acccording to the nature and
value of the offence and damage, seize and bring away
any of that plantation of Indians that shall interteine, protect or rescue the offender, though it should
bee in another Jurissdiction, when through distance of

place, commission or direction cannot bee had, after
notice and due warning giuen them, as actors, or at
least accessary to the iniurye and damage done to the
English, onely women and children to bee sparingly
seized, vnless knowne to bee some way guilty. And
because it will bee chargeable keeping Indians in
prison, and if they should escape they are like to
prove more insolent and dangerous after, It was thought
fitt that vppon such seizure, the delinquent or satisfaction bee againe demaunded of the Sagamore or plantation of Indians guilty or accessory as before; and if
it bee denyed, that then the Magistrates of the Jurissdiction deliuer vp the Indian seized to the party or
partyes endammaged, either to serue or be shipped out
and exchanged for neagers, as the case will justly
beare. And though the Comissioners foresee that such
severe though just proceeding may provoake the Indians
to an vniust seizing of some of ours, yet they could
not at present finde no better meanes to preserue the
peace of the Colonyes, all the aforementioned outrages
and insolences tending to an open warr: Onely they
thought fitt that before any such seizure bee made in
any plantation of Indians, the ensuing Declration bee
published, and a Coppye giuen to the perticular Sagga-
mores:

the Commissioners for the Vnited Colonyes, considering how peace with righteousness may bee preserued
betweixt all the English and the severall plantations
of the Indians, thought fitt to declare and publish, as
they will doe no iniurye to them, so if any Indian or
Indians of what plantation so euer, doe any willfull
dammage to any of the English colonyes, vppon proofe,
they will in a peaceable way require just satisfaction,
according to the nature of the offence and dammage.
But if any Saggamore or plantation of Indians, after
notice and due warninge, interteine, hyde, protect,
keepe, conuey away or further the escape of any such
offendor or offendors, the English will require satisfaction of such Indian and Saggamore or Indian plantation; and if they deny it, they will right themselues
as they may, vppon such as so meinteine them that doe
the wrong, keeping peace and all tearmes of Amity and
Greement with all other Indians.

INNKEEPERS

Forasmuch as there is a necessary vse of howses of
Common Interteinment in euery Common wealth, and of
such as retaile wine, beare and victualls, yet because
there are so many abuses of that lawfull liberty, both
by persons interteining and persons interteined, there
is allso need of strict lawes and rules to regulate
such an imployment;

It is therefore ordered by this Courte and Authority thereof, that no person or persons licensed for
Common Interteinement shall suffer any to bee drunken
or drinke excessiuely, viz: aboue halfe a pointe of
wyne for one person at one tyme, or to continue tipling
aboue the space of halfe an houre, or at vnseasonable
times, or after nine of the clock at night, in or about
any of theire howses, on penalty of fiue shillings for
euery such offence. And euery person found drunken,
viz: so that hee bee thereby bereaued or dissabled in
the vse of this vnderstanding, appearing in his speech
or gesture, in any of the said howses or elsewhere,
shall forfeitt ten shillings; and for excessive drinking, three shillings, foure pence; and for continnuing
aboue halfe an houre tipling, two shillings six pence;
and for tipling at vnseasonable times, or after nien a
clock at night, fiue shillings, euery offence in these
perticulars, being lawfully convicted thereof; and for
want of payment, such shall bee imprisoned vntill they
pay, or bee set in the stocks, one houre or more, in
some open place, as the weather will permitt, not
exceeding three houres at one time; Provided notwithstanding, such licensed persons may interteine sea-
faring men or land trauellers in the night season when
they come first on shoare, or from theire journye, for
theire necessary refreshment, or when they prepare for
theire voyage or journeye the next day early, [if
there] bee no dissorder amongst them; and allso strangers and other persons in an orderly way may continnue
[in] such howses of Common Interteinement during m[eal]
times or vppon lawful buisines, what time their occasions shall require . . .

JURYES AND JURORS

It is ordered by the Authority of this Courte, that in all cases wch are entred vnder forty shillings, the sute shall bee tryed by the Courte of Magistrates as they shall judge most agreeable to equity and righteousness. And in all cases that are tryed by Juries, it is left to the Magistrates to impannell a Jury of sixe or twelue, as they shall judge the nature of the case shall require; and if four of sixe, or eight of twelue, agree, the verdict shall bee deemed to all intents and purposes sufficient and full; vppon wch judgement may bee entred and execution graunted, as if they had all concurred; but if it fall out that there bee not such a concurrence as is before mentioned, the Jurors shall returne the case to the Courte with theire reasons, and a speciall verdict is to bee drawne therevpon, and the voate of the greater number of Magistrates shall carrye the same; and the judgement to bee entred and other proceedings as in case of a verdict by a Jury . . .

GRAND JURY

It is ordered and decreed, that there shall bee a Grand Jury of twelue or fourteene able men warned to appeare euery Courte yearely in Septembr, or as many and oft as the Gouernor or Courte shall thinke meete, to make presentments of the breaches of any Lawes or orders or any other misdemeanors they shall know of in this Jurissdiction . . .

MAGISTRATES

This Courte being sensible of the great dissorder growing in this Common wealth, through the contempts cast vppon the Civill Authority, wch willing to prevent, doe order and decree:

That whosoeuer shall henceforth openly or willingly defame any courte of Justice, or the sentences and proceedings of the same, or any of the Magistrates or judges of any such Courte, in respect of any Act or sentence therein passed, and being thereof lawfully convicted in any Generall Courte or Courte [of] Magis-

trates, shall bee punnished for the same by fyne,
imprisonment, dissfranchisement or bannishment, as the
quality and measure of the offence shall deserue.

MARRIAGE

Forasmuch as many persons intangle themselues [by]
rashe and inconsiderate contracts for theire future
joininge in Marriage Covenant, to the great trouble and
greife of themselues and theire freinds; for the
preventing thereof,
It is ordered by the Authority of this Courte, that
whosoeuer intends to joine themselves in Marriage
Covenant shall cause theire purpose of contract to bee
published in some publique place, and at some publique
meeting in the severall Townes where such persons
dwell, at the least eight dayes before they enter into
such contract whereby they ingage themselues each to
other, and that they shall forbeare to joine in Marriage Covenant at least eight dayes after the said
contract . . .

SCHOOLES

It being one chiefe project of that old deluder
Sathan, to keepe men from the knowledge of the Scriptures, as in former times keeping them in an unknown
tongue, so in these latter times by perswading them
from the vse of Tongues, so that at least the true
sence and meaning of the originall might bee clouded
with false glosses of saint seeming deceiuers; and that
Learning may not bee buried in the Graue of or Fore-
fathers, in Church and Common wealth, the Lord assisting our indeauers, -- It is therefore ordered by this
Courte and Authority thereof, that euery Towneshipp
within this Jurissdiction, after the Lord hath increased them to the number of fifty houshoulders, shall
then forthwith appoint one within theire Towne to teach
all such children as shall resorte to him, to write and
read, whose wages shall bee paid either by the parents
or masters of such children, or by the Inhabitants in
generall by way of supplye, as the maior parte of those
who order the prudentialls of the Towne shall appointe;
provided that those who send theire children bee not
oppresed by more than they can haue them taught for in

other Townes. And it is further ordered, that where
any Towne shall increase to the number of one hundred
families or housholders, they shall sett vp a Grammer
Schoole, the masters thereof being able to instruct
youths so farre as they may bee fitted for the Vniver-
sity. And if any Towne neglect the performance hereof
aboue one yeare, then euery such Towne shall pay fiue
pounds pr Annum, to the next such Schoole, till they
shall performe this order.

The propositions concerning the maintenance of
Schollars at Cambridge, made by the Commissioners is
confirmed. And it is ordered, that two men shall bee
appointed in euery Towne, within this Jurissdiction,
whoe shall demaund what euery familye will giue, and
the same to bee gathered and brought into some roome in
March, and this to continue yearly as it shall be
considered by the Commissioners.

SECRETARY

It is ordered and decreed, that within twenty dayes
after the session of euery Generall Courte, the Secretary thereof shall send forth Coppies of such Lawes and
orders as are or shall bee made at either of them, wch
are of generall concernement for the gouernement of
this Commonwealth, to the Constables of each Towne
within this Jurissdiction, for them to publish within
fourteene dayes more, at some publique meeting in
theire seuerall Townes, and cause to bee written into a
Booke and kept for the Vse of the Towne. And once
euery yeare the Constables in each Towne shall read or
caue to bee read in some publique meeting all the
Capitall Lawes, and giue notice to all the Inhabitants
where they may at any time see the rest of the Lawes
and orders and acquaint themselues therewith: And the
Secretary of the Courte Shall haue twelue pence for the
Coppy of the orders of each Session aforesaid, from
each of the Townes . . .

TOBACKO

Forasmuch as it is obserued that many abuses are
crept in and committed by frequent taking of Tobacko,
It is ordered by the Authority of the Courte, that no
person vnder the age of twenty yeares, nor any other

that hath not allready accustomed himselfe to the use
thereof, shall take any Tobacko, vntill hee hath
brought a certificate vnder the hands of some who are
approued for knowledge and skill in phisick, that it is
usefull for him, and allso that hee hath receiued a
lycense from the Court for the same. And for the
regulating of those whoe either by theire former taking
it haue to theire owne aprehensions made it necessary
to them, or vppon due advice are perswaded to the vse
thereof, It is ordered, that no man within this Colonye, after the publication hereof, shall take any
Tobacko publiquely in the street, high wayes, or any
barne yards, or vppon training dayes in any open
places, vnder the penalty of six pence for each offence
against this order in any the perticulares thereof, to
bee paid without gainsaying vppon conviction, by the
testimony of one wittness that is without just exception, before any one Magistrate. And the Constables in
the severall Townes are required to make presentment to
each particular courte of such as they doe vnderstand
and euict to bee transgressors of this order . . .

VOATES

It is ordered by this Courte and decreed, that if
any person within these Libberties haue been or shall
be fyned or whipped for any scandalous offence, hee
shall not bee admitted after such time to haue any
voate in Towne or Common wealth, nor to serue on the
Juiry untill the Courte shall manifest theire satisfaction . . .

DOCUMENT 59:   The Cambridge Agreement of October 4, 1652

Text, complete and with the original spelling, is taken from *The Records of the Town of Cambridge (Formerly Newtowne) Massachusetts, 1630 - 1703, Vol. II* (Cambridge: University Press, John Wilson and Son, 1901), 99-100. This agreement is simultaneously a reformation of the civil polity and a set of instructions form the town meeting to those individuals selected to act in the name of the town meeting between meetings. The practice of town meetings giving instructions to its elected officers and representatives was a common one in the colonies, and was extended to colony wide, adn later state wide, representative bodies. Often it was to press for specific legislation, but many, as in this case, were designed to formalize fundamental community values and principles to guide the actions of those in government. The letter "f" has been transcribed as the letter "s" where appropriate.

At a Genrall meeting of the Towne ye 4th (10) 1652.
    Theis prpositions here under written were voted, and joyntly agreed uppon by the Inhabitants, for the instructions to be giyen to the Townsmen.
        That wt eur worke or buissines is by order of Court assigned to the Townsmen or injoyned on the Town That the Townsmen shall make due care to effect the same so as may best conduce to a publique good and no damage by neglect thereof
2.   That as often as they shall see needfull, they shall giue publique notice to the inhabitants to meet together and wt eur orders or determinations shalbe passed by a publique vote of the Towne, or are already made by the Towne or ye select men, that the Townsmen

take due care to execute fullfill and accomplish the
same with out respect of any mans person, according to
yr best wisdome.
3. That wt eur damage they shall conceiue or apprehend
to come to the Towne, by any person with in or with out
the Towne by appropriating intruding or damnifying or
exceeding there owne due prportion in any wise, any of
the Commons, landes or woodes, or other publique stocke
liberties or interests of the Towne according to there
best discretion they shall prvent and remoue the same.
4. That they take due care for the maintenance and
reparation and well ordering of all such thinges wherin
the Towne hath a Common interest, as the meeting house
Common gates and high wayes, Common heards and ye like.
5. That they make such wholesome orders and impose
such Penalties, and duly publish and execute the same
as may best effect the execution of the premises.
6. That the necessary charges yt shalbe expended in ye
execution of the premises be yearly discharged by an
equall rate, made by the Townsmen, and leuied by the
Custable on ye seurall Inhabitants
7. That The Cunstables giue in a yearly account of wt
they receiue of the publique stocke of the Towne by
rate or otherwise, and how they haue disbursed the
same, the same to be done before ye yearly Election of
the Townsmen, and kept uppon Record in a booke fairely
written and in case the Cunstables shall faile herein,
then to Continue in there office another yeare, except
the Towne shall see meet otherwise to dispose.
8. That the Surveyours of the high wayes take due care
for the reparation of all the Comon high wayes with in
ye towne, and keep uppon Record the names of Such
persons as are improued therein during ye yeare, and
deliur the same in a list fairely written to the
Townsmen then in place at ye end of there year [   ]
that so no man may be wronged in doing more than his
due proportion.
    At the same time the buissines about stinting[2] ye
Cow Comon was debated, and by a publicke Voted agreed
that it should be refferred to ye magestrates of the
next County Cort in Midlesex, to determine wheth[   ]
or Cow Common were already lawfully stinted.
    also there is chosen for a committe to effect this
buissines with the Magestrates by prsenting ye true

state of the buissines, mr Joseph Cooke John Bridge, Gregory Stone, Edward Goffe Ri: Jacson and Edward Winship.

DOCUMENT 60: Puritan Laws and Liberties, September 29, 1658

The text is based on the one found in David Pulsifer, ed., *Records of the Colony of New Plymouth: Vol. II, Laws 1623 - 1682* (Boston: The Press of William White, 1861), pp. 147-167. The text is here reproduced only in part since the document is a revision of The Pilgrim Code of Law (Document 20) and therefore repeats much of what is found in the earlier document. The shorthand in the earlier document was tortuous, so some changes have been made for the modern reader. The letter "l" with a short line through it ( ) has been replaced by either "ly" or "li," and the symbol " " replaced by the word "and."

The Booke of the Generall Lawes and Liberties of the Inhabitants of the Jurisdiction of New Plymouth Collected out of the Records of the generall Court; and lately Reuised and established and deposed into an Alphabeticall order and published by the Authoritie of the generall Court held att New Plymouth the 29th day of September: Anno i658

Bee Subject to every
ordinance of Man for
the Lords sake
1 peter 2cond 13th

To our beloued bretheren and Naighbours the Inhabitants of the Jurisdiction of New Plymouth; the Gour: Assistants and Deputies assembled att the generall Court of that Jurisdiction held att the Towne of Plymouth the 29th day of September Anno: Dom: i658, wisheth grace and peace in our Lord Jesus Chrift;

it was the great privilidge of Israell of old and
soe was acknowlidged by them Nehemiah the 9:13 That God
gaue them right Judgments and true lawes; for God being
the God of order and not of confusion hath Comaunded in
his word; and put man into a capasitie in some measure
to obserue and bee guided by good and wholsome lawes
which are soe fare good and wholsome; as by how much
they are deriued from and agreeable to; the Ancient
platforme of Gods lawe; for although sundry pticulares
in the Judiciall law which was of old jnioyned to the
Jewes: did more especially (att least in some cercom-
stances) befitt their Pedagogye; yett are (they for the
maine) soe exemplary being grounded on principalls of
morall equitie as that all men; (Christians especially)
ought alwaies to haue an eye thervnto; in the framing
of theire Politique Constitutions; and although seuerall of the heathen National whoe were Ignorant of the
true God and of his lawe haue bine famous in theire
times for the enacting and execution of such lawes as
haue proued profitable for the Gourment of theire
Comonwealth in the times wherin they liued; yett
notwithsatnding theire exelencye appeered so fare; as
they were founded vpon grounds of morall equitie which
hath its originall from the lawe of God; and accordingly wee whoe haue bine actors in the framing of this
smale body of lawes together with other vsefull Instruments who are gone to theire rest; can safely say; both
for ourselues and them; that wee haue had an eye
principally and primarily vnto the aforsaid platforme;
and Secondaryly vnto the Right Improuement of the
liberteis graunted vnto vs by our Superiours the state
of England att the first begining of this infant
plantation which was to enact such lawes as should most
befitt a state in the nonage therof; not rejecting or
omiting to obserue such of the lawes of our Natiue
Countrey as would conduce vnto the good and grouth of
soe weake a begining as ours in this Wilderness as any
Impartiall eye not forestaled with prejudice may eazely
descerne in the pusall of this smale booke of the lawes
of our Collonie; The prmises duely considered might
worke euery consiencious sperit to faithfull obei-
dience; and although wee hold and doe affeirme that
both Courts of Justice and Majestrates; whoe are the
minnesters of the lawe are esencially Ciuill; Notwithstanding wee conceiue that as the Majestrate hath his

power from God soe vndoubtedly hee is to Improue it for
the honor of God; and that in the vphoulding of his
worship and seruice and against the contrary; with due
respect alsoe to bee had vnto those that are really
consciencious; though differing and discenting in some
smaller matters; but if any really or in the pretence
of consience shall professe that which eminently
tendeth to the Invndation of Ciuill State and violation
of Naturall bonds or the ouerthrow of the Churches of
God or of his Worship; that heer prudence is to bee
Improued in a speciall manor in the enacting and
execution of lawes; It hath bine our endeauors in
framing of our lawes that nothinge should bee found
amongst them but that which fall vnder the same pticulares; wee haue likewise reduced them to such order as
they may most conduce to our vtillitie and profitt;
posibly it may bee that weaknes may appeer in the
composure of sundry of them for want of such plenty of
able instruments as others are furnished withall;
howeuer lett this suffice the gentle Reader; that our
ends are to the vtmost of our powers; in these our
endeauors to promote both Church and State both att the
psent and for the future; and therfore soe fare as wee
haue aimed att the glory of God and comon good; and
acted according to God; bee not found a Resister but
obeidient; least therby thou Resist the ordinance of
God and soe Incurr the displeasure of God vnto damna-
tion; Romans 13:2:

A Declaration demonstrating the warrantable grounds
and proceedings of the first associates of the Gourment
of New Plymouth in theire laying the first foundation
of the Gourment in this Jurisdiction for makeing of
lawes and disposing of lands and all such thinges as
shall or may Conduce to the welbeing of this Corporation of New Plymouth;

Whereas John Carver William Bradford Edward Winslow
William Brewster Isacke Allerton and diuers others the
subjects of our late Sour: Lord Kinge James by the
grace of God Kinge of England Scotland ffrance and
Ireland Defendor of the faith   did in the eighteenth
yeare of his Raigne of England ffrance and ireland; and
of Scotland the fifty fourth which was in the year of
our Lord God one thousand six hundred adn twenty;
vndertake a voyage into that pte of America called
Verginnia or New England thervnto adjoyning; there to

erect a plantation and Collonie of English; Intending
the Glory of God the enlargment of his Maties dominnions and the speciall good of the English Nation.
  And Wheras by the good Prouidence of God the said
John Caruer William Bradford Edward Winslow William
Brewster Isacke Allerton and theire associates ariued
in New England aforsaid in the harbour of Cape Cod or
Paomett Scittuate and being in New England aforsaid;
where all the said psons entered into a Ciuill Combination; being the eleuenth day of Nouember in the yeare
aforemencioned; as the subjects of our said Sour: Lord
the Kinge; to become a body Pollitique binding our
selues to obserue such lawes and ordinances and obey
such officers as from time to time should bee made and
Chosen for their well ordering and guidance; and
thervpon by the fauor of the Almighty; began the first
Collonie in New England; there being then none other
within the said Continent; att a place Called by the
Natiues Apaum alliis Patuxett; and by the English New
Plymouth; all which Lands being void of Inhabitants;
Wee the said John Carver William Bradford Edward
Winslow William Brewster Isacke Allerton and the rest
of our Associates; entering into a league of Peace with
Massasoiett since called Woosamequen Prince or Sachem
of these ptes; hee the said Massasoiett freely gaue
them all the lands adjacent to them; and theire heires
for euer, acknowlidging himselfe content to become the
subject of our Sour Lord the Kinge aforsaid his heires
and Successors and takeing protection of vs the said
John Carver William Bradford Edward Winslow William
Brewster Isacke Allerton and theire Associates the
naturall subjects of our Sour: Lord the Kinge aforsaid
But haueing noe speciall letters Patents for the said
ptes of New England but onely the generall leaue and
libertie of our Consiences in the publicke worship of
God where euer wee should settle; being therefore now
settled and requiring speciall lycence and Comission
from his Matie for the ordering of our affaires vnder
his graciouse protection; had sundry Comissions made
and Confeirmed by his Maties Councell for New England
to John Peirse and his associates; whose names wee
onely made vse of and whose associates wee were in the
late happy and memorable Raigne of our said Sour: Lord
King James; But finding our selues still straightened;
and a willingnes in the honoble Councell aforsaid to

enlarge vs; ptely in regard of the many difficulties
wee had vndergone; and ptely in regard of the good
service wee had done; as well in releiueing his Maties
Subjects as otherwise wee procured a further enlarge-
ment vnder the name of Willam Bradford aforsaid and his
Associates whose names wee likewise vsed; and whose
associates as formerly wee still. are; By vertue of
which said letters Pattents libertie is giuen to vs
deriuatory from our Sour: Lord King Charles bearing
date the thirteenth of January 1629 being the fift
yeare of his raigne of England Scotland ffrance and
Ireland &c and signed by the Right honoble Robert Earle
of Warwicke in the behalfe of his Maties said Councell
for New England; and sealed with theire Comon seale to
frame and make orders ordinances and Constitutions for
the ordering disposing and Gouning of our psons and
distributeing of our Lands within the said Lymetts To
bee holden of his Matie his heires and successors as of
his mannor of East greenwich in the County of Kent in
free and Comon Soccage and not in Capite nor by Knights
seruice, viz: all that pte of America and tract and
tracts of land that lyeth within or between a sertaine
Rivolett or Rundelett comonly called Coahassettt alliis
Conahassett towards the north; and the Riuer called
Narrangansett Riuer towards the south and the great
Westeren Ocean towards the East; and within and between
a straight line directly extending into the maine
towards the west; from the mouth of the said Riuer
called Narranganssett Riuer to the vtmost bounds and
lymetts of a Countrey or place in New England called
Pocanacutt alliis Puckanakicke alliis Sowamsett doth
extend; together with the one halfe of the said Riuer
called Narrangansetts; and the said Riuolett or Rundelett called Coahassett allis Conahassett; and all lands
Riuers waters hauens creekes ports ffishings fowlings;
and all heredetiments profitts Comodities and emolu-
ments whatsoeuer; Scittuate lying and being arising
within or between the said lymetts or bounds or any of
them; furthermore all that Tract or pte of land in New
England or pte of america aforsaid which lyeth within
or between; and extendeth it selfe from the vtmost
lymetts of Cobbasecontee alliis Comacecontee which
adjoyneth to the Riuer of Kennebecke alliis Kenne-
bekicke towards the westeren Ocean; and a place called
the falls at Nequamkicke in America aforsaid; and the

space of fifteen English miles on each side of the said
Riuer comonly called Kenebecke Riuer; that lyeth within
the said bounds Eastwards Westwards Northwards and
southwards last aboue mentioned; and all lands grounds
soyles Riuers waters ffishings heridetiments and
proffitts whatsoeuer scittuate lying and being arising
happening or accrewing in or within the said lymetts or
bounds or either of them; together with free Ingresse
egresse and Regresse with shipps boates shallops and
other vessels from the sea called the westeren ocean;
to the Riuer called Kennebecke and from the said Riuer
to the said Westeren Occean; together with all proro-
gatiues Rights Royalties Jurisdictions priuilidges
franchises liberties and amunities and alsoe marine
liberties with the escheats and causualties therof; the
Admiraltie Jurisdiction excepted; with all the Interest
right title claime and demaund whatsoeuer which the
said Councell and theire successors now haue or ought
to haue or may haue or require heerafter in or to any
of the said Tract or portion of lands heerby mencioned
to bee graunted; or any the pmises in as free large
ample and benificiall manor to all Intents and con-
structions whatsoeuer as the said Councell by vertue of
his Maties said letters may or can graunt; To haue and
to hold the said Tract and tracts of land and all and
singulare the pmises aboue mencioned to bee graunted
with theire and euery of theire appurtenances; To the
said Willam Bradford his heires associates and assignes
for euer To the onely proper vse and absolute behoofe
of the said Willam Bradford his heires associates and
assignes for euer; yeilding and paying vnto our said
Sour: Lord the Kinge his heires and successors for
euer; one fift pte of the Oare of the mines of Gould
and siluer; and one other fift pte therof to the
presedent and Councell; which shalbee had posessed and
obtained within the precincts aforsd for all seruices
and demaunds whatsoeuer; allowing the said Willam
Bradford his associates and assignes and euery of them
his and theire agents tenants and servants; and all
such as hee or they shall send or Imploy about his said
pticulare plantation; shall and may from time to time
freely and lawfully goe and returne trad or trafficke
as well with the English as any the Natiues within the
precincts aforsaid; with libertie of fishing vpon any
pte of the sea coast and sea shores of any the seas or

Ilands adjacent; and not being Inhabited or otherwise
disposed of by order of the said Presedent and Councell
forbiding all others to traffick with the Natiues or
Inhabitants in any of the said Lymetts; without the
speciall leaue of the said Willam Bradford his heires
and associates; and allowing the said Willam Bradford
his heires and associates to take apprehend seize and
make prise of all such psons theire Shipes and goods as
shall attempt to Inhabite or trad with the salvage
people as aforsaid;

Morouer Wheras in the first begining of this
Collonie diuers Marchants and others of the Citty of
London and elsewhere adventured diuers sumes of money
with the said John Caruer William Bradford Edward
Winslow William Brewster Isacke Allerton and the rest
of theire asosiates on certaine tearmes of ptenorship
to continew for the tearme of seauen yeares the said
tearm being expired; the plantation by reason of
manifold losses and Crosses by sea and land in the
begining of soe great a worke being largly Indebted and
noe meanes to pay the said debtes but by the sale of
the whole and the same being put vpon sale; the said
William Bradford Edward Winsow William Brewster Isacke
Allerton and other our associates the Inhabitants of
New Plymouth and elswhere being loth to bee depriued of
our labours bought the same; for and in consideration
of eighteen hundred pounds sterling viz: all and
singulare the priuilidges lands goods Chattles ordinance amunition or whatsocuer appertained to the said
plantation or the adventures; with all and singulare
the priuilidges thervnto belonging; as appeers by a
deed between the said Isacke Allerton then agent for
the said William Bradford and his Associates on the one
pte; and John Pococke Robert Keine Edward Basse James
Sherley and John Beachamp on the other pte being
thervnto deputed by the said Marchants and the rest
adventuring as aforsaid; as appeers by a Deed bearing
date the sixt of Nouember in the third yeare of the
Raigne of our Sour: Lord Charles by the grace of God
Kinge of England Scotland ffrance and Ireland

Anno Dom: i627 one thousand six hundred twenty and
seauen; Bee it Knowne vnto all men by these psents that
according to our first Intents for the better effecting
the glory of God; the Inlargment of the dominnions of
our said Sour: Lord the Kinge, and the speciall good

of his subjects by vertue as well of our Combination
aforsaid; as alsoe the seuerall graunts by vs procured;
in the Names of John Peirce and William Bradford theire
heires and associates together with our lawful right in
rsepect of vacancye donation or Purchase of the Natiues
and our full purchase of the adventures before expressed; haue giuen vnto and alloted assigned and
graunted to all and euery pson and psons whose name or
names shall follow vpon this publicke Record such
proportion or proportions of Grounds with all and
singulare the priuilidges thervnto belonging as aforsaid to him or them his or theire heires and Assignes
Successiuely for euer to bee holden of his Maties of
England his heires and Successors as of his manor of
East greenwich in the Countey of Kent in free and comon
Sockage and not in Capitie nor by Knights Service
yeilding and paying to our said Sou: Lord the Kinge
his heires and Successors for euer one fift pte of the
Oare of the mines of Gould and siluer and one other
fift pte to the psedent and Councell which shalbee had
possesed and obtained as aforsaid and whatsoeuer lands
are graunted vnto any by the said William Bradford
Edward Winslow William Brewster Isaack Allerton or
their heires or Associates as aforsaid being acknowlidged in publicke Court and brought to this booke of
Records of the seuerall Inheritances of the Subjects of
our Soueraigne Lord the King within this Gouerment; It
shalbee lawfull for the Gour of New Plymouth aforsaid
from time to time and att all times for all Intents and
purposes; the said ptie or pties his or theire heires
or assignes for euer; To haue and to hold the said
portion of lands soe graunted bounded and recorded as
aforsaid with all and singulare the Apurtenances
thervnto belonging to the onely proper and Absolute
vse and behoofe of the said ptie or pties his or theire
heires and Assignes for euer;
     Wee the Associates of New Plymouth coming hether as
freeborne Subjects of the State of New England Indowed
with all and singulare the privilidges belonging to
such being Assembled Doe ordeine constitute and enacte
that noe acte Imposition law or ordinance bee made or
Imposed vpon vs att prsent or to come but such as
shalbee made and Imposed by consent of the body of the
Associates or theire Representatives legally assembled,

which is according to the free liberties of the State of England;

It is further enacted

That all our Courts bee kept att the Towne of Plymouth except the Gour and Assistants shall see Reason to keep som Courts of Assistants elswhere within this Gourment.

Whereas by the first Associates of this Gourment the Courts of Election were held in the month of January Anually and afterwards in the month of March Anually; By reason of the vnseasonablenes of those times of the yeare; It is enacted by the Court and the Authoritie therof That the election Courts bee holden the first Tusday in June Annually; And the other Generall Courts bee holden the first Tusday in October and the first Tusday in March Anually; and that the Courts of Assistants bee holden the first Tusday in August the first Tusday in December the first Tusday in ffebrewary and the first Tusday in May Anually.

It is enacted by the Court and the Authoritie therof that all such as shalbee admited freemen of this Corporation shall stand one whole yeare propounded to the Court viz: to bee propounded att one June Court and to stand so propounded vntill the June Court following and then to bee admited if the Court shall not see cause to the Contrary.

Wheras A Comittee was chosen viz: Mrh Tho: Prence Mr Willam Collyare Mr Tho: Dimmacke Mr James Cudworth Mr Josias Winslow John Dunham senir. Gorge Soule and Constant Southworth to consider of the proposition propounded by the deputies att the Court held in October i650 concerning the major pte of the Courts to order the adjournments and desolutions of the generall Courts and the makeing and repealing of lawes they the said Comittee declared theire minds to bee that matters in the aforsaid respects to rest vnaltered as they were and that for the future as formerly in the makeing and repealing of lawes and adjornment of Courts wherin Comittes are resquisite the majestrates and deputies bee considered as one body.

Wheras diuers actes and orders touching the making and repealing of lawes att June Courts and the adjourn-ments therof is rendered with a dubiouse Interpreta-tion; and this Court haueing by propositions to the freemen of the seuerall Townships desired theire

answares in order to the regulateing therof but not
receiueing any answare from sundry of them haue seen
cause to declare theire owne sence therof and therfor
doe enact That fitt and able psons bee anually chosen
out of the freemen to attend June courts and the
seuerall adjornments therof by the approued Inhabitants
quallified as in such case is prouided of this Jurisdiction in theire respectiue townshipps for deputies
vnto whom with the majestrates as the body Represen-
tatiue is comitted full power for the makeing and
repealing of all lawes as vpon theire seriouse considerations they shall find meet for the publicke weale
of this Jurisdiction and that then onely such lawes bee
enacted or repealed except the Gour for the time being
shall see waightey and nessesary cause by the complaint
of the freemen or otherwise to call a special Court
either of the whole body of the ffreemen or theire
deputies; the freemen of this Jurisdiction being left
to theire liberties to send theire voate by proxey for
the choise of Gour Assistants Comissioners and Treasurer in such way as by order of Court is alreddy
prouided and this order to stand in full force till the
whole body of ffreemen shall take further order therin;
It is alsoe further provided that vpon notice giuen in
an orderly way to the Gour by the major pte of the
ffreemen of this Jurisdiction of theire apprehensions
of a nessesitie of the body of ffreemen to come together; then the Gour for the time being shall take the
first oppertunitie to Summon in the body of ffreemen to
aduise and acte ther as the matter shall require;

The Oath of a ffreeman.

You shalbee truely Loyall to our Sour Lord the King
his heires and Successors. You shall not speake or doe
deuise or aduise Any thinge or things Act or Actes
directly or Indirectly by Land or Water that doth shall
or may tend to the destruction or ouerthrow of these
prsent plantations or Townshipes of the Corporation of
New Plymouth neither shall you suffer the same to bee
spoken or done but shall hinder oppose and descouer the
same to the Gour And assistants of the said Collonie
for the time being; or some one of them; you shall
faithfully Submitt vnto such good and wholsome Lawes
and ordinances as either are or shalbee made for the

ordering and Gourment of the same; and shall Indeuor to
aduance the grouth and good of the seuerall townshipes
and plantations within the Lymetts of this Corporation
by all due meanes and courses; All which you pmise and
Sweare by the Name of the great God of heauen and earth
simply truely and faithfully to pforme as you hope for
healp from God who is the God of truth and punisher of
falchood.

It is enacted by the Court and the Authoritie
therof; That on the first Tusday in June anually there
shalbee a Gour and seauen Assistants chosen to Rule and
Gouerne the said plantations and Townshipes within the
Lymetts of this Corporation and this election to bee
made onely by the ffreemen therof;

And that the Gour in due season by warrant directed
to the seuerall Cunstables in the Name of his Matie
giue warning to the ffreemen either to make their
psonall appeerance att the Courts of election or to
send theire voates by proxey for the choise of officers
according to the following order; and that all our
Courts warrants Summons and comaunds bee all done
directed and made in the Name of our Sour Lord the King

Wheras in regard of age disabilletie of body vrgent
occations and other Inconveniencies that doe acrew
sundry of the ffreemen are hindered that they can not
appeer att Courts of election, In consideration wherof
it is enacted by the Court and the Authoritie therof
that any freeman of this Corporation shall haue libertie to send his voate by proxey for the choise of Gour
Assistants Comissioners and Treasurer; And that the
deputies of the seuerall townes chosen to attend the
Courts of election and the seuerall adjournments therof
shall in the towne meeting in which they are chosen
they or either of them giue notice vnto the freemen
that those that Intend not to make theire psonall
appeerance att the Court of election are now to giue in
theire voates Sealed vp for the chosing of Gour Assistants Comissioners and Treasurer; and the said deputies
to obserue by a list of their Names whoe hath voted and
whoe hath not; The which voates soe brought in to bee
ymediately Sealed vp and brought vnto and deliuered in
open Court by the said deputies.

It is enacted by the Court that att Courts of
election the voates of all the ffreemen prsent bee
first read and Next after them the deputies of the

suerall townes shall orderly prsent the proxey of
theire owne towne.

It is enacted by the Court and the Authoritie
therof that other public offecers besides Gour and
Assistants bee chosen and established att the Court in
June Anually viz: Comissioners and Treasurrer; and
that other Inferior officers; as Cunstables grand-
jurymen and Survayors for the highwaies bee then alsoe
confeirmed if approued by the Court.

It is enacted by the Court and the Authoritie
therof that incase there shalbee occation for a Cor-
roner that the Next majestrate where such accedent
falls shall sitt as Corrowner and execute that office
according to the Custome of England as near as may bee.

It is enacted by the Court and the Authoritie
therof that all our Courts summons and comaunds bee all
done directed and made in the Name of his Matie of
England our dread Sour and alsoe that all Ciuill
officers and minnesters of Justice in this Jurisdiction
to be sworne in his said Maties name and alsoe that the
oath of fidelitie and all other oathes shall goe in
that tenure.

The office of the Gour:

The office of the Gour for the time being consisteth in the execution of such lawes and ordinances as
are or shalbee made and established for the good of
this Corporation according to the bounds and Lymitts
therof viz: in calling together or aduising with the
Assistants or Councell of the said Corporation vpon
such matteriall occations (or soe seeming to him) as
time shall bring forth, In wch Assembly and all other
the Gour to propound the Occation of the Assembly and
haue a double voyce therin; if the Assistants Judge the
case too great to bee desided by them and refer it to
the Genrall Court then the Gourr to Summon a Courty by
warning all the ffreemen that are then extant; as alsoe
incase the major pte of the ffreemen seeing waighty
cause for the whole body to meet together and in an
orderly way acquaint him with theire desires therof;
Then hee shall Summon the whole body of ffreemen
together with all convenient Speed; and there alsoe to
propound causes and goe before the Assistants in the
examination of pticulares and to propound such Centance

as shalbee determined; further It shalbee lawfull for
him to Arrest and comitt to Ward any offendors; provided that with all Convenient Speed hee shall bring
the cause to hearing either of the Assistants or
generall Court according to the nature of the offence;
Alsoe it shalbee lawfull for him to examine any suspicious psons for euill against the Collonie as alsoe
to Interupt or oppose such letters as hee conceiueth
may tend to the ouerthrow of the same; and that this
office continew one whole yeare and noe more without
renewing by election;

The Oath of the Gour:

You Shalbee truely Loyall to our Sour Lord King
Charles his heires and Successors Also according to
that measure of Wisdome vnderstanding and deserning
giuen vnto you shall faithfully Equally and Indifferently without respect of psons Adminnester Justice
in all Cases coming before you as the Gour of New
Plymouth; You shall in like manor faithfully duely and
truely exequte the Lawes and ordinances of the Same;
and shall laboure to Advance and further the good of
The Townshipes and plantations within the Lymitts
therof to the vtttermost of youer power and oppose any
thing that shall seeme to hinder the same Soe healp you
God whoe is the God of truth and the punisher of
falshood.

The Office of Ann Assistant.

The office an an Assistant for the time being
consisteth in appeering att the Gournors Summons and in
giueing his best advise both in publicke court and
private Councell with the Gour for the good of the
seuerall Townships and plantations within the lymetts
of this Gourment; not to disclose but to keep secrett
such things as concerne the publique good and shalbee
thought meet to bee concealed by the Gour and Councell
of Assistants in haueing a speciall hand in the examination of publicke offendors and in contriueing the
affaires of the Collonie to haue a voyce in the censuring of such offendors as shalbee brought to publicke
Court; That if the Gour haue occation to bee absent
from the Collonie for a short time by the Gour with

concent of the rest of the Assistants hee may bee
deputed to Gouerne in the absence of the Gour alsoe it
shalbee lawfull for him to examine and comitt to ward
where any occation ariseth where the Gour is absent
prouided the pson bee brought to hearing with all
convenient Speed before the Gour and the rest of the
Assistants ; alsoe it shalbee lawfull for him in his
Maties Name to direct his warrants to any Cunstable
within the Gourment whoe ought faithfully to execute
the same according to the Nature and tenure therof and
may bind ouer psons for matters of crime to the Nature
and tenure therof and may bind ouer psons for matters
of crime to answare att the next ensueing Court of his
said Mtie after the fact comitted or the pson apprehended;

The Oath of an Assistant.

You shall all sweare to bee truely Loyall to our
Sour Lord King Charles his heires and Successors you
shall faithfully truely and Justly according to the
measure of deserning and descretion God hath giuen you
bee Assistant to the Gour for this prsent yeare for the
execution of Justice in all cases and towards all psons
coming before you without parciallitie according to the
Nature of the Office of an Assistant read vnto you;
Morouer you shall dilligently duely and truely see that
the Lawes and ordinances of this Corporation bee duely
executed and shall labour to Advance the good of the
seuerall plantations within the lymetts therof and
oppose any thinge that shall hinder the same by all due
meanes and courses Soe healp you God whoe is the God of
truth and punisher of falshood;

It is enacted by the Court and the Authorite
thereof that the Gour and two of the Assistants at the
least shall as occation shalbee offered in time convenient determine in such triviall cases viz. vnder
forty shillinges between man and man as shall come
before them as alsoe in offences of smale Nature shall
determine doe and execute as in wisdome God shall
direct them;

It is enacted by the Court and the authoritie therof
That att euery election Court some one of the
Assistants or some other suficient man bee chosen
Treasurer for the yeare following whose place it
shalbee to demaund and receiue in whatsoeuer sume or
sumes shall appertaine to the Royaltie of the place

either coming in by way of fine Amercment or otherwise
and shall Improue the same for the publicke benefitt of
this Corporation by order of the Gourment.

It is further enacted by the Court that the Treasurer shall att the election Courts Anually giue in his
accounts of his receipts and paiments for his yeare to
any that the Court shall appoint and to bee entered
vpon Record and thervpon to bee discharged.

It is likewise enacted by the Court that the
Treasurer by vertue of his said office shall take order
that all debts due to the Countrey bee seasonbly
brought in vnto such place or places as hee shall
appoint that soe all dues and debts due vnto any pson
or psons from the Contrey may bee seasonably and
Satisfactorily defrayed except the publice officers
wages which is otherwise prouided for.

It is enacted by the Court that iss halbee in the
libertie of the Treasurer after a month is past after
Judgment by his warrant to require in any fine as hee
shall see reason;

Wheras the Court haue taken notice that diuers of
the ffreemen of this Corporation doe neither appeer att
Courts of election nor send theire voates by proxey for
the choise of majestrates   It is enacted by the
Court and the authoritie therof That whosoeuer of the
ffreemen of this Corporation that shall not appeer att
the Court of election att Plymouth in June annually nor
send theire voate by proxey according to order of Court
for the Choise of Gour Assistants Comissioners and
Treasurer shall be fined to the Collonies vse the sume
of ten shillinges for euery such default; vnlesse some
vnavoidable Impediment hinder such in theire appeerance.

Memorand that an oath bee formed for the Treasurer
and next entered.

The oath of the Treasurer.

You shall faithfully serue in the office of the
Treasurer in the Jurisdiction of New Plymouth for this
prsent yeare during which time you shall dillegently
enquire after demaund and receiue whatsoeuer sum or
sumes shall appertaine to this Gourment; arising by way
of fine amersment Royaltie or otherwise and shall
faithfully Improue the same for the vse of the Gourment
and according to order dispose therof as occasion shall
require you shalbee reddy to giue in a true account

vnto the Court of youer actings in youer said office
yearly att June Courts; Soe healp you God
                    The oath of a Grandjuryman.
    You shall true prsentment make of all thinges giuen
you in charge you shall prsent Nothing of Mallice or
illwill youer owne Councell and youer fellowes in
reference to this oath you shall well and truely keep
soe healp you God.
                The oath of the Clarke of the Court.
    You shall faithfully serue in the office of the
Clarke of the Court for the Jurisdiction of New Plymouth You shall attend the Generall Courts held for
this Gourment att Plymouth Aforsaid and the suerall
Adjournments therof; and the Courts of Assistants and
there Imploy youerselfe in such occations as are
behoofull to youer said place and office you shall
likewise Attend such other meetings of the majestrates
of like Nature as aboue expressed that shall or may
fall out in the Interims of time betwixt the said
Courts you shall not disclose but keep secrett such
things as concerne the Publicke good and shalbee
thought meet to bee Concealled by the Gour and Councell
of Assistants You shall fiathfully Record all such
thinges as you shall haue order from Authoritie to
Comitte to publicke Record and shall faithfully keep
the publicke Records of this Jurisdiction Soe healp you
God who is the God of truth and the punisher of falshood; . . . .

DOCUMENT 61:   An Act of the General Court
                June 10, 1661

The charter of 1629 creating the Massachusetts Bay
Company not only had the standard provision providing
for local self-government, it also had the peculiarity
of failing to make any specific reference to Parlia-
mentary authority. This was interpreted to mean, at
least by the colonists, that the English Parliament had
no power over the colony. Among other documents, the
Massachusetts Body of Liberties (1641) implied that the
colony was bound only by laws of its own choosing.
This document was passed by the Massachusetts General
Court in a bold attempt to essentially declare their
autonomy from allegiance to the King as well, or at
least to render that allegiance so tenuous as to make
it meaningless. This move to enlarge the liberties of
the colonies is one more major attempt by the colonists
to create a political foundation based completely upon
their own consent. The Crown eventually revoked the
colony' charter in 1684, and this document was a major
reason for that royal action. The text is taken from
Nathaniel B. Shurtleff, ed., *Records of the Governor
and Company of the Massachusetts Bay in New England,
Vol. IV,*   (Boston, 1854), part 2, pp. 25-26.

CONCERNING OUR LIBERTIES

    1.   We conceive the patent (under God) to be the
first and main foundation of our civil polity here, by
a Governor and Company, according as is therein expressed.
    2.   The Governor and Company are, by the patent, a
body politic, in fact and name.
    3.   This body politic is vested with power to make
freemen.

4.   These freemen have power to choose annually a governor, deputy governor, assistants, and their select representatives or deputies.

5.   This government has power also to set up all sorts of officers, as well superior as inferior, and point out their power and places.

6.   The governor, deputy governor, assistants, and select representatives or deputies have full power and authority, both legislative and executive, for the government of all the people here, whether inhabitants or strangers, both concerning ecclesiastics and in civils, without appeal, excepting law or laws repugnant to the laws of Englad.

7.   The government is privileged by all fitting means (yea, if need be, by force of arms) to defend themselves, both by land and sea, against all such person or persons as shall at any time attempt or enterprise the destruction, invasion, detriment, or annoyance of this plantation, or the inhabitants therein, besides other privileges mentioned in the patent, not here expressed.

8.   We conceive any imposition prejudicial to the country contrary to any just law of ours, not repugnant to the laws of England, to be an infringement of our right.

CONCERNING OUR DUTIES OF ALLEGIANCE TO OUR
SOVEREIGN LORD, THE KING

1.   We ought to uphold and, to our power, maintain his place, as of right belonging to Our Sovereign Lord, The King, as holden of His Majesty's manor of East Greenwich, and not to subject the same to any foreign prince or potentate whatsoever.

2.   We ought to endeavor the preservation of His Majesty's royal person, realms, and dominions, and so far as lies in us, to discover and prevent all plots and conspiracies against the same.

3.   We ought to seek the peace and prosperity of Our King and nation by a faithful discharge in the governing of his people committed to our care.

First, by punishing all such crimes (being breaches of the First or Second Table) as are committed against the peace of Our Sovereign Lord, The King, his Royal Crown, and dignity.

Second, in propagating the Gospel, defending and upholding the true Christian or Protestant religion according to the faith given by our Lord Christ in His word; our dread sovereign being styled "defender of the faith."

The premises considered, it may well stand with the loyalty and obedience of such subjects as are thus privileged by their rightful sovereign (for Himself, His Heirs, and Successors forever) as cause shall require, to plead with their prince against all such as shall at any time endeavor the violation of their privileges . . . And, also, that the General Court may do safely to declare that in case (for the future) any legally obnoxious, and flying from the civil justice of the state of England, shall come over to these parts, they may not here expect shelter.

DOCUMENT 62:   A Letter from Governor Richard Nicolls to
               the Inhabitants of Long Island, February,
               1665

Taken from E.B. O'Callaghan, ed., *Documents Relating to
the Colonial History of the State of New York* (15
vols., Albany, N.Y.; 1883), XIV, 564-5. The text is
complete with the spelling as found in O'Callaghen.

Whereas the Inhabitants of Long Island, have for a
Long time groaned under many grievous inconveniences,
and discouragements occasioned partly from their
subjection, partly from their opposition to a forraigne
Power, in which distracted condition, few or no Lawes
could bee putt in due Execution, Bounds and Titles to
Lands disputed, Civill Libertyes interrupted, and from
this Generall Confusion, private dissentions and
animosityes, have too much prevailed against Neighborly
Love, and Christian Charity; To the preventing of the
future growth of like Evils, his Majesty as a signall
grace and honor to his subjects upon Long Island, hath
at his owne charge reduc't the forraigne Power to his
obedience and by Pattent hath invested his Royall
Highness the Duke of York with full and absolute Power,
in and over all and every the Particular Tracts of Land
therein mentioned, which said Powers by Comission from
his Royall Highnesse the Duke of York, I am deputed to
put in execution. In discharge therefore of my Trust
and Duty, to Settle good and knowne Laws within this
government for the future, and receive your best advice
and Information in a General Meeting, I have thought
fitt to Publish unto you, That upon the last day of
this present February, at Hempsteed upon Long Island,
shall be held a Generall Meeting, which is to consist
of Deputyes chosen by the major part of the freemen

only, which is to be understood of all Persons rated
according to their Estates, whether English, or Dutch,
within your severall Towns and precincts, whereof you
are to make Publication to the Inhabitants, foure dayes
before you proceed to an Election appointing a certain
day to that purpose; You are futher to impart to the
Inhabitants from mee, that I do heartily recommend to
them the choice of the most sober, able and discreet
persons, without partiality or faction, the fruite &
benefitt whereof will return to themselves in a full
and perfect settlement and composure of all contro-
versyes, and the propagation of true Religion amongst
us. They are also required to bring with them a
Draught of each Towne Limits, or such writings as are
necessary to evidence the Bounds and Limitts, as well
as the right by which they challenge such Bounds and
Limits, by Grant or Purchase, or both, as also to give
notice of this meeting to Sachems of the Indyans, whose
presence may in some cases bee accessary. Lastly I do
require you to Assemble your Inhabitants and read this
Letter to them, and then and there to nominate a day
for the Election of two Deputyes from your Towne, who
are to bring a certificate of their due election, (with
full power to conclude any cause or matter relating to
their serveral Townes) to mee at Hempsteed upon the
last day of February, where (God willing) I shall
expect them.

DOCUMENT 63:   General Assembly of Rhode Island Is
               Divided Into Two Houses, March 27, 1666

Taken from John Russell Bartlett, ed., *Records of the
Colony of Rhode Island and Providence Plantations in
New England: Vol. II, 1664 - 1677* (Providence, R.I.:
A. Crawford Greene and Brother, State Printers, 1857).

The Assembly having taken notice of the motion from
the townes of Portsmouth and of Warwick, desiring the
Assembly would order that the deputyes may sitt apart
from the magistrates as a House by themselves; and
consequently the magistrates to sitt as a House by
themselves; and that of these two houses may consist
the law makeing power, called in the Charter the
Gennerall Assembly, of this body, collony, or copo-
ration of Rhode Island and Providence Plantations. At
this present Assembly haveing well weighed such con-
veniances, and such consideratiiones as may perswade to
grant the same, and yett to provide against such
inconveniancyes as may for want of mature and sound
advice proceed therefrom, doe in this presant Assembly
enacte and declare that it is freely agreed, that the
request of the townes aforesaid, be granted and ordered, that the magistrates sitt by themselves, and the
deputyes by themselves, and that each house soe sitting
have equal power and priviledge in the proposeing,
composing and propagating any act, order and law in
Gennerall Assembly; and that neither house in Gennerall
Assembly shall have power without the concurrance of
the majour part of the other House, to make any law or
order to be accounted as an acte of the Gennerall
Assembly. This in gennerall, is fully ordered, with a
recommendation of the more pertickelar and methodicall
settleing the ways and circumstances of ordering and

regulating the afaires in each house and addresses, &c., from the one house to the other, vnto the consideration of the Gennerall Assembly, that is to sitt the first Wednesday in the month of May, now next ensuinge: where it is hopefully expected the matter may be fully debated and sett in a good way vpon more deliberation than this presant time can afford. The Court haveing alredye sate long on other weighty matters that lay before them.

Ordered, that the Recorder shall have for his atendance on the Gennerall Assembly in October, and for the Assembly now in March, 1666, for coppies of both, twenty five shillings from each towne.

Ordered, that coppies shall spedily goe forth vnder the seale to each towne.

DOCUMENT 64:   Preface to the General Laws and Liberties
of Connecticut Colony Revised and
Published by Order of the General Court
Held at Hartford in October 1672

The text is from J. Hammond Trumbull, ed., *Public
Records: Colony of Connecticut prior to the union
with New Haven Colony May, 1665* (Hartford: Brown and
Parsons, 1850).

To our Beloved Brethren and Neighbours, the Inhabitants of the Colony of Connecticut, The GENERAL COVRT
of that Colony with Grace and Peace in our Lord Jesus.
The Serious Consideration of the Necessity of the
Establishment of wholesome Lawes, for the Regulating of
each Body Politick, Hath enclined us mainly in Obedience unto JEHOVAH the Great Law-giver: Who hath been
pleased to set down a Divine Platforme, not onely of
the Morall but also of Judicial Lawes, suitable for the
people of Israel; As also in conformity to the manifest
Pleasure of our Soveraign Lord the King, in his Majesties Gracious Charter, requiring and Granting Liberty
thereby of makeing of Laws and Constitutions suiting
our State & condition, for the Safety & Welfare of the
people of the Colony of Conecticut. We say the sense
of these Weighty Inducemnts hath moved us, notwithstanding the exceeding great difficulties of the Work,
Looking up to God for wisedom and strength to engage in
this solemn Service, To Exhibit and take care concerning the sufficient Promulgation of such needfull
Lawes, that a more full and plain way may be set for
execution of, and judgement thereby.
Wherefore although in our former Initial times
(while this Colony was deemed distinct in Jurisdiction
from that of New-haven,) We contented ourselves with
keeping our Lawes in Manuscripts, and in the

Promulgation of them by written Copies sent unto those
Townes who then acknowledg themselves to be setled
within our Limits, But since by Divine Providence We
and New-haven have agreed, according to his Majesties
Pleasure manifested in our Patent, to vnite as one Body
Politick: From whence and from other increasings of
Plantations and Persons, together with the addition of
more Lawes and Orders, an occasion is given to think it
convenient if not necessary for further or full Publication, that so as well Forreigners occasionally
comming hither, as the more settled Inhabitants, may
have ready meanes in forming how to demean themselves
and observe.

From hence and such like Considerations urging,
This Court have seen cause to put these our Lawes in
Print, so far as they are at present prepared; Being
willing that all concerned by this Impression may know
what they may expect at our hands as Justice, in the
Administration of our Government here. We have endea-
voured not onely to Ground our Capital Laws upon the
Word of God, but also all our other Laws upon the
Justice and Equity held forth in that word, which is a
most perfect Rule.

Now in these our LAWS, although we may seem to vary
or differ, yet it is not our purpose to Repugn the
Statute Laws of England, so far as we understand them;
professing ourselves alwayes ready and willing to
receive Light for Emendation or Alteration as we may
have oportunity: Our whole aim in all being to Please
and Glorifie God, to approve ourselves Loyal Subjects
to our Soveraign, and to promote the Welfare of this
People in all Godliness and Honesty, in Peace, which
will be the more establishing to his Majesties Crown
and Dignity, and best Answer his Religious Directions
to us in our Charter: And that pure Religion and
undefiled before God, according to the Gospel of our
Lord Jesus, may be maintained amongst us, which was the
end of the first Planters, who settled these Foundations; and ought to be the endeavours of those that
shall succeed to Vphold and Encourage unto all Genera-
tions.

We need no other Inducments to lay before you, to
bespeak your Obedience to what follows but that of the
apostle, 1 Pet. 2, 13, 17. submit yourselves to every

Ordinance of man for the Lord's sake, &c., Love the Brotherhood, Fear God, Honour the King.

By order of the General Court,
John Allin, Secrt.

DOCUMENT 65:   General Laws and Liberties of New
                Hampshire, 1680

This document is here reproduced completely and with
the original spelling to permit comparison with similar
documents such as the Pilgrim code of Law (Document
21), the Laws and Liberties of Massachusetts, 1647
(Document 52), the Connecticut Code of Laws, 1650
(Document 57), the Puritan Laws and Liberties, 1658
(Document 60), and the revision of this document the
Laws and Liberties of New Hampshire, 1682 (Document
71).   The text is taken from *Provincial Papers,
Documents, and Records Relating to the Providence of
New Hampshire: Vol. I, 1623-1686* (1867).

                    Province Laws.
    The Generall Lawes and Liberties of the Province of
New Hampshire, made by the Generall Assembly in Portsmo
the 16th of March 1679/80 and approved by the Presidt
and Councill.
    For as much as it hath pleased our Sovereigne Lord
the King, out of his Princely Grace and favour, to take
vs, the Inhabitants of New Hampshire, into his imediate
Governmt and Protection, the wch, as we are ever bound
to acknowledge wth great thankfulnesse, soe we have
great reason to hope and believe yt his Majesty will
still continue to countenance and incourage vs with ye
Injoymt of such Libertyes, Imunities and ppties as
belong to free borne Englishmen, and whereas his
Majesty hath been pleased by his Letters Pattents, sent
to vs, to confer such power upon ye Generall Assembly
as to make such Lawes and ordinances as may best sute
wth ye good Governmt and quiet settlemt of his Majesties subjects within this Province:
    It is therefore ordered and inacted by this Gene-
rall Assembly and the authority thereof, that no Act,

Imposition, Law or Ordinance by made or imposed upon us but such as shall be made by the said Assembly and approved by the Presidt and Councill from time to time. That Justice and Right be equally and imparshally administered vnto all: not sold, denied or causelessly deferred unto any. 9 Hen. 3, 29 Stat.; 2 Edw. 3, 8 State.; 5 Edw. 3, 9 Stat; 14 Edw. 28: Edw. 3, 3 Stat.; 11 R. 2, 10, 17; Caro. 1, 10,

---

Cappitall Laws.

IDOLLITRY.
1.   It is enacted by ye Assembly and ye authority thereof, yt if any pson having had the knowledge of the true God, openly and manifestly have or worship any other God but the Lord God, he shall be put to death. Ex. 22:20; Deu. 13; 6 and 10.

BLASPHEMY.
2.   If any pson wthin ye Province professing ye true God shall wittingly and willingly presume to blaspheme the wholly name of God, Father, Son or Holy Ghost, wth direct, express, presumptions or high-handed blasphemy, either by willful or obstinate denying ye true God or his creation or Governmt of ye world, or shall curse God, Father, Son, or Holy Ghost, such pson shall be put to death. Levit. 24: 15 and 16.

TREASON.
3.   Treason against ye pson of our Souereigne, ye King, the State, and Comon Wealth of England, shall be punished wth death.

PUBLIQUE REBELLION.
4.   If any man conspire and attempt any Invasion or insurrection or Publique Rebellion against this his Majesties Province, or shall endeavor to surprise any towne or townes, fort or forts therein, or shall treacherously or perfidiously attempt the alteration and subversion of the fundamental frame of ye Government, according to his Majesties constitution by his Letters Pattents, every such pson shall be put to death, or otherwise greveously punished.

5.   If any pson shall comitt wilfull murther by
killing any man, woe; or child, upon premeditated
malice, hatred or cruelty, not in a way of necessary
and just defence, nor by casualty against his will, he
shall be put to death.

6.   If any pson slayeth another pson sudenly, in
his anger and cruelty of passion, he shall be put to
death.

7.   If any pson shall slay another through guile,
either by pysoning or other such devilish practice, he
shall be put to death.

WITCHCRAFT.

8.   If any Christian, soe called, be a witch, yt
is, hath or consulted wth a familiar spirit, he or they
shall be put to death.

BEASTIALITY.

9.   If any man lie wth a beast or bruite creature
by carnall copulation, they shall surely be put to
death, and ye beast shall be slaine and buried, and not
eaten.

BUGGERY.

10.   If any man lieth with mankind as he lieth wth
a woman, both of them hath committed abomination; they
shall be surely put to death, unless the one pty were
forced or be vnder 14 years of age; and all other
sodomitical filthiness shall be severally punished
according to the nature of it.

FALSE WITNESS.

11.   And if any pson rise up by false witness, and
of purpose to take away a man's life, he shall be put
to death.

MAN STEALING.

12.   If any man stealeth mankind, he shall be put
to death or otherwise grieviously punished.

CURSING PARENTS.

13.   If any child or children above 16 years old,
of competent understanding, shall curse or smite their
natural father or mother, he or they shall be put to
death, unless it can be sufficiently testified that the

parents have been very unchristianly negligent of ye
education of such children, or soe provoked them by
extreme cruell correction yt they have been forced
thereunto to preserve themselves from death or maiming.

A REBELLIOUS SON.

14. If any man have a rebellious or stubborne son
of sufficient years and vndersetanding, viz. 16 years
of age or upwards, wch shall not obey ye voyce of his
father or ye voyce of his mother, yt when they have
chastened him will not hearken vnto them, then shall
his father and mother, being his naturall parents,
bring him before the Majestrates assembled in court,
and testifie vnto them that theire son is rebelleous
and stubborne, and will not obey theire voyce and
chastizemt but lives in sundry notorious crimes, such
son shall be put to death, or otherwise severely
punished.

RAPED.

15. If any man shall ravish a maid or woeman by
committing carnal copulation wth her, that is above 10
years of age, or if she were vndr 10 years of age,
though her will was gained by him, he shall be punished
wth death, or some other greivous punishmt as the fact
my be circumstanced.

WILFUL BURNING.

16. Whoseover shall wilfully or on purpose burn
any house, ship, or barque, or any other vessell of
considerable value, such pson shall be put to death, or
otherwise greviously punished, as ye case may be
circumstanced.

Criminall Laws.

1. It is orderedd by the Assembly and the authority thereof that wt pson soever is to answer any
criminal ofence, whether they be in prison or under
baile, his case shall be heard and determined at the
court yt hath cognizance therof.

ADULTERY.

2.   It is Inacted by this Assembly that whosoever shal comitt Adultery wth a married woe: or one betrothed to another man, both of them shall be sevearly punished by whiping two severall times, not exceeding 40 lashes, vizt., once when ye Court is sitting at wch they were convicted of the fact, and ye 2d time as the court shall order, and likewise shall ware 2 cappitall letter A.D. cut out in cloth and sowed on theire upermost garmts on theire arms or back, and if at any time they shall be found wthout the said letters so woren whilst in this Governmt, to be forthwth taken and publiquely whiped, and so from time to time as often they are found not to weare them.

FORNICATION.

3.   It is ordered by this Assembly and the authority thereof that if any man comit Fornication with any single woe: they shall be punished, either by injoyning marriage, or fine or corporall punishmt, or all or any of these, as ye judges of ye court yt hath cognizance of ye case shall appoint, and if any comitt carnall copulation after contract before marriage, they shall be amerced each of them 50s. and be imprisoned, if the court see reason; and if any cannot and will not pay ye fine, then to be punished by whiping. And for ye more discountenancing this prevailing evill, the Assembly hath further determined yt such as transgress in any of these wayes, shall be convicted in publique court, theire fines shall be paid in money.

BURGLARY.

4.   For as much as many psons of late years have been and are apt to be injurious to the Lives and Goods of others, notwithstanding all Laws and means to prevent the same, it is therefore ordered by this Assembly and ye authority thereof yt if any pson shall comitt Burglary by breaking vp any dwelling house or ware house, or shall foreceably robb any pson in ye field or high wayes, such offenders shall for the first offence be branded on the right hand wth ye letter B; and if he shall offend in the like kind a 2d time he shall be branded on the other and be sevearly whiped, and if either were comitted on ye Lord's day his brand shall be sett on his forehad, and if he shall fall into

the like offence the 3rd time he shall be put to death as being incoragable, or otherwise greviously punished, as ye court shall determine.

FELLONY.

5.   And whosoever shall steale or attempt to steale any ship, barque or vessell of burden, or any publique amunition, shall be sevearly punished according to the nature of such a fact, provided it extends not to Life or Limb.

6.   That if any strangers or inhabitants of this Province shall be legally convicted of stealing or purloyning any horses, chattels, money, or other goods of any kind, he shall be punished by restoring 3 fold to the ptie wronged, and a fine or corporall punishmt, as the court or 3 of the councell shall determine. Provided that such sentance, where not given by ye court, it shall be at the liberty of ye delinquent to appeale to ye next court, putting in due caution there to appeare and abide a Tryall.

COUNCIL'S POWER IN CRIMINALS.

7.   That any one of ye Councill may heare and determine such small thefts and pilferings as exceeds not ye damage or fine of 40s., or penalty of stocking or whipping not exceeding 10 strypes, or only legall admonition, as he shall see cause, saveing liberty of appeale to the delinquent as aforesd.

SWEARING.

8.   It is ordered by this Assembly and the authority thereof yt if any pson wthin this province shall sweare rashly or vainly by the holy name of God, or other oathes, he shall forfeit to the common Treasury for every such offence 10s., and it shall be in the power of any member of the Councill by warrant to ye Constable to call such pson before him, and vpon suffissient profe, to sentence such offenders and to give orders to levy ye fine; if such pson be not able or shall refuse the said fine, he shall be comitted to the stocks, there to continue for a time not exceeding 3 hours, nor less than 1 houre; and if any pson shall sweare more oathes than one at a time before they remove out of the roome or company where hee soe sweared, he shall then pay 20s., the like penalty shall

be inflicted for profane and wicked cursings of any pson or creature, and for multiplying the same as it is appoynted for profaine swearing; and in case any pson so offending by multiplying oathes or curses shall not pay his or theire fine forthwith, they shall be whipped or comitted to prison till they shall pay the same, at the discresion of ye Court or Judges that shall have cognisence thereof.

PROFANING THE LORD'S DAY.

9.   Upon information of sundry abuses and misde-meanors comitted by divers persons on ye Lord's Day, It is therefore ordered and inacted by this Generall Assembly, That wt pson soever wthin this Governmt shall pfane ye Lord's Day, by doeing unnessary servell worke or travell, or by sports or recreations, or by being at ordinarys in time of publique worship, such pson or psons shall forfeite 10s., or be whipt for every such offence, and if it appeares yt ye sin was proudly or presumptiously, and wth a high hand, comitted against the known comand and authority of ye Blessed God, such person therein dispising and reproaching ye Lord, shall be sevearly punished, at ye Judgmt of ye Court.

CONTEMPT OF GOD'S WORD, OR MINISTERS.

10.   It is inacted c., for as much as ye open contempt of God's word and ye messengers thereof, is ye desolating sin of sevell States and Churchs, It is therefore enacted, that if any Christian, so called, in this Province, shall speak contempteously of the Holy Scriptures, or of ye holy penmen thereof, such pson or psons shall be punished by fine or corporall punishmt, as ye Court shall see reason, so as it extend not to life or limbe, or shall behave himself contempteously toward the Word of God preached, or any minister thereof called and faithfully dispensing ye same in any congregation, either by manifest interrupting him in his ministeriall dispensations, or falsely or perem-torily charging him with teaching error, to ye dis-paragmt and hinderance of ye work of Christ in his hands; or manifestly or contempteously reproach ye wayes, churches or ordinances of Christ, being duely convicted thereof, he or they, for the first trans-gression, be amerced 20s. to the province use, or to sett in ye stocks not exceeding 4 hours; but if he or

they go on to transgres in ye same kind, then to be
amerced 40s., or to be whiped for every such trance-
gression.

FORCIBLE DETAINING POSSESSION.

11.   It is ordered c., yt where a judgement is
given in any Court, for any pson, or house, or lands,
upon ye tryal of the title thereof, or other just
cause, if the pson against whome ye Judgmt is given
doth either forceably detaine possesion thereof, either
against the officer impowered to serve an execution
thereon, or otherwise after execution served, enter
upon it again, and soe retain possession by force, he
shall be accounted a high offendr against ye Law, and
breaker of the publique peace; therefore, speedily to
redress such a criminall offence, every of the Councill
is impowered, and by his place hath power to give
warrant and comand to ye Marshall, officer and other
men whome he thinks meet to be imployed in the case or
business, the Marshall or other officers requiring aid
greater or lessas need require to suppress ye force and
give possession to ye owner, and to imprission such as
doe appear to be delinquents and their aiders and
abettors, to be forth coming at ye next Court, yt did
give ye Judgmt in the case, there to make their answer,
and whom the court doth find guilty, to sett such fine
or other punishmt upon them, as the merit of their
severall cases doth require.

CONSPIRICIE AGAINST THIS PROVINCE, ETC.

12.   It is ordered &c., That whosoever shall
disturb or undermine the peace of this Province or
Inhabitants thereof, by plotting wth others, or by his
own tumultuous and offenceive carrage, traducing,
quarreling, challenging, or assaulting, or any other
way tending to publicque disturbance, in wt place
soever it be done, or shall defame any Court of Justice, or any of his Majesties councill, or Judges of
any court in this Province, in respect of any act or
sentence therein passed, every such offender upon due
proof made shall be by ye Councill punished by fine,
imprisonmt, binding to ye peace or good behaviour,
according to the quality and measure of the offence or
disturbance to them, seeming just and equall.

And that such as beate, hurt or strike an other
person, shall be lyable to pay unto ye ptie hurt or

stricken, together wth such fine to the Province, as, on consideration of the ptie smiting or being smitt, and wth wt instrument, danger more or less, time, place, provocation, c., shall be judged just and reasonable, according to the nature of the offence.

FORGERY OF DEEDS.

13.   It is ordered, &c., yt if any pson shall forge any deed or conveiance, testimt, bond, bill, release, acquittances, letters of attourney, or any writing, to the injury of another, to prevent equity and justice, he shall pay ye ptie agreived double damage, and be fined so much himself, to ye Province's vse, and if he cannot pay it, to be publiquely whiped and be branded with a Roman F in ye forehand.

DEFACING RECORDS.

14.   Be it also enacted, yt if any notary, or keeper of publique records or writings, shall wilfully imbazle or make away any such records or writings of concernmt comitted to his keeping and trust, or shall on ppose falsefie or deface them by raceing out, adding to them, or otherwise, such corrupt officer shall loose his office, be disfranceized and burned in the face, according to ye circumstances of the case

NONE TO ENDEAVOR TO CORRUPT YE OFFICERS.

15.   And if any person shall endeavour to corrupt any officer yt keepeth such publique records or paps of conernmt, to procure him to deface, corrupt, alter, imbazle any of them, he shall be sevearly punished by fine, imprisonmt or corporall punishmt, as ye matter may be circumstanced.

LYING.

16.   It is inacted by this Assembly, c., That wt pson soever, being 16 yeares of age, or upward, shall wittingly or willingly make or publish any lie wch may be tending to ye damage or hurt of any pticular pson, or wth intent to deceive and abuse the people with false news or reports, shall be fined for every such defalt 10s., and if ye ptie cannot or will not pay ye fine, then he shall sit in ye stocks as long as the court shall think meete; and if the offenders shall come to any one of councill aforesd to execute ye law upon him where he liveth, and spare his appearance at ye Court, but in case when ye lie is greatly prnitious

to ye comon weale, it shall be more sevearly punished
according to the nature of it.

BURNING FENCES.

17.   It is inacted by this Assembly, c., That if
any pson shall willfully, and of sett purpose, burn any
man's fence, he shall make good the damage to the ptie
wronged, and be amerced 40s. and be bound to the good
behavior, if the court so meets.

BREAKING DOWN FENCES.

18.   It is further ordered, That if any pson shall
wilfully and on purpose brake down an other man's
fence, gate or bridge, to ye anoyance either of a
pticular person or a neighborhood, he shall make up
such fence, gate or bridge, at his own charge, pay
ye damage thereby sustained, and be amersed according
to the nature of the offence, sauing the right of him
yt pulls up a fence sett on his land without his
approbation.

DEFACING LANDMARKS.

19.   And whosoever shall willfully pluck up, remove
or deface any Landmark or bound betweene ptie and ptie,
yt hath been or shall be orderly set up by psons
therunto appointed, he or they shall be fined from 20s.
to 5 pounds, as the offence may be circumstanced.

UNLAWFUL GAMING IN PUBLIQUE HOUSES.

20.   Be it inacted by this Assembly, c., That noe
Innhoulder or publique house keeper shall suffer any
unlawful games, nor any kind of gaming, in or about his
house, for money or moneys worth liquors, wine, beer or
the like, on forfeit of 40s., to be paid by the master
or keepof such house, and 10s. by each gamester for
every such default.

LOTTERY.

21.   Be it further inacted, yt no pson in this
Province shall play at cards, dice, or any such unlawful games wherein there is Lottery, at any private
house or elsewhere in the Province, on penalty of 10s.
fine, to be paid by evry one yt soe playeth, and 20s by
the master or head of a family yt shall know of and
suffer any such gameing where he hath to command.

DRUNKENNESS.

22.   For as much as it is observed yt ye sin of
drunkenness doth greatly abound, to the dishonor of
God, improverishing of such as fall into it, and grief
of such as are sober minded, for ye prevention of ye

growing and prevailing evill, It is inacted by this
Assembly, and ye authority thereof, yt wtsoever pson
shall be found drunk at any time in any Taverne,
ordinary, alehouse, or elsewhere in this Province, and
be legally convicted thereof, he or they shall for ye
first defalt be fined 5s. to ye use of the Province--
for the 2d defalt 10s.; and if he or they will not or
can not pay ye fine, then to be sett in ye Stocks not
exceeding 2 houres, and for the 3d transgression to be
bound to ye good behavior; and if he shall transgress a
4th time, to pay 5 pounds or be publickly whipt, and so
from time to time as often as they shall be found
trancegressors in that kind. By drunkenness is to be
understood one yt lisps or falters in his speach by
reason of over much drink, or yt staggers in his going,
or yt vomits by reason of excessive drinking, or that
cannot by reason thereof follow his calling.

FIREING WOODS.

23. Whereas many have sustained great damage by
indiscreet and untimely fireing of the woods, It is
ordered, that none shall fire ye woods at any time but
between ye 1st of March and ye latter end of April; and
if any shall unnessesarily fire the woods, or not
observe this order, damnifie any, he shall make good
the damage and be fined 10s., or sett in the Stocks.

COUNCILL'S POWER IN CRIMINALS.

24. It is hereby inacted, yt it shall be in ye
power of any member of the councill to hear and determine all criminall cases where the fine doth not exceed
40s., or ye punishment 10 stripes or committing to
stocks, always allowing liberty to the delinquent of
appeale to ye next Court for tryalls of actions wthin
ye Province; and further, in cases doubtful or difficult, it shall be in ye power of ye Judge before whom
ye pson is convicted, to bind them over to the next
Court in this Province, to comitt to prison as ye fact
may deserve, allowing also for entering Judgmt and
fileling evidences 2s. 6d.

PRISON KEEPER'S CHARGE.

25. It is ordered by this Assembly and ye authority thereof, yt no Prison keeper wthin this Province
shall suffer any pson to goe wthout the presinks of the
prison, yt is delivered unto them for debt, by virtue
of any execution, and it is further ordered the houses
and yards of the said keepers shall be allowed &

accounted the presinks of the sd prison, and yt it
shall be lawful for any officer wthin this Province, if
he have occation to carry any prisoner to the neerest
Prison in the Province, and yt if any Prison keeper
shall suffer any such prisoner to goe wthout the
presinks of ye sd prison, they shall be liable to
satisfie the whole debt for wch ye sd Prisoner was
imprisoned, and the sd keeper's fees shall be 5s. for
turning the key, to be paid by the person imprisoned,
before he be set at liberty.

MARSHALLS.

26. It is ordered by this Assembly and the authority thereof, yt it shall be lawful for either of the
marshalls in this Province to levy executions, attachmt
and warrants in any pt of ye sd Province, and yt feese
for serving attachmt wthin theire owne towns shall be
2s. for every attachmts, to be paid by them yt imploy
them before they shall be compelled to serve it, and 2
for a warrt: for warrts served upon criminal offenders.

JUDGMT AND EXECUTION TO STAND GOOD YT
WERE BEFORE YE LATE CHANGE.

27. It is ordered by this Generall Assembly and
that authority thereof, yt all Judgmts and Executions
granted on any civill or criminal cases by former
Courts of Justice wthin this Province, or ye County
Court of Norfolk to any of our Inhabitants within this
Province, shall be held as good and vallued for and
against any pson as when they were granted by the Court
at the time of tryall.

General Lawes.

Townships, &C, Confirmed.

1. To prevent contention that may arise amongst
vs by reason of the late change of Governmnt, it is
ordered by this Assembly and the authority thereof yt
all land, Townships, Town grants, wth all other grants
lying wthin the limitts of this Province, and all other
rights and prop'ties, shall stand good, and are hereby

confirmed to ye townes and psons concerned, in the same
state and condition as they did before this late
alteration. 33 Ed: 1.

CONTROVERSIES OF LAND TO BE TRIED BY A JURY.

2.   And it is further ordered, yt if any difference or controversy shall hereafter arise amongst us
about the titles of land wthin this Province, it shall
not be finally determined but by a Jury of 12 able men,
chosen by the freemen of each towne according to law
and custome, and sworne at ye Quarter Court wch shall
take cognisance of the case.

CONTRACTS TO BE PAID IN SPECIA.

3.   For preventing deceite in trade, yt all men
may be on a certainty in matters of contracts and
bargains, It is ordered by this Generall Assembly and
the authority thereof, that all contracts, agreemts or
covenants for any specia whatsoever shall be paid in
the same specia bargained for, any law, vseage or
custome to the contrary notwithstanding.

HORSES.

4.   It is ordered by this Assembly and ye authority thereof, that ye brand markets mentioned in the
Law, title horses, to brand horses wth, shall be as
followeth: for the towne of Portsmouth P, for ye towne
of Hampton H. for ye towne of Dover D, and for the
towne of Exeter E.
For the preventing of damage being done by horses
wthin this Province, by reason of ye goeing upon our
lands and pastures wthout some fettering, it is ordered
by this Assembly and ye authority thereof yt no horse
or horse kind shall be suffered to goe vpon any of our
lands and pastures wthout fence wthin this Province,
from ye 1st day of May vnto ye 1st of 8ber, without a
sufficient pr of iron fetters on his feete, or a clog
equivelent, vpon ye penalty for evry owner of any such
horse or horse kind yt shall be taken doeing damage, or
wthin any man's corne field, meadowes or inclosures,
paying 5s. in mo, besides all damage to yt ptie yt
impounded them; and if they be found doing damage

wthout ye towne brande to wch they belong, ye owners of them shall pay 20s. in mony; and it is likewise ordered yt every towne wthin this Province shall have a distant brand marke, wch they shall brand theire horses wth all yt goe in ye comons from time to time.

It is further ordered that no horse or horses shall be suffered to goe vpon any of our lands and pastures wthout fense wthin this Province yt is known to be vnruly, wthout the approbation of ye selectmen, or ye major pt of them of ye severall townes, vnder ye penalty of every owner of such horse paying 10s. in money to ye ptie yt soe find them contrary to this order, or loose his ye sd horse soe taken.

TIME AND PLACE FOR KEEPING COURTS.

5.   For the better adminstration of justice, It is ordered by this Assembly and the authority thereof, yt these courts following shall be annually kept wthin this Province: A GENERALL ASSEMBLY, to meete at Portsmo ye 1st Tuesday in March, to make and constitute such Lawes and ordinances as may best conduce to ye good governmt of this his Majesties Province, as allso wth the Presidt and Counll, to heare and determine all actions of appeale from Inferior Court, whither of civill or ciminall nature. Alsoe, there shall be 3 other courts held at time and place hereafter mentioned by ye Presidt and Councll, or any 6 of ye Councll, whereof ye Presidt or his Deputy be one, together wth a Jury of 12 honest men, chosen and called as ye law directs, for such as desire to be tried by a Jury; evry of wch Courts shall have full power to heare and determine all cases, civill and criminall, allowing one liberty of appeale from such sentence or judgmt as shall be passed in sd Court or Courts, to ye residt and Councll, together with the Generall Assembly as above sd, provided such appellant give bond to prosecute according to law. The time and place for holding such shall be as followeth:

At Dover ye first Tuesday in June; at Hampton ye first Tuesday in 7ber; at Portsmo the first Tuesday in 10ber.

ALL TRYALLS BY JURY.

6. It is further enacted yt all tryalls, whether capitall, criminal, or between man and man, both respecting meritine affairs as well as others, be tryed by a Jury of 12 good and lawfull men, according to the good & commendable custome of England, except the ptie or pties concerned doe refer it to the bench, or some express law doth refer it to their judgmt and tryall, or the tryall of some other court where jury is not, in wch case any ptie agreived may appeale, and shall have tryall by a jury; and it shall be in ye liberty of both plant and defendt, or any delinquent yt is to be tryed by a jury, to challenge any of ye jury, and if ye challenge be found just and reasonable by ye bench, it shall be allowed him, and others wthout just exception shall be impanelled in theire roome; and if it be in case of life and death the prisoner shall have libertye to except against 6 or 8 of ye jury wthout giving any reason for his exceptions.

CONSTABLES TO CLEAR THEIR RATE IN THE YEAR.

7. For the better clearing of ye arrears in the hands of the constables.
It is ordered yt if any Constable shall faile to clear vp his rates wthin his yeare, he shall be lyable to have his estate distrained by warrt from ye Treasr, directed to ye Marshall or Marshalls wthin this Province; and for all rates for ye ministry and other towne rates, ye selectmen shall direct their warrts to ye Constables next chosen, to distraine upon the estates of such Constables as shall faile of their duties therein.

FREEMEN.

8. It is ordered by this Assembly and the authority thereof, yt all Englishmen, being Protestants, yt are settled Inhabitants and freeholders in any towne of this Province, of ye age of 24 years, not viceous in life but of honest and good coversation, and such as have 20. Rateable estate wthout heads of persons having also taken the oath of allegiance to his Majs, and no others shall be admitted to ye liberty of being

freemen of this Province, and to give theire votes for
the choic of Deputies for the Generall Assembly,
Constables, Selectmen, Jurors and other officers and
concernes in ye townes where they dwell; provided this
order give no liberty to any pson or psons to vote in
the dispossion or distribution of any lands, timber or
other properties in ye Towne, but such as have reall
right thereto; and if any difference arise about sd
right of voting, it shall be judged and determined by
ye Presidt and Councill wth the Genll Assembly of this
Province.

MARRIAGE.

9.   As the ordinance of Marriage is Honrable
amongst all, so should it be accordingly solemnized.
It is therefore ordered by this Assembly and the
authority thereof, that any member of ye Councill shall
have liberty to joyne any persons together in marriage;
and for prevention of unlawfull marriages it is ordered
yt no pson shall be joyned in marriage before the
intention of the pties pleeding therein have been 3
times published, at some publique meeting in ye townes,
where ye pties, or either of them doe ordinarily
reside, or be sett up in writing upon some post of
theire meeting house door, in publique view, there to
stand soe as it may be easily read, by ye space of 14
dayes.

MAKING RATES.

10.   That thear may be a just and eaquall way of
raising means for defraying ye publique charge, boath
in church and civill affairs, whereof every pson doth
or may receive ye benefit, their persons and estates
shall be asseassed or rated as followeth, vizt: to a
single rate of a penny in ye pound, every male person
above the age of 16 yeares, is vallued at 18 l., and
all land within fense, meddow or marsh, mowable, shall
be at 5s. [per] acres; all pasture lands without fence,
rate free; all oxen 4 yeares old and upward, 3 l.;
steers, cows and heiffers of 3 yeare old, at 40s.,
steers and heiffers, of 2 yeares old, at 25s.; year-
lings at 10s.; horses and mares of 3 yeares old and
upward, at 20s., sheepe above 1 yeare old, at 5s.;

swine above one yare old at 10s.; and all other estates
whatsoever in ye hands of whome it is at ye time when
it shall be taken, shall be rated by some equall
proportion, by ye selectmen of each towne, wth grate
care yt pticulars be not wronged; and all ships,
ketches, barques, boates, and all other vessells
wchsoever, shall be rateable, as allso, all dwellings
houses, ware houses, wharffs, mills, and all handy-
crafts men, as carpenters, masons, joiners, shoemakers,
taylors, tanners, curriers, butchers, bakers, or any
other artificers, victuallers, merchts and inn keepers
shall be rated by estymation. If any persons be greved
at their being over-rated, they shall have liberty to
complain to ye next quarr Court, who shall give them
all just reliefe.

SELECTMEN TAKE ACCOUNTS.

11. For ye more eaquall and imparshall valluing
of houses and ships and other estates of mrchts,
traders, handycraft, wch must necessarily be rated by
estymatyon --

Be it enacted by this Assembly and the authority
thereof, yt ye selectmen of ye severall townes shall
forthwth take an accot of all such estates, wth ye
vallue tehreof according to theire ordinary way of
rating; a list of wch estates, so taken and vallued,
shall be trancmitted to a committee of 4 men chosen by
this Assembly out of Dover, Portsmo, Hampton and
Exetor, together wth 2 of ye Counll, wch comitte shall
examine and compare sd list and bring sd estates to an
equall valluation, having respect to the places where
they lie, yt no towne or psons be burthened beyond
proportion; wch act of said committee in the vtion of
sd estates shall stand as a rule, according to which
rates and asseasmts shall be made for ye future; ye
psons chosen for this Comittee are Richd Walderne,
Esqr, Elias Stileman, Esqr, Mr. Ro: Elliott, Mr.
Anthony Nutter, Mr. Ralph Hall, Mr. Edward Gove, and ye
time of meeting ye 2d Tuesday in Aprill in Portsmoo.

A LIST OF MALES AND ESTATES TO BE TAKEN.

12. It is ordered by this Generall Assembly yt
warrts be forthwith ishued out to ye Selectmen of ye
severall townes wthin this Province, yt they doe
forthwth take a list of all ye male psons of 16 yeares
old and vpward in theire respective townes, wth ye
valluation of all their estates, according to such
rules as are past this court; and all psons yt are so
rated are to be rated by estymatyon and make returns
thereof to ye commitee appointed for yt affaire, at or
before the 2d Tuesday in Aprill next.

BOUNTY FOR KILLING WOOLF.

13. It is ordered by this Assembly yt evry psons
wthin this Province yt shall, after ye date hereof,
kill any woolfe wthin this Province, they shall forthwth carry the head of every such woulfe unto ye constable of ye same towne, who shall bury or deface the
same by cutting the eares off, and ye sd constable
shall give ye sd ptie a sirtifficate, attested under
his hand, of ye day and ye rect thereof; and ye sd ptie
procuring such a surtificate shall be allowed by ye
Treasurer of ye Province for every woulfe soe killed
40s. out of ye next rate made for the Province, but if
the ptie be an Indian that killed ye woulfe, he shall
be allowed but 10s., and the sd Indian shall make proof
that he killed ye sd woulfe wthin this sd Province.

FORMER LAWS TO STAND.

14. For a presant settlemt of matters in civill
and criminall proceedings, and directions to Courts,
Judges and all other officers, it is ordered that those
Lawes wch we have fformrly been directed and governed
by, shall be a rule to vs in all Judiciall proceedings,
soe far as they will sute our constitution and be not
repugnante to ye Laws of England, vntill such acts and
ordinances as have beene or shall be made by this
assembly and approved by ye Hond Presdt and Council,
may be drawned up and legally published. The like
lawes shall be a rule to all the selectmen in each
towne for ye managmt of all theire prudenciall affaires, according to the lawdable customs hitherto
vsed.

PROVINCE RATE.

15. For defraying to ye publique charge of the
Province, It is ordered by this Assembly and ye authority thereof, yt a rate be made of 11/2d. in ye pound,
upon all psons and estates (ye Presdt and Council,
ministers and elders of churches excepted), in this
Province, according to ye valuation made by this
Assembly, and yt ye Selectmen in ye severall Towns doe
forthwth pforme the duty of theire places in ye valuation made by this Assembly, and yt ye Selectmen in ye
severall Towns doe forthwth pforme the duty of theire
places, in ye making such rates and comitting them to
the respective constables, to be imediately collected,
and the same to be transmitted to the Treasr of the
Province. This rate is to be paid in the speatiaes at
ye prices following, vizt:

M'ble boards at any mills in Piscataqua Rivr at ye
vsiall place of delivery, at 30s. p. M. M'ble wt oak
pipestaves, at some convenient landing place, where yye
constable shall apoint,

	at 3 l. p.M.
R: o: P: l Staves p supra,	at 30s. p.M.
R: o: hhd: ditto p supra,	at 25s. p.M.
Indian Corne	at 2½s. p. bush
Wheate	at 5s. p. bush
Malt	at 4s.
Fish	at price currt.

And whosoever shall pay theire rates in shall be abated
1/3 pt.

CONSTABLES TO CLEAR THEIR RATES WITHIN THE YEAR.

16. It is inacted by this Assembly and the
authority thereof, That whereas ye Constables of the
severall Townes are injoyned to cleare their rates, on
penalty of making good ye same out of theire owne
Estates --

PENALTY FOR REFUSING TO PAY.

17.   It is therefore ordered yt if any pson or
psons wthin this Province, rateable, shall refuse to
pay his rate or rates, or discover any estate to the
Constable, yt the Constable shall have power to seize
his person and carry him to the next prison, there to
remaine till he pay his sd rates, or give good security
soe to doe.

MARSHALLS TO LEVY FINES.

18.   It is further ordered, yt every marshall in
ye Province shall diligently and faithfully collect and
levy all such fines and sums of money, of every person
for wch he shall have arrt or execution signed by the
Treasurer, or other authority constituted by his
Majesty in ye Province, and sd sums soe leyed he shall
wyth all convenient speed deliver to ye sd Treasurer or
ptie, or attorney yt obtained ye Judgmt or executions
wyth wt hee hath done by vertue thereof, vnder his
hand, at the next Quart Court, or Sessions in ye
Province, after ye receipt thereof vnto ye Treasurer,
Secty or Clark yt granted ye same; to be by him kept,
and if ye execution or warrt be not fully satisfied the
sd Secty,, Clark, or treasurer may grant execution for
ye remainder.

MARSHAL'S FEES.

19.   And it is hereby ordered yt ye Marshall's
fees shall be as followeth: For all executions and
warrs levyed by them vnder five pound, five shillings;
for all executions not exceeding tenn pounds, twelve
pence in ye pound; for all executions above tenn pounds
and not exceeding forty pound, 10s. for ye 10 l., and
six pence in ye pound for evry pound above forty, and
one penny in ye pound for every pound abouve 100 l.,
out of the estate of ye pson the execution is served
upon, over and above, besides ye execution, and in all
cases where ye above sd fees for levying executions or
fines will not answer the Marshall's travell, & other
necessary charge, he shall have power to demand 6d. p.
mile, and vpon refusall or nonpayment to levy the same,
togeather wyth his other fees.

MARSHALLS MAY CALL FOR ASSISTANCE.

20. And whereas the sd Marshalls have oftentimes need of Assistance in the execution of ye office, it is therefore ordered yt ye Marshall or Contables wthin ye Province shall and have liberty to charge any pson to assist them in ye execution of yt office, if they see need; and whosoever shall neglect or refuse to assist them when thereunto required, the ptie soe refusing, complaint being made vnto any member or members of ye Councill or Court, he shall pay such a fine in money, vnto yye Treasurer of the Province, as Judge or Court yt hath cognisance thereof shall determine, according to the nature of the offence.

WHERE MARSHALS SHALL MAKE DEMANDS.

21. And in all cases of fines and assesmts to be levyed, and upon execution in civil actions, the Marshall or Constable shall make a demand at ye place of the pties vsiall abode, if it be knowne, and of the ptie if he be there to be found; if not, the marshall or Constable so employed shall leave at ye sd house his demand of ye same, and lyable to be paid by virtue of sd execution, rate or warrt, for fine attested under his hand; and upon refusal or nonpaymt accordingly, the officer or Marshall shall have power, calling assistance, if they see cause to break open the door of any house, chest or place, where he shall have notice yt any goods lyable to such levyes or execution shall be; and if he be to take ye pson, he may do ye like, if ypon demand he shall refuse to surrender himself. And wtsoever charge the officer shall nessessarily be put vnto upon any such occasion, he shall have power to levy the same as he doth debt, rate, fine or execution, And where the officer shall levy any such goods vpon execution, yt cannot be conveyed to ye place where ye ptie dwells, for whome such execution shall be levyed (if they be to be there delivered), wthout considerable charge, shall levy ye sd charge also wth ye execution, and in no case shall any officer be put to seek out any man or estates, farther yn hisplace of abode; but if ye ptie will not discover his estate, the officer may take this pson, and if any officer shall doe injury to any

by couller of this office, in this or any other case,
he shall be lyable vpon complaint of the ptie wronged,
by action or information, to make full resstitution,
and no marshall or constable shall in any case make a
deputy.

FINES TO BE PAID FORTHWITH.

22.   It is farther ordered yt whn any Delinquents
are fined to ye Province, they shall forthwth pay their
fines in money, or yt wch is equivalent, or give good
security to the Treasurer for the same, or ye pson
shall be secured till they do it.

NEAR RELATIONS NOT TO VOTE.

23.   For preventing all occation of ptiallity in
Courts of Justice, and avoiding of jellousies, It is
ordered yt in all civill cases betweene ptie and ptie,
where the judges or jurors are neerly related to either
ptie, as ye relation of ffather and son, either by
nature or marriage, brother and brothrs, vnkle and
nephew, landlord and tennant, yt judge or juror soe
related shall not vote or give sentence in any case
wherein his relations are ye pties concerned.

NO IMPRISONMENT BEFORE SENTENCE.

24.   Be it farther enacted yt no man's pson shall
be restrained or imprisoned by any authority wtsoever
before the law hath sentenced him therevnto, if he can
and will put in suffisient security, bail or maine
price, for his appearance and good behavior in ye mean
time, vnless it be in crimes captall, or contempt in
open Court, but in such cases where some express act of
court doth allow it.

LEGAL NOTICE IN CASE OF ATTACHMENT.

25.   And it is farther ordered, yt in all
attachmts of goods and chattells, Land or Heredittem ts
by ye officer, notice shall be given to the ptie
against whom the suite is comenced, either by reading
ye attachmt to him, or leaving a sumons or a copia of

ye attachmt, vnder ye hand of ye officer, at his house
or place of vsiall abode, or else ye case shall not
proceed; but if ye ptie be out of ye Province and not
like to return before ye court, ye case shall proceed
to triall, but judgmt shall not be entered, untill a
month after, and execution shall not be granted vntil
ye plaintife have given suffissient security to
respond, if ye defendant shall reverse ye judgment
wthin the space of one year.

YE FREEMEN OF EACH TOWNE TO CHUSE THEIR OFFICERS AND MAKE ORDERS FOR THEIR TOWNES. -- PENALTY FOR OFFENCES.

26.   Whereas pticular Townes have many things wch
concerne only themselves and ye ordering of yr owne
affairs of disposing of business in their owne Towne,
It is therefore ordered yt ye freemen of every towne
shall have power to chuse yr owne pticular officers, as
Consta: Grand Juror, and Jury of Tryalls, Surveyors
for ye highways, and like, annually, or otherwais as
need requires, and to make such laws and constitutions
as may concerne ye well fare of ye towne; provided they
be not of a criminall but of a prudenciall nature, and
yt the penalty exceed not 20s. for one offence, and
that they be not repugnante to ye publique laws and
orders of this Province; and if any Inhabitant shall
neglect or refuse to observe them, they shall have
power to levy the appointed penalty by distress; and if
any man shall behave himself offencively at any town
meeting, ye rest yr present shall have power to
sentence him for such offense, soe as ye penalty exceed
not 20s.

PRUDENTIAL OFFICERS.

27.   And ye freemen of every towne shall have
power to chuse yearly, or for a less time, a convenient
number of fitt men to order ye prudenciall affairs of
ye Towne, provided nothing be done by them contrary to
ye Lawes and orders of this Province, and yt ye number
doe not exceed 7 for one towne; and ye selectmen in
evry town shall take care from time to time to order
and dispose all single psons and inmates wthin yr

townes to service or otherwise; and if any pson be
greived at any such order or disposall, they have
liberty to appeale to the next court of this Province,
yt by law hath prop. cognicence thereof.

NONE TO CAST BALLAST INTO THE RIVER.

28. It is ordered yt no ship or other vessell
shall cast out any ballast in ye channel, or other
place inconvenient, in any Harbor or River wthin this
Province, upon ye penalty of tenn pounds.

AGE TO MAKE A VALID ACT.

29. It is ordered by the Generall Assembly, &c,
That no pson in this Province shall have power to pass
away lands, Herridittamts, or any other estates, or
make any legall or vallued act, or be capable of suing
or being sued in any of our Courts, in his or her own
pson, vntill they attaine vnto ye age of 21 years; but
any orphan may choose yr Gardean, to act for them at ye
ate of 14 years, to secure or Defend yr estates During
ye minority; also yt all parents and masters shall have
power in all civill cases to prosecute and Defend ye
Rights of yr children or sevants during the time of
their nonage, and in all criminal cases every person,
younger as well as elder, shall be Lyable to answer in
yr owne person for any misdemeanures charged upon them,
and may also Inform against any other person to any
Court, member of ye Counll, or Grand Jury man wthin
this Province.

ANY MEMBER OF YE COUNCIL OR CLARK TO GRANT
ATTACHMTS, AND HOW ATTACHMENTS ARE TO BE SERVED.

30. And it is further ordered, yr it shall be in
ye Power of any member of ye Counll or any Clarke of ye
writs allowed of by any of our gen. Courts, to grant
sumons and attachmts in all civil proceedings.
It is ordered, yt all sumons or attachmts shall be
served 6 days inclusively before ye court where ye case
is to be tryed, and ye cause or ground of ye action
shall in ye said process be briefly Declared, and wt
capassity ye Plaintiffe sheweth, whither in his owne

name, or as Attorney, assigne, gardian, executr, Adminr, Agent, or such like: or in Defect thereof, if exception be taken before ye pties Joyne Ishew, it shall be accoumpted a Legall barr, and ye Plaintiff shall be lyable to pay Cost, but no circumstantiall error in a sumons or attachmt where ye ptie and case intended may be Rationaly understood, shall be taken as a sufficeint ground for a nonsuit.

PLANT. OR DEFENDT NOT APEARING, TO BE NONSUITED.

31. And if either plaintif or Defendant doe make default of appearing, having been 3 times distinctly called by ye Marshall, or other office appointed by ye court to call, the plaintiff shall be nonsuited and Lyable to pay the Defendant Cost.

YE DEFENDT NOT APEARING, YE SURETY OR GOODS ATTACHED TO STAND.

32. It is enacted by ye General Assembly and authority yrof, yr if ye Defendant faile of his appearance, if it apears by ye process yt goods were attached or surety or sureteis bound for his apearance after ye surety hathe been 3 times called, ye action shall proceed to tryall, and if ye Judgmt be granted to ye plaintif, execution shall Ishew forthe against ye Defendant, and ye surety or goods attached shall stand good for 1 moth after Judgmt., but if the execution be not extended wthin one moth after judgment, ye goods attached or suretys bound shall be Released.

NO OFFICER TO BAILE ANY WTHOUT GOOD SURETY.

33. And yt no pson may Loose or be Defrauded of his Just debt, it is ordered yt no Marshall, Constable or other officer shall baile any pson yt he hath attached, wthout sufficient surety; vizt, one or more yt is a settled inhabitant wthin this province, and yt hathe a visible Estate to be Responsible, according to ye bond Required.

JUDGMENT TO BE ACKNOWLEDGED BEFORE 2 OF
YE COUNLL, &C.

34.   It is further enacted, yt any pson yt is attached to our gen. Court, and desirous to prevent farther charge, shall have Liberty, upon notice given to ye plaintiff or his attorney, to appear before 2 of ye members of ye Counll and ye Clark or Recorder of any gen. Court wthin this province, and acknowledge a Judgment, wch shall stand good and valid in Law, provided yt ye goods attached or surety bound shall not be Released till a month after ye acknowledgmt of such Judgmt, unless ye Crr give under his hand yt he is satisfied, and yt such pson as Live out of ye province, the acknowledgmt of a Judgmt shall not free ym. unless they shall produce a sufficient surety yt is a settled inhabitant wthin ye Judgmt, and ye Execution to stand good against ye surety for a full month after.

PERSONS NOTIFIED NOT APEARING, YE PENALTY.

35.   Be it farther enacted, that if any pson summoned to answer any presentmt, or for any fact or misdemeanor, do not appear at ye time appointed, he or they shall be proceeded aginst for contempt, except it appears they have been prevented by the hand of God.

PLAINT. MAY WTHDRAW HIS ACTION.

36.   It is also enacted, yt it shall be at ye Liberty of the Plaintiff to wthdraw his action at any time before ye Judge or Jury have given in yr verdict in ye case, in wch case he shall pay full Cost to ye Defendant.

NONE TO PRETEND GREAT DAMAGE TO VEX HIS ADVERSARY.

37.   And yt no pson, in his suit or plaint against another, shall falsely pretend great damage or debts, to vex or discredit his adversary, and if it appears to ye Court yt any plaintife hath wittingly wronged ye Defendant in vexatious suits or complaints, he shall pay ye Defendant double cost, and be fined to ye province 40s. or more, according to the demerrit of his fact.

ACTIONS MAY BE REVIEWED.

38.   It is further enacted, yt it shall be in ye liberty of any pson to review any suit or action wherein he hath been plaintife or Defendant in any Court wthin this province, but if any ptie be tweice Cast upon a Review, and shall still persist in a Course of Law, if he be Cast a 3d time his Case shall be Judged vexatious, and shall pay double Cost and such fine as ye Court shall award, not exceeding five pounds.

INNKEEPERS TO SELL NO STRONG DRINKS TO CHILDREN OR SERVANTS.

39.   Be it also enacted, yt no ordinary or Innkeeper suffer any Servants, or Children vnder family governmt, to buy (or to set drinking of) any Liquor, wine or other drink, in their houses or where they have to doe, or to spend their time there, wthout ye Leave of yr parents or Masters, unless it be in Case of necessity, on pain of 10s. forfeiture for every offence, ½ to ye informer and ye other to ye poore of ye towne.

A PERSON BEING 3 Mos IN TOWN SHALL BE AN INHABITANT, EXCEPT.

40.   Likewise it is further orderrd, yt if any pson come into any town wthin this province, and be there reced & entertained 3 moths, if such person fall sick or Lame, he shall be relieved by yt towne where he was so long entertained, but if ye Constable of yt Towne, or any of ye selectmen, have given warning to such psons wthin ye space of 3 moths yt ye towne will not admit of him, if such pson shall stand in need of Reliefe ye towne shall supply his necessity, until ye Prest and Counll can dispose of him, as to ym shall seem most just and Equall.

PERSONS SENT FROM OTHER TOWNS, YE TOWNS THEY ARE SENT FROM TO PAY THE CHARGE.

41.   It is also ordered, yt if any Children or elder pson shall be sent or come from one towne to another, to school, or to nurse, or otherwise to be

educated, or to a phisition or Chirurgion, to be cured
or healed, if such shall stand in need of Relief they
shall be Relieved at the charge of ye towne from whence
they came or doe belong, and not by ye towne to wch
they are sent; and in case they be sent from any towne
wthout ye Province, the taker, nurse, phisition or
Chirurgion to whome they are sent, shall take good
security to save ye town and Province chargless, or
shall be Responcable themselves, for such as need
Releife.

PRESIDENT OR DEPUTY TO HAVE CASTING VOTE.

42. It is further ordered, yt ye Presidt, or in
his absence his Deputy, shall have a Casting vote,
whensoever there shall be an Equivote, either in ye
General Assembly, genl Courts, or Councll.

NONE TO BRING IN OR ENTERTAIN STRANGERS
WTHOUT LEAVE.

43. Be it also enacted yt no pson, mstr of any
vessell, or other, do bring into any of our townes
wthin this Province, any pson or psons, wthout ye
approbation of ye Prest or 3 of any pson or psons,
wthout ye approbation of ye Prest or 3 of ye Counll, or
ye, selectmen of each Towne, nor yt any Inhabitant
wthin this Province, doe entertaine in his family any
pson yt is not soe allowed, for more than one weeke,
wthout giving notice thereof to 1 of ye Counll or to ye
Selectmen of ye towne to wch they belong, on penalty of
forfeiting 5 l. to ye towne, and be lyable to be sued
and give bond to free ye towne from Damage. Provided
this ordr shall not hinder any man from taking of any
apprentice or Cov'ent servant, for a year or yeares, yt
is at present sound and well; and if such servant shall
fall sick or Lame he shall be maintained by his Master
during ye Date of his Indentures or Covenant, and
afterwards by ye towne, in case of necessity.

CONSTABLES TO WARN FREEMEN'S MEETINGS TO CHOOSE DEPUTIES.

44.   It is enacted by this assembly and the authority thereof, yt ye severall constables in each towne of ye province doe warne and call together the free men of theire Respective townes, on ye first Monday in february, annually, and from among themselves to make their election of Deputies for ye Genll Assembly, who are to meet at Portsmo on ye first Tuesday of March, by 10 of ye Clock in ye forenoone, and ye number of Deputies for each towne to be as followeth, vizt: 3 for ye towne of Portsmo, 3 for ye towne of Dover, 3 for ye towne of Hampton, and 2 for ye towne of Exeter, whose names, after their election and acceptance, ye severall Consas shall make Return of to ye Assembly, as above vnder their hands; and if any Constable neglect his Duty in calling the free men together, or making Returns of ye names of ye Deputies chosen as above, he shall pay ye sum of 5 1. to ye Treasurer, for ye use of ye Province, for every such neglect; and if any Deputy, after his Election and acceptance, shall neglect his attendance at ye time and place of meeting, or absent himself form ye said Assembly wthout Leave, he shall pay a fine of 20s. to the Province, for Every Dayes absence, and so proportionably for every pr. of a day, vnless some Enevatable provindence or such other occation Hinder, as shall be judged by ye Majr pt of sd Assembly a sufficient excuse for sd absence.

PAY FOR ENTRY OF ACTIONS.

45.   And it is ordered, that for ye entry of all actions of appeale from ye qrtr Courts, shall be paid 20s. in money.

DOCUMENT 66:   Fundamentals of West New Jersey, 1681

The text is reproduced as found in Francis N. Thorpe, ed., *The Federal and State Constitutions, Colonial Charters, and Other Organic Laws of the United States* (Washington, D. C.: Government Printing Office, 1907), pp. 2565 - 2567.

Forasmuch as it hath pleased God, to bring us into the Province of West New Jersey, and settle us here in safety, that we may be a people to the praise and honour of his name, who hath so dealt with us, and for the good and welfare of our posterity to come, we the Governor and Proprietors, freeholders and inhabitants of West New Jersey, by mutual consent and agreement, for the prevention of innovasion and oppression, either upon us or our posterity, and for the preservation of the peace and tranquility of the same; and that all may be encouraged to go chearfully in their several places: We do make and constitute these our agreements to be as fundamentals to us and our posterity, to be held inviolable, and that no person or persons whatsoever, shall or may make void or disanul the same upon any pretence whatsoever.

    I.   That there shall be a General Free Assembly for the Province aforesaid, yearly and every year, at a day certain, chosen by the free people of the said Province, whereon all the representatives for the said Province, shall be summoned to appear, to consider of the affairs of the said Province, and to make and ordain such acts, and laws, as shall be requisite and necessary for the good government and prosperity of the free people of the said Province; and (if necessity shall require) the Governor for the time being, with the consent of his Council, may and shall issue out

writts to convene the Assembly sooner, to consider and
answer the necessities of the people of the said
Province.

II. That the Governor of the Province aforesaid,
his heirs or successors for the time being, shall not
suspend or defer the signing, sealing and confirming of
such acts and laws as the General Assembly (from time
to time to be elected by the free people of the
Province aforesaid) shall make or act for the securing
of the liberties and properties of the said free people
of the Province aforesaid.

III. That it shall not be lawful for the Governor
of the said Province, his heirs or successors for the
time being, and Council, or any of them, at any time or
times hereafter, to make or raise war upon any accounts
or pretence whatsoever, or to raise any military forces
within the Province aforesaid, without the consent of
the General Free Assembly for the time being.

IV. That it shall not be lawful for the Governor
of the said Province, his heirs or successors for the
time being, and Council, or any of them, at any time or
times hereafter, to make or enact any law or laws for
the said Province, without the consent, act and
concurrence of the General Assembly; and if the
Governor for the time being, his heirs or successors
and Council, or any of them, shall attempt to make or
enact any such law or laws of him or themselves without
the consent, act and concurrence of the General
Assembly; that from thenceforth, he, they, or so many
of them as shall be guilty thereof, shall, upon legal
conviction, be deemed and taken for enemies to the free
people of the said Province; and such act so attempted
to be made, to be of no force.

V. That the General Free Assembly from time to
time to be chosen as aforesaid, as the representatives
of the people, shall not be prorogued or dissolved
(before the expirance of one whole year, to commence
from the day of their election) without their own free
consent.

VI. That it shall not be lawful for the Governor
of the said Province, his heirs or successors for the
time being, and Council, or any of them, to levy or
raise any sum or sums of money, or any other tax

whatsoever, without the act, consent and concurrence of the General Assembly.

VII. That all officers of State, or trust, relating to the said Province, shall be nominated and elected by the General Free Assembly for the time being, or by their appointment; which officer and officers shall be accountable to the General Free Assembly, or to such as the said Assembly shall appoint.

VIII. That the Governor or the Province aforesaid, his heirs, or successor for the time being, or any of them, shall not send ambassadors, or make treaties, or enter into an alliance upon the publick account of the said Province, without the consent of the said General Free Assembly.

IX. That no General Free Assembly hereafter to be chosen by the free people of the Province aforesaid, shall give to the Governor of the said Province for the time being, his heirs or successors, any tax, or custom for a longer time than for one whole year.

X. That liberty of conscience in matters of faith and worship towards God, shall be granted to all people within the Province aforesaid; who shall live peaceably and quietly therein; and that none of the free people of the said Province shall be rendered uncapable of office in respect of their faith and worship.

Upon the Governors acceptance and performance of the proposals herein before expressed, we the General Free Assembly Proprietors and freeholders of the Province of West New Jersey aforesaid, do accept and receive Samuel Jenings as Deputy Governor.

In testimony whereof I have hereunto put my hand and seal, the day and year above written.

SAMUEL JENNINGS,
Deputy Governor.

Thomas Ollive, Speaker, to the General Free Assembly per order and in the name of the whole Assembly.

The fundamentals aforesaid being signed and sealed by the Deputy Governor, were ordered and appointed by the said Deputy Governor, and General Free Assembly, to be recorded the day and year first aforesaid, by me Thomas Revell, clerk to the General Assembly.

DOCUMENT 67:   Concessions to the Province of
               Pennsylania -- 1681

Text is taken from *Votes and Proceedings of the House
of Representatives of the Province of Pennsylvania,
Vol. I*   (Philadelphia: B. Franklin and D. Hall,
printers, 1752), pp. xxiv - xxvi.

Certain conditions, or concessions, agreed upon by
William Penn, Proprietary and Governor of the province
of Pennsylvania, and those who are the adventurers and
purchasers in the same province, the eleventh of July,
one thousand six hundred and eighty-one.

FIRST

     That as soon as it pleaseth God that the abovesaid
persons arrive there, a certain quantity of land, or
ground plat, shall be laid out, for a large town or
city, in the most convenient place, upon the river, for
health and navigation; and every purchaser and
adventurer shall, by lot, have so much land therein as
will answer to the proportion, which he hath bought, or
taken up, upon rent: but it is to be noted, that the
surveyors shall consider what roads or high-ways will
be necessary to the cities, towns, or through the
lands. Great roads from city to city not to contain
less than forty foot, in breadth, shall be first laid
out and declared to be for high-ways, before the
dividend of acres be laid out for the purchaser, and
the like observation to be had for the streets in the
towns and cities, that there may be convenient roads
and streets preserved, not to be encroached upon by any
planter or builder, that none may build irregularly to
the damage of another. In this, custom governs.

II. That the land in the town be laid out
together after the proportion of ten thousand acres of
the whole country, that is, two hundred acres, if the
place will bear it: however, that the proportion be by
lot, and entire, so as those that desire to be
together, especially those that are, by the catalogue,
laid together may be so laid together both in the town
and country.

III. That, when the country lots are laid out,
every purchaser, from one thousand, to ten thousand
acres, or more, not to have above one thousand acres
together, unless in three years they plant a family
upon every thousand acres; but that all such as
purchase together, lie together; and, if as many as
comply with this condition, that the whole be laid out
together.

IV. That, where any number of purchasers, more or
less, whose number of acres amounts to five or ten
thousand acres, desire to sit together in a lot, or
township, they shall have their lot, or township, cast
together, in such places as have convenient harbours,
or navigable rivers attending it, if such can be found;
and in case any one or more purchasers plant not
according to agreement, in this concession, to the
prejudice of others of the same township, upon
complaint thereof made to the Governor, or his Deputy,
with assistance, they may award (if they see cause)
that the complaining purchaser may, paying the survey
money, and purchase money, and interest thereof, be
entitled, enrolled and lawfully invested, in the lands
so not seated.

V.   That the proportion of lands, that shall be
laid out in the first great town, or city, for every
purchaser, shall be after the proportion of ten acres
for every five hundred acres purchased, if the place
will allow it.

VI. That nowithstanding there be no mention made,
in the several deeds made to the purchasers; yet the
said William Penn does accord and declare, that all
rivers, rivulets, woods, and underwoods, waters,
watercourses, quarries, mines, and minerals, (except
mines royal) shall be freely and fully enjoyed, and
wholly by the purchasers, into whose lot they fall.

VII. That, for every fifty acres, that shall be
allotted to a servant, at the end of his service, his
quit-rent shall be two shillings per annum, and the
master, or owner of the servant, when he shall take up
the other fifty acres, his quit-rent, shall be four
shillings by the year, or, if the master of the servant
(by reason of the indentures he is so obliged to do)
allot out to the servant fifty acres in his own
division, the said master shall have, on demand,
allotted him, from the governor, the one hundred acres,
at the chief rent of six shillings per annum.

VIII.   And, for the encouragement of such as
are ingenious and willing to search out gold and silver
mines in this province, it is hereby agreed, that they
have liberty to bore and dig in any man's property,
fully paying the damages done; and in case a discovery
should be made, that the discoverer have one-fifth, the
owner of the soil (if not the discoverer) a tenth part,
the Governor two-fifths, and the rest to the public
treasury, saving to the king the share reserved by
patent.

IX. In every hundred thousand acres, the Governor
and Proprietary, by lot, reserveth ten to himself, what
shall lie but in one place.

X.   That every man shall be bound to plant, or
man, so much of his share of land as shall be set out
and surveyed, within three years after it is so set out
and surveyed, or else it shall be lawfull for new
comers to be settled thereupon, paying to them their
survey money, and they go up higher for their shares.

XI.   There shall be no buying and selling, be it
with and Indian, or one among another, of any goods to
be exported, but what shall be performed in public
market, when such places shall be set apart, or
erected, where they shall pass the public stamp, or
mark.   If bad ware, and prized as good, or deceitful in
proportion or weight, to forfeit the value, as if good
and full weight and proportion, to the public treasury
of this province, whether it be the merchandize of the
Indian, or that of the planters.

XII. And forasmuch, as it is usual with the
planters to over-reach the poor natives of the country,
in trade, by goods not being good of the kind, or
debased with mixtures, with which they are sensibly

aggrieved, it is agreed, whatever is sold to the Indians, in consideration of their furs, shall be sold in the market place, and there suffer the test, whether good or bad; if good, to pass; if not good, not to be sold for good, that the natives may not be abused, nor provoked.

XIII. That no man shall, by any ways or means, in word, or deed, affront, or wrong any Indian, but he shall incur the same penalty of the law, as if he had committed it against his fellow planter, and if any Indian shall abuse, in word, or deed, any planter of this province, that he shall not be his own judge upon the Indian, but he shall make his complaint to the governor of the province, or his lieutenant, or deputy, or some inferior magistrate near him, who shall, to the utmost of his power, take care with the king of the said Indian, that all reasonable satisfaction be made to the said injured planter.

XIV. That all differences, between the planters and the natives, shall also be ended by twelve men, that is, by six planters and six natives; that so we may live friendly together as much as in us lieth, preventing all occasions of heart-burnings and mischief.

XV. That the Indians shall have liberty to do all things relating to improvement of their ground, and providing sustenance for their families that any of the planters shall enjoy.

XVI. That the laws, as to slanders, drunkenness, swearing, cursing, pride in apparel, trespasses, distriesses, replevins, weights, and measures, shall be the same as in England, till altered by law in this province.

XVII. That all shall mark their hogs, sheep and other cattle, and what are not marked within three months after it is in their possession, be it young or old, it shall be forfeited to the governor, that so people may be compelled to avoid the occasions of much strife between the planters.

XVIII. That, in clearing ground, care be taken to leave one acres of trees for every five acres cleared, especially to preserve oak and mulberries, for silk and shipping.

XIX. That all ship-masters shall give an account of their countries, names, ships, owners, freights and passengers, to an officer to be appointed for that purpose, which shall be registered within two days after their arrival, and if they shall refuse so to do, that then none presume to trade with them, upon forfeiture thereof; and that such masters be looked upon as having an evil intention to the province.

XX. That no person leave the province, without publication being made thereof, in the market place, three weeks before, and a certificate from some justice of the peace, of his clearness with his neighbours and those he dealt withal, so far as such an assurance can be attained and given: and if any master of a ship shall, contrary hereunto, receive and carry away any person, that hath not given that public notice, the said master shall be liable to all debts owing by the said person so secretly transported from the province.

Lastly, That these are to be added to, or corrected, by and with the consent of the parties hereunto subscribed.

WILLIAM PENN.

Sealed and delivered in the presence of --

WILLIAM BOELHAM,
HARBERT SPRINGET,
THOMAS PRUDYARD.

Sealed and delivered in the presence of all of the proprietors, who have hereunto subscribed, except Thomas Farrinborrough and John Goodson, in presence of --

HUGH CHAMBERLEN,
R, MURRAY,
HARBERT SPRINGET,
HUMPHREY SOUTH,
THOMAS BARKER,
SAMUEL JOBSON,
JOHN JOSEPH MOORE,

WILLIAM POWEL,
RICHARD DAVIE,
GRIFFITH JONES,
HUGH LAMBE,
THOMAS FARRINBORROUGH,
JOHN GOODSON.

DOCUMENT 68:   Laws and Liberties of New Hampshire,
               1682

Taken from *Provincial Papers, Documents, and Records
Relating to the Province of New Hampshire: Vol. I,
1623 - 1686*   (1867).   See Document 68.

Laws made by the Honorable, the Governor, with the
     advice and consent of the Council and General
     Assembly, held at Portsmouth the 14th of November,
     1682.

     1.   Be it enacted by the Governor, by and with
the advice and consent of the Council and Assembly, and
it is hereby enacted by the authority aforesaid, that
justice and right be equally and impartially
administered unto all men, not sold, denied, or
carelessly deferred unto any.
     2.   Be enacted, &c., That whosoever shall commit
adultery with a married woman, or one betrothed to
another man, both of them shall be fined: namely, ten
pounds apiece; and shall wear two capital letters;
namely, A D. cut out in a cloth and sewed upon their
uppermost garments, on their arm or back; and if, at
any time, any person so offending shall appear without
the said letters, he or she shall be liable to pay a
fine of five pounds as often as the offender shall be
so found.
     3.   Be it enacted, &c, That if any man commit
fornication with any single woman, they shall both be
punished by paying each a fine not exceeding five
pounds; and in case any commit carnal copulation after
contract, before marriage, they shall be amerced fifty
shillings apiece.

4.   Forasmuch as many persons of late years have
been and are apt to be injurious to the lives and goods
of others, notwithstanding all laws and means to
prevent the same, it is therefore enacted, &c., that if
any person commit burglary by breaking open any
dwelling house, warehouse, or shall forcibly rob any
person in the field or highways, such offenders shall,
for the first offence, be branded on the right hand
with the letter B, or R; and if he shall offend in the
like kind a second time, he shall be put to death, or
otherwise grievously punished, as the court shall
determine.

5.   Be it enacted, &c., That if any person in
this Province shall be legally convicted of stealing or
purloining horses, cattle, money, or other goods of any
kind, he shall be punished by restoring three-fold to
the party wronged, and a fine not exceeding twenty
shillings, or corporal punishment, to be inflicted as
the nature or circumstance of the case may require.

6.   Be it enacted, &c., That whosoever shall
steal, or attempt to steal, any ship, barkue, or vessel
of burden, or any public ammunition, shall be severely
punished, according to the nature of such a fact,
provided it extend not to life or limb.

7.   Be it enacted, &c., That whosoever shall
profane the sacred and blessed name of God, by vain
swearing or cursing, shall pay a fine of ten shillings,
or be set in the stocks an hour.

8.   Be it enacted, &c., That if any person, being
sixteen years of age or upward, shall wittingly or
willingly make or publish any lie, which may tend to
the damage or hurt of any particular person, or with
intent to deceive or abuse the people with false news
or reports, he shall be fined for every such offence
ten shillings, or sit an hour in the stocks.

9.   Be it enacted, &c., That whosoever shall be
found drunk shall pay a fine of ten shillinngs, or sit
an hour in the stocks; and whosoever shall drink to
excess, so as thereby to disguise himself, discovering
the same by speech or behaviour, he shall pay a fine of
three shillings and four pence, or sit in the stocks
half an hour.

10.   Be it enacted, &c., For prevention of the
prophanation of the Lord's day, that whosoever shall,

on the Lord's day, be found to do unnecessary servile labor, travel, sports, or frequent ordinaries in time of public worship, or idly straggle abroad, the person so offending shall pay a fine of ten shillings, or be set in the stocks an hour; and for discovery of such persons it is ordered that the constable, with some other meet person whom he shall choose, shall, in the time of public worship, go forth to any suspected place within their precincts, to find out any offender as above, and when found to return their names to some justice of the peace, who shall forthwith send for such offender, and deal with him according to law.

11. Be it enacted, &c., That whosoever shall speak contemptuously of the scriptures, or holy penmen thereof, shall be punished by fine not exceeding five pounds; and whosoever shall behave himself contemptuously toward the word of God preached, or any minister thereof, called and faithfully dispensing the same in any congregation, either by manifest interrupting of him in his ministerial dispensation, or falsely charging him with teaching error; such offender shall pay a fine of 20s., or sit two hours in the stocks.

12. Be it enacted, &c., That if any person do willfully and on purpose, burn down any man's fence, he shall make good the damage to the party wronged, and be amerced forty shillings, and be bound to ye good behaviour for six months.

13. Be it enacted, &c., That whosoever shall willfully pluck up, remove, or deface any landmarks or bounds, between party or party, that hath been or shall be orderly made or set up, by persons thereunto appointed in the several towns, he or they shall be fined not exceeding five pounds for such offence.

14. Forasmuch as sundry dissolute persons are too ready to run into ye transgression of such laws, unto which fines are annexed, and perhaps are so indigent as the paying of fines may be very injurious to themselves and families; be it therefore enacted, that every person so offending, not having five pound ratable estate, according to the valuation stated by law; or parents, or master or masters under whose government they are, that will forthwith pay the fine, shall be liable to be whipt: viz., for an offence where the

fine does not exceed twenty [ten] shillings, 5 stripes, where the fine doth not exceed twenty shillings, ten stripes; where the fine doth not exceed five pound, twenty stripes; and where the fine doth not exceed ten pound, thirty stripes or upward, not exceeding forty stripes.

15. Be it enacted, &c., That if any constable shall fail to clear his province rates within his year, or such time as shall be limited him by the trustees or overseers of the town, he shall be liable to have his estate distrained, by warrants from the treasurer directed to the marshal of the province, for the sum not gathered, and for all town rates made and committed to the constable, by the trustees or overseers of the town, to be collected within the time limited, the constable failing of his duty herein shall be liable to have his estate distrained, by warrant from the trustees, or overseers, directed to the marshal, for the sum not gathered.

And where to constables of the several towns are enjoined to clear their rates, on penalty of making good the same out of their own estates, it is ordered, that if any person or persons within this Province, rated, shall refuse to pay his rate or rates, and discover his own estate to the constable, he shall have liberty to seize the person and carry him to the next prison, there to remain till he pay the same, or give good security so to do.

16. For defraying the present charges arisen in the several towns, for the support of the ministers of the gospel, as also for payment of the necessary expenses of the Assembly men of each town, during their sitting, and other necessary occasions relating to the town;

17. Be it enacted, &c., That the trustees or overseers, hitherto called selectmen, in the respective towns where they live, do make such rates upon all persons and estates in the several towns, to be forthwith collected by the constable, as may answer the occasions aforesaid, until further orders, that particular care be taken with reference to all arrearages of rates, that the same may be forthwith collected and paid to the person to whom they are due.

18. For defraying the public charges of the
Province, be it enacted, &c., that a rate be made of
four pence in the pound, upon all persons and estates
within the Province, according to valuation thereof
last set, and that the trustees or overseers in the
several towns do forthwith effect it, committing the
same into the hands of the respective constables, to be
collected and transmitted into the hand of the Province
treasurer, in the species at the prices following:
viz.

Mer'ble pine boards at any convenient landing place in Piscataqua river,	at 26s. p. M.
Ditto white oak pipe staves, at any convenient landing, where the constable shall appoint,	at 50s. p. M.
Ditto red oak pipe staves, ut supra,	at 35s. p. M.
Beafe,	at 2d. per lb.
Poarke,	at 3d. per lb.
Indian corne,	at 3s. per bush'll.
Wheate,	at 5s. per bush'll.
Pease,	at 4s. per bush'll.
Malte,	at 3s. per bush'll.
ffish,	at price current.

19. And whosoever will pay their rates in money
shall be abated one third part: The said rate being
paid into the treasury, that comes not in money, to be
converted into money, and applied to the uses
following: viz., a present of two hundred pounds, in
money, to our honored Governor, as soon as the said
rate can be collected and converted into money, and the
remainder to answer any other province [purpose?] that
doth and may arise.

20. For bringing plenty of money into the
Province, by putting a value on foreign coin, be it
enacted, &c., that the several sorts of foreign coin
herein after named, shall pass here in all payments at
the value here set upon them; that is to say, the price
of eight ryalls of Spain, or dollars of Seville,
Mexico, and pillar and all lesser pieces, provided they

be good silver, at six shillings eight pence pr. the ounce, Troy weight, provided that all monyes payable upon former contracts be paid in specie, according to agreement.

21.   Whereas a bill was lately passed for regulation of the choice of jurors, assembly men, trustees, or overseers for the respective towns, and it appearing that the manner of choice of jurors therein expressed is absolutely contrary to the known laws and statutes of the kingdome of England, Be it therefore enacted by the Honorable Edward Cranfield, Esq., Lieutenant Governor and Commander-in-Chief of his Majesty's Province, with the advice and consent of the Council and General Assembly thereof, and it is hereby enacted by the authority aforesaid, that the clause in the said bill relating to the choice of jurors be repealed, and that for the future, jurymen shall be empaneled by the sheriff or marshal of the Province for the time being, and summoned and returned to the court of pleas, as it is customary in England and all other his Majesty's plantation; and whosoever is legally returned of the jury, and appears not, and this appears by the oath of the marshal, shall pay twenty shillings for this default, unless sickness or other necessity prevent, such as shall give the judge satisfaction.

22.   That no person may be a loser through the officer's neglect, Be it enacted that no marshal, constable, or other officer, shall bail any person that he hath attached, without sufficient security: viz., one or more that is settled inhabitants in the Province, and that hath a visible estate to be responsible according to the bonds required, provided no man's person be imprisoned that shall tender to the officer sufficient security by his own estate to answer the attachment, unless in such case where the law allows neither bail nor main-prize.

23.   Be it enacted, &c., That any person who is plaintiff in any court within this province shall have liberty at any time before verdict is given to withdraw his action, in which case he shall pay full costs to the defendant.

24.   Be it enacted, &c, That if any person do make default of appearance in any court where he is plaintiff, having been three times distinctly called by

the marshal or other officer appointed thereto, he shall be nonsuited and liable to pay the defendant costs; and if the defendant fail to make his appearance, if it appears by the process that goods were attached, or surety or sureties bound for his appearance, after the surety hath been three times called, the cause shall proceed to trial; and if judgment be given for the plaintiff, execution shall issue forth against the defendant, and the surety of goods attached shall stand good for a month after judgment; but if the execution be not levied within one month after judgment, the goods attached or sureties shall be discharged.

25. Be it enacted, &c., That every justice of the peace in the respective towns where he dwells shall have the power hereby to hear and determine any civil action where the debtor's damages exceed not forty shillings, provided attachments and summons are made out or signed by the clerk of the court of pleas for the time being; and it shall be lawful for the party aggrieved by such determination to appeal to the next court of pleas, or to the Governor and Council, giving security to prosecute such appeal, and abide the order therein.

26. Be it enacted, &c., That all summons and attachments shall be served six days before the court where the case is to be tried, and the cause or grounds of the action shall in the said process be briefly declared, and in what capacity the plaintiff sueth, whether in his own name, or as assignee, guardian, executor, administrator, agent, or such like, or in defect thereof, if exception be taken before parties join issue, it shall be counted a legal bar, and the plaintiff shall be liable to pay cost, but no circumstantial errors in a summons or attachment where the person and cause intended may be rationally understood, shall be taken as a sufficient ground for a nonsuit.

27. Be it enacted, &c., That any person attached, desiring to prevent further charge, shall have liberty, at any time before the sitting of the court where he is to answer, upon notice given to the plaintiff or his attorney, to appear before the judge and clerk of the said court and acknowledge judgment, which shall stand

good and valid in law, provided that the goods attached
or sureties bound shall not be discharged till a month
after the acknowledgment of such judgment, unless the
creditor give under his hand that he is satisfied;
provided, also, such acknowledgment of judgment, by any
person or persons not inhabiting within this province,
shall not free them unless they produce a sufficient
surety that he is a settled inhabitant within the
limits of this Province, to engage with him or them in
the acknowledgment of the said judgment and execution,
to stand good against the surety for a full month
after.

Vera Copia from the original laws.

    Attest: RICHARD CHAMBERLAIN.

DOCUMENT 69:   Frame of Government of Pennsylvania --
                1682

Taken from *Votes and Proceedings of the House of Representatives of the Province of Pennsylvania, Vol. I*
(Philadelphia: B. Franklin and D. Hall, printers,
1752), pp. xxvii-xxviii.

The frame of the government of the province of
Pensilvania, in America: together with certain laws
agreed upon in England, by the Governor and divers
freemen of the aforesaid province. To be further
explained and confirmed there, by the first provincial
Council that shall be held, if they see meet.

THE PREFACE

    When the great and wise God had made the world, of
all his creatures, it pleased him to chuse man his
Deputy to rule it: and to fit him for so great a
charge and trust, he did not only qualify him with
skill and power, but with integrity to use them justly.
This native goodness was equally his honour and his
happiness; and whilst he stood here, all went well;
there was no need of coercive or compulsive means; the
precept of divine love and truth, in his bosom, was the
guide and keeper of his innocency. But lust prevailing
against duty, made a lamentable breach upon it; and the
law, that before had no power over him, took place upon
him, and his disobedient posterity, that such as would
not live comformable to the holy law within, should
fall under the reproof and correction of the just law
without, in a judicial administration.
    This the Apostle teaches in divers of his
epistles: "The law (says he) was added because of

transgression:" In another place, "Knowing that the
law was not made for the righteous man, but for the
disobedient and ungodly, for sinners, for unholy and
prophane, for murderers, for whoremongers, for them
that defile themselves with mankind, and for
man-stealers, for lyers, for perjured persons," &c.,
but this is not all, he opens and carries the matter of
government a little further: "Let every soul be
subject to the higher powers; for there is no power but
of *God*.   The powers that be are ordained of *God*:
whosoever therefore resisteth the power, resisteth the
ordinance of *God*.   For rulers are not a terror to good
works, but to evil: wilt thou then not be afraid of
the power? do that which is good, and thou shalt have
praise of the same." "He is the minister of God to
thee for good." "Wherefore ye must needs be subject,
not only for wrath, but for conscience sake."

This settles the divine right of government beyond
exception, and that for two ends: first, to terrify
evil doers: secondly, to cherish those that do well;
which gives government a life beyond corruption, and
makes it as durable in the world, as good men shall be.
So that government seems to me a part of religion
itself, a thing sacred in its institution and end.
For, if it does not directly remove the cause, it
crushes the effects of evil, and is as such, (though a
lower, yet) an emanation of the same Divine Power, that
is both author and object of pure religion; the
difference lying here, that the one is more free and
mental, the other more corporal and compulsive in its
operations: but that is only to evil doers; government
itself being otherwise as capable of kindness, goodness
and charity, as a more private society. They weakly
err, that think there is no other use of government,
than correction, which is the coarsest part of it:
daily experience tells us, that the care and regulation
of many other affairs,more soft, and daily necessary,
makeup much of the greatest part of government; and
which must have followed the peopling of the world, had
Adam never fell, and will continue among men, on earth,
under the highest attainments they may arrive at, by
the coming of the blessed *Second Adam,* the *Lord*   from
heaven. Thus much of government in general, as to its
rise and end.

For particualar *frames* and *models* it will become
me to say little; and comparatively I will say nothing.
My reasons are:

First.   That the age is too nice and difficult
for it; there being nothing the wits of men are more
busy and divided upon. It is true, they seem to agree
to the end, to wit, happiness; but, in the means, they
differ, as to divine, so to this human felicity; and
the cause is much the same, not always want of light
and knowledge, but want of using them rightly. Men
side with their passions against their reason, and
their sinister interests have so strong a bias upon
their minds, that they lean to them gainst the good of
the things they know.

Secondly. I do not find a model in the world,
that time, place, and some singular emergences have not
necessarily altered; nor is it easy to frame a civil
government, that shall serve all places alike.

Thirdly.   I know what is said by the several
admirers of *monarchy, aristocracy* and *democracy,*
which are the rule of one, a few, and many, and are the
three common ideas of government, when men discourse on
the subject. But I chuse to solve the controversy with
this small distinction, and it belongs to all three:
Any government is free to the people under it
(whatever be the frame) *where the laws rule, and the*
people are a party to those laws, and more than this
is tyranny, oligarchy, or confusion.

But, lastly, when all is said, there is hardly one
frame of government in the world so ill designed by its
first founders, that, in good hands, would not do well
enough; and story tells us, the best, in ill ones, can
do nothing that is great or good; witness the and
states. Governments, like clocks, go from the motion
men give them; and as governments are made and moved by
men, so by them they are ruined too. Wherefore
governments rather depend upon men, than men upon
governments. Let men be good, and the government
cannot be bad; if it be ill, they will cure it. But,
if men be bad, let the government be never so good,
they will endeavor to warp and spoil it to their turn.

I know some say, let us have good laws, and no
matter for the men that execute them: but let them
consider, that though good laws do well, good men do

better: for good laws may want good men, and be
abolished or evaded [invaded in Franklin's print] by
ill men; but good men will never want good laws, nor
suffer ill ones. It is true, good laws have some awe
upon ill ministers, but that is where they have not
power to escape or abolish them, and the people are
generally wise and good: but a loose and depraved
people (which is the question) love laws and an
administration like themselves. That, therefore, which
makes a good constitution, must keep it, viz: men of
wisdom and virtue, qualities, that because they descend
not with wordly inheritances, must be carefully
propagated by a virtuous education of youth; for which
after ages will owe more to the care and prudence of
founders, and the successive magistracy, than to their
parents, for their private patrimonies.

These considerations of the weight of government,
and the nice and various opinions about it, made it
uneasy to me to think of publishing the ensuing frame
and conditional laws, foreseeing both the censures,
they will meet with, from men of differing humours and
engagements, and the occasion they may give of
discourse beyond my design.

But, next to the power of necessity, (which is a
solicitor, that will take no denial) this induced me to
a compliance, that we have (with reverence to God, and
good conscience to men) to the best of our skill,
contrived and composed the frame and laws of this
government, to the great end of all government, viz:
*To support power in reverence with the people, and to
secure the people from the abuse of power;*   that
they may be free by their just obedience, and the
magistrates honourable, for their just adminstration:
for liberty, without obedience is confusion, and
obedience without liberty is slavery. To carry this
evenness is partly owing to the constitution, and
partly to the magistracy: where either of these fail,
government will be subject to convulsions; but where
both are wanting, it must be totally subverted; then
where both meet, the government is like to endure.
Which I humbly pray and hope *God* will please to make
the lot of this Pensilvania. Amen.

WILLAM PENN.

The Frame, &c -- April 25, 1682

To all Persons, to whom these presents may come. WHEREAS king Charles the Second, by his letters patents, under the great seal of *England* bearing date the fourth day or March in the Thirty and Third Year of the King, for divers consideration therein mentioned, hath been graciousy pleased to give and grant unto me *William Penn,* by the name of *William Penn,* Esquire, son and heir of Sir *William Penn,* deceased, and to my heirs and assigns forever, all that tract of land, or Province called *Pennsylvania,* in *America,* with divers great powers, pre-eminences, royalties, jurisdictions, and authorities, necessary for the well-being and government thereof: Now know ye, that for the well-being and government of the said province, and for the encouragement of all the freemen and planters that may be therein concerned, in pursuance of the powers aforementioned, I, the said *William Penn* have declared, granted, and confirmed, and by these presents, for me, my heirs and assigns, do declare, grant, and confirm unto all the freemen, planters and adventurers of, in and to the said province, these liberties, franchise, and properties, to be held, enjoyed and kept by the freemen, planters, and inhabitants of the said province of *Pennsilvania* for ever.

Imprimis. That the government of this province shall, according to the powers of the patent, consist of the Governor and freemen of the said province, in form of a provincial Council and General Assembly, by whom all laws shall be made, officers chosen, and public affairs transacted, as is hereafter respectively declared, that is to say --

II. That the freemen of the said province shall, on the twentieth day of the twelfth month, which shall be in the present year one thousand six hundred eighty and two, meet and assemble in some fit place, of which timely notice shall be before hand given by the Governor or his Deputy; and then, and there, shall chuse out of themselves *seventy-two* persons of most note for their wisdom, virtue and ability, who shall meet, on the tenth day of the first month next ensuing,

and always be called, and act as, the provincial
Council of the said province.

III. That, at the first choice of such provincial
Council, one-third part of the said provincial Council
shall be chosen to serve for three years, then next
ensuing; one-third party, for two years then next
ensuing; and one-third party, for one year then next
ensuing each election, and no longer; and that the said
third part shall go out accordingly; and on the
twentieth day of the twelfth month, as aforesaid,
yearly for ever afterwards, the freemen of the said
province shall, in like manner, meet and assemble
together, and then chuse twenty-four persons, being
one-third of the said number, to serve in provincial
Council for three years: it being intended, that
one-third part of the whole provincial Council (always
consisting, and to consist, of seventy-two persons, as
aforesaid) falling off yearly, it shall be yearly
supplied by such new yearly elections, as aforesaid;
and that no one person shall continue therein longer
than three years: and, in case any member shall
decease before the last election during his time, that
then at the next election ensuing his decease, another
shall be chosen to supply his place, for the remaining
time, he has to have served, and no longer.

IV. That, after the first seven years, every one
of the said third parts, that goeth yearly off, shall
be uncapable of being chosen again for one whole year
following: that so all may be fitted for government
and have experience of the care and burden of it.

V. That the provincial Council, in all cases and
matters of moment, as their arguing upon bills to be
passed into laws, erecting courts of justice, giving
judgment upon criminals impeached, and choice of
officers, in such manner as is hereinafter mentioned,
not less than two-thirds of the whole provincial
Council shall make a *quorum* and that the consent and
approbation of two-thirds of such *quorum* shall be had
in all such cases and matters of moment. And moreover
that, in all cases and matters of lesser moment,
twenty-four Members of the said provincial Council
shall make a *quorum* the majority of which twenty-four
shall, and may, always determine in such cases and
causes of lesser moment.

VI. That, in this provincial Council, the Governor or his Deputy, shall or may, always preside, and have a treble voice; and the said provincial Council shall always continue, and sit upon its own adjournments and committees.

VII. That the Governor and provincial Council shall prepare and propose to the General Assembly, herafter mentioned, all bills, which they shall, at any time, think fit to be passed into laws, within the said province; which bills shall be published and affixed to the most noted places, in the inhabited parts thereof, thirty days before the meeting of the General Assembly, in order to the passing them into laws or rejecting of them, as the General Assembly shall see meet.

VIII. That the Governor and provincial Council shall take care, that all laws, statutes and ordinances, which shall at any time be made within the said province, be duly and diligently executed.

IX. That the Governor and provincial Council shall, at all times, have the care of the peace and safety of the province, and that nothign be by any person attempted to the subversion of this frame of government.

X. That the Governor and provincial Council shall, at all times, settle and order the situation of all cities, ports, and market towns in every county, modelling therein all public buildings, streets, and market places, and shall appoint all necessary roads, and high-ways in the province.

XI. That the Governor and provincial Councill shall, at all times, have power to inspect the management of the public treasury, and punish those who shall convert any part thereof to any other use, than what hath been agreed upon by the Governor, provincial Council, and General Assembly.

XII. That the Governor and provincial Council, shall erect and order all public schools, and encourage and reward the authors of useful sciences and laudable inventions in the said province.

XIII. That, for the better management of the power and trust aforesaid, the provincial Council shall, from time to time, divide itself into four distinct and proper committees, for the more easy administration of the affairs of the Province, which

divides the seventy-two into four eighteens, every one
of which eighteens shall consist of six out of each of
the three orders, or yearly elections, each of which
shall have a distinct portion of business, as
followeth: *First,* a committee of plantations, to
situate and settle cities, ports, and market towns, and
high-ways, and to hear and decide all suits and
controversies relating to plantations. *Secondly,* a
committee of justice and safety, to secure the peace of
the Province, and punish the mal-administration of
those who subvert justice to the prejudice of the
public, or private, interest. *Thirdly,* a committee of
trade and treasury, who shall regulate all trade and
commerce, according to law, encourage manufacture and
country growth, and defray the public charge of the
Province. And, *Fourthly,* a committee of manners,
education, and arts, that all wicked and scandalous
living may be prevented, and that youth may be
successively trained up in virtue and useful knowledge
and arts: the *quorum* of each of which committees
being six, that is, two out of each of the three
orders, or eyarly elections, as aforesaid, make a
constant and standing Council of *twenty-four* which
will have the power of the provincial Council, being
the quorum of it, in all cases not excepted in the
fifth article; and in the said committees, and standing
Council of the Province, the Governor, or his Deputy,
shall, or may preside, as aforesaid; and in the absence
of the Governor, or his Deputy, if no one is by either
of them appointed, the said committees or Council shall
appoint a President for that time, and not otherwise;
and what shall be resolved at such committees, shall be
reported to the said Council of the province, and shall
be by them resolved and confirmed before the same shall
be put in execution; and that these respective
committees shall not sit at one and the same time,
except in cases of necessity.

XIV. And, to the end that all laws prepared by the
Governor and provincial Council aforesaid, may yet have
the more full concurrence of the freemen of the
province, it is declared, granted and confirmed, that,
at the time and place or places, for the choices of a
provincial council, as aforesaid, the said freemen
shall yearly chuse Members to serve in a General

Assembly, as their representatives, not exceeding two
hundred persons, who shall yearly meet on the twentieth
day of the second month, which shall be in the year one
thousand six hundred eighty and three following, in the
capital town, or city, of the said province, where,
during eight days, the several Members may freely
confer with one another; and, if any of them see meet,
with a committee of the provincial Council (consisting
of three out of each of the four committees aforesaid,
being twelve in all) which shall be, at that time,
purposely appointed to receive from any of them
proposals, for the alterations or amendment of any of
the said proposed and promulgated bills: and on the
ninth day from their so meeting, the said General
Assembly, after reading over the proposed bills by the
Clerk of the provincial Council, and the occasions and
motives for them being opened by the Governor or his
Deputy, shall give their affirmative or negative, which
to them seemeth best, in such manner as hereinafter is
expressed. But not less than two-thirds shall make a
quorum in the passing of laws, and choice of such
officers as are by them to be chosen.

XV. That the laws so prepared and proposed, as
aforesaid, that are assented to by the General
Assembly, shall be enrolled as laws of the Province,
with this stile: *By the Governor, with the assent and
approbation of the freemen in provincial Council and
General Assembly.*

XVI. That, for the establishment of the government
and laws of this province, and to the end there may be
an universal satisfaction in the laying of the
fundamentals thereof: the General Assembly shall, or
may, for the first year, consist of all the freemen of
and in the said province; and ever after it shall be
yearly chosen, as aforesaid; which number of two
hundred shall be enlarged as the country shall increase
in people, so as it do not exceed five hundred, at any
time; the appointment and proportioning of which, as
also the laying and methodizing of the choice of the
provincial Council and General Assembly, in future
times most equally to the divisions of the hundreds and
counties, which the country shall hereafter be divided
into, shall be in the power of the provincial Council
to propose, and the General Assembly to resolve.

XVII. That the Governor and the provincial
Council shall erect, from time to time, standing courts
of justice, in such places and number as they shall
judge convenient for the good government of the said
province. And that the provincial Council shall, on
the thirteenth day of the first month, yearly, elect
and present to the Governor, or his Deputy, a double
number of persons, to serve for Judges, Treasurers,
Masters of Rolls, within the said province, for the
year next ensuing; and the freemen of the said
province, in the county courts, when they shall be
erected, and till then, in the General Assembly, shall,
on the three and twentieth day of the second month,
yearly, elect and present to the Governor, or his
Deputy, a double number of persons, to serve for
Sheriffs, Justices of the Peace, and Coroners, for the
year next ensuing; out of which respective elections
and presentments, the Governor or his Deputy shall
nominate and commissionate the proper number for each
office, the third day after the said presentments, or
else the first named in such presentment, for each
office, shall stand and serve for that office the year
ensuing.

XVIII. But forasmuch as the present condition of
the province requires some immediate settlement, and
admits not of so quick a revolution of officers; and to
the end the said Province may, with all convenient
speed, be well ordered and settled, I,   do
therefore think fit to nominate and appoint such
persons for Judges, Treasurers, Masters of the Rolls,
Sheriffs, Justices of the Peace, and Coroners, as are
most fitly qualified for those employments; to whom I
shall make and grant commissions for the said offices,
respectively, to hold to them, to whom the same shall
be granted, for so long time as every such person shall
well behave himself in the office, or place, to him
respectively granted, and no longer. And upon the
decease or displacing of any of the said officers, the
succeeding officer, or officers, shall be chosen, as
aforesaid.

XIX. That the General Assembly shall continue so
long as may be needful to impeach criminals, fit to be
there impeached, to pass bills into laws, that they
shall think fit to pass into laws, and till such time

as the Governor and provincial Council shall declare that they have nothing further to propose unto them, for their assent and approbation: and that declaration shall be a dismiss to the General Assembly for that time; which General Assembly shall be, notwithstanding, capable of assembling together into laws, and till such time as the Governor and provincial Council shall declare that they have nothing further to propose unto them, for their assent and approbation: and that declaration shall be a dismiss to the General Assembly for that time; which General Assembly shall be, notwithstanding, capable of assembling together upon the summons of the provincial Council, at any time during that year, if the said provincial Council shall see occasion for their so assembling.

XX. That all the elections of members, or representatives of the people, to serve in provincial Council and General Assembly, and all questions to be determined by both, or either of them, that relate to passing of bills into laws, to the choice of officers, to impeachments by the General Assembly, and judgment of criminals upon such impeachments by the provincial Council, and to all other cases by them respectively judged of importance, shall be resolved and determined by the ballot, and unless on sudden and indispensible occasions, no business in provincial Council, or its respective committees, shall be finally determined the same day that it is moved.

XXI. That at all times when, and so often as it shall happen that the Governor shall or may be an infant, under the age of one and twenty years, and no guardians or commissionrs are appointed in writing, by the father of the said infant, or that such guardians or commissioners shall be deceased; that during such minority, the provincial Council shall, from time to time, as they shall see meet, constitute and appoint guardians or commissioners, not exceeding three, one of which three shall preside as deputy and chief guardian, during such minority, and shall have and execute, with the consent of the other two, all the power of a Governor, in all the public affairs and concerns of the said province.

XXII. That, as often as any day of the month,
mentioned in any article of this charter, shall fall
upon the first day of the week, commonly called the
            The business appointed for that day shall
be deferred till the next day, unless in case of
emergency.

XXIII. That no act, law, or ordinance whatsoever,
shall at any time hereafter, be made or done by the
Governor of this province, his heirs or assigns, or by
the freemen in the provincial Council, or the General
Assembly, to alter, change, or diminish the form, or
effect, of this charter, or any part, or clause
thereof, without the consent of the Governor, his
heirs, or assigns, and six parts of seven of the said
freemen in provincial Council and General Assembly.

XXIV. And lastly, that I, the said for myself, my
heirs and assigns, have solemnly declared, granted and
confirmed, and do hereby solemnly declare, grant and
confirm, that neither I, my heirs, nor assigns, shall
procure to do any thing or things, whereby the
liberties, in this charter contained and expressed,
shall be infringed or broken; and if any thing be
procured by any person or persons contrary to these
premises, it shall be held of no force or effect. In
witness whereof, I, the said *William Penn* have unto
this rpesent character of liberties set my hand and
broad seal, this five and twentieth day of the second
month, vulgarly called April, in the year of our
            one thousand six hundred and eighty-two.

WILLIAM PENN.

Laws Agreed Upon in England, &c.

I. That the charter of liberties, declared,
granted and confirmed the five and twentieth day of the
second month, called April, 1682, before divers
witnesses, by *William Penn,* Governor and chief
Proprietor of *Pensilvania,* to all the freemen and
planters of the said province, is hereby declared and
approved, and shall be for ever held for fundamental in
the government thereof, according to the limitations
mentioned in the said charter.

II. That every inhabitant in the said province, that is or shall be, a purchaser of one hundred acres of land, or upwards, his heirs and assigns, and every persons who shall have paid his passage, and taken up one hundred acres of land, at one penny an acre, and have cultivated ten acres threof, and every person, that hath been a servant, or bondsman, and is free by his service, that shall have taken up his fifty acres of land, and cultivated twenty thereof, and every inhabitant, artificer, or other resident in the said province, that pays scot and lot to the government; shall be deemed and accounted a freeman of the said province: and every such person shall, and may, be capable of electing, or being elected, representatives of the people, in provincial Council, or General Assembly, in the said province.

III. That all elections of members, or representatives of the people and freemen of the province of *Pensilvania,* to serve in provincial Council, or General Assembly, to be held within the said province, shall be free and voluntary: and that the elector, that shall receive any reward or gift, in meat, drink, monies, or otherwise, shall forfeit his right to elect: and such person as shall directly or indirectly give, promise, or bestow any such rewrd as aforesaid, to be elected, shall forfeit his election, and be thereby incapable to serve as aforesaid: and the provincial Council and General Assembly shall be the sole judges of the regularity, or irregularity of the elections of their own respective Members.

IV. That no money or goods shall be raised upon, or paid by, any of the people of this province by way of public tax, custom or contribution, but by a law, for that purpose made; and whoever shall levy, collect, or pay any money or goods contrary thereunto, shall be held a public enemy to the province and a betrayer of the liberties of the people thereof.

V. That all courts shall be open, and justice shall neither be sold, denied or delayed.

VI. That, in all courts all persons of all persuasions may freely appear in their own way, and acording to their own manner, and there personally plead their own cause themselves; or, if unable, by their friends: and the first process shall be the

exhibition of the complaint in court, fourteen days
before the trial; and that the party, complained
against, may be fitted for the same, he or she shall be
summoned, no less than ten days before, and a copy of
the complaint delivered him or her, at his or her
dwelling house. But before the complaint of any person
be received, he shall solemnly declare in court that he
believes, in his conscience, his cause is just.

VII. That all pleadings, processes and records in
courts, shall be short, and in English, and in an
ordinary and plain character, that they may be
understood, and justice speedily administered.

VIII. That all trials shall be by twelve men, and
as near as may be, peers or equals, and of the
neighborhood, and men without just exception; in cases
of life, there shall be first twenty-four returned by
the sheriffs, for a grand inquest, of whom twelve, at
least, shall find the complaint to be true; and then
the twelve men, or peers, to be likewise returned by
the sheriff, shall have the final judgment. But
reasonable challenges shall be always admitted against
the said twelve men, or any of them.

IX. That all fees in all cases shall be moderate,
and settled by the provincial Council, and General
Assembly, and be hung up in a table in every respective
court; and whosoever, shall be convicted of taking
more, shall pay twofold, and be dismissed his
employment; one moiety of which shall go to the party
wronged.

X. That all prisons shall be work-houses, for
felons, vagrants, and loose and idle persons; whereof
one shall be in every county.

XI. That all prisoners shall be bailable by
sufficient sureties, unless for capital offences, where
the proof is evident, or the presumption great.

XII. That all persons wrongfully imprisoned, or
prosecuted at law, shall have double damages against
the informer, or prosecutor.

XIII. That all prisons shall be free, as to fees,
good and lodging.

XIV. That all lands and goods shall be liable to
pay debts, except where there is legal issue, and then
all the goods, and one-third of the land only.

XV. That all wills, in writing, attested by two witnesses, shall be of the same force as to lands, as other conveyances, being legally proved within forty days, either within or without the said province.

XVI. That seven years quiet possession shall give an unquestionable right, except in cases of infants, lunatics, married women, or persons beyond the seas.

XVII. That all briberies and extortion whatsoever shall be severely punished.

XVIII. That all fines shall be moderate, and saving men's contenements, merchandize, or wainage.

XIX. That all marriages (not forbidden by the law of God, as to nearness of blood and affinity by marriage) shall be encouraged; but the parents, or guardians, shall be first consulted, and the marriage shall be published before it be solemnized; and it shall be solemnized by taking one another as husband and wife, before credible witnesses; and a certificate of the whole, under the hands of parties and witnesses, shall be brought to the proper register of that county, and shall be registered in his office.

XX. And, to prevent frauds and vexatious suits within the said province, that all charters, gifts, grants, and conveyances (except leases for a year or under) and all bills, bonds, and specialties above five pounds, and not under three months, made in the said province, shall be enrolled, or registered in the public enrolment office of the said province, within the space of two months next after the making thereof, else to be void in law, and all deeds, grants, and conveyances of land (except as aforesaid) within the said province, and made out of the said province, shall be enrolled or registered, as aforesaid, within six months next after the making thereof, and settling and constituting an enrolment office or registry within the said province, else to be void in law against all persons whatsoever.

XXI. That all defacers or corrupters of charters, gifts, grants, bonds, bills, wills, contracts, and conveyances, or that shall deface or falsify any enrolment, registry or record, within this province, shall make double satisfaction for the same; half whereof shall go to the party wronged, and they shall be dismissed of all places of trust, and be publicly disgraced as false men.

XXII. That there shall be a register for births, marriages, burials, wills, and letters of administration, distinct from the other registry.

XXIII. That there shall be a register for all servants, where their names, time, wages, and days of payment shall be registered.

XXIV. That all lands and goods of felons shall be liable, to make satisfaction to the party wronged twice the value; and for want of lands or goods, the felons shall be bondmen to work in the common prison, or work-house, or otherwise, till the party injured be satisfied.

XXV. That the estates of capital offenders, as traitors and murderers, shall go, one-third to the next of kin to the sufferer, and the remainder to the next of kin to the criminal.

XXVI. That all witnesses, coming, or called, to testify their knowledge in or to any matter or thing, in any court, or before any lawful authority, within the said province, shall there give or delivery in their evidence, or testimony, by solemnly promising to speak the truth, the whole truth, and nothing but the truth, to the matter, or thing in question. And in case any person so called to evidence, shall be convicted of wilful falsehood, such person shall suffer and undergo such damage or penalty, as the person, or persons, against whom he or she bore false witness, did, or should, undergo; and shall also make satisfaction to the party wronged, and be publicly exposed as a false witness, never to be credited in any court, or before any Magistrate, in the said province.

XXVII.   And, to the end that all officers chosen to serve within this province, may, with more care and dilligence, answer the trust reposed in them, it is agreed, that no such person shall enjoy more than one public office, at one time.

XXVIII.   That all children, within this province, of the age of twelve years, shall be taught some useful trade or skill, to the end none may be idle, but the poor may work to live, and the rich, if they become poor may not want.

XXIX.   That servants be not kept longer than their time, and such as are careful, be both justly and kindly used in their service, and put in fitting equipage at the expiration thereof, according to custom.

XXX.   That all scandalous and malicious reporters, backbiters, defamers and spreaders of false news, whether against Magistrates, or private persons, shall be accordingly severely punished, as enemies to the peace and concord of this province.

XXXI.   That for the encouragement of the planters and traders in this province, who are incorporated into a society, the patent granted to them by *William Penn,* Governor of the said province, is hereby ratified and confirmed.

XXXII.   *   *   *

XXXIII.   That all factors or correspondents in the said province, wronging their employers, shall make satisfaction, and one-third over, to their said employers: and in case of the death of any such factor or correspondent, the committee of trade shall take care to secure so much of the deceased party's estate as belongs to his said respective employers.

XXXIV.   That all Treasurers, Judges, Masters of the Rolls, Sheriffs, Justices of the Peace, and other officers and persons whatsoever, relating to courts, or trials of causes, or any other service in the government; and all Members elected to serve in provincial Council and General Assembly, and all that have right to elect such Members, shall be such as possess faith in Jesus Christ, and that are not convicted of ill fame, or unsober and dishonest conversation, and that are of one and twenty years of age, at least; and that all such so qualified, shall be capable of the said several employments and privileges, as aforesaid.

XXXV.   That all persons living in this province, who confess and acknowledge the one Almighty and eternal God, to be the Creator, Upholder and Ruler of the world; and that hold themselves obliged in conscience to live peaceable and justly in civil society, shall, in no ways, be molested or prejudiced for their religious persuasion, or practice, in matters of faith and worship, nor shall they be compelled, at

any time, to frequent or maintain any religious
worship, place or ministry whatever.

XXXVI.   That, according to the good example of
the primitive Christians, and the case of the creation,
every first day of the week, called the Lord's day,
people shall abstain from their common daily labour,
that they may better dispose themselves to worship God
according to their understandings.

XXXVII.   That as a careless and corrupt
administration of justice draws the wrath of God upon
magistrates, so the wildness and looseness of the
people provoke the indignation of God against a
country: therefore, that all such offences against
God, as swearing, cursing, lying, prophane talking,
drunkenness, drinking of healths, obscene words,
incest, sodomy, rapes, whoredom, fornication, and other
uncleanness (not to be repeated) all treasons,
misprisions, murders, duels, felony, seditions, maims,
forcible entries, and other violences, to the persons
and estates of the inhabitants within this province;
all prizes, stage-plays, cards, dice, May-games,
gamesters, masques, revels, bull-baitings,
cock-fightings, bear-baitings, and the like, which
excite the people to rudeness, cruelty, looseness, and
irreligion, shall be respectively discouraged, and
severely punished, according to the appointment of the
Governor and freemen in provincial Council and General
Assembly; as also all proceedings contrary to these
laws, that are not here made expressly penal.

XXXVIII.   That a copy of these laws shall be hung
up in the provincial Council, and in public courts of
justice: and that they shall be read yearly at the
opening of every provincial Council and General
Assembly, and court of justice; and their assent shall
be testified, by their standing up after the reading
thereof.

XXXIX.   That there shall be, at no time, any
alteration of any of these laws, without the consent of
the Governor, his heirs, or assigns, and six parts of
seven of the freemen, met in provincial Council and
General Assembly.

XL.   That all other matters and things not herein
provided for, which shall, and may, concern the public
justice, peace, or safety of the said province; and the

raising and imposing taxes, customs, duties, or other charges whatsoever, shall be, and are, hereby referred to the order, prudence and determination of the Governor and freemen, in provincial Council and General Assembly, to be held, from time to time, in the said province.

Signed and sealed by the Governor and freemen aforesaid, the fifth day of the third month, called one thousand six hundred and eighty-two.

DOCUMENT 70:   Freedom of Conscience, December 7, 1682

Text is from J.T. Mitchell and H. Flanders, eds.,
Statutes at Large of Pennsylvania, Vol. I, pp.
107-109. The sections are mis-numbered in the original
so that there is no section IV.

Wheras the glory of almighty God and the good of
mankind is the reason and end of government and,
therefore, government in itself is a venerable
ordinance of God. And forasmuch as it is principally
desired and intended by the Proprietary and Governor
and the freemen of the province of Pennsylvania and
territories thereunto belonging to make and establish
such laws as shall best preserve true christian and
civil liberty in opposition to all unchristian,
licentious, and unjust practices, whereby God may have
his due, Caesar his due, and the people their due, from
tyranny and oppression on the one side and insolence
and licentiousness on the other, so that the best and
firmest foundation may be laid for the present and
future happiness of both the Governor and people of the
province and territories aforesaid and their posterity.
  Be it, therefore, enacted by William Penn,
Proprietary and Governor, by and with the advice and
consent of the deputies of the freemen of this province
and counties aforesaid in assembly met and by the
authority of the same, that these following chapters
and paragraphs shall be the laws of Pennsylvania and
the territories thereof.
  Chap. I. Almighty God, being only Lord of
conscience, father of lights and spirits, and the
author as well as object of all divine knowledge,
faith, and worship, who can only enlighten the mind and
persuade and convince the understandings of people. In

due reverence to his sovereignty over the souls of mankind;

Be it enacted, by the authority aforesaid, that no person now or at any time hereafter living in this province, who shall confess and acknowledge one almighty God to be the creator, upholder, and ruler of the world, and who professes him or herself obliged in conscience to live peaceably and quietly under the civil government, shall in any case be molested or prejudiced for his or her conscientious persuasion or pratice. Nor shall he or she at any time be compelled to frequent or maintain any religious worship, place, or ministry whatever contrary to his or her mind, but shall freely and fully enjoy his, or her, christian liberty in that respect, without any interruption or reflection. And if any person shall abuse or deride any other for his or her different persuasion and practice in matters of religion, such person shall be looked upon as a disturber of the peace and be punished accordingly.

But to the end that looseness, irreligion, and atheism may not creep in under pretense of conscience in this province, be it further enacted, by the authority aforesaid, that, according to the example of the primitive Christians and for the ease of the creation, every first day of the week, called the Lord's day, people shall abstain from their usual and common toil and labor that, whether masters, parents, children, or servants, they may the better dispose themselves to read the scriptures of truth at home or frequent such meetings of religious worship abroad as may best suit their respective persuasions.

Chap. II. And be it further enacted by, etc., that all officers and persons commissioned and employed in the service of the government in this province and all members and deputies elected to serve in the Assembly thereof and all that have a right to elect such deputies shall be such as profess and declare they believe in Jesus Christ to be the son of God, the savior of the world, and that are not convicted of ill-fame or unsober and dishonest conversation and that are of twenty-one years of age at least.

Chap. III. And be it further enacted, etc., that whosoever shall swear in their common conversation by

the name of God or Christ or Jesus, being legally
convicted thereof, shall pay, for every such offense,
five shillings or suffer five days imprisonment in the
house of correction at hard labor to the behoof of teh
public and be fed with bread and water only during that
time.

Chap. V. And be it further enacted, etc., for the
better prevention of corrupt communication, that
whosoever shall speak loosely and profanely of almighty
God, Christ Jesus, the Holy Spirit, or the scriptures
of truth, and is legally convicted thereof, shall pay,
for every such offense, five shillings or suffer five
days imprisonment in the house of correction at hard
labor to the behoof of the public and be fed with bread
and water only during that time,

Chap. VI.   And be it further enacted, etc.,
that whosoever shall, in their conversation, at any
time curse himself or any other and is legally
convicted thereof shall pay for every such offesne five
shillings or suffer five days imprisonment as
aforesaid.

DOCUMENT 71:   Charter of Liberties and Privileges,
                October 30, 1683.

Complete text is taken from *The Colonial Laws of New
York, Vol. I* , pp. 111 - 116. For the circumstances
surrounding this document and the similar charter of
1691, see Charles M. Andrews, *The Colonial Period of
American History, Vol. III,* chapter 3; and David S.
Lovejoy, "Equality and Empire: The New York Charter of
Libertyes, 1683," *William and Mary Quarterly,* third
series, Vol. 21 (1964), pp. 493 - 515.

ffOR The better Establishing the Government of this
province of New Yorke and that Justice and Right may be
Equally done to all persons within the same.
BEE It Enacted by the Governour Councell and
Representatives now in General Assembly mett and
assembled and by the authority of the same.
THAT The Supreme Legislative Authority under his
Majesty and Royall Highnesse James Duke of Yorke Albany
&c Lord proprietor of the said province shall forever
be and reside in a Governour, Councell, and the people
mett in General Assembly.
THAT The Exercise of the Cheife Magistracy and
Administration of the Government over the said province
shall bee in the said Governour assisted by a Councell
with whose advice and Consent or with at least four of
them he is to rule and Governe the same according to
the Lawes thereof.
THAT in Case the Governour shall dye or be absent out
of the province and that there be noe person within the
said province Comissionated by his Royal Hignesse his
heirs or Successours to be Governour or Comander in
Cheife there That then the Councell for the time being
or Soe many of them as are in the Said province doe

take upon them the Administration of the Governour and
Execution of the Lawes thereof and powers and
authorityes belonging to the Governour and Councell the
first in nomination in which Councell is to preside
untill the said Governour shall returne and arrive in
the said province againe, or the pleasure of his Royall
Highnesse his heires or Successours Shall be further
knowne.
THAT According to the usage Custome and practice of the
Realme of England a session of a Generall Assembly be
held in this province once in three yeares at least.
THAT Every ffreeholder within this province and
ffreeman in any Corporation Shall have his free Choise
and Vote in the Electing of the Representatives without
any manner of constraint or Imposition. And that in
all Elections the Majority of Voices shall carry itt
and by freeholders is understood every one who is Soe
understood according to the Lawes of England.
THAT the persons to be Elected to sitt as
representatives in the Generall Assembly from time to
time for the severall Cittyes townes Countyes Shires or
Divisions of this province and all places within the
same shall be according to the proportion and number
hereafter Expressed that is to say for the Citty, and
County of New Yorke four, for the County of Suffolke
two, for Queens County two, for Kings County two, for
the County of Richmond two for the County of West
Chester two.
        for the County of Ulster two for the County of
Albany two and for Schenectade within the said County
one for Dukes County two, for the County of Cornwall
two and as many more as his Royall Highnesse shall
think fitt to Establish.
THAT All persons Chosen and Assembled in manner
aforesaid or the Major part of them shall be deemed and
accounted the Representatives of this province which
said Representatives together with the Governour and
his Councell Shall forever be the Supreame and only
Legislative power under his Royall Hignesses of the
said province.
THAT The said Representatives may appoint their owne
Times of meeting dureing their sessions and may
adjourne their house from time to time to such time as
to them shall seeme meet and convenient.

THAT The said Representatives are the sole Judges of the Qualifications of their owne members, and likewose of all undue Elections and may from time to time purge their house as they shall see occasion dureing the said sessions.

THAT noe member of the general Assembly or their servants dureing the time of their Sessions and Whilest they shall be goeing to and returning from the said Assembly shall be arrested sued imprisoned or any wayes molested or troubled nor be compelled to make answere to any suite, Bill plaint, Declaration or otherwise, (Cases of High Treason and felony only Excepted) provided the number of the said servants shall not Exceed three.

THAT All bills agreed upon by the said Representatives or the Major part of them shall be presented unto the Governour and his Councell for their Approbation and Consent All and Every which Said Bills soe approved or Consented to by the Governour and his Councell shall be Esteemed and accounted the Lawes of the province, Which said Lawes shall continue and remaine of force untill they shall be repealed by the authority aforesaid that is to say the Governour Councell and Representatives in General Assembly by and with the Approbation of his Royal Highnesse or Expire by their owne Limittations.

THAT In All Cases of death or removall of any of the said Representatives The Governour shall issue out Sumons by Writt to the Respective Townes Cittyes Shires Countryes or Divisions for which he or they soe removed or deceased were chosen willing and requireing the ffreeholders of the Same to Elect others in their place and stead.

THAT Noe freeman shall be taken and imprisoned or be disseized of his ffreehold or Libertye or ffree Customes or be outlawed or Exiled or any other wayes destroyed nor shall be passed upon adjudged or condemned But by the Lawfull Judgment of his peers and by the Law of this province. Justice nor Right shall be neither sold denyed or deferred to any man within this province.

THAT Noe aid, Tax, Tallage, Assessment, Custome, Loane, Benevolence or Imposition whatsoever shall be layed assessed imposed or levyed on any of his Majestyes Subjects within this province or their Estates upon any

manner of Colour or pretence but by the act and Consent
of the Governour Councell and Rpresentatives of the
people in Generall Assembly mett and Assembled.
THAT Noe man of what Estate or Condition soever shall
be putt out of his Lands or Tenements, nor taken, nor
imprisoned, nor dishereited, nor banished nor any wayes
distroyed without being brought to Answere by due
Course of Law.
THAT A ffreeman Shall not be amerced for a small fault,
but after the manner of his fault and for a great fault
after the Greatnesse thereof Saveing to him his
freehold, And a husbandman saveing to him his Wainage
and a merchant likewise saveing to him his merchandize
And none of the said Amerciaments shall be assessed but
by the oath of twelve honest and Lawfull men of the
Vicinage provided the faults and misdemeanours be not
in Contempt of Courts of Judicature.
ALL Tryalls shall be by the verdict of twelve men, and
as neer as many be peers or Equalls And of the
neighbourhood and in the County Shire or Division where
the Fact Shall arise or grow Whether the Same be by
Indictment Information Declaration or otherwise against
the person Offender or Defendant.
THAT In all Cases Capitall or Criminall there shall be
a grand Inquest who shall first present the offence and
then twelve men of the neighbourhood to try the
Offender who after his plea to the Indictment shall be
allowed his reasonable Challenges.
THAT In all Cases whatsoever Bayle by sufficient
Suretyes Shall be allowed and taken unlesse for treason
or felony plainly and specially Expressed and menconed
in the Warrant of Committment provided Alwayes that
nothing herein contined shall Extend to discharge out
of prison upon bayle any person taken in Execution for
debts or otherwise legally sentenced by the Judgment of
any of the Courts of Record within the province.
THAT Noe ffreeman shall be compelled to receive any
Marriners or Souldiers into his house and there suffer
them to Sojourne, against their willes provided Alwayes
it be not in time of Actuall Warr within this province.
THAT Noe Comissions for proceeding by Marshall Law
against any of his Majestyes Subjects within this
province shall issue forth to any person or persons
whatsoever Least by Colour of them any of his Majestyes

Subjects bee destroyed or putt to death Except all such
officers persons and Soldiers in pay throughout the
Government.

THAT from hence forward Noe Lands Within this province
shall be Esteemed or accounted a Chattle or personall
Estate but an Estate of Inheritance according to the
Custome and practice of his Majesties Realme of England.

THAT Noe Court or Courts within this province have or
at any time hereafter Shall have any Jurisdiction power
or authority to grant out any Execution or other writt
whereby any mans Land may be sold or any other way
disposed of without the owners Consent provided Alwayes
That the issues or meane proffitts of any mans Lands
shall or may be Extended by Execution or otherwise to
satisfye just debts Any thing to the Contrary hereof in
any wise Notwithstanding.

THAT Noe Estate of a feme Covert shall be sold or
conveyed But by Deed Acknowledged by her in Some Court
of Record the Woman being secretly Examined if She doth
it freely without threats or Compulsion of her husband.

THAT All Wills in writeing attested by two Credible
Witnesses shall be of the same force to convey Lands as
other Conveyances being registered in the Secretaryes
Office within forty dayes after the testators death.

THAT A widdow after the death of her husband shall have
her Dower And shall and may tarry in the Cheife house
of her husband forty dayes after the death of her
husband within which forty dayes her Dower shall be
assigned her And for her Dower shallbe assigned unto
her the third party of all the Lands of her husband
dureing Coverture, Except shee were Endowed of Lesse
before Marriage.

THAT All Lands and Heritages within this province and
Dependencyes shall be free from all fines and Lycences
upon Alienations and from all Herriotts Ward Shipps
Liveryes primer Seizins yeare day and Wast Escheates
and forfeitures upon the death of parents and Ancestors
naturall unaturall casuall or Judiciall, and that
forever; Cases of High treason only Excepted.

THAT Noe person or persons which professe ffaith in God
by Jesus Christ Shall at any time be any wayes molested
punished disquieted or called in Question for Difference
in opinion or Matter of Religious Concernment, who doe
not actuall disturb the Civill peace of the province,
But that all and Every such person or prsons may from

time to time and at all times freely have and fully
enjoy his or their Judgments or Consciencyes in matters
of Religion throughout all the province, they behaveing
themselves peaceably and quietly and not useing this
Liberty to Lycentiousnesse nor to the civill Injury or
outward disturbance of others provided Alwayes that
this liberty or any thing contained therein to the
Contrary shall never be Construed or improved to make
void the Settlement of any publique Minister on Long
Island Whether Such Settlement be by two thirds of the
voices in any Towne thereon which shall alwayes include
the Minor part Or by Subscriptions of perticuler
Inhabitants in Said Townes provided they are the two
thirds thereon Butt that all such agreements Covenants
and Subscriptions that are there already made and had
Or that hereafter shall bee in this Manner Consented to
agreed and Subscribed shall at all time and times
hereafter be firme and Stable And in Confirmation
hereof It is Enacted by the Governour Councell and
Representatives; That all Such Sumes of money soe
agreed on Consented to or Subscribed as aforesaid for
maintenance of said public Ministers by the two thirds
of any Towne on Long Island Shall alwayes include the
Minor part who shall be regulated thereby And also Such
Subscriptions and agreements as are before mentioned
are and Shall be alwayes ratified performed and paid,
And if any Towne on said Island in their publick
Capacity of agreement with any Such minister or any
perticuler persons by their private Subscriptions as
aforesaid Shall make default deny or withdraw from Such
payment Soe Covenanted to agreed upon and Subscribed
That in Such Case upon Complaint of any Collector
appointed and Chosen by two thirds of Such Towne upon
Long Island unto any Justice of that County Upon his
hearing the Same he is here by authorized impowered and
required to issue out his warrant unto the Constable or
his Deputy or any other person appointed for the
Collection of Said Rates or agreement to levy upon the
goods and Cattles of the Said Delinquent or Defaulter
all such Sumes of money Soe covenanted and agreed to be
paid by distresse with Costs and Charges without any
further Suite in Law Any Lawe Custome or usage to the
Contrary in any wise Notwithstanding.
PROVIDED Alwayes the said sume or sumes be under forty
shillings otherwise to be recovered as the Law directs.

AND WHEREAS All the Respective Christian Churches now in practice within the City of New Yorke and the other places of this province doe appeare to be priviledged Churches and have beene Soe Established and Confirmed by the former authority of this Government BEE it hereby Enacted by this Generall Assembly and by the authority thereof That all the Said Respective Christian Churches be hereby Confirmed therein And that they and Every of them Shall from henceforth forever be held and reputed as priviledged Churches and Enjoy all their former freedomes of their Religion in Divine Worshipp and Church Discipline And that all former Contracts made and agreed upon for the maintenances of the severall ministers of the Said Churches shall stand and continue in full force and virtue And that all Contracts for the future to be made Shall bee of the same power And all persons that are unwilling to performe their part of the said Contract Shall be Constrained thereunto by a warrant from any Justice of the peace provided it be under forty Shillings Or otherwise as this Law directs provided allsoe that all Christian Churches that Shall hereafter come and settle within this province shall have the Same priviledges.

DOCUMENT 72:   Articles of Agreement Between the
Members of the Frankfort Company, for
the Settlement of Germantown,
Pennsylvania, November 12, 1686

Text is taken from *Pennsylvania Magazine of History,*
Vol. XV, pp. 205 - 211.

In the name and to the glory of God!

We underwritten, witness and confess hereby, whereas we
altogether have jointly purchased five and twenty
thousand acres of unseparated land, English measure, in
the American province of Pennsylvania, each of us
having effectually paid his share, as appears by the
accounts thereof, viz.,

Jacob van de Wallen	2500	
Caspar Merian, now Jacob		
van de Wallen	883 1/3	5000
and Daniel Behagel	1666 2/3	
Lieutenant Johan Jacob		
Schutz	4000	
Johan William Uberfeld,		5000
now Francis		
Daniel Pastorius	1000	
Jacob van de Wallen	1666 2/3	
George Strauss, now		
Johana Elenora von		5000
Merlau, wife of Johan		
William Peters	1666 2/3	
Daniel Behagel	1666 2/3	
D. Gerhard von Mastricht	1666 2/3	
D. Thomas von Wilich	1666 2/3	5000
and Johanes le Brun	1666 2/3	
Balthasar Jawert	3333 1/3	
Johanes Kemler	1666 2/3	5000

That we, concerning this estate, for ourselves, our respective wives, children, and heirs, in the name of God, have entered into and agreed upon a communion or society in manner and form folloiwng.

1.   The above said land, wherever they are or hereafter shall be assigned jointly and asunder, as also the lots in the city, which over and above the aforementioned belong unto us, to wit four or six places in the city of Philadelphia, for to build new houses upon, and a matter of 300 acres in the city's liberty situate before and above Philadelphia, and the land which of late has been bought upon the Skulkill for a brick kiln, together with all and every edifices and other improvements which are now and hereafter shall be made in any place and quarter of all Pennsylvania, as also victuals, commodities, cattle, household stuff, etc., which we have sent thither, or were bought or otherwise acquired there; and the present and future real rights and privileges shall now and hereafter be and remain common in equal right, according to everyone's above specified share which he has in the said company.

2.   All and every expenses for the cultivating, improvement, and buildings; items for transporting of servants, tenants, and other persons, as also commodities, victuals, tools, etc., and there in the said province for tradesmen and laborers, etc. and universally all charges of what name soever, which hitherto have been spent in America and Europe or herafter at the next mentioned manner may be spent, shall be at common costs after the rate of everyone's share.

3.   Per contra, all profits, revenues, and whatsoever there is got, built, planted, tilled, and brought forth, either in products of the ground, slaves, cattle, manufactures, etc., nothing at all excepted, shall be common among all the partners pro rato of the number of acres.

4.   Concerning the affairs of this company, the five head-stems, every 5000 to be accounted for a head-stem, or as hereafter it may be otherwise agreed upon, shall consult among themselves and by the plurality of votes, each thousand acres having ten votes, conclude with all convenient speed.

5.   There in the said province there shall be always an attorney for the company and in case of his decease, absence, and unableness a substitute be apointed unto him with a salary in writing executed by both parties. Both these shall yearly, under both their hands and the company's seal, make an orderly inventory of all the company's effects there, specifying the cultivated and uncultivated acres, meadows, waters, woods, houses, the bounds thereof, as also the servants, tenants, cattle, fruits, victuals, commodities, debts active and passive, ready money etc., and send the same over with their accounts of costs and profits, receipt and disbursement, decrease and increase in all particulars by one and another following vessel with a second original, and likewise, in manner aforesaid, commuincate the state of things to him unto whom at the time the correspondency of the company shall be committed.

6.   Here in these parts there shall be always ordained, by the plurality of vote in writing, two clerks of the company, either of the companions or strangers, who shall attend the company's accounts and correspondence in America, open the letters which belong to them, and communicate the contents thereof by way of extract, or, if need be, a copy to the 5 head-stems, by and from whom further all and every partners are to receive, do, and perform theirs, write down with short words, yet clearly and diligently, in a diary of the Pennsylvanian affairs out of the letters coming from thence or the occurrencies happening here; make peculiar memorandums of what is to be done and observed, adjust every year, ultimo decembris, the accounts, together with the revision of inventories and the annotation of increase and decrease by day and date, as far as may be had by letters or otherwise, and being approved of by the five head-stems or their attorneys, record them in a book, and keep them under two locks in good order according to their table or index, together with the company's documents and original writings ascribing day and date, as also the copies of the letters which they send away, in a certain place as the company pleases, and now for the present time at Frankfort upon the Main, where this work did first begin, and whereunto as yet the greatest part does belong and in all, without the special

consent of the five head-stems, not undertake nor
dispatch anything of importance. Further, they shall
enjoy for all their labor some moderate recompence from
the company. Moreover, each head-stem may, for himself
and the partners thereunto belonging, extract out of
such letters what he pleases; but the originals shall
be kept in the archive.

    7.   Hereafter the company shall sign their
letters and contracts with a peculiar seal to be kept
along with the aforesaid original documents; and shall
send another seal somewhat different in bigness and
circumscription to their factors in Pennsylvania, there
to make the like use thereof. Without such seals no
letters or contracts shall be sent in the company's
name thither or hither nor be esteemed firm and good.

    8.   In case any of us or of our heirs should go
to Pennsylvania, or send an attorney for himself
aforehand to prepare him a settlement and would give
him, or take along with himself, several proper things
for his use, he or they may do the same at their own
costs and risk; afterwards, after the rate of his
share, for every thousand acres, choose from himself
sixty in one tract of uncleared land, so as we receive
the same of the Governor, and therefore he shall pay
yearly a recognition as rent to the company, for every
ten acres, one English shilling; and if this land be
not enough but too narrow for him, there shall be
further allowed unto him, proportionably to his share,
60 acres as aforesaid, in consideration of each
thousand, for the moiety of the price for which the
company uses to let it at that time upon rent unto
strangers; and in case he should still desire more
land, if the company can spare it, at the price and on
such conditions as to a stranger. Now upon these lands
which one or the other settles for himself alone in
manner aforesaid, he may act at his pleasure and use
and enjoy all sort of goods immoveable and moveable
which we have in common there before other strangers;
nevertheless, that all this be unprejudicial to the
common best of the company. And those companions which
dwell in Pennsylvania shall pay the usual rent, wages,
payment, or value of all what they use of the common
things for themselves to the company's factor there,
whereof they are, at the following repartition, to
receive back their share. But if the whole company do

generally find good to let go over any of their
companions for their common service and at their common
costs, there shall in that case be made a particular
agreement. But in every case and in all parts
whatsoever the companions there and their heirs shall
be obliged no less than those in Europe to stand to
this contract and to the further orders of the most
votes.

9. If the clerks or else one more by the
company's approbation, as aforesaid, should disburse
money, such debtors shall be obliged to repay the thus
disbursed principal sum at the utmost within the space
of one year with the yearly interest of five per cent,
and therefore their share shall hereby in the best form
of law be engaged as a special pledge.

10. If any of us or ours soon or late shall die
without wife and heirs begotten in matrimony of his
body, not having expressly and particularly declared by
testament or credible disposition in writing, or by
word of mouth, what he would have done with his share
of these common goods after his decease, his share
shall accrue and be herewith assigned to the whole
company, proportionably to each's respective share, and
shall not be otherwise accounted than as if he had
reserved to himself only the use of such goods for the
term of his life, and presently in the beginning
incorporated the true property to the company. And all
deceases of the companions and who are their heirs in
this work shall, by the clerks then being, in credible
form either under the attestation of all the nearest
relations of the deceased or of other credible persons,
be advised with all speed, or until the certainty
thereof, the name of the deceased be continued in
accounts and books. And his contingent which falls to
him be kept in the company's case along with the
original documents.

11. It's not lawful for any that is a partner in
this company to alien his land or right thereof, all or
in part, to any without the company, unless he have the
company's consent, or at least made the first offer to
the same; but if one or other of us, our wives,
children, or whoever shall be hereafter a partner of
the company, should be willing, soon or late, to
alienate his share or portion and none of the company

to acquire or buy the same, then and not otherwise the
seller shall have liberty to sell it to any other; yet
with this proviso, that always the company, or, if they
will not have it, any of the company within three
months after the alienation is made known, shall have
liberty to take to themselves that what is sold, paying
down the consideration money, and for their profit to
deduct or give less than such new purchaser bought the
part aliened for ten per cent of the consideration
money, the price whereof both seller and buyer shall be
obliged to declare upon their conscience.

12. In case which we do not expect, be it soon or
late, there should happen any misunderstanding or cause
or contention between us, our heirs, and successors,
concerning these goods and what thereon does depend,
the same shall be deterined among the members of the
company, or if both parties do not account them wholly
impartial, by other two honest persons unanimously
chosen by the differing parties and these two chosen
persons shall have power to take unto them the third,
if they think it necessary, in form and manner
hereafter described, viz., the chosen arbitrators on an
appointed day and place in the presence of the
differing parties or their attorneys, after the
invocation of divine assistance and ripe consideration
of the matter, shall determine the business by their
award according to their best knowledge and sentiment
in case they cannot bring the parties to a composition;
but if these three cannot agree or find out the most
votes, they shall send for advice to one or two of the
head partners and then conceive and pronounce their
award; to the contrary whereof afterwards in no matter
or ways any thing shall be done, acted, or admitted by
right or force of no judge or man in the whole world,
in Europe or America; and if any should presume to
oppose himself hereunto, eo ipso (or by so doing), he
shall forfeit his whole share, and besides pay a fine
of 200 rix dollars to the public almonry, or to the
poor, ipso facto, without any exception or futher
declaration.

All faithfully and without covin. In true witness
this present contract, to which all partners after a
ripe consideration did unanimously consent, is twelve
times under all and everyone's own hand and seal set

forth, and an exemplar thereof delivered to each, and
one laid up with the common documents. Given at
Frankford upon Main the 12th November anno 1686.

Gerhard von Mastrick,	Daniel Behagel,
Francis Daniel Pastorius,	Jacobus van den Wallen,
Thomas von Wylich,	Johan Wilhelm Petersen,
Johan le Brun,	Johannes Kemler,
Johan Jacob Schutz,	Balthasar Jawert.

DOCUMENT 73:   Division of the Connecticut General
               Assembly Into Two Houses, October 13,
               1698

Taken from J.H. Trumbull and C.J. Hoadly, eds., *The
Public Records of the Colony of Connecticut: Vol. IV,
1636 - 1776* (Hartford: Brown and Parsons, 1850), p.
267.

It is ordered by this court, and the authority thereof,
that for the future its general assembly shall consist
of two houses The first shall consist of the governor,
or, in his absence of the deputy-governor, and
assistants, which shall be known by the name of the
Upper House. The other shall consist of such deputies
as shall be legally returned from the several towns
within this colony to serve as members of this general
assembly, which shall be known by the name of the Lower
House wherein a speaker chosen by themselves shall
preside. Which houses so formed shall have a distinct
power to apoint all needful officers and to make such
rules as they shall severally judge necessary for the
regulating of themselves. And it is further ordered
that no act shall be passed into a law of this colony,
nor any law already enacted be repealed, nor any other
act proper to this general assembly, but by the consent
of both houses.

DOCUMENT 74:   Act to Ascertain the Manner and Form of
               Electing Members to Represent the
               Inhabitants of This Province in the
               Commons House of Assembly, 1721

Text is taken from T. Cooper, ed., *Statutes at Large of South Carolina*, Vol. *III*, pp. 135 - 140.

Whereas the choosing members of the Commons House of Assembly for this province by parishes or precincts has been found by experience to be the most just and least expensive method that can be devised, and approaches nearest to the form and method of choosing or electing members in other his Majesty's dominions and plantations, and not liable to the inconveniencies that attend any other method heretofore used or practiced in this province; therefore, for preserving the same inviolable, we humbly pray your most sacred Majesty that it may be enacted,

I.   And be it enacted by his Excellency Francis Nicholson, Esq., Governor, etc., by and with the advice and consent of his Majesty's honorable Council and the Assembly of this province, and by the authority of the same, that the persons who shall be chosen to serve as members of Assembly after the ratification of this act shall be elected and chosen after the manner and at the places appointed by this act.

II.   And be it further enacted, by the authority aforesaid, that all writs for the future elections of members of Assembly shall be issued out by the Governor and Council for the time being, and shall bear date forty days before the day appointed for the meeting of the said members, and shall be directed to the church warden or church wardens of the several parishes hereafter named, or in case there should be wanted

church wardens in any parish then to such other proper
persons as the Governor and Councill shall think fit to
nominate in the said writs to manage such elections,
every one of whom are hereby empowered and required to
execute the said writs faithfully according to the true
intent and meaning of this act, to which every person
shall be sworn by any one justice of the peace for the
county, who is hereby required to administer such oath
without fee or reward and shall give public notice in
writing of all and every such writs two Sundays before
the appointed time of election at the door of each
parish church, or at some other public place as shall
be appointed in the said writs in such parishes as have
yet no churches erected, to the intent the time and
place of election may be better and more fully made
known; which writs shall be executed upon the same days
at all places where elections are appointed.

    III. And be it further enacted, by the authority
aforesaid, that every free white man, and no other
person, professing the christian religion, who has
attained to the age of one and twenty years and has
been a resident and an inhabitant in this province for
the space of one whole year before the date of the
writs for the election he offers to give his vote at,
and has a freehold of at least 50 acres of land, or has
been taxed in the precedent year twenty shillings, or
is taxed twenty shillings the year present to the
support of this government, shall be deemed a person
qualified to vote for and may be capable of electing a
representative or representatives to serve as a member
or members of the Commons House of Assembly for the
parish or precinct wherein he actually is a resident,
or in any other parish or precincts wherein he has the
like qualification.

    IV. And for the preventing of frauds in all
elections as much as possible, it is hereby enacted, by
the authority aforesaid, that the names of the electors
for members of the Commons House of Assembly shall be
fairly entered in a book or roll, for that purpose
provided by the churchwardens or other persons
appointed for managing elections, to prevent any
person's voting twice at the same election; and the
manner of their voting shall be as herein after is
directed, shall put into a box, glass, or sheet of

paper, prepared for that purpose by the said church
wardens or other persons, as is above directed, a piece
of paper rolled up, wherein is written the names of the
representatives he votes for, and to which paper the
elector shall not be obliged to subscribe his name; and
if upon the scrutiny two or more papers with persons
written thereon for members of Assembly be found rolled
up together, or more person's names be found written in
any paper than ought to be voted for, all and every
such paper or papers shall be invalid and of no effect;
and that those persons who, after all the papers and
votes are delivered in and entered as aforesaid, shall
be found, upon the scrutiny made, to have the majority
of votes, are and shall be deemed and declared to be
members of the succeeding Commons House of Assembly, so
as they be qualified as is hereinafter directed.

V.   And be it further enacted, by the authority
aforesaid, that the said election shall not continue
longer than two days and that the said elections shall
begin at nine in the morning and end at four in the
evening, and that at adjourning of the poll at
convenient hours, in the time of the aforesaid election
the church wardens, or other persons, as foresaid,
empowered to manage the said elections, shall seal up
the said box, glass, or paper wherein are put all the
votes then delivered in and rolled up by the electors,
as aforesaid, with their own seals and the seals of any
two or more of the electors that are there present, and
upon opening the poll shall unseal the said box, glass,
or paper in the presence of the said electors, in order
to proceed in the said elections.

VI.   And be it further enacted, by the authority
aforesaid, that the said church wardens, or other
persons appointed in each parish to manage the
elections aforesaid, shall, within seven days after the
scrutiny is made, give public notice in writing at the
church door, or at such other public places in the
parishes that have no churches where the election was
made, to the person or persons so elected that the
inhabitants of the said parish have made choice of him
or them to serve as their representative or
representatives in the next succeeding Commons House of
Assembly, under the penalty of one hundred pounds
current money of this province for his default or

neglect therein, to be recovered and disposed of in
such manner and form as is hereafter in this act
directed.

VII. And be it further enacted, by the authority
aforesaid, that the inhabitants of the several parishes
in this province qualified to vote for members of
Assembly, as is before in this act directed, shall,
upon the day of the election, according to the
Governor's and Council's precept for the time being,
meet at their respective parish churches, or at some
other public place in such parishes as have not yet any
churches erected in them, as shall be appointed by the
said precept, and there proceed to choose their
representatives according to the number following; that
is to say, the parish of St. Philip's Charlestown, five
members; for the parish of Christ church, two members;
for the parish of St. John's three members; for the
parish of St. Andrew's, three members; for the parish
of St. George's two members; for the parish of St.
James Goose Creek, four members; for the parish of St.
Thomas and St. Dennis, three members, the election to
be made at the parish church of St. Thomas; for the
parish of St. Paul's four members; for the parish of
St. Bartholomew's, at such place in the said parish as
shall be appointed by the governor and Council's
precept, until the parish church is erected, four
members; for the parish of St. Helena, four members,
the election to be made at Beauford in the said parish;
and for the parish of St. James Santee, with Winyaw,
two members. And the said several members who, upon a
scrutiny, are found to have the majority of votes, so
as they are qualified as is hereinafter directed, shall
be and they are hereby declared and adjudged to be the
true repreentatives for the said parish.

VIII. And be it further enacted, by the
authority aforesaid, that every person who shall be
elected and returned, as is before directed by this
act, to serve as a member of the Commons House of
Assembly, shall be qualified as follows; viz., he shall
be a free born subject of the kingdom of Great Britain,
or of the dominion thereunto belonging, or a foreign
person naturalized by act of Parliament in Great
Britain or Ireland, that has attained to the age of
twenty-one years, and has been resident in this

province for twelve months before the date of the said
writs; and having in this province a settled plantation
or freehold, in his own right, of a leave 500 acres of
land, and ten slaves, or has in his own proper person
and in his own right, to the value of 1,000 in houses,
buildings, town lots, or other lands in any part of
this province.

IX. And be it further enacted, by the authority
aforesaid, that any of his Majesty's justices of the
peace returned to serve as a member of the said Commons
House of Assembly shall read over to the rest of the
members returned to serve in the said house, before
they be admitted to sit as such, the last mentioned
qualifying clause, and then each member, before he be
admitted to sit as such in the said house, shall take
the following oath on the holy evagelists. I, AB, do
sincerely swear that I am duly qualified to be chosen
and serve as a member of the Commons House of Assembly
of this province for the parish of ....,
according to the true intent and meaning of this act.
So help me God.

X.   And be it further enacted, by the authority
aforesaid, that if any member or members hereafter
chosen to serve in any Commons House of Assembly should
die or depart this province, or refuse to qualify him
of themselves as in this act directed, or be expelled
by the said House of Commons, then and in such cases
the said House shall by message to the Governor and
Council for the time being desire them to issue out a
new writ or writs, and the said Governor and Council
shall, on such a message to them presented, issue out a
new writ or writs, directed as before in this act is
appointed, for choosing another person or persons to
serve in the place or places of such member or members
so dead or departed this province, or who shall refuse
to qualify him or themselves, or be expelled as
aforesaid. Which person or persons, so chosen and
summoned as before directed, shall attend the Commons
House of Assembly, as by the precept is directed, under
the same fines and penalties the several church wardens
or other persons appointed to manage elections
according to the directions of this act are liable to
the said act.

XI. And be it further enacted, by the authority aforesaid, that all and every member and members of the Commons House of Assembly of this province, chosen by virtue of this act, shall have as much power and privilege to all intents and purposes as any member or members of the Commons House of Assembly of this province heretofore of right had, might, could, or ought to have in the said province; provided the same are such as are according to his Majesty's thirty-fifth instruction.

XII. And be it further enacted, by the authority aforesaid, that if any person or persons appointed by this act to manage any election for a member or members of the Commons House of Assembly, as aforesaid, shall willingly or knowingly admit of or take the vote of any person not qualified according to the purpose of this act, or, after any vote delivered in at such election, shall open or suffer any person whatsoever to open any such vote before the scrutiny is begun to be made, or shall make an undue return of any person for a member of the Commons House of Assembly, each person so offending, shall forfeit for each such vote taken and admitted of, opened, or suffered to be opened, as aforesaid, and for each such return, the sum of one hundred pounds current money of this province, to be recovered and disposed of in such manner and form as hereafter in this act is directed.

XIII. And be it further enacted, by the authority aforesaid, that all and every person or persons appointed to take votes, or to manage elections of members to serve in the Commons House of Assembly, as aforesaid, shall for that purpose attend at the time and place of election according as he or they are directed by the said writs and attend likewise on the said Commons House of Assembly the two first days of their sitting, unless he or they have leave sooner to depart, to inform them of all such matters and disputes that did arise or may have arisen about the election of any member or members to serve as aforesaid, or at any place or places where the same was or were appointed to be managed, and shall show to said House the list of the votes of every person returned to be a representative to serve as aforesaid, or which otherwise ought to have been returned as such, if any

complaint of a false return has been made to the
Commons House of Assembly; and every person appointed
to take votes, as aforesaid, who shall omit or refuse
to attend at either of the times and places, as
aforesaid, shall forfeit the sum of ten pounds current
money of this province, to be recovered and disposed of
in such manner and form as is hereafter directed by
this act.

XIV. And be it further enacted, by the authority
aforesaid, that if any person or persons whatsoever
shall, on any day appointed for the election of a
member or members of the Commons House of Assembly as
aforesaid, presume to violate the freedom of the said
election by any arrest, menaces, or threats, or
endeavor or attempt to over-awe, fright, or force any
person qualified to vote against his inclination or
conscience, or otherwise by bribery obtain any vote, or
who shall, after the said election is over, menace,
despitefully use, or abuse any person because he has
not voted as he or they would have had him, every such
person so offending, upon due and sufficient proof made
of such his violence or abuse, menacing or threatening,
before any two justices of the peace, shall be bound
over to the next general sessions of the peace, himself
in fifty pounds current money of this province, and two
sureties, each in twenty-five pounds of like money, and
to be of good behaviour, and abide the sentence of the
said court, where, if the offender or offenders are
convicted and found guilty of such offense or offenses,
as aforesaid, then he or they shall each of them
forfeit the sum of fifty pounds current money of this
province, and be committed to jail without bail
mainprize till the same be paid; which fine so imposed
shall be paid unto one of the church wardens of the
parish where the offense was committed for the use of
the poor thereof; and if any person offending as
aforesaid shall be chosen a member of the Commons House
of Assembly, after conviction of illegal practices
proved before the said House, shall by a vote of the
said House be rendered uncapable to sit or vote as a
member of that Commons House of Assembly.

XV. And be it further enacted, by the authority
aforesaid, that no civil officer whatsoever shall
execute any writs or other civil process whatsoever

upon the body of any person qualified to vote for
members of the Commons House of Assembly, as before in
this act is directed, either in his journey to or in
his return from the place of such election, or during
his stay there on that account, or within forty-eight
hours after the scrutiny for such elections is
finished, under the penalty of twenty pounds current
money of his province, to be recovered of and from the
officer which shall arrest or serve any process, as
aforesaid, after such manner and form and to be
disposed of as hereinafter is directed; and all such
writs or warrants executed on the body of any person
either going to or being at, within the time limited by
this clause, or returning from the place of such
election is appointed to be managed, he being qualified
to give in his vote thereat, are hereby declared void
and null.

XVI.   And be it further enacted, by the authority
aforesaid, that every justice of the peace who shall
refuse or neglect to do his duty in and by this act
enjoined and required shall, for every default, forfeit
the sum of one hundred pounds current money of this
province, to be recovered and disposed of as is
hereinafter directed by this act.

XVII.   And be it further enacted, by the authority
aforesaid, that in any succeeding Commons House of
Assembly, no less than nineteen members duly met shall
make an House to transact the business of the same; and
for passing any law therein, there shall not be less
than ten affirmatives; nor shall a less number than
seven members of the said House met together have power
to adjourn, which number are hereby declared to have
power, in the absence of the speaker, to choose a
chairman to adjourn the members from day to day and to
summon by their messenger any absenting member or
members to appear and give their attention in the said
House.

XVIII.   But forasmuch as, by the great distance of
the habitation of several of the members of
Charlestown, through bad weather and other accidents it
may often happen that such a number may not meet to
make an adjournment, be it, therefore, enacted, by the
authority aforesaid, that in case none of the members
of the Commons House of Assembly, or a less number than

seven of them, should appear in the said House
according to the directions of the writs appointing
their first meeting; or to their last prorogation or
adjournment, that then and in such case it shall be and
it is hereby declared lawful for the governor for the
time being, with the advice and consent of his council,
to name a further day for the meeting of the Said
Commons House of Assembly, and that the said House
shall not be dissolved by their not meeting as
aforesaid, any law, custom, or usage to the contrary
thereof in anyway notwithstanding.

XIX. And be it further enacted, by the authority
aforesaid, that whosoever for the future shall be
elected a member to serve in the Commons House of
Assembly, before he be permitted to sit and vote in the
said house, shall further qualify himself for the same
by taking the usual oaths and make and sign the
declaration appointed by several acts of Parliament of
Great Britain.

XX. And be it further enacted, by the authority
aforesaid, that all the fines and forfeitures mentioned
in this act and not before particularly disposed of,
the one-half thereof shall be to his Majesty for the
use of the poor of the parish of St. Philip's
Charlestown, to be paid to the church wardens of the
said parish, and the other half to him or them that
will sue for the same by action of debt, suit, bill,
plaint, or information in any court of record in this
province, wherein no essoign, protection, privilege, or
wager of law, or stay of protection shall be admitted
or allowed of.

XXI. And be it further enacted by the authority
aforesaid, that this present General Assembly shall
determine and be dissolved at the expiration of three
years next after the date of the writs issued out for
calling the same, and that every General Assembly
hereafter called by virtue of any writs, as aforesaid,
shall determine and be dissolved every three years next
after the date of the respective writs by which they
were called, except sooner dissolved by the Governor.

XXII. And be it further enacted, by the authority
aforesaid, that the sitting and holding of General
Assemblies shall not be discontinued or intermitted
above six months, but shall within that time, from and

after the determination of this or any other General
Assembly, or oftener if occasion require, new writs to
be issued out by the Governor for the time being for
calling, assembling, and holding of another General
Assembly.

XXIII. And be it further enacted and declared
that this present Assembly, having been elected and
called together by virtue of his Majesty's royal
commissions and instructions to his Excellency Francis
Nicholson, Esq., his Majesty's Governor and
Commander-in-Chief of this his province of South
Carolina, shall in all things whatsoever be deemed and
held to be a true and lawful Assembly, and all acts and
ordinances duly passed by them, by and with the consent
of his Majesty's honorable Council and assented to by
his Excellency, shall be deemed and accounted laws and
orders of the said province, anything in any former act
of this province heretofore made notwithstanding.

XXIV. And be it further enacted, by the authority
aforesaid, that all former acts of Assembly of this
province relating to or concerning the elections of the
members to serve in the Commons House of Assembly be,
from and after the ratification of this act, repealed,
and they are hereby declared void and repealed.

                                   James Moore,
                                   Speaker

Charlestown, [. . .] 19, 1721.
Assented to by Francis Nicholson, Governor

APPENDIX

A number of the documents written by Americans that qualify as instruments of political foundation could not be reproduced in this volume because of space limitations. They have been identified by a double asterisk in the analysis of the documents found on pp. 29 and 30 in the introductory essay. The ones excluded were chosen on the basis of two criteria: 1) they tended to be redundant in content   documents that were reproduced; and 2) they are more or less readily available in any reasonable university library, whereas the ones reproduced in this volume are difficult to find or too important to leave out. The documents left out on the basis of these criteria are identified below with the easiest source available for public scrutiny.

The Charter of Connecticut -- 1662; Benjamin Perley Poore, comp., Federal And State Constitutions, Colonial Charters, and Other Organic Laws of the United States (Washington: Government Printing Office, 1878), pp. 252 - 257.

The Charter of Rhode Island and Providence Plantations -- 1663; Poore, comp., Federal and State Constitutions . . ., pp. 1595 - 1603.

The Concession and Agreement of the Lords Proprietors of the Province of New Caesarea, or New Jersey, to and With all and Every the Adventurers and All Such as Shall Settle or Plant There -- 1664; Francis N. Thorpe, ed., *The Federal and State Constitutions, Colonial Charters, and Other*

Organic Laws of the United States (Washington: Government Printing Office, 1907), pp. 2535 - 2544.

The Concessions and Agreement of the Proprietors of Carolina with the Prospective Settlers -- January 1665; William L. Saunders, ed., The Colonial Records of North Carolina: Vol. I, 1662 - 1712 (Raleigh: P.M. Hale, Printer to the State, 1886).

The Concessions and Agreement of West New Jersey -- March 3 - 13, 1677; Keith W. Kavenagh, ed., Foundations of Colonial America: A Documentary History (New York; Chelsea House, 1973), 175 - 183.

The Frame of Government of Pennsylvania -- 1683; Francis N. Thorpe, pp. 3064 - 3069.

Laws of Personal Freedom - 1683; J. T. Mitchell and H. Flanders, eds., Statutes at Large of Pennsylvania, Vol. I, pp. 114 - 153.

The Fundamental Constitutions for the Province of East New Jersey in America, Anno Domini 1683; Francis N. Thorpe, pp. 2574 - 2581.

Admonition for Reformation -- March 13, 1689; Cotton Mather, Magnalia Christi Americana: The Ecclesiastical History of New England originally published in seven volumes in 1852 , and reprinted in two volumes in 1967 by Russell and Russell in New York. See pp. 334 - 336 in volume one of this reprinting.

The Frame of Government of Pennsylvania -- 1696; Francis N. Thorpe, pp. 3070 - 3076.

Charter of Privileges Granted by William Penn, Esq. to the Inhabitants of Pennsylvania and Territories -- 1701; Francis N. Thorpe, pp. 3076 - 3080.

One of the essential points being made by this volume is that American constitutionalism did not result from an appropriation of theory from major European thinkers such as John Locke and Montesquieu as much as it derived from the documents written and evolved by Americans during their colonial period. To satisfy himself or herself on this point, the careful student will want to examine closely the early state constitutions written before the United States Constitution of 1787. These early state constitutions can be found in the seven volume compilation by Francis N. Thorpe cited earlier in this appendix. One can sort out the early foundation documents of a given colony and watch the documentary evolution reaching culmination in the state constitutions written by the state that emerges from the colony. Other documents found in Thrope, such as the Massachusetts Explanatory Charter of 1725 will help fill out the picture. In effect, this volume is designed to supplement Thorpe's volumes to show that the organic documents of the seventeenth century belong in his volumes as well as those of the eighteenth century. A few of the early documents reproduced here will also be found in Thrope, but his record of the colonial history of foundation documents has gaping holes it is hoped will be filled by the present volume.

Although the compiler and editor of this volume has attempted to uncover every foundation document of the seventeenth century that is still available in records surviving to this day, he has focued his attention upon the seventeenth century. It should not be assumed that Americans stopped writing foundation documents after the state constitutions became the dominant form of foundation document. On the frontier that was moving westward across the continent, and in territories not yet formally admitted to the Union, Americans continued to write covenants and compacts to bind themselves together on nothing more than their individual, respective consent. As just one example of many that could be reprinted, the Cubmerland Compact is reproduced here to illustrate the continuing practice of Americans to write their own documents of political foundation when no other was operative in their lives.

DOCUMENT 75:   The Cumberland Compact -- 1780

By 1780 the original thirteen states were in the midst
of writing or rewriting constitutions derived from a
long history of foundation documents written over the
previous century and a half.   It is interesting to
note, then, that on the frontier we find communities
being founded and governed in a fashion similar to that
of the original colonies in the seventeenth century.
Each of the new states claimed land to the west of
their recognized borders, and the conflicting claims
meant that settlers on the frontier were not certain to
whom they owed allegiance, if anyone.   The present
document is typical in that it shows a people governing
themselves at the local level using a document of
political foundation of their own making.   The actual
drafter of the document was Richard Henderson, leader
of the Transylvania Company which purchased the land in
question from the Cherokees.   The text is as found in
the *History of Tennessee (Nashville, 1886),*   pp. 184
- 88.

        Lands shall be reserved for the particular person
in whose name they shall be entered, or their heirs,
provided such persons shall remove to this country and
take possession of the respective place or piece of
land so chosen or entered, or shall send a laborer or
laborers and a white person in his or her stead to
perform the same on or before May, 1781; and also
provided such land so chosen and entered for is not
entered and claimed by some person who is an inhabitant
and shall raise a crop of corn the present year at some
station or place convenient to the general settlement
in this country.   But it is fully to be understood that
those who are actually at this time inhabitants of this

country shall not be debarred of their choice or claim on account of the right of any such absent or returning person or persons.

It is further proposed and agreed that no claim or title to any lands whatsoever shall be set up by any person in consequence of any mark, or former improvement, unless the same be entered with the entry taker within twenty days from the date of this association and agreement. And that when any person hereafter shall mark or improve land or lands for himself, such mark or improvement shall not avail him, or be deemed an evidence of prior right, unless the same be entered with the entry taker in thirty days from the time of such mark or improvement. No other person shall be entitled to such land so as aforesaid to be reserved in consequence of any purchase, gift, or otherwise.

If the entry taker to be appoitned shall neglect or refuse to perform his duty, or be found by the said judges or a majority of them to have acted fraudlently to the prejudice of any person whatsoever, such entry taker shall be immediately removed from his office and the book taken out of his possession by the said judges, until another shall be appointed to act in his room.

As often as the people in general are dissatisfied with the doings of the judges or triers, so to be chosen, they may call a new election at any of the said stations and elect others to act in their stead, having due respect to the number now agreed to be erected at each station, which persons so to be chosen shall have the same power with those in whose room or place they are or may be chosen to act.

As no consideration money for the lands on Cumberland River within the claim of the said Richard Henderson and Company, which is the subject of association, is demanded or expected by the said company until a satisfactory and indisputable title can be made, we think it reasonable and just that the 26 13s. 4d., current money, per hundred acres, the price proposed by the said Richard Henderson, shall be paid according to the value of money on the 1st day of January last, being the time the price was made public and settlement was encouraged thereon by said

Henderson. Richard Henderson on his part does hereby
agree that, in case of the rise or appreciation of
money, an abatement shall be made in the sum according
to its raised or appreciated value.

When any person shall remove to this country with
intent to become an inhabitant and shall depart this
life, either by violence or in the natural way, before
he shall have performed the requisites necessary to
obtain lands, the child or children of such deceased
person shall be entitled to his or her room to such
quantity of land as such person would have been
entitled to in case he or she had lived to obtain a
grant in their own name. And if such death be
occasioned by the Indians, the said Henderson does
promise and agree that the child or children shall have
as much as amounts to their headrights gratis,
surveyors' and other incidental fees excepted.

Whereas from our remote situation and want of
proper offices for the administration of justice, no
regular proceedings at law can be had for the
punishment of offenses and attainment of right, it is
therefore agreed that until we can be relieved by
government from the many evils and inconveniences
arising therefrom, the judges or triers to be appointed
as before directed, when qualified, shall be and are
hereby declared a proper court or jurisdiction for the
recovery of any debt or damages; or where the cause of
action or complaint has arisen or hereafter shall
commence for anything done or to be done among
ourselves within this, our settlement on Cumberland
foresaid or in our passage hither; where the laws of
our country could not be executed or damages repaired
in any other way, that is to say, in all cases where
the debt or damages or demand does or shall not exceed
$100. Any three of the said judges or triers shall be
competent to make a court and finally decide the matter
in controvery. But if for a larger sum, and either
party shall be dissatisfied with the judgement or
decision of such court, they may have an appeal to the
whole twelve judges or triers. In which case, nine
members shall be deemed a full court whose decision, if
seven agree in one opinion upon the matter in dispute,
shall be final and their judgment carried into
execution in such manner and by such person or persons

as they may appoint. The said courts respectively shall have full power to tax such costs as they may think just and reasonable, to be levied or collected with the debt or damage so to be awarded.

It is further agreed that a majority of the said judges, triers, or general arbitrators shall have power to punish in their discretion, having respect to the laws of our country, all offenses against the peace, misdemeanors, and those criminal or of a capital nature, provided such court does not proceed with execution so far as to effect life or member. In case any should be brought before them whose crime is or shall be dangerous to the state or for which the benefit of clergy is taken away by law, and sufficient evidence or proof of the fact or facts can probably be made, such courts or a majority of the members shall and may order and direct him, her, or them to be safely bound and sent under a strong guard to the place where the offense was or shall be committed or where legal trial of such offense can be had. This shall accordingly be done and the reasonable expense attending the discharge of this duty ascertained by the court and paid by the inhabitants in such proportion as shall be hereafter agreed on for that purpose.

As this settlement is in its infancy, unknown to government and not included within any county in North Carolina, the state to which it belongs, so as to derive the advantages of those wholesome and salutary laws for the protection and benefits of its citizens, we find ourselves constrained from necessity to adopt this temporary method of restraining the licentious and supplying, by unanimous consent, the blessings flowing from a just and equitable government, we declare and promise that no action or complaint shall be hereafter instituted or lodged in any court of record within this state or elsewhere for anything done, or to be done, in consequence of the proceedings of the said judges or general arbitrators, to be chosen and established by this our Associaton.

As the well-being of this country entirely depends, under Divine Providence, on uninimity of sentiment and concurrence in measures, and as clashing interests and opinions without being under some restraint will most certainly produce confusion, discord, and almost certainly ruin, we think it our duty to associate and hereby form ourselves into one society for the benefit of present and future settlers. Until the full and proper exercise of the laws of our country can be in use and powers of government exerted among us, we do most solmenly and sacredly declare and promise to each other that we will faithfully and punctually adhere to, perform, and abide by this our Association, adn will at all times, if need be, compel by our united force a due obedience to these rules and regulations. In testimony whereof we have hereunto subscribed our names in token of our entire approbation of the measures adopted.

Document 1: Articles, Laws, and . . . in Virginia

[1]Calling down evil upon a person.

[2]A small dagger or stiletto.

[3]Open defiance.

[4]Treatment.

[5]Provisions.

[6]Materials for barter or exchange.

[7]An officer who supervised the store or provision house of a fort.

[8]The master of the provisions, who also provided the soldiers' allowance.

[9]Spirits, or alcoholic beverages.

[10]Not a mariner, a countryman.

[11]Seeing that.

[12]Bleach clothes.

[13]Palisades.

[14]Rinse.

[15]Used to remove trees, etc.

[16]A powerful chief of an Indian confederation south of the Potomac River.

[17]A werowance was an Indian chief.

[18]A vessel used in sheltered water near the shore.

[19]Boil.

Document 5: Plymouth Oath

[1]The words "a true christian" were later struck out and the phrase in brackets substituted so that the last sentence read: ". . . to perform as you hope for help from God," etc.

Document 7:   Agreement of the Massachusetts Bay Co.

[1]Hindrance, obstruction, or delay.

[2]The archaic symbol for an English pound.

Document 17:   Salem Oath for Residents

[1]In the late Middle Ages, to convent someone meant to call him to an assembly.

Document 26:   Government of Pocasset

[1]Clerk.

Document 32:   Fundamental Orders of Connecticut

[1]The calendar in use at the time began the new year on March 24. Thus, in today's calendar system, this date is 1639. The dates internal to the documents are always left as is, while the dates in the titles are given according to today's system. Another peculiarity was that March dates prior to the 24th were still considered part of the first month. So, for example, the second day of the first month was March 2, not March 25.

Document 38:   Agreement of the Settlers at Exeter

[1]Both Hammond and Belknap transcribe this as "derived," whereas C.H. Bell transcribes it as "directed." The former version is used here.

Document 39:   Plantation Agreement at Providence

[1]Pence.

Document 41:   Massachusetts Body of Liberties

[1]Provision of military equipment by a feif.

[2]Maintenance allowance provided by a feif.

[3]Tax paid by the eldest to retain title to property.

[4]Inheritance tax.

Document 45:   Government of Guilford

[1]Foeffee: The person to whom a freehold estate in
land is conveyed by a foefment. A foefment is the
action of investing a person with a feif, or putting
him in legal possession.

Document 49:   Massachusetts Ordinance on the Legislature

[1]Sheire, or shire, is another word for county.
"Sheire town" is county seat.

Document 56:   Maryland Toleration Act

[1]Christian. Also, an "X" followed by a subscript
"p" was a common symbol for Christ.

[2]In the practice of the day, a line over a letter
meant that one or more letters to follow have been
ommitted.

[3]Lieutenant.

[4]Two shillings and six pence.

Document 59:   The Cambridge Agreement

[1]What ever.

[2]Making an allotment, apportioning, setting limits
to.

ABOUT THE EDITOR

Donald S. Lutz is Professor of Political Science at the University of Houston. He is the author of *Popular Consent and Popular Control: Whig Political Theory in the Early State Constitutions*, co-author (with Charles S. Hyneman) of *The Founding Era in America: Its Fundamental Convictions and Assumptions*, and co-editor (with Charles S. Hyneman) of *American Political Writing During the Founding Era, 1760-1805*.

DATE DUE

SEP 01 1995			